BETWEEN HISTORY AND HISTORIES:
THE MAKING OF SILENCES AND COMMEMORATIONS

Since the 1980s historians have been influenced by two anthropological concepts: cultural distance and awareness of small-scale interactions. Recent work, however, has shifted away from these notions. We now see that cultures cannot be studied as units with internal coherence and that the microcosm does not represent a cultural whole.

This book proposes an alternative. Differentiation is the keyword that lets us focus on ruptures, contradiction, and change within a society. It drives us to recognize many different *histories* both along with and opposed to *history*. The case studies in *Between History and Histories* use this new approach in historical anthropology to examine how certain events are silenced in the shadow of others that are commemorated by monuments, ceremonies, documents, and storytelling. The first set of studies explores cases around the world where the official construction of the past has been contested. The second set describes the silences that emerge in the midst of such disputes.

For students, this collection provides a useful overview of interaction between two disciplines. For historians and anthropologists, it offers an alternative vision of the production of history.
(Anthropological Horizons)

GERALD SIDER is professor of anthropology at the City University of New York. GAVIN SMITH is professor of anthropology at University College, University of Toronto.

ANTHROPOLOGICAL HORIZONS

Editor: Michael Lambek, University of Toronto

This series, begun in 1991, focuses on theoretically informed ethnographic works addressing issues of mind and body, knowledge and power, equality and inequality, the individual and the collective. Interdisciplinary in its perspective, the series makes a unique contribution in several other academic disciplines: women's studies, history, philosophy, psychology, political science, and sociology.

Published to date:

JUN 1 5 1999

EDITED BY GERALD SIDER AND GAVIN SMITH

Between History and Histories: The Making of Silences and Commemorations

UNIVERSITY OF TORONTO PRESS
Toronto Buffalo London

© University of Toronto Press Incorporated 1997
Toronto Buffalo London
Printed in Canada

ISBN 0-8020-0901-8 (cloth)
ISBN 0-8020-7883-4 (paper)

Printed on acid-free paper

Canadian Cataloguing in Publication Data

Main entry under title:

Between history and histories : the making of silences
and commemorations

(Anthropological horizons)
ISBN 0-8020-0901-8 (bound)   ISBN 0-8020-7883-4 (pbk.)

1. Memorials.   2. History.   3. Public history.
4. Historiography.   I. Sider, Gerald M.   II. Smith, Gavin A.
III. Series.

D21.3.B48 1997   909   C97-931421-6

University of Toronto Press acknowledges the financial assistance to its publishing
program of the Canada Council for the Arts and the Ontario Arts Council.

Contents

Preface

The papers in this volume were presented, in early draft form, at a conference called 'The Production of History: Silences and Commemorations.' This was one of a series of round-table conferences organized by the working group in anthrolopogy and history at the Max-Planck-Institut für Geschichte in Göttingen and co-sponsored by the Maison des Sciences de l'Homme in Paris, the fourth conference series of the working group. The first two were single conferences; the latter two were series of meetings on a specific topic. In these series we first met as a small group to formulate some of the issues in our topic and to invite a number of papers that would explore possibilities for research and discussion. During and after this exploratory conference we narrowed the focus of our topic and invited papers for the final conference. At the final conference extensive protocols of the discussions were made by the participants, and the protocols of the entire conference discussions, together with the editors' comments, were circulated to all the participants for use in revising their papers – the labour theory of value applied, to the extent that it is applicable to this kind of work.

From the first conference on work processes, in 1978, we have sought to develop *grounded* analytical tools. Our first conference focused on 'work processes' rather than production: how canoes were built by villagers on a Pacific island, how trees were cut down in early-twentieth-century England. The point of this emphasis was not a retreat into microscopic, descriptive 'history.' Indeed, in that perspective what we were doing was not even as large-scale as the usual 'microhistory'; it was more like historical electron microscopy. The point of this project was to reconsider some familiar larger issues, particularly how social reproduction is organized and how reproduction becomes transformation. The papers from this conference developed into a volume on class and culture – *Klassen and Kulture: Sozialanthropologische Perspektiven in der Geschichtsschreibung*, ed. Robert Berdahl et al. (Frankfurt am Main: Syndikat, 1982).

The second conference (1980) used the framework 'material interest and emotion' to explore kinship in history and anthropology (Hans Medick and David Sabean, eds., *Interest and Emotion: Essays on the Study of Family and Kinship* [New York: Cambridge University Press, 1984]). In this project the study of the microspecificity and concrete materiality of social relations became a way of taking culture seriously – not as the thickly describable quaint and curious customs of strange and different peoples, but as a domain of socially transformative tensions and struggles.

Our third project was a series of conferences in 1982–4 on the subject 'Herrschaft als soziale Praxis.' This title is almost impossible to translate directly: in essence, it means 'lordship and authority and/as the range of usual, expected, and unexpected responses of its subjects.' (The resulting book, edited by Alf Lüdtke, is *Herrschaft als soziale Praxis: historische und sozialanthropologische Studien* [Göttingen: Vandehoeck und Ruprecht, 1991]). The conferences addressed the interweaving of domination and legitimation, in order to understand circumstances and processes where the *de*legitimation of domination becomes part of its reproduction, and to understand situations where accommodation, collusion, and resistances are so intermingled that even to give them separate names is to misunderstand how power works. If power, like electricity, flows through resistance, then the contestability of its legitimacy can become crucial to both the reproduction and the transformation of the relationships that domination engenders. The following series of meetings, between 1985 and 1989, on 'the production of history: silences and commemorations,' were very densely interwoven with the conferences on *Herrschaft*, and are taken up in the Introduction.

No endeavour is concluded without debts, and an edited book comes with an especially heavy burden. Because we have been the editors of a collection of work that has arisen from interchanges of greater or lesser formality – from round tables to hallway conversations to notes passed hither and thither – our debts are especially widespread; indeed, they are not debts as much as the bricks and mortar that have built this book on a noisy and conversational building site. Alberta Arthurs of the Rockefeller Foundation and the staff at the Bellagio Center on Lake Como in Italy were generous in their hospitality when they hosted the conference from which these papers emerged. Generous too were Maurice Aymard, Director of the Maison des Sciences de l'Homme, and Rudolph Vierhaus, Director of the Max-Planck-Institut für Geschichte, who co-sponsored the conference as well as the several preparatory meetings. Johns Hopkins University and the College of Staten Island provided release time for David William Cohen and Gerald Sider to organize the conference.

We are all grateful to David William Cohen, who wrote the conference-call paper that helped to set our initial agenda. Each of the papers published here has been enhanced by the significant contributions of those participants in the conference and the pre-conference meetings who are not directly represented in this collection: Robert Berdahl, Utz Jeggle, Bogumil Jewsiewicki, Orvar Lofgren, Shula Marks, David Sabean, and Katherine Verdery.

Several of the themes discussed in the Introduction were developed in the Cultural Pluralism Seminar at Columbia University, and we are very grateful to the Columbia University Seminars program for a grant in aid of the preparatory work for publication. We would also like to thank Michael Lambek for his encouragement in carrying this project to fruition, and Glynis George for her careful work – against all odds – in bringing it to closure.

BETWEEN HISTORY AND HISTORIES:
THE MAKING OF SILENCES AND COMMEMORATIONS

Introduction

GERALD SIDER AND GAVIN SMITH

The Changing Dialogue between Anthropology and History

This book brings together anthropologists and historians to address questions of how commemorations and the silences that surround them come into being and are institutionalized. As the specific issue for interweaving anthropology and history, the focus on silences and commemorations expresses a subtle but pervasive shift in the two disciplines over the years. Here in the introduction we take stock of the past dialogue and use the essays in the volume to suggest new perspectives and methods. This part highlights some of the significant ways in which the conjunction of anthropology and history has changed over the years.

One early conjunction of the two disciplines came through the British Marxist social historians' sympathy for anthropology. Eric Hobsbawm's *Primitive Rebels* (1959) was in part his response to the invitation to participate in Max Gluckman's seminar in the anthropology department at Manchester. (We might speculate, too, that Gluckman's never-completed shift toward a more historically informed ethnography in his *Analysis of the Social Situation in Modern Zululand* [1958] arose in part from this interchange.) One reason for these historians' 'anthropological turn' was their revised notion of the project of social history: to give voice to the silent and the silenced.

Since that time we find troubling questions arising about the role of guild historians and anthropologists in representing the people whom they study: giving voice to the silent and oppressed is not without its problems. Questions arise: Do such voicings constrain or nourish the powerful? Does the fact of powerlessness imbue voice with some special authenticity *sui generis?* We return to these questions in a moment.

Then, some twenty years after that Manchester seminar, the anthropologist Bernard Cohn initiated another influential exchange. Reflecting on it later, he called attention to the responsibility of scholars in their production of knowledge, given the realities of power: 'Anthropological historians and historical anthropologists cannot deal with history only as the reconstruction of what has happened, and as the explication of the natives' own understanding of the encounter with Europeans. They must also deal with the fact that events have consequences for those people who are our "subjects" up to and including their total destruction' (1981:252). Yet, it has to be said that historians continued to use anthropology as a means for escaping, rather than confronting, issues of global and local power differentials, by invoking it in ways that opened a breach in social history between the dynamics of class and the collective expression of artisans, villagers, and the urban poor seen in terms of the curiosities of 'culture.'

In that exchange Carlo Ginzburg and Natalie Zemon Davis reflected on what the anthropological craft had to offer social historians. While Ginzburg referred to anthropology's concern with other cultures, for Zemon Davis the anthropological method had to do with (among other things) the scale at which ethnographers worked. Writing after the meeting, Ginzburg suggested, 'Two features of anthropologists' work have had a powerful impact on a good number of historians, the emphasis on *cultural distance*, and the attempt to overcome it by emphasizing the *inner coherence* of every aspect of societies widely different from our own' (Ginzburg 1981:277 [emphasis added]). After noting four features that make anthropological writings useful for historians, Zemon Davis stressed, 'Ethnographic studies have also given historians a new awareness of *informal and small-scale interactions* which can express important linkages and conflicts' (Davis 1981:269 [emphasis added]).

It probably remains true that the anthropological craft is still widely associated with the two specific features of *cultural distance* and a focus on *small-scale interactions*, and these features remain central, though problematic, to most of the contributors here. What *has* noticeably changed in the intermediate years, though, is two other features. First, very few anthropologists today (and very few historians familiar with contemporary anthropology) would be happy with the suggestion that societies different from our own are usefully thought of as having inner coherence. Rather, anthropologists have become increasingly interested in differences within cultures (Sahlins 1987; Smith 1989; Thomas 1991), the often violently constitutive dialogue between cultures (see Donham 1992 and Polier 1994; cf. Clifford and Marcus 1986 and Hannerz 1991), and the role that this differentiation *within*, and dialogue *between*, plays in the reproduction of culture and class.

Second, the publication of Wolf's *Europe and the People without History* (1982) brought to the fore an issue that had been brewing among anthropologists for some time, one that began as 'the question of authenticity' (see, for example, Cohn 1981) and became 'the questioning of authenticity' (O'Brien and Roseberry 1991:1–19). Western historians and anthropologists had colluded in the often-unacknowledged assumption that the authenticity of other people's claim to cultural distinctiveness lay in their unimpeachable historical difference lost in the mists of time and coming down to us as *survivals* against the currents of change in the modern world: it was in being survivals that the authenticity of people's cultures lay, and claims to land, cultural rights, ancestral remains, and even citizenship continue to be couched in such a 'natural language.' This perspective has shaped not only the ways in which native peoples have been allowed or encouraged to make their claims but also anthropology itself.

Bernard Cohn put the issue very succinctly as he reflected on the earlier conference:

The anthropologist projected by these historians is concerned with stability, structure, regularity, the local, the common, the small scale, and the expressive, symbolic, and magical. These features are typical of immobile or slow moving societies, which Lévi-Strauss terms 'cold' societies. In societies in which change seems cumulative, rapid and transformative of the structures, then the anthropological-influenced historians look for those groups or categories within these 'hot' societies *who maintain aspects of this more immobile past* – the engulfed and marginalized peasantry, the stubborn working classes, women who are mired in domesticity, and such semi-closed communities as academics, artists, and bandits. (1981:243 [emphasis added]).

Yet, as Cohn says, this is a projection, and it is a poor one, for the stress on anthropology as the study of survivals is misleading. Since the publication of Wolf's book, of Hobsbawm and Ranger's *The Invention of Tradition* (1983), and of Benedict Anderson's *Imagined Communities* (1991), to name just the best known, it has become increasingly difficult for anthropologists or historians to hold the view that cultural difference is, above all, simply the result of 'survivals' from a pristine past. Rather, 'the modern transformation has involved the constant creation of new expressions of cultural difference as well as fundamental redefinitions of old ones' (O'Brien and Roseberry 1991:1).[1]

This issue of the more or less self-conscious *construction* of histories by our subjects and by ourselves has now become the most well travelled bridge between anthropologists and historians. 'They have moved, or at least now suggest the potential of moving, from being audience to one another to being audience together to the lively, critical telling, writing and using of history in settings and times outside the control of the crafts and guilds of historical disciplines' (David W. Cohen 1988:26). The implications of this understanding are far-reaching. As we think of the interface between professional anthropologists and historians and their subjects engaged in *historical production,* understood in a wider sense to include claims to the past as part of the very process of grasping some leverage over the making of history now, in the present, and toward the future – as we think in these terms, so it becomes clear that the features of anthropology identified by Ginzburg and Davis have to be rethought too.

Medick's influential article (1987) on the linkages between anthropology and history suggests one modification to Ginzburg's assertion that historians have much to learn from the way that anthropologists handle *cultural distance.* Medick raises challenges to hermeneutic questions about the accessibility of subjective experience: 'For hermeneutic historians, the primary goal had been the access – however critically approached – to an existing tradition, a tradition which, it was presumed, the historian and his object share alike' (Medick 1987:84). It is a procedure only sustainable so long as a 'shared context' is assumed between the historian and his or her subject. Social historians, Medick noted, 'had all too quickly reduced the alien to the familiar.' Against this, he quoted Ginzburg: 'The fundamental instrument [of a newer historical method] is that of alienation, making strange, the ability to make the familiar alien – and not the reverse, as historians usually do' (Ginzburg 1983; quoted in Medick 1987:84).

What is being called for here is a technique – be it at the moment of scholarly apprehension of some historical data or in the subsequent writing up of a text – which 'increases the duration of perception' at the very least to make historians more self-conscious of the work that they are doing as they try to make sense of what they confront. For Medick, Clifford Geertz's use of 'thick description' can serve such a purpose and hence becomes a corrective for social historians. Yet the false familiarity with their subjects that historians felt, for which Medick offers this anthropological remedy, is not, as he says, found so predominantly among anthropologists – raising the provocative question as to whether anthropologists might not need a corrective of precisely the opposite kind: one that would take them over the same path but in the opposite direction, asking, for example, what investment they have as professionals in the reproduction of difference and strangeness, and how their own discourses have been taken up to this effect by non-anthropologists (see Stolcke 1995).

Yet the point here is not so much our preferences or our perspectives, as our alliances with and our grasp on the world around us. Anthropology, so profoundly enmeshed in notions of almost taken-for-granted *difference* and *distance* between scholar and subject, is now forced to examine a much more complex process in the formation of strangeness and difference, in the form of the pervasive transformation of production toward increasingly violent national and international forms of regulation. Under such conditions, methods for the interpretation of a pre-existing, taken-for-granted native difference may be less valuable than those that help us to understand the socio-genesis of difference under varying historical conditions.

Zemon Davis, as we have seen, raises a different issue: anthropology's interest in *informal and small-scale interactions*. In the pieces collected here it becomes clear that a focus on the small-scale now has very much less to do with trying to see what the microcosm can say (as representative of some cultural whole possessed of *inner coherence*), than with the role of *heterogeneity within cultures*.

Faced with the challenges to our methodological and conceptual baggage provided by the contemporary world, then, the dialogue between anthropologists and historians, which once could well be centred on issues of cultural distance, questions of scale in our respective studies, and a range of problems and disquietudes grouped under the label of 'authenticity,' has now blown apart. Thus David William Cohen's original conference-call paper provoked us in this manner: 'The stories, the discussions of contests and contexts of history production, are offered as montage, eclectic, open-sided, rough-edged, with contradictions and ambiguities gaping from the text. In a sense, part of "our position" is that the "production of history" is a complex medium of things rough, muddled, misunderstood, askew, incomplete, warped, and tendentious, yet a medium which few – whether among the powerful or the powerless – choose to cease attempting to make their own' (Cohen 1988:30).

And here lies, at least in part, the value of a focus on *commemorations*, precisely inasmuch as they are attempts at closure, at decisiveness and imposition, like the sharp report of a field gun at a military commemoration and the ringing silence that follows it: *this* is the sound of remembrance, *this* the silence. So, although anthropologists and historians have always shown a professional interest in rituals and symbols of remembrance, it is by seeing them against the backdrop of the kind of imagery captured here by David William Cohen that we wanted to stimulate discussion amongst us.

And just such discussion seems to be what has happened as our very different contributions have taken form. We were at pains from the beginning to remind ourselves that our concern was *not* with 'memory,' collective or individual (see, for example, Halbwachs 1992; Schwartz 1982; Middleton and Edwards 1990; Fentress and Wickham 1992), or with forgetting, but with the way that silences and commemorations lie in different kinds of relationship to one another. It will become clear to the reader that we each took different notions of 'commemorating' and hence, by extension, of commemorations' silent hinterlands. Yet each of the pieces that follow works over this issue: the impossible task that we all attempt – to make a moment or space of closure within and against the march of time.

Through the variety of these cases, one is struck by a deep ambivalence in modern societies with respect to their attitudes to the past, an ambivalence that is reproduced in the strange institutions of public remembering formed around the nexus of some physical memorial, now surely a feature of every national state in the world, from Saddam's great arch to the eternal flame at France's Place d'Étoile. There is surely some truth to Pierre Nora's (1989) observation that such commemorative symbols invoke less a sense of *identity* with those remembered than a (very modernist) sense that we should remember them *precisely so as not to be like them.*

So, as memorial sites multiply to the point where they almost compete with one another for attention to *this* rather than *that* memory, so also does a body of literature on memorials and commemorations – as though to deny, to work against, to break down, the silencing effect of closure brought by these memorials. From James Young's powerful study of Holocaust memorials (1993) to Henry Rouso's *Vichy Syndrome* (1991; see also Gillis 1994: Koonz 1994)[2] we see not just studies *about* these things (as we might find studies of Bauhaus architecture or Balinese marriage rites) but studies that in some way seek to work *against* the dead weight of modernism's cynical distancing of itself from the past, captured in the notion of 'progress.' 'Let us not forget, lest we do it again'; thereby follows progress.

Yet Marx long ago noted of the Hegelians that no amount of good concepts guarantee a better reality, and sadly, good memory is not itself a guarantee against bad practice in the present. In the section that follows, and drawing on the papers to come, we propose new ways of conjoining anthropology and history, ways that encourage different analytical methods and perspectives and a different sense of the problems before us.

History and Histories, Silences and Commemorations

Carlo Ginzburg, as we noted above, focused his vision of the utility of anthropology for historians on two 'real world' features that anthropologists have characteristically addressed: the 'distance' between cultures and 'the attempt to overcome ... [this distance] by emphasizing the inner coherence of every society different from our own.' Our project is situated between the realization of the inadequacy of both these components and the difficulty of constructing an alternative. The ways in which we separate and combine history and histories and the perspectives that we have developed on silences and commemorations introduce a different historical anthropology.

The two components of Ginzburg's bridge between anthropology and history – in shorthand, distance and coherence – have become inadequate both as representation of the world and as analytical or methodological frameworks. To begin, we are not so much dealing with any abstract, historically static quality – distance, otherness, 'alterity' – but rather with processes of differentiation. These processes simultaneously create and destroy various kinds of differences both between and within societies, and they turn out to be based as much or more on closeness and intimacy as on any imagined (or more, desired) difference.

When, for instance, the English naturalist Thomas Hariot was sent to observe and report upon Sir Walter Raleigh's 1586 attempted settlement of the Virginia coast, he ended his 'Brief and True report of the New Found Land of Virginia' (1590) with a description of the 'Natural Inhabitants' and the settlers' relations with them. The settlers had just burned a native village and destroyed the natives' store of corn because they thought that the natives had stolen a silver goblet from one of them; it was the end of summer, and this action would cause substantial continuing suffering. Despite – or in the midst of – this brutalization, Hariot claimed that the native people could be brought to 'honor, obey, fear and love us.'

This is the woman's side of the Christian marriage contract, with the addition of fear: men promised to love, honor, and cherish. At the very time the British were beginning the process of converting native people from the same kinds of settled, village farmers as peopled the European countryside to alien 'forest rovers,' to be displaced and enslaved as unworthy savages, they were using an amended version of the marriage contract to delineate their relationship to these 'original inhabitants.' Differentiation – which includes such violent, transformative intimacies – and not distance, is the effective concept to understand not only the relations between the settlers and the native peoples, but also the changing relations between native societies and among natives and settlers.

With the realization that the processes which create, harness, trivialize, destroy – in sum, continually transform – differentiation are necessarily both uneven and multiplex, the whole notion of 'coherence' both as a feature of social systems and as a means of overcoming distance breaks down, and we come to focus on the fractures, tensions, and contradictions of any society as central for understanding its historical dynamic. More, the crucial loss of innocence about difference (an innocence that was implicit in the notion of distance) should also take from us the desire to 'overcome' the presumed space of difference. A travel brochure in suburban New York City for a photo safari in the east African 'jungle' (i.e., savannah) calls relatively prosperous American people to come and witness 'tribal dances' and simultaneously 'make new friends' with African people – in three days and presumably with the rural people whose farm and grazing lands have largely been taken from them for game parks, without adequate compensation, leaving them impoverished, desperate, and dancing, so that more cosmopolitan Africans might graze and harvest tourists.

Our project is not to help people make new friends with the oppressed (however noble a sentiment that might, in its ignorance, be) but to contribute to transforming the world that oppresses both us and them, at first by better understanding its processes.

While the distinction between 'distance' and 'differentiation' turns us toward process, our simultaneous focus on fractures and contradictions, rather than coherence, substantially complicates the task of conceptualizing a historical dynamic. From a straightforward Marxist (or even Hegelian) perspective it might well be claimed that understanding a social system in terms of its contradictions is far from an impossible task; indeed, the whole of *Capital* is a demonstration of how to do this. But the fundamental – or better, the necessary – fractures and contradictions are far from being simply about class, or between classes, or even 'about' gender and ethnicity. As the papers here show, these ruptures emerge and develop their significance within, as well as between, the component elements of fundamental social antagonisms.

Reflecting upon the conference papers, we propose a distinction between 'history' and 'histories' as a way of conceptualizing societies in terms of their changing ruptures and contradictions. We are, in this approach, seeking to develop a historical anthropology of and for social systems that reveal themselves by how they do not fit together. In this way the irreducible ambivalences and ambiguities of both silences and commemorations – their changing, multiple valences and their fundamental, often purposeful unclarity and non-specificity of their meanings – are a crucial route toward seeing the fractures from which this new kind of historical anthropology will emerge.

So, as the editors of this volume, once we came to consider historically significant silences and historically focused commemorations, the importance of distinguishing histories from history increasingly became a central problem for us. Indeed, we learned to see this separation not only as an analytical abstraction but as a real-world field of high-consequence battles. And then we began to see the distinction between history and histories to be deeply related to the further idea that power must be understood as engendering chaos and havoc – conceptual, cultural, and social-relational – as much as it does order. Two illustrations will help to clarify our understanding of the connection between power, order, and chaos and the characteristic practices of power that produce both order and chaos. These same illustrations can also delineate the often-antagonistic separation between history and histories.

The first illustration sketches a history of class alliances across the enmities of war. At the end of the Second World War, German officer prisoners of war in American prisons in France were used to replace rapidly demobilized American soldiers as guards in the military jails for American enlisted men (non-officers). After all the boundless horrors of the war this is a very tiny and insignificant incident, unless one happened to be a prisoner in such a jail after spending several years at the fronts, seeing one's comrades wounded and killed and seeing oneself become focused on wounding and killing – or even unless one was the youthful, upper-class 'liberal' German officer telling this story, shaken by the experience of being told to guard, in an American military jail, the 'same' American troops who had captured and come close to killing him.

When this story is understood as part of a larger history, it teaches us little that we do not already know, except perhaps that the attempt by those with power to order the world along lines of class is rather more pervasive – and more expansive – than we might have imagined. It is only when we leave the terrain of 'history' and read this small story through the eyes of its 'inhabitants' that we begin to understand that power creates both order and chaos simultaneously, and that people must struggle against both.[3]

The inescapable emergence of such struggles, and the chaos that power routinely brings, can be illuminated with an example again drawn from that paragon of presumed bureaucratic orderliness, the military's treatment of its own current and former soldiers in peacetime. Consider the situation of the more than 5,000 American soldiers exposed to 'nerve gas' in the U.S. destruction of an Iraqi military storage facility in early 1991. Most of those who were exposed to these chemicals have had long-lasting neural ailments, and genetic problems have emerged among a substantial percentage of the children subsequently born to them. Five years later, in 1996, the U.S. government admitted, under pressure, the occurrence of this incident and the likelihood that it was related to the troubles of those who were exposed. Although this admission is the prerequisite for the government's accepting responsibility for treatment of the afflicted, nothing substantial has yet been done. For the victims and their families, is it the order or the chaos that power brings, or both together, which must be fought?

In such contexts we can neither privilege nor deny either a 'grand narrative history' or multiple specific histories. Yet it is not particularly useful simply to associate 'history' with 'large systems and large processes' and 'histories' with the specific and the particular – the ethnographic, as it were. So by invoking plural *histories*, we are suggesting that these histories emerge both within and against larger social processes – against 'history' – and also, in significant ways, *against the local and the locally known as well*. The following brief incident illustrates the point:

A young German girl, about seven years old at the end of the Second World War, living in a small, mostly Catholic farming village and suffering, with her family, very severe hunger in the disruptions at the end of the war, went gleaning potatoes in the village convent's fields at the end of the harvest, the long-standing right of her village's poor and needy.[4] This is, of course, only a local instance of a widely replicated practice, but here as elsewhere the right of some poor, always including children, to glean was a key element in the construction of a presumably 'moral' community. The harvest had been very thorough; several hours of her gleaning produced only a small, but very special, sack of potatoes. At the end of the day, when she was about to go home, a nun came out of the convent, demanded the bag, and struck her hard, taking it when it was not given.

The chaos that such assaults produce in people's lives is at least as useful to contemplate as any 'ordering' or unifying pattern or process, and equally large and politically crucial issues are at stake. Although the story here is about taking a small bag of potatoes from a little girl, the situation is more general: The chaos in people's lives that power creates, in its arrogance and its violence and in the full range of its ordinary daily practices and claims – including 'allowing' the poor to glean – is as much the precondition for continued accumulation, both of goods and of further power, as is any transient, apparent, or even actual order that may emerge from the exercise and 'legitimation' of power.

It is this chaos – the turmoil and tumult created by the cultural and physical violence that is always crucial to the continuing exercise of power – which enables us to use the distinction between history and histories without privileging 'history.' And it should also provoke us to think anew about the ways in which we seek to put anthropology and history together. All the recurrent, shifting ruptures we have seen in our own lives – different kinds of wars, different kinds of economic booms and busts, all with vastly different consequences from those that came before and those that will follow – should have long ago taught us to call into question our conceptual apparatus for a 'historical social science.' 'Social organization,' 'culture,' 'social relations of production,' 'text' – all such concepts name, at their best, the fundamental struggles that characterize social life.

It would thus be a serious mistake to create a concept of 'history' that is intrinsically and ordinarily (rather than episodically and partially) the domain of order, rationality, pattern, progress, development, and linear change. 'History' is used in ways that misleadingly imply the majesty of systemic coherence, over and against the seemingly more random and incoherent expressions of a multitude of people's claims, concerns, and actions. It is heuristically important, therefore, to see the distinction between histories and history, as we use it here, as at least *beginning* on a playing field, with neither side assumed to be more responsible for maintaining, reproducing, or transforming the social order. This distinction is not ordinarily made or used in such a way, but the difference is crucial, we feel, to the papers collected here.

We began this part of the introduction by saying that both anthropology and history might gain from addressing more thoroughly the issue of cultural differentiation. Attending to processes of differentiation becomes more than just adding another topic to a list of anthropological and historical interests. Rather, processes of differentiation centre our analyses upon what we might provocatively call 'the rents of culture': what a culture takes and appropriates, and from whom; the tears across the still-being-woven fabrics of social life: in sum, culture history.

We need to develop ways of seeing 'culture,' and in particular the splits, tensions, and antagonisms within a culture, not simply *in* history but *as* history: the continual formation of culture and cultures through the assertions, rejections, and necessarily incomplete acceptance of the forms of knowledge and ways of being that power creates. We have found that the making and breaking of silences and commemorations calls our attention to those aspects of culture that are not simply shared – or unshared – 'values'; more, that a close attention to silences and commemorations broadens, in analytically very useful ways, our concepts of necessary struggle.

Silences and commemorations call our attention to forms of struggle within, as well as between, classes, or more broadly, among oppressed and exploited people, as well as between them and those who dominate. In the largest sense the issue before us is not simply struggle but necessary struggle – not necessary in any simple mechanical, predetermined way, but as one outcome of antagonisms that are crucial to the organization and reproduction of a society.

We can amplify and clarify our point by distinguishing a direct consideration of silences and commemorations from the social-historical project, particularly salient in the last three decades or so, of 'giving voice' to the silent and silenced. By choice, progressive forms of social and cultural anthropology have been closely associated with this social-historical project and anthropology has been widely, if somewhat unspecifically, invoked by historians in their search for voices to give. Much as this whole project has been an extraordinary gain over what went before, broadening our sense of social processes, it has some peculiar and limiting twists that can be found right at the outset of its conceptual and methodological pathways. The related anthropological project of speaking for the oppressed reveals, in its more salient and unavoidable difficulties, some of the key problems with the historical project of giving voice to the silent/silenced.

Ethnographers face some issues about silence and voice that are rightly of not much concern to historians, save to those of the very recent past: giving voice to people whose well-being or lives depend upon silence. And this issue goes far beyond the presentation of any specific critique of power. The French ethnologist Georges Condominas, speaking in tears to the 1972 plenary session of the American Anthropological Association annual meetings, told how his monograph analysing and celebrating the music and ethnomusicology of Montaignard people in the Vietnamese highlands was used by the American Central Intelligence Agency to uncover lines of social alliance in these highlands and to identify and kill several of his key 'informants' (an anthropological term from a more innocent age).

But ethnographers, in the midst of the extreme pressures upon them to consider and to invoke their own silences, have a special advantage over most social historians: the 'voice' that they seek to give to the unheard has a double presence, even if the distinction is often unclear. Ethnographers can speak *about* the unheard to one another and to their readers, and on the basis of their extensive residence among the people whom they study, they can record and re-present the (often mutually antagonistic) words of diverse groups among 'the people' themselves.

Without entering into the useful, but increasingly diversionary, discussions of how the ethnographer often imposes his or her own modalities upon 'native' voices, we here address a more salient issue for historians as well as anthropologists. This second component of what anthropologists do – re-presenting local voices – has led, and increasingly forcefully still leads, directly to the issue of making these voices matter. Otherwise we are pushed back to an anthropology that is little more than a description of the quaint or violent customs of other people, or a social history that calls talking to each other about the vulnerable giving them voice. Far more often than we have admitted, it is not simply the silence of the vulnerable that matters – they are as likely as not to scream and wail when their children die – but the silence of the dominant society, and other groups of the poor and the oppressed, about their or each other's suffering. Aldous Huxley put the issue clearly: 'Screams of pain and fear go pulsing through the air at the rate of eleven hundred feet per second. After traveling for three seconds they are perfectly inaudible'.

There is a historical myth, widespread among and important to progressive American historians, which seems to delineate our strategy for coping effectively with silences. This myth developed from a tale spun in the late 1970s by Paul Cowan, a reporter for the New York City *Village Voice*, about the aftermath of the 1912 'Bread and Roses' strike in Lawrence, Massachusetts (Cowan 1979, 1980). His story centres on the family history of Camella Teoli, who as a thirteen-year-old girl working in a mill in Lawrence in 1911, the year before the strike, had her scalp torn off by a yarn-twisting machine. The myth that developed from this incident, retold by Herbert Gutman in several influential contexts, including his 1982 presidential address to the American Historical Association (see Gutman 1987), can be divided into two major allegories. The first concerns the family relations of the working class and claims that Camella Teoli never told her children about her scalping or about her dramatic post-strike testimony in a congressional inquiry; it further claims that this silence, this lack of knowledge of one's own family history, was both widely replicated and a serious obstacle to the development of class consciousness.

The second major allegory in this myth focuses on the development, beginning in 1980, of a 'Bread and Roses' day of public commemoration in Lawrence, with music, speeches, and food and with a special place of honour for Camella Teoli, including giving her name to a pathway in the town park where the commemorations are held. Historians, especially Paul Cowan, played a key role in the development of this Bread and Roses commemoration, as also did a progressive union and a church group, both with headquarters in New York City. As Gerald Sider has shown (1996), all the major components of this myth about 'giving voice to the silenced' are not only factually wrong but also wrong in ways that matter a very great deal to the working people of Lawrence. Camella Teoli's children in fact knew their mother's history in great detail long before they first met Paul Cowan; the crucial silence that we need strategically to consider is not their silence with each other but their silence before Paul Cowan's widely believed, insistent, and totally false assertion, both to them and publicly, that he was giving them their history, rather than imposing a history.

The commemoration of the Bread and Roses strike, at its beginning in 1980, was largely designed and financed by outsiders, with the worthy goal of enhancing class consciousness by 'giving people back' their history. But in 1980 the last textile mill had been closed for twenty-six years, and the city was largely, and the public schools predominantly, Hispanic. The entire governance of the city, all the city jobs, and the whole school board were in the hands of the remaining White ethnic population. Far from simply being 'about' teaching class consciousness, the commemoration and glorification of the 'history' of workers – but particularly the non-Hispanic workers – quickly became embedded in a politics that culminated during the elections of 1986, in the successful mayoral candidate's slogan 'Give Lawrence back to the people who made it' – even though the Whites still then had it all, and still now have almost all there is left to have. Some historians, emphasizing the importance of collectively self-referential ways of looking at 'texts' and paying elaborate attention to the relations that historians have to one another and to their 'audiences' (rather than emphasizing what is and has been happening in the outside world), have regarded the interweaving of fact and fancy in this myth and its commemoration and the political significance of getting the story right as 'ludic' (see Cohen, this volume, and more generally Montgomery, Buhle, Stansell, and Cameron in their rejoinders published along with Sider 1996). The struggles that rage just out of sight of our 'gift of history' to the workers of Lawrence are far less ludic to the Hispanic people there, a great many of whom rioted against their treatment in 1984, triggering a wave of arson that went far beyond the arson rate of any other city in New England and lasted until the early 1990s.

The mythic interpretations of the long history of labour struggles in Lawrence seemed worse than ludicrous to the remnants of the old White working class, who have outspokenly regarded the subsequently imposed 'Bread and Roses' label for the strike (a slogan that was never used by the strikers themselves) as a travesty and a trivialization of their hunger, their suffering, and their need. In 1989 people involved in labour struggles in Lawrence in the 1930s and 1940s were interviewed about their sense of their own history. One said that 'calling the 1912 mill strike the Bread and Roses strike is ludicrous. It was not a glamorous occasion. I used to see the men come out of the Arlington mill half-naked to the waist. They were drowned in sweat and looking at them you felt they were about to collapse ... I never saw people suffer like that ... It left a terrible impression' (this woman's full statement is presented and discussed in Sider 1996:67). When we speak of silence or when we speak 'for' or to the silenced, we must ourselves first do a much better job of listening. As the transformations of our attempts to bring our version of class consciousness to the 'silenced' workers of Lawrence shows, the process of listening to, and for, silences must also be the process of rethinking some of our most cherished and romantically compelling concepts and collective self-perceptions. The silenced, as with Camella Teoli's children, may be particularly silent *precisely to us*, and that silence, rather than what we might wish it, may be politically significant component of their consciousness of class – their consciousness both of their class and of ours and the multiple kinds of connections, spaces, and silences within and between theirs and ours.

Speaking about the fact that throughout the mid-twentieth century the non-White infant mortality rate in the United States has been three times as high as that of White infants, James Baldwin told us, 'All those children died in silence.' When we think about this silence, we find it to be not at all the silence of their parents, nor simply the silence of those who, like us, lived apart from the kinds of struggles entailed in such deaths. Rather, this 'silence' names the active, and in some ways the actively enforced and often exceptionally noisy, relationships between those infants, their parents, ourselves, and our dominant social institutions. All those very specific children died both in silence and, as Baldwin implied, from silence, and when we look closely at those silences, we find them to be in crucial ways both embedded in and also continually reborn from our praxis and from our inability to listen.

We need then to think about a broader range of necessary struggles and alliances than those revealed by the actually multiple – but often seemingly polar – antagonisms of class, gender, or ethnicity. On this basis we can begin to work on the problems of what it means to 'give voice' to the vulnerable and the oppressed. We could also consider what else we might need to do, analytically and politically (besides a more or less 'thick' description of others' works and days), to engage with the struggles, in addition to class, that must be fought and to make the alliances that need to be made.

Historians' invocation of anthropology to describe the 'otherness' of the people whom they study (see, for example, Lowenthal 1995) runs the risk of homogenizing their subjects of study, reducing the changing internal dynamics to a few stereotypical distinctions – male or female, working or unemployed, religion a or b, black or white – distinctions that may or may not, at any given time and place, have any significant part in the transformative tensions that wreak havoc, change, and hope (hope, for the vulnerable, being as much a terror as a joy) among the dominated and the oppressed.

The issue before us, in sum, ought no longer to be the 'otherness' of the people whom we study and work with, but the ways that differentiation, like silence, can be both imposed and chosen, and how differentiation, like commemoration, involves attempts from both 'above' and 'below,' as it were, to claim and impose a past upon the future and upon each other.

The Contributors

The papers in this book are divided into two sections. Though all the authors address the role of different forms of power in indexing what are to be taken as historical truths, the papers in the first group refer to contests over the social constructions of the past, while those in the second explore the shape and textures of silences that result from the contestation of commemorations – oral, structural, and textual.

Part I: History and Histories

Michel-Rolph Trouillot, a scholar from a community that has not dominated the discourse of Western historiography, warns us to be suspicious of the ways in which this dominant discourse has produced a single truth about History (written with a capital 'H'). Yet by referring, in the opening chapter, to Haitian urban elites who prefer that certain ghosts are 'best left undisturbed' (40), he reminds us that we should not be too hasty in passing the baton of 'truth' to elite guild historians beyond the West.

Trouillot's argument is that asking the question about what history is or what it should be is misguided; rather, we should be trying to explore *how history works*, and he identifies at least four essential stages in this process: the making of *sources*, of *archives*, of *narratives*, and finally 'the moment of retrospective significance (the making of *history* in the final instance).' He points out that we should take care not to focus too closely on the later of these stages to the exclusion of the selective processes that occur in the first two. His article then gives us a profound and intricate exploration of what we find when such a genuinely *critical* history is undertaken. Trouillot reminds us time and again of the limitations of his own endeavour: history for him, as for all the contributors, is eternally an unfinished task, not just *whether* our gaze is turned back to the past or on to the future, but *because* our gaze can never be singularly directed to the one or the other.

In the chapter that follows, Gerald Sider returns again to struggles over the way that history is produced, in 'Against Experience: The Struggles for History, Tradition, and Hope among a Native American People.' Here he addresses the formation of specific experiences of being Indian and of sharecropping in terms of how people claim their history not only *from* but, as crucially, *against* their own experiences. The issue at the core of this analysis of an ongoing ethnic history is the simultaneous formation of tradition and class – against and within the histories that are claimed, that people are forced to live, that people must oppose. Out of the diversity of interlocked struggles that we have named 'history' and 'tradition,' people form and also deny both their own cultures and their experiences.

Next, Gavin Smith's essay, 'Pandora's History,' illuminates profound differences between the ways that Peruvian peasants and urban intellectuals –

journalists, historians, government officials – organize both specific stories of their confrontations and land occupations, and chains of interwoven stories. We are not dealing here with anything that can simply be reduced to the notion of 'resistance' ideologies or practices. The fundamental issue is how ordinary people *continue* – continue their ways, their practices, their beliefs, their life itself – and how they talk to one another about their 'history,' in ways that keep them going, keep them talking to one another – against the ways that their history is organized for them by those with far more political and cultural power.

The themes of dispute and difference in the production of histories are taken up again in Sumit Sarkar's 'Renaissance and Kaliyuga: Time, Myth, and History in Colonial Bengal,' in which we find the author worrying that Edward Said's path-breaking book attacking western Orientalism has itself resulted in a counter-orthodoxy that relies too closely on 'simplistic impact-response frameworks' vis-à-vis colonial hegemonic discourses. The result, he suggests, is that 'a vague "community-consciousness" can now be postulated as relatively free of internal tension or structures of oppression: *an indigenism that can become extremely retrogressive in its political implication*s' (emphasis ours). The relevance of this observation is made clear near the end of the essay, when we find the author turning from the writing of his piece to the communal violence engulfing the India he lives in today.

Sarkar chooses as his ground a small item in the historical records: a pamphlet describing a court case. A high-caste rural gentleman had invited a wandering Brahman and two of his untouchable followers into his home, and murder and mayhem had resulted. The court case that resulted provides inconclusive flashes of light on a complex reality. For Sarkar, any discussion of the so-called post-colonial discourse is faced with an almost insuperable task. Hitherto, he suggests, it has resolved the problem by focusing almost exclusively on classes that leave the most vivid historical traces, notably the Indian middle class. The issue is far more complex, however, and Sarkar tackles it by setting up for us a number of crucial characteristics of the period that he is dealing with, among them the very rapid introduction of clock time to Bengal and of office discipline among the lower middle classes moving from rural to urban settings. What we discover in his intricate account is that not only was the colonial encounter experienced differently by different groups in Bengali society, but so too was the supposedly 'Bengali' indigenous history to which actors turned in their everyday worlds.

But this is only part of the problem, for people's access to and use of the four stages of historical production which we saw Trouillot identifying are very far from uniformly distributed through late nineteenth-century Bengali society. Sarkar the historian is not able to deal with his 'informants' on an equal basis: as his vividly drawn untouchable, Prasanna, cynically remarks to the judge in the court case, 'If I had known how to write, why, then, I would have become a judge and earned five to seven hundred rupees.' So even though he has sensitized himself to the multiplicity of voices, the very materiality of the historical resources themselves impels Sarkar – and all of us – toward what? A kind of forgery? (See Medick's chapter below.) Yet Sarkar and Trouillot, in the opening chapter, are alike in their forceful insistence that the threatened *traisons des clercs* involved in a constructivist view of historical 'reality' lie above all else in political timidity.

Karin Hausen's 'The "Day of National Mourning" in Germany,' illuminates a history of the spaces between personal grief and public mourning, and shows how in this space grief and mourning are simultaneously shaped, denied, and appropriated. The starting point of this history is the substitution of 'fallen' for 'killed' and the continual eradication of the victims of the killed soldiers. The history develops through the multiple struggles of families, veterans' associations, and the re-emergent state against the idea of 'deaths for nothing' in the loss of the First World War. This struggle was also lost – the struggle to learn something productive 'from history' – and in this loss we can see the processes through which the mass 'industrial' slaughters of armies in the First World War were broken into thinkable pieces in ways that create culture by making and denying both memory and understanding.

Part II: Silences and Commemorations

At the core of Alf Lüdtke's essay, 'Histories of Mourning: Flowers and Stones for the War Dead, Confusion for the Living,' is his rejection of any attempt to produce a 'coherent picture' of the contestations in the histories of mourning. Rather, his purpose is to portray the 'fractured realities' of public and private histories across the division and reunification of East and West Germany, and to use the lines of fracture to draw out paradoxes in the commemorations of the German war dead – commemorations simultaneously 'negating and appropriating public and private grief.' The mass graves and ordered cemetery at Halbe become both 'sites of memory' (*lieux de mémoire*, in Pierre Nora's 1989 phrase) and also, crucially, sites of the denial of memory and a focal point for the struggles of people with their own specific memories, as well as the memories and memory-projects of others. Memory and history are torn apart, one from the other, both before our eyes and again almost out of sight. Indeed, one of the achievements of this essay is to show how what we do and do not see as history takes, and loses, shape.

David William Cohen and E.S. Atieno Odhiambo, in 'Silences of the Living, Orations of the Dead,' examine the struggles in Kenya over the burial of S.M. Otieno. These struggles began with Otieno's wife and his brother each claiming the body for burial and developed through seven court battles, major public demonstrations, and an outpouring of correspondence and commentary in the national newspapers. On the surface a conflict between 'tradition' and 'modernity,' the debate quickly developed into confrontations over the historical construction of culture and authority. The power of this piece lies precisely in its ability to show us the creation and destruction both of such abstractions as 'culture' and 'authority' and also simultaneously of actual people, especially Wambui, Otieno's wife.

The struggles over the construction of memory and the connections between a remembered past and an impending future are directly engaged by Gadi Algazi in his study of village assemblies in late-medieval western Germany, 'Lords Ask, Peasants Answer: Making Traditions in Late Medieval Village Assemblies.' In these assemblies, subject peasants were forced by their lords to both state and agree to the laws that constituted the rights of the lord over and against them, and that specified the rights of the peasants as well. In ritualized 'visits' to the peasant communities, lords would ask a series of formal questions to the peasants' spokesperson(s). These interrogations often began quite simply – 'Am I your lawful lord?' – but they soon progressed, under the watchful eyes of both the lord's armed retainers and the peasant inhabitants of the village, to questions about rents and dues. Most of the questions took the form of enquiries into – which is to say, statements about and constructions of – the customs of the continuing past. 'Remembering' emerged as part of a dialogue between people of unequal power. Although – and because – the lord could not claim what the peasant would not state, and the peasant could not respond to what was not asked, peasants had the power of memory and lords the power to call it forth or press it back. In such contexts, memory was not that domain of the self that could seem to be partly isolated from lordship, and tradition could be a burden. More to the point, both memory and tradition were the products of fundamentally antagonistic confrontations – as elsewhere, although elsewhere the processes that create such outcomes are ordinarily more diffuse.

History and histories are always being used and reused, asserted and denied. But not all uses and denials are of the same ethical kind. This is especially striking in the pieces by Jane and Peter Schneider and Louise Lamphere, which raise and extend this issue in the contexts of commemorations and silences. As the Schneiders introduce us to the world of contemporary Sicily in the next chapter, we learn of a variety of anti-mafia groups who differ above all in the ways in which they seek to confront mafia in the present. We learn that within

the everyday social relationships through which people get things done now –
today, tomorrow, at a birthday, in a local government office – it is hard to draw
the line between practicality and morality.

But then as we turn to the backlash with which the various expressions of
anti-mafia have been faced in Sicily, we discover that the apparently mundane
and present-day focus of people's dilemmas is pre-eminently a product of the
way that Sicilian history has been and is being produced. Against the rational
individualism of peace and Green activists who talk of the universal good of
'the rule of law,' there is another side, even among many anti-mafia activists
themselves, who simultaneously feel nostalgia for an intimate past of awkward
Italian dialect while recognizing that there is nothing universal or 'blind' about
the liberal 'rule of law' in its real, daily application, particularly as they witness their landscape transformed by the gentle and thorough predations of a
liberal international capital.

What is the essence of a good Sicily – something we can be fond of without
feeling guilty or treacherous? And what really were those quotidian moments
of toil and joy, jealousy and love, that we experienced, or wished that we had
experienced, in our youth (or our grandparents in theirs)? These seem to be
conjoined questions. Against the insistence of historians and lawyers on 'truth,'
we all reserve the right to demonize or romanticize elements of our intimate
past (and to switch our views, too, from one day to the next), even despite –
perhaps precisely because of – what somebody else tells us is the evidence.

For one thing, that 'someone else,' as we have seen in the pieces by Trouillot
and Sarkar and are shortly to see in Medick's piece, always has *some* agenda of
his or her own which we may or may not know. In Lamphere's study of a plant
in New Mexico whose workers are faced with management plans to introduce
'high involvement' work schemes, the agendas of those who describe the past
daily practices of work to each other are not obscure, even if they are not
always consistent or clear. The introduction of these new methods of organizing shop-floor work inevitably assumes a certain way of interpreting what has
happened in the past, the version differing greatly depending on where you are
in the company. Although management may have seen the Taylorist schemes
of the past as problematic, they nonetheless saw within them well-intentioned
attempts to get labour to work more productively by using management's
suggested methods. The workers, on the other hand, felt that they had always
wanted to 'get involved' and, indeed, had often suggested ideas to management, but were never taken seriously. And these are not just academic disputes
over 'what really happened'; how you see what the past labour process was
really all about very much determines the shape that you give to the new
'Japanese plan.'

For, although workers may believe that they have as much stake as management in making the factory work properly, their shared desire to improve *productivity* (against foreign competition) translates ultimately into whether or not each of them has a job – a job that comes to be defined as much by its increasingly brutalizing demands as by the wage – on the one hand, and whether or not management can pay dividends to the shareholders, on the other. So new versions of 'corporate culture' involve a quite specific reading of what is most relevant in the history of capitalism. In 'corporate *culture*' the term 'culture' is taken very much in its old anthropological sense: a shared set of meanings (and goals) and a common sense of belonging, in which the 'we versus they' lines are forged not between management and labour but between our firm and theirs. Lamphere's piece illustrates very clearly the deep personal and social splits and woundings created and then obscured by such a construction.

The piece by Hans Medick is especially provocative in a collection on the production of history, for it deals with a document full of 'thick description' of the famine in the Swabian Alps of Germany at the beginning of the last century. Long a rich source for professional historians of this period, the document turns out to have been a forgery with a complex ideological agenda, including anti-Semitism. Near the end of his chapter Medick questions why the author of the piece might have chosen to undertake his very dubious enterprise. Among his hypotheses is that this obscure rural schoolteacher wished to 'establish in a written text the oral memory of the famine years,' which he felt to be disappearing in the face of the modern age. Because this was at a time when such histories had little legitimacy among German professional historians, Medick suggests, perhaps the teacher chose to mask his retrospective sentiments in the guise of thick description. But symbolic capital turns out to be like any other form of capital: it draws its own vitality from other people's lives.

In a sense, then, the teacher may have chosen the route of forgery because there was no professional guild of social historians (or anthropologists) who would or could provide a cover of professional respectability for his work. What Medick hypothesizes that the teacher may have been doing was trying to find a means that would reproduce as closely as possible the oral tradition of the people whom he felt himself to be representing. And what resulted was 'a forgery.' By calling his article 'An Example of the Fiction of the Factual,' Medick draws our attention to the extent to which historians and anthropologists seeking a means to *represent* the world of their subjects always run the risk of slipping into forgery. It is a theme taken up in different ways by Trouillot, Sarkar, and the Schneiders.

Reflecting on his own position paper (circulated as part of the call for these essays) in the final chapter, David W. Cohen brings us back to the strategic implications of our attempts to understand 'the production of history,' by alluding to a separation between struggles for historical knowledge and other kinds of struggle, particularly in contexts where these other kinds of struggle 'are not usually susceptible to elaboration.'

The project of this collection of essays is, at its most general and most fundamental, the reformulation of our concepts of class and class struggle. Edward Thompson – whose absence is a space in our hearts, whose presence inspired much of the hope that fuels our own work – taught us specifically to understand the priority of struggle; from struggle came class and class consciousness, not vice versa. These essays take up that point of view, but in the context of struggles that are both about class and necessarily also very much broader. More and different rough beasts are now slouching towards Bethlehem to be born; our concepts of class, in this perspective, seem almost too innocent and too neat for the battles that must now be fought.

What each and every paper in this collection tries to confront is the issues of dispute and struggle within and against ordered fields of power, not always the powerful interested in order and the weak opposed to it, but often the weak seeking (their) order against chaos imposed by domination. It is hardly surprising, then, that the pieces themselves speak with and against each other, to form what we as editors hope will be a continually unfinished dialogue between history and histories.

NOTES

1 O'Brien and Roseberry's book is among the best recent treatments of the relationship between anthropology and history, as also is Comaroff and Comaroff 1992.
2 We do not claim to be exhaustive here. Studies of collective memory, as well as the role of personal ways of remembering, can be found in sociology, psychology, anthropology, and history and also in emerging interdisciplinary fields such as gender studies, cultural studies, and ethnicity studies. Especially important are the works of Vincent (1981), Samuel and Thompson (Samuel 1981, 1989; P. Thompson 1982; Samuel and Thompson 1990), Swindells (1985), Steedman (1986, 1988), Passerini (1987), the Personal Narratives Group (1989), Tonkin (1991), Portelli (1991), Terradas (1992), and Lüdtke (1995). That the exemplary work of Ronald Fraser (1972, 1973, 1979) is rarely referred to in (con)texts such as this one demonstrates the continued hegemony of university-based research and disciplinary fortresses.
3 Rosaldo (1989) has suggested the importance of 'the space between order and chaos,' which is a similar distinction that he uses for much different purposes. Rosaldo is trying to 'go beyond' the dichotomy of order and chaos to focus on 'nonorder.' Here we emphasize people's unavoidable confrontations with the chaos that power engenders.
4 The fact that the 'right' to glean – and related practices, such as using dead wood from the forest or hunting small mammals and birds – was long and bitterly contested is not the point

here; at the time of this story the contest had been won by the needy villagers, and won as if it were a 'traditional' right.

REFERENCES

Anderson, Benedict
    1991 Imagined Communities: Reflections on the Origin and Spread of Nationalism. Rev. ed. London: Verso
Berdahl, Robert, et al.
    1982 Klassen und Kultur: Sozialanthropologische Perspektiven in der Geschichtsschreibung. Frankfurt am Main: Syndikat.
Clifford, James, and George Marcus, eds.
    1986 Writing Culture: The Poetics and Politics of Ethnography. Berkeley: University of California Press
Cohen, David William
    1988 The Production of History. Conference-call paper for Bellagio conference.
    1994 The Combing of History. Chicago: University of Chicago Press.
Cohn, Bernard
    1981 Anthrolopogy and History in the 1980s: Toward a Rapprochement. Journal of Interdisciplinary History 12: 227–52.
Comaroff, John, and Jane Comaroff
    1992 Ethnography and the Historical Imagination. Boulder, CO: Westview.
Cowan, Paul
    1979 Whose America Is This? Village Voice, 2 April.
    1980: A City Comes Alive. Village Voice, 9–15 July.
Davis, Natalie Zemon
    1981 Anthropology and History in the 1980s: The Possibilities of the Past. Journal of Interdisciplinary History 12: 267–75.
Donham, Donald L.
    1992 Revolution and Modernity in Maale: Ethiopia, 1974 to 1987. Comparative Studies in Society and History 34:28–57.
Fentress, James, and Chris Wickham
    1992 Social Memory. Oxford: Blackwell.
Fraser, Ronald
    1972 In Hiding: The Life of Manuel Cortes. Harmondsworth: Penguin.
    1973 The Pueblo. London: Allen Lane.
    1979 Blood of Spain: An Oral History of the Spanish Civil War. New York: Pantheon
Gillis, John R.
    1994 Memory and Identity: The History of a Relationship. In Commemorations: The Politics of National Identity, Gillis, ed. Princeton: Princeton University Press.
Ginzburg, Carlo
    1981 Anthropology and History in the 1980s: A Comment. Journal of Interdisciplinary History 12:277–8.
Gluckman, Max
    1958 Analysis of the Social Situation in Modern Zululand. Manchester: Manchester University Press.

Gutman, Herb
    1987 Power and Culture: Essays on the American Working Class, Ira Berlin, ed. New York: New Press.

Halbwachs, Maurice
    1992 On Collective Memory. Lewis Coser, ed. and trans. Chicago: University of Chicago Press.

Hannerz, Ulf
    1991 Scenarios for Peripheral Cultures. *In* Culture, Globalization and the World System, Anthony King, ed. Albany: State University of New York Press.

Hobsbawm, Eric J.
    1959 Primitive Rebels. New York: Norton.

Hobsbawm, Eric J., and Terrance Ranger
    1983 The Invention of Tradition. Cambridge: Cambridge University Press.

Keesing, Roger
    1987 Anthropology as Interpretive Quest. Current Anthropology 28:161–76.

Koonz, Claudia
    1994 Between Memory and Oblivion: Concentration Camps in German Memory. *In* Commemorations: The Politics of National Identity, John R. Gillis, ed. Princeton: Princeton University Press.

Lowenthal, David
    1985 The Past Is a Foreign Country. Cambridge: Cambridge University Press.

Lüdtke, Alf
    1990 Herrschaft als Sozial Praxis. Göttingen: Vandenhoeck und Ruprecht.

Lüdtke, Alf, ed.
    1995 The History of Everyday Life: Reconstructing Historical Experiences and Ways of Life. Princeton: Princeton University Press.

Medick, Hans
    1987 'Missionaries in a Rowboat'? Ethnological ways of knowing as a challenge to social history. Comparative Studies in Society and History 29.

Medick, Hans, and David Sabean, eds.
    1984 Interest and Emotion: Essays on the Study of Family and Kinship. New York: Cambridge University Press.

Middleton, David, and Derek Edwards, eds.
    1990 Collective Remembering. London: Sage.

Nora, Pierre
    1989 Between Memory and History: Les lieux de mémoire. Representations 26.

O'Brien, Jay, and William Roseberry
    1991 Golden Ages, Dark Ages. Berkeley: University of California Press.

Ortner, Sherry B.
    1984 Theory in Anthropology since the Sixties. Comparative Studies in Society and History 26:126–66.

Passerini, Luisa
    1987 Fascism in Popular Memory. Cambridge: Cambridge University Press.

Personal Narratives Group
    1989 Interpreting Women's Lives: Feminist Theory and Personal Narratives. Midland: Indiana University Press.

Polier, Nicole
    1994 A View from the 'Cyanide Room': Politics and Culture in a Mining Township in Papua New Guinea. Identities: Global Studies in Culture and Power 1:63–84.

Portelli, Alessandro

    1991 The Death of Luigi Trastulli and Other Stories: Form and Meaning in Oral History. Albany: State University of New York Press.

Raphael, Samuel

    1989 Theatres of Memory. London: Verso.

Rosaldo, Renato

    1989 Culture and Truth. Boston: Beacon.

Roseberry, William

    1989 Anthropologies and Histories. New Brunswick, NJ: Rutgers University Press.

Rousso, Henry

    1991 The Vichy Syndrome. Arthur Goldhammer, trans. Cambridge: Harvard University Press.

Sahlins, Marshall

    1987 Islands of History. Chicago: University of Chicago Press.

Samuel, Raphael

    1981 People's History and Socialist Theory. History Workshop. London: Routledge.

Samuel, Raphael, and Paul Thompson, eds.

    1990 The Myths We Live By. History Workshops. London: Routledge.

Schwartz, Barry

    1982 The Social Context of Commemoration: A Study in Collective Memory. *Social Forces* 61:374–97.

Sider, Gerald M.

    1993 Lumbee Indian Histories: Race, Ethnicity and Indian Identity in the Southern United States. New York: Cambridge University Press.

    1996 Cleansing History: Lawrence, Massachusetts, the Strike for Four Loaves of Bread and No Roses, and the Anthropology of Working Class Consciousness. Radical History Review 65: 48–83. Published with responses by David Montgomery, Paul Buhle, Christine Stansell, and Ardis Cameron and a reply.

Smith, Gavin

    1989 Livelihood and Resistance: Peasants and the Politics of Land in Peru. Berkeley: University of California Press.

Steedman, Carolyn

    1986 Landscape for a Good Woman. London: Virago.

    1988 The Radical Soldier's Tale. London: Routledge.

Stolcke, Verena

    1995 Talking Culture: New Boundaries, New Rhetorics of Exclusion in Europe. Current Anthropology 36:1–15.

Swindells, Julia, and Lisa Jardine

    1990 What's Left? Women in Culture and the Labour Movement. London: Routledge.

Terradas, Ignasi

    1992 Elisa Kendall: reflexiones sobre una anti-biografia. Barcelona: Universidad de Barcelona.

Thomas, Nicholas

    1991 Against Ethnography. Cultural Anthropology 6:306–22.

Thompson, Edward P.

    1968 The Making of the English Working Class. New York: Pantheon.

    1972 Anthropology and the Discipline of Historical Context. Midland History 1:41–55.

    1991 Customs in Common. London: Merlin Press

Thompson, Paul, ed.
  1982 Our Common History: The Transformation of Europe. London: Pluto.
Tonkin, Elizabeth
  1991 Narrating Our Pasts: The Social Construction of Oral History. Cambridge: Cambridge
        University Press.
Vincent, David
  1981 Bread, Knowledge and Freedom. London: Methuen.
Wolf, Eric
  1982 Europe and the People without History. Berkeley: University of California Press.
  1990 Distinguished Lecture: Facing Power – Old Insights, New Questions. American
        Anthropologist 92: 586–96.
Young, James
  1993 The Texture of Memory: Holocaust Memorials and Meaning. New Haven: Yale
        University Press.

PART I:
HISTORY AND HISTORIES

Silencing the Past: Layers of Meaning in the Haitian Revolution

MICHEL-ROLPH TROUILLOT

Sans Souci: The Palace

In the northern mountains of the Republic of Haiti, there is an old palace called Sans Souci that many urbanites and neighbouring peasants revere as one of the most important historical monuments of their country. The palace – what remains of it – stands on a small elevation between the higher hills surrounding the town of Milot. It is impressive if only because of its size, or what one can now guess to have been its size. It was built to instil a long-lasting deference, and it still does, in part because its occasional visitors expect fascination. One does not stumble upon these ruins: they are both too remote and too often mentioned within Haiti for the encounter to be fully accidental. Anyone who comes here, enticed by the posters of Haiti's Département du Tourisme or by one or another narrative of glory, is at least vaguely familiar with the country's past and assumes history to be dormant within these crumbling walls. Anyone who comes here knows that this huge dwelling was built in the early nineteenth century, for a black king, by blacks barely out of slavery. Thus the traveller is soon caught between the sense of desolation that moulds Sans Souci's present and a furtive awareness of bygone glory. There is so little here to see and so much to infer. Anyone who comes here comes too late, after a climax of which little has been preserved, yet early enough to dare imagine what it might have been.

What it might have been is not left entirely to the visitor's imagination. Soon enough a peasant of the area will force himself upon you and serve as your impromptu guide. He will take you through the ruins, and for a small fee, he will talk about Sans Souci. He will tell you that the palace was built by Henry Christophe, a hero of the Haitian Revolution who fought against slavery and became king of Haiti soon after the French defeat and the independence of

1804. He may or not mention that Haiti was then cut into two states, with Christophe ruling the northern one. He may or not know that Millot was an old French plantation that Christophe took over and managed for some time during the revolution; but he will surely relate the fabulous feasts that went on at Sans Souci after Christophe became king, the opulent dinners, the dances, the brilliant costumes. He might tell you that the price was heavy, both in currency and in human blood: the king was both rich and ruthless. Hundreds of Haitians died building his favourite residence, the surrounding town, and the neighbouring Citadel Henry, either because of the harsh labour conditions or because they faced the firing squad for a minor breach of discipline.

At this point, you may start wondering if Sans Souci was worth the price. But the peasant will keep on describing the property, oblivious to your query. He will insist on its immense gardens now denuded, its dependencies now gone, and especially the waterworks. In the words of an old hand who took me around the ruins, 'Christophe made water flow within these walls.' If your guide is seasoned enough, he will preserve his main effect until the very end: having seduced your imagination, he will conclude with a touch of pride that this extravagance was meant to impress the *blan* (whites or foreigners), meant to provide the world with irrefutable evidence of the ability of the black race.

On these and many other points, the printed record – the pictures and the words left behind by those who saw Sans Souci and the town of Milot before the 1842 earthquake that precipitated its ruin – corroborates the crux of the peasant's story and some of its amazing details. Geographer Karl Ritter, who drew a sketch of the palace a few days after Christophe's death, found it 'very impressive to the eye' (Ritter 1836:77). British visitor John Candler (1842), who saw a deserted building that he judged to be in poor style, admitted that it must have been 'splendid' in Christophe's time. U.S. physician Jonathan Brown (1837:186) wrote that Sans Souci had 'the reputation of having been one of the most magnificent edifices of the West Indies.' Writers also preserved passing descriptions of the waterworks: Christophe did not make water flow within the walls, but Sans Souci did have an artificial spring and numerous waterworks.

Similarly, the king's ruthless reputation is well established in books, some of which were written by his contemporaries; professional historians are uncertain only about the actual number of labourers who died during the construction of the palace. Christophe's racial pride is also well known: it exudes from what remains of his correspondence (e.g., Sanders 1816); it inspired Caribbean writers as various as Martiniquan Aimé Césaire ([1963] 1970) and Cuban Alejo Carpentier ([1949] 1983). Long before this pride was fictionalized, one of Christophe's closest advisers, Baron Valentin de Vastey, chancellor of the kingdom, evoked the 1813 completion of Sans Souci and the adjacent Royal

Church of Milot in grandiose terms: 'These two structures, erected by descendants of Africans, show that we have not lost the architectural taste and genius of our ancestors who covered Ethiopia, Egypt, Carthage, and old Spain with their superb monuments' (Vastey 1823:137).

Though the written record and the oral history transmitted by the local guides match quite closely on most substantial points, there is one topic of importance on which the peasants remain more evasive than the writers. If asked about the name of the palace, even a neophyte guide will reply, quite correctly, that *san sousi* means 'carefree' in Haitian (as *sans souci* does in French) and that the words are commonly used to qualify someone who worries about little. Some may even add that the expression aptly describes the king himself, or at least that side of him that sought for relaxation and the easy life of Sans Souci. Others may recall that during Christophe's reign the name of Sans Souci was extended to the town newly built around the palace, now a rural burg more often referred to as Milot. Few guides, however, are prone to volunteer the fact that Sans Souci was also the name of a man and that this man was killed by Henry Christophe himself.[1]

The War within the War

The circumstances surrounding the death of Sans Souci the man are often mentioned – though always in passing and rarely in detail – in historical works dealing with the Haitian war of independence. The main storyline of the Haitian Revolution, which augured the end of American slavery and eventuated in the birth of Haiti from the ashes of French Saint-Domingue, will receive only a summary treatment here. It took thirteen years for the revolution to unfold, from the initial slave uprising of August 1791 in northern Saint-Domingue to the proclamation of Haitian independence in January 1804. The stretch that most concerns us, which lasted less than a year, starts with the landing in 1802 of the French forces sent by First Consul Napoleon Bonaparte with secret instructions to re-establish slavery in Saint-Domingue. What follows is a synopsis of the undisputed facts.

The French expedition was led by General Charles Leclerc, Napoleon's brother-in-law. The revolutionary forces were commanded by a Creole black, General Toussaint Louverture, who had emerged as the nearly uncontested leader of the revolutionary slaves since 1794. From 1797 to 1801 Louverture had ruled over the colony like an independent monarch, though nominally in the name of France. He had consolidated the fragile freedom gained in the early 1790s with the backing of a 'colonial' army, composed mainly of former slaves and comprising at times in excess of 20,000 men. One key figure of

Louverture's army in the north of the country was Henry Christophe, a former freedman born in neighbouring Grenada and with an already extensive life experience for a black man at the times: he had been, in turn, a scullion, a major-domo, and a hotel manager. He had been slightly wounded in Georgia, at the battle of Savannah, while fighting on the side of the American Revolution in the Comte d'Estaing's regiment.

After a few months of bloody engagements, Leclerc's forces broke down many of the revolutionaries' defences. Henry Christophe then left Louverture and joined the French in April 1802. Soon after Christophe's defection, other prominent black officers (including Louverture's most important second, General Jean-Jacques Dessalines) surrendered, quite probably with Louverture's consent. In early May 1802 Louverture himself capitulated. Even though a number of former slaves rejected that ceasefire and maintained isolated pockets of armed resistance, Leclerc used the limited calm to entrap Louverture. The black general was captured in June 1802 and sent to jail in France.

Armed resistance had not stopped completely with the successive submissions of Christophe, Dessalines, and Louverture. It escalated after Louverture's exile, especially when Leclerc ordered the disarmament of all former slaves who did not belong to the 'colonial' regiments now formally integrated within his army. Many cultivators and soldiers who had seen in Louverture's arrest a testimony of Leclerc's treachery viewed the disarmament decree as additional proof of the intention by the French to re-establish slavery. They joined the resistance in increasing numbers in August and September 1802. By October most of the Louverture followers who had formally accepted Leclerc's authority the previous summer rejoined the resistance with their troops. These black officers forged a new alliance with light-skinned free coloureds who had up to then supported the expedition. By November 1802 Dessalines had become the leader of the alliance with the blessing of the most prominent of the free coloureds, mulatto general Alexandre Pétion, a former member of Leclerc's army. A year later the reconstituted revolutionary troops gained full control of the colony, the French acknowledged defeat, and Haiti became an independent country with Dessalines as its first chief of state.

Historians generally agree on most of these facts, with the Haitians usually insisting on the courage of their ancestors, and the foreigners, especially white foreigners, usually emphasizing the role of yellow fever in weakening the French troops. Both groups mention only in passing that the Haitian war of independence involved, in fact, more than two camps. The army first put together by Toussaint Louverture and reconstituted by Dessalines did not only fight against the French expeditionary forces. At crucial moments of *the* war, black officers turned also against their own, engaging in what was, in effect, *a war within the war.*

The series of events that I call the 'war within the war' stretches from about June 1802 to mid-1803. It comprises mainly two major campaigns: the one led by the black officers reintegrated under Leclerc's command against the former slaves who had refused to surrender to the French (June–October 1802) and the one led by the same generals and the free coloured officers associated with Pétion against the former slaves who refused to acknowledge the revolutionary hierarchy and the supreme authority of Dessalines (November 1802–April 1803). Crucial to the story is the fact that in both campaigns the first group is composed mainly of black Creoles (natives of the island or of the Caribbean) and the dissident groups are composed of – and led by – Bossales (African-born slaves), mainly from the Congo. The story of Jean-Baptiste Sans Souci ties together these two campaigns.

Sans Souci: The Man

Colonel Jean-Baptiste Sans Souci was a Bossale slave, probably from the Congo, who played an important role in the early days of the uprising, commanding the rebel camp of Cardinaux in 1791 (Gros 1793; cited by Thibau 1989:311). Like other Congo military leaders, he excelled at the guerrilla-type tactics, reminiscent of the Congo civil wars of the eighteenth century (Thornton 1991), which were critical to the military evolution of the Haitian Revolution. After Toussaint Louverture unified the revolutionary forces, Sans Souci became one of Christophe's immediate subalterns. At the time of the French invasion, he was military commander of the *arrondissement* of Grande Rivière, an important district in the north of Saint-Domingue that included his original Cardinaux camp. Between February and April 1802 he repeatedly defeated the French expeditionary forces in the areas that he controlled. Like many other black officers, however, he tacitly accepted Leclerc's victory after Louverture's surrender. I do not know of a document indicating Sans Souci's formal submission, but for the month of June at least, the French referred to him by his 'colonial' grade, which suggests his integration within Leclerc's military organization.

Sans Souci's presence in the French camp, however formal, was quite short, lasting less than a month. Leclerc, who had reports that the colonel was covertly reorganizing the 'colonial' troops and calling on cultivators to join a new rebellion, gave a secret order for his arrest on 4 July 1802. French general Philibert Fressinet, a veteran of Napoleon's Italian campaigns (then, nominally at least, the superior of both Christophe and Sans Souci, who were technically French 'colonial' officers) took steps to implement that order. But Sans Souci did not wait for Fressinet. He defected with most of his troops, launching a vigorous attack on a neighbouring French camp on 7 July. Fressinet then wrote to Leclerc: 'I am warning you, General, that *le nommé* [the so-called] Sans Souci has just rebelled and tries to win to his party as many cultivators as he can. He is even now encircling the Cardinio [Cardinaux] camp. *General* Henry Christophe is marching against him' (Auguste and Auguste 1986:189; italics mine).[2]

Between early July and November, troops from both the 'colonial' and expeditionary forces, led in turn by Christophe, Dessalines, and Fressinet himself among others, tried unsuccessfully to overpower Sans Souci. The African, meanwhile, gained the loyalty of other blacks, soldiers and cultivators alike. He soon became the leader of a substantial army, at least one powerful enough to give constant concern to the French. Using primarily guerilla-type tactics, Sans Souci exploited his greater knowledge of the topography and his troops' better adaptation to the local environment to keep at bay both the French and the colonial forces still affiliated to Leclerc. While Christophe, Pétion, and Dessalines managed to subdue other foci of resistance, the extreme mobility of Sans Souci's small units made it impossible for them to dislodge him from his moving retreats in the northern mountains (Auguste and Auguste 1986:188–98).

In early September 1802 Leclerc ordered French general Boudet to launch an all-out effort against Sans Souci with the backing of French general Brunet and Dessalines himself, then recognized by the French as the most capable of the native higher ranks. Brunet alone led 3,000 troops. Sans Souci's riposte was brisk and fierce. Commenting soon after on the massive offensive of 15 September, Leclerc wrote to Napoleon, 'This day alone cost me 400 men.' By the end of September Sans Souci and his most important allies, Makaya and Sylla, had nearly reversed the military situation in the northern part of the country. They never occupied any lowland territory for long, if at all, but they made it impossible for the French troops and their native allies to do so securely.[3]

The sustained resistance of various dissident groups (composed mainly of Africans and among which those controlled or influenced by Sans Souci were the most important) and their continuous harassment of the French created an untenable situation for both Leclerc and the Creole officers under his command. On the one hand, an ailing and exasperated Leclerc (he in fact died before the end of the war) took much less care to hide his ultimate plan: the deportation of most black and mulatto officers and the restoration of slavery. On the other hand, the native officers themselves, constantly suspected by the French to be in connivance with Sans Souci or one or another leader of the resistance, found themselves under increasing pressure to defect. By November 1802 most 'colonial' officers had turned once more against the French, and Dessalines was acknowledged as the military leader of the new alliance forged between himself, Pétion, and Christophe.

But just as some former slaves had refused to submit to the French, some (often the same) contested the new revolutionary hierarchy. Jean-Baptiste Sans Souci notably declined the new leaders' repeated offers to join ranks with them, arguing that his own unconditional resistance to the French exempted him from obedience to his former superiors. He would not serve under men whose adhesion to the cause of freedom was, at the very least, dubious, and he especially resented Christophe, whom he considered a traitor.

It is in this second phase of the war within the war that Sans Souci marched to his death. Within a few weeks the Creole generals defeated or won out over most of the dissidents. Sans Souci resisted longer than most, but eventually agreed to negotiations with Dessalines, Pétion, and Christophe about his role in the new hierarchy. At one of these meetings he virtually assured Dessalines that he would recognize his supreme authority, thus in effect reversing his opposition but without appearing to bow to Christophe personally. Still, Christophe asked for one more meeting with his former subaltern. Sans Souci showed up at Christophe's headquarters on the Grand Pré plantation with only a small guard. He and his followers fell under the bayonets of Christophe's soldiers.

Sans Souci's existence and death are mentioned in most written accounts of the Haitian war of independence. Likewise, professional historians who deal with Christophe's rule always note the king's fondness for grandiose constructions and his predilection for the Milot palace, his favourite residence. But few writers have puzzled over the palace's peculiar name. Fewer have noted the obvious similarity between that name and the patronymic of the man killed by Christophe ten years before the erection of his royal residence. Fewer even have noted, let alone emphasized, that there were three, rather than two Sans Soucis: the man and *two* palaces. Six decades before Christophe's coronation, Prussian emperor Frederick the Great, had built himself a grandiose palace on top of a hill in the town of Potsdam, a few miles from Berlin. That palace, a *haut lieu* of the European Enlightenment, which some observers claim to have been part inspiration for the purpose – if not for the architectural design – of Milot, was called Sans Souci.

Sans Souci Revisited

With their various layers of silences, the three faces of Sans Souci provide a multiplicity of vantage points from which to examine the means and process of historical production. Most of us know (or should now know) that history is constructed, that it is never just – if at all – an accurate picture of what happened in the past. Yet most of us suspect that not just any fiction can pass for history at any point in time. Thus between the mechanically 'realist' and naively 'constructivist' extremes, there is the more serious task of determining not *what history is* – a hopeless goal if phrased in essentialist terms – but *how history works*. For if 'the production of history' is more than an elegant metaphor with economistic undertones, then this 'production' is a process that puts together certain components to form something new. If history is 'produced,' we need to illuminate this production process, understand its mechanisms, and classify its components.

Silences are among many of such components. They are inherent in the process, both as part of production itself and as part of its result. They are active and concrete, both means and products of historical production (M.-R. Trouillot 1990). As such, they can be used to illuminate the entire process, though, clearly, from specific viewpoints. They can be used to reveal the differential power of various groups of agents in producing history: the differential access of these agents to the means of historical production and (allowing for equal access) their differential control of these means. Silences enter historical production at four specific moments: the moment of fact creation (the making of *sources*), the moment of fact collection (the making of *archives*), the moment of fact retrieval (the making of *narratives*), and the moment of retrospective significance (the making of history in the final instance).[4] Although I see the distinction between the first and second moments as crucial for many reasons (including a necessary distinction between history and fiction), I will blend the two in the passages immediately following. First, the creation of sources and archives is sometimes simultaneous, and my case includes such instances. Second, the creation of silences within archives has been exposed quite well elsewhere (e.g., Foucault 1969; Certeau 1974).[5]

Silences obtain in the creation of sources, regardless of who notes what and regardless of the chronological distance between an occurrence and its transformation as 'fact' by way of this engraving.[6] Some occurrences are noted from the start; others are not. Some are engraved in individual or collective bodies; others are not. Some leave physical traces; others do not.

The materiality of this first moment (the combined creation of sources and facts) is so obvious that we tend to neglect it. It does not imply that facts, or

even statements of fact, about an occurrence are engraved from the start, meaningless repositories waiting to be discovered, but rather, more modestly, that
history begins with bodies and artefacts: living brains, fossils, texts, buildings.
Oral history does not escape that law, except that in the case of oral transmission, the first moment of fact collection is continually carried over in the very
bodies of the individuals who partake in that transmission. The *source* is alive.

As they stand now, the three faces of Sans Souci typify this materiality by
their very contrast. They span a continuum of physical presence or absence that
goes from extreme concreteness to complete disappearance. The palace at
Potsdam is still standing. The Milot palace is a wreck. The body of the colonel
is missing. The mass of stone and mortar at Potsdam has retained most of its
shape and weight, and it is still furnished with what passes for the best of
rococo elegance. Indeed, Frederick's successor started its historical maintenance, its transformation into an *archive* of a sort, by reconstructing Frederick's
room the very year of his death! The emperor's own body, in his well-kept
coffin, has become a marker of German history. Hitler stood at his Potsdam
grave to proclaim the Third Reich. Devoted German officers removed the
coffin from Potsdam as the Soviet army moved into Berlin. Chancellor Kohl
had the coffin reinterred in Potsdam recently as a tribute to German reunification. Two centuries after Frederick's death, both he and his palace have a
materiality that history needs to reckon with.

In contrast, the walls of the Milot palace were breached by civil war, neglect, and natural disasters. They testify to a physical decline that started the
very year of Christophe's death and accelerated over time. He had no political
heir, certainly no immediate successor anxious and able to preserve his personal quarters. He committed suicide in the midst of an uprising, and the
republicans who took over his kingdom had no wish to transform Sans Souci
into a monument. Although Christophe's stature as myth preceded his death,
his full-fledged conversion into a national hero came much later. Still, just like
Frederick, he is also buried in his most famous construction, the Citadel Henry,
now a UNESCO World Heritage landmark not far away from Sans Souci. The
Sans Souci palace has also been turned into a monument, though one that
reflects both the limited means and the determination of the Haitian government to invest in historical preservation. The surrounding town of Milot, in
turn, has lost historical significance. As for the body of the colonel, it is
somewhat misleading to describe it as 'missing,' for it was never reported as
such. As far as we know, no one ever claimed it, and its memory does not even
live in the bodies of his descendants, if any, in or around Milot.

Thus the presences and absences embodied in sources (artefacts and bodies
that turn an event into fact) or archives (facts collected, thematized, and

Sans Souci–Milot today

processed as documents and monuments) are neither neutral or natural. They are created. As such, they are not mere presences and absences, but mentions or silences of various kinds and degrees. Mentions and silences are active, dialectical counterparts of which history is the synthesis. Almost every mention of Sans Souci the palace, the very resilience of the physical structure itself, effectively silences Sans Souci the man, his political goals, his military genius.

At the beginning at least, mentions and silences are not created by historians. Actors within any sequence of events already have unequal control over whatever becomes the means of historical production long before the historian

Henry I, king of Haiti, by British painter Richard Evans

(qua collector, narrator, or interpreter) comes to the scene.[7] Romantic re-evaluation of the weak and defeated notwithstanding, the starting points are different. Sans Souci–Potsdam is knowable in ways that Sans Souci–Milot will never be. Similarly, we know what both Christophe and Frederick looked like because each had the wish and the power to have his features engraved for posterity. The royal painting of Henry I by Richard Evans, reproduced in so many recent books, remains a source that Colonel Sans Souci has yet to match.

But if lived inequalities yield unequal historical power, they do so in ways that we have yet to determine. The distribution of historical power does not necessarily replicate the inequalities (victories and setbacks, gains and losses of various kinds) lived by the actors. Historical power is not a direct reflection of a past occurrence or a simple sum of past inequalities measured from the actors' perspective or from the viewpoint of any 'objective' standard, even at the first moment. The French superiority in artillery, the strategic superiority of Sans Souci, and the political superiority of Christophe can all be demonstrated, but no such demonstration would enable us to predict their relative significance then and now. Similarly, sources do not encapsulate the whole range of significance of the occurrences to which they testify.

Further, the outcome itself does not determine in any linear way how an event or a string of events enters into history. The French expeditionary forces lost the Haitian war. (They *thought* they did, and they *did*.) Similarly, Colonel Sans Souci was the loser and Christophe the ultimate winner, both politically and militarily within the black camp. Yet the papers preserved by General Donatien Rochambeau (Leclerc's successor as commander of the French expedition) show more than fifty entries about French general Fressinet in spite of the fact that he was, by anyone's standard, a quite minor figure in the Saint-Domingue campaigns. In comparison, there are eleven entries about Christophe, whom we know gave both Leclerc and Rochambeau much more to think about than Fressinet ever did. Sans Souci, in turn, who came close to upsetting the plans of *both* the French and the colonial officers and indeed forced both to change tactics in mid-course, received a single entry (Monti 1972).[8]

Still, we need not understand fully the mechanisms by which inequalities experienced by the actors lead to uneven historical power in the creation of sources to recognize that the physical traces of the past, once turned into sources, privilege some events over others. They are instances of inclusion, the other face of which is, of course, what is left out. This may now be obvious enough to those of us who have learned (though more recently than we care to remember) that sources imply choices. But the conclusion that we tend to draw that some occurrences have the capacity (a physical one, I would insist) to enter history and become 'fact' at the first stage while others do not is much too general and is ultimately useless in its ecumenical form. That some peoples and things are absent *of* history is much less relevant to the historical practice than the fact that some peoples and things are absent *in* history and that this absence itself is constitutive of the process of historical production.

Silences are inherent *in* history because any single event, however defined, enters history with *some* of its constituting parts missing.[9] *Some* thing is always left out, while another one is recorded. There is no perfect closure of any event, however one chooses to define the boundaries of that event. Thus whatever becomes *fact* does so with its own inborn absences, specific to its production. In other words, the very mechanisms that make any historical recording possible also ensure that historical facts are not created equal. They reflect differential control of the means of historical production at the very first engraving that transforms an event into a fact.[10]

Silences *in* the Historical Narrative

The dialectics of mentions and silences obtain also at the third moment of the process, when events that have become facts (and may have been processed through archives) are retrieved. Even if we assume instances of pure historical 'narrativity,' that is, accounts that describe the past in a way analogous to a sportscaster's blow-by-blow description of a game (Dray 1982:203), even if we postulate a recording angel – with no stakes in the story – who would dutifully note all that was mentioned and collected, any subsequent narrative (or any corpus of such narratives) would demonstrate to us that retrieval and recollection proceed unequally. Occurrences equally noted and supposedly not yet subject to interpretation in the most common sense of the word exhibit in the historical corpus an unequal frequency of retrieval, unequal (factual) weight – indeed, unequal degrees of factualness. Some facts are recalled more often than others; some strings of facts are recalled with more empirical richness than others even in blow-by-blow recountings.

Every fact recorded in the summary narrative given above is part of the available record in relatively accessible form since I have used only sources found in multiple copies: memoirs, published accounts, and so-called secondary sources, that is, material already produced *as history*. But the frequency with which they appear in the total corpus from which the narrative was drawn varies. So does the material weight of mention, that is, the sheer empirical value of the string within which any single fact is enmeshed.

That Colonel Sans Souci was not the leader of an impromptu or marginal rebel band but an early leader in the slave uprising and then a high-ranking officer of Louverture's army turned dissident has been a constant *fact* within the published record from the early nineteenth century to our times (e.g., Gros in Thibau 1989; Lacroix 1819; Ardouin [1853–60] 1958; Cole 1967). But that fact remained largely unused until recently: its frequency of retrieval was low, its empirical elaboration defective in terms of the information already available in that corpus. Sans Souci was most often alluded to without mention of grade or origins, without even a first name, all facts available within the corpus. Little was said about the size of his troops, the details of his death, or his few stated positions.[11] Yet there was enough to sketch a picture of Sans Souci, even if a very fleeting one, though certainly not as elaborate as that of Christophe himself.

Still, materials of that sort had to re-enter the corpus, so to speak, quite slowly and in restricted ways, for instance, as part of a catalogue of documents within which they remained more or less inconspicuous (Monti 1972). Only recently have they surfaced as (re)discoveries in their own right within a narrative (Auguste and Auguste 1986). Thus, to many readers who had access to most of this corpus and who may or may not have different stakes in the narrative, the extent of Sans Souci's dissident resistance, if not that of his existence, is likely to be apprehended as 'news.' So is (for a different group of readers, overlapping and as substantial as the first one) the suggestion that the palace at Milot may have been modelled after the one at Potsdam to an extent still undetermined.

Now, the individuals who constructed this corpus came from various times and backgrounds, sought to offer various interpretations of the Haitian Revolution, and passed at times opposite value judgments on either the revolution itself or Christophe. Given these conflicting viewpoints, what explains the greater frequency of certain silences in the corpus?

Let us go back to the analogy with the sportscaster's account. That account is a blow-by-blow description, but only of the occurrences that matter to the game. Even if it is guided mainly by the seriality of occurrences, it tends to leave out from the series witnesses, participants, and events generally considered marginal. The audience enters primarily when it is seen as influencing the players. Players on the bench are left out, and those in the field are mentioned mainly when they capture the ball, or at least when they try to capture it or are meant to do so. Silences are necessary to the account, for if the sportscaster told us every 'thing' that happened at each and every moment, we would not understand anything. If the account was indeed comprehensive, it would be incomprehensible. Further, the selection of what matters, the dual creation of mentions and silences, is premised on an understanding of the rules of the game by broadcaster and audience alike. In short, blow-by-blow accounts are restricted in terms of what may enter them and in terms of the order in which these elements may enter: they follow a plot.

Historical narratives, like any narrative (fictional or not), are 'emplotted' (White 1978). They tell their story according to a limited number of plot structures. They are, in part, literary artefacts. It does not follow that they are 'fiction' in the most common sense, as some constructivists argue, that the historian may impose upon them the significance of her or his choice (White 1978, 1987). *If history is indeed 'a fable agreed upon,' not all fables can pass for history.*[12] But we can agree with the constructivists that historical narratives obey stated and unstated conventions and procedures. And unless we take the stance that such conventions and procedures are rooted in the human mind, then ways of telling a story *as history* reflect the dominations that have marked the evolution of particular discourses and disciplines, including history itself. Certain ways of telling the story inherently silence others (M.-R. Trouillot 1990, 1995).

In historical narratives, as elsewhere, even a blow-by-blow account is premised on previous understandings. In the case of Haitian historiography, as for most Third World countries, these previous understandings have been profoundly shaped by Western conventions and procedures. The writing and reading of Haitian historiography implies literacy and formal access to a Western, primarily French, language and culture, two prerequisites that already exclude the majority of Haitians from direct participation in its production.[13] Regardless of their training and the degree to which they may be considered members of a guild, Haitian and foreign narrators aim to conform to guild practices.[14] Previous understandings here include an acknowledgment of the now-global academic division of the labour as shaped by the particular history of Western Europe and by the ways in which Europeans came to view their history. Here, as elsewhere, previous understandings also include the narrator's assessment of information accumulated before the ongoing account. Just as the sportscaster assumes the audience's limited knowledge of the players (who is who; what are the two sides), so does the historian build any narrative on the shoulders of previous ones.

This paper itself exemplifies the point. My narrative assumed both a certain way of reading history and the reader's greater knowledge of French than of Haitian history. However correct these assumptions, they reflect a presumption about the unevenness of historical power. But if they were correct, the narrative had to present an overview of the last year of the Haitian Revolution. Otherwise the story of Sans Souci would not *make sense* to most readers. I did not feel the need to add that Haiti is in the Caribbean and that Afro-American slavery had been going on in that region for exactly three centuries when these events occurred. These mentions would have added to the empirical weight of the narrative, but the story still made sense without them. Further, I assumed that most of my readers knew these facts, an assumption that I would not dare make if all of my readers were North American undergraduates. I did not report that Louverture's capture (which I qualified as an entrapment) occurred on 7 June 1802 because the exact date did not seem to matter much in the narrative. But if I had done so, I would have used, as I do now, the Christian calendar, the time indexation system that the West inherited from Dionysius Exiguus, rather than, say, an ancient eastern system. Nowhere in this text do I use the *calendrier républicain* (the system that indexed most of the primary documents of this story) because it did not prevail in post-revolutionary narratives. Even individuals who were forced to learn its correspondence with Dionysius' system at an early age (as I was in school) would take some time to ascertain that 'le 18 prairial de l'an dix' was indeed 7 June 1802. In short, I bowed to some rules, inherited from a history of uneven power, to ensure the accessibility of my narrative.

Thus, in many ways, my account followed a conventional line, but only up to a certain point because of my treatment of Sans Souci. Up to now, indeed, the combined effect of previous understandings about plot structures and common empirical knowledge eventuated in a partial silencing of the life and death of the colonel. Players have been distributed according to the major leagues, and the event-units of Haitian history have been cut into slices that cannot be easily modified. Thus 'the war within the war' has been subsumed under accounts of the war between the French and the 'colonial' troops, rarely (if ever) detailed as a narrative in its own right. In that sense, indeed, it never constituted a complete sequence, a blow-by-blow account of any 'thing.' Rather, its constituting events were retrieved as marginal subparts of other accounts, and the life and death of Sans Souci himself as a smaller segment of these subparts. To unearth Colonel Sans Souci as more than a negligible figure within the story of Haiti's emergence, I chose to add a section that recast his story as a separate account after the chronological sketch of the revolution. This was a choice based on both possible procedures and assessment of my readers' knowledge. To be sure, I could have highlighted the figure of the colonel in a different way. But I had to resort to a procedure of emphasis based on both content and form. I could not leave to chance the transformation of some silences into mentions with increased retrospective significance. In short, this unearthing of Sans Souci, however sketchy itself, required extra labour not so much in the production of new facts as in their transformation by way of new positioning.

Silences within Silences

The unearthing of silences, their replacement by mentions of which the historian emphasizes the retrospective significance, requires extra labour and most often a project linked to an interpretation. This is so because the combined

silences accrued through the first three steps of the process of historical production intermesh and solidify at the fourth and final moment, when retrospective significance itself is produced. To call this moment 'final' is not to suggest
that it follows the chronological disappearance of the actors. Retrospective
significance can be created by the actors themselves, as a past within their past
or as a future within their present. Henry I killed Sans Souci twice: first,
literally, during their last meeting, and second, symbolically, by naming his
most famous palace Sans Souci. This killing *in history* was as much for his
benefit as it was for our wonder. It erased Sans Souci from Christophe's own
past, and it erased him from his future, what has become the historians' present.
It did not erase Sans Souci from Christophe's memory or even from the sources.
Historian Hénock Trouillot, one of the few Haitians to emphasize the similarity
between the two names, suggests that Christophe may even have wanted to
perpetuate the memory of his enemy as the most formidable one he had defeated. In other words, the silencing of Sans Souci could be read as an engraving of Christophe himself, the ultimate victor over all mortal enemies and over
death itself. Trouillot writes:

In erecting Sans Souci at the foothills of Milot, did Christophe want to prove how
solidly his power was implanted in this soil? Or else, was he dominated by a more
obscure thought? For a legend reports that a diviner foretold Christophe that he would
die by the hand of a Congo. Then, superstitious as he was, having satisfied his propensity for magic, did he believe that in erecting this town he could defy destiny? ... We do
not know. (H. Trouillot 1972:29)[15]

But we know that the silencing was effective, that Sans Souci's life and death
have been endowed with only marginal retrospective significance, while
Christophe's apologists and detractors alike cannot fail to mention both his
thirst for glory and the extent to which he achieved it in his lifetime and
thereafter. The 'legend' of the diviner may one day be transformed into fact. But
Trouillot's references to 'superstition' notwithstanding, the real 'magic' remains
this dual production of a highly significant mention of glory and an equally
significant silence. Christophe indeed defied the future with this silencing.

Silencing here is an erasure more effective than the simple absence of
memory, faked or genuine.[16] French general Pamphile de Lacroix had no particular reason to take publicly the side of either man at the time that he wrote
his memoirs. He knew them both. His own life intersected with theirs in ways
that usually inscribe events in memory: they were both his enemies and his
subalterns at different points in time in a foreign war about which he was half-
convinced and which he ended up losing. He is the only human being we know

to have left records of a conversation with Christophe about Colonel Sans Souci. That exactly sixty pages after the report of this conversation de Lacroix mentions by name the favourite palace of Henry I without underlying the similarity between that name and the colonel's patronymic testifies to the effectiveness of Christophe's silencing (Lacroix 1819:227, 287).[17]

Indeed, de Lacroix's silence typifies an obliteration that may have gone beyond Christophe's wishes, for in many non-Haitian circles, the disappearance of Sans Souci the man tied the entire significance of the palace at Milot to Sans Souci–Potsdam. Jonathan Brown, a U.S. physician who visited Haiti a decade after Christophe's death and failed to note the connection between the colonel and the palace, wrote that Christophe 'was particularly delighted with history, of which his knowledge was extensive and accurate; and Frederick the Great of Prussia was a personage with whom above all others he was captivated, the name of Sans Souci having been borrowed from Potsdam' (Brown 1837, 2: 216). Christophe would have approved of the praise; but phrased in these terms, it deprives him of any originality, surely an intended consequence for a common man turned king with such an acute sense of his past trajectory and of his future place in history.

The excerpt from Brown is one of the earliest written mentions of a relationship between the two palaces and the most likely source for subsequent writers in the English language. The connection is weak if all that supports it is the homonymy.[18] The only reference to Potsdam prior to Brown in the corpus covered here is buried in a diatribe against Christophe by Haitian writer and politician Hérard Dumesle. He does *not* say that the Milot palace was designed or named after Potsdam. Rather, he emphasizes a fundamental contradiction between what he perceives as Frederick's love for justice and Christophe's tyranny (Dumesle 1824:225–6). Elsewhere in the book, Dumesle also compares Christophe with Nero and Caligula. He derides Christophe's ceremonial corps of *amazons*, who, in his view, were much less graceful than the real Amazons of pre-conquest South America! In short, as mentioned by Dumesle, the connection between Potsdam and Milot is purely rhetorical. Has history turned this rhetoric into a source? Hubert Cole, who wrote an important biography of Christophe, expands on the theme of German influence on Haitian architecture of the time and claims that 'German engineers' built the citadel. Just like Brown, he does not cite sources for his suggestions.

Implicitly contradicting Brown and Cole, Haitian historian Vergniaud Leconte (1931:273) credits Christophe's military engineer, Henri Barré, for the design of the citadel and one Chéri Warloppe for the design and building of Sans Souci. Leconte examined most of the writings available at the time about Christophe and claimed to have used new documents as well as oral sources, but except for locating Warloppe's grave in a cemetery in northern Haiti, he does not tie his data to specific archives or sources. Leconte does not allude to any German influence. Did someone dream of the German connection?

There were German – and other European – residents in Christophe's kingdom. There were Haitians fluent in German – and in other European languages – in the king's personal service (Harvey 1827). Moreover, Christophe did hire German military engineers to strengthen the defences of his kingdom. Charles Mackenzie, the British consul in Haiti and a self-avowed spy, describes the case of two of these Germans whom Christophe jailed in order to prevent them from divulging military secrets (Mackenzie 1830:II, 209). Yet Mackenzie, who visited and described Sans Souci less than ten years after Christophe's death, does not connect the two palaces (Mackenzie 1830:I, 169–79).

Still, given what we know of Henry I and given the presence of German military architects in his kingdom, it is more than probable that he was aware of Potsdam's existence and that he knew what it looked like. That Frederick contributed to the design of Potsdam, wrote poetry, received in his palace celebrities of his time, men such as Johann Sebastian Bach and Voltaire, also suggests an example that could have inspired Christophe. Henry I indeed supervised personally the construction of Sans Souci–Milot and maintained there the closest Haitian equivalent to an intellectual *salon*, thus reproducing, willingly or not, aspects of the dream of Potsdam. None of this, however, authenticates a strong Potsdam connection. Having compared numerous images of the two palaces, which include sketches of Sans Souci before 1842, I find that they reveal some similarities both in general layout and in some details (the cupola of the church, the front arcades). But I will immediately confess that my amateurish associations require at least *a suspicion of influence*. How grounded is such a suspicion?

The strongest evidence against a strong Potsdam connection is yet another silence. Austro-German geographer Karl Ritter, a seasoned traveller and a keen observer of peoples and places, visited Sans Souci eight days after Christophe's death. He (1836:81) climbed a hill and drew a picture of the palace. His text describes in detail a building that was 'built entirely according to European taste' (Ritter 1836:77) and insists upon such features as Christophe's bathroom and the 'European' plants in the garden (ibid.:78). Indeed, the word 'European' returns many times in the written description, but nowhere is there the suggestion of an affinity between Christophe's residence and that of Frederick.

Ritter had the benefit of both immediacy and hindsight. Most resident foreigners had been kept away from the road to the citadel and therefore from Sans Souci during Christophe's tenure. A few days after the king's suicide,

Sans Souci–Milot, a nineteenth-century engraving

some European residents rushed to discover by themselves Christophe's two most famous constructions. Ritter joined that party. Thus he visited the palace in the company of other whites at a time when Sans Souci 'triggered so much interest' among the few white residents of Haiti that 'every white had to talk about it' (Ritter 1836:76). Ritter does not report these conversations, but one can presume that he took them into consideration while writing his text. At the same time, since that text was published much later, indeed after those of Dumesle and Mackenzie, he could have picked up from either of these two very different authors hints as to a German connection. Yet Ritter never alludes to a specifically 'German' or 'Prussian' influence on Sans Souci–Milot (Ritter 1836:77–82). Either he had never heard of it, even from fellow German speakers, or he thought it inconsequential both then and later. How interesting, in light of this silence, that later writers gave Potsdam so much retrospective significance.

Hubert Cole is one of the few authors to have noted explicitly the connection between Potsdam, Milot, and the colonel. But he depreciates the link between the latter two and makes Potsdam pivotal (Cole 1967:207). Cole spends a single sentence on the three faces of Sans Souci to produce a more eloquent silence than many would in three paragraphs.[19] The coincidence between Sans Souci–Milot and Sans Souci the man was an accident that the king easily bypassed. The colonel had no symbolic significance (I am aware of being redundant in phrasing it this way), only a factual one. In retrospect, only Potsdam mattered, though Cole does not say why it should matter so much. In so stressing Potsdam, he not only silences the colonel, but he also denies Christophe's own attempt to silence Sans Souci the man. Cole's silencing thus produces a Christophe who is a remorseless murderer, a tasteless potentate, a bare mimic of Frederick, a man who consumes his victim and appropriates his war name, not through a ritual of reckoning but by gross inadvertence.[20]

Such a picture is not convincing. A 1786 map of northern Saint-Domingue (Phelipeau 1786) shows the main Grand Pré plantation to be adjacent to the Millot estate. Christophe used both places as headquarters. Given the size of the palace and its dependencies, the royal domain may have run over part of Grand Pré. In other words, Christophe built Sans Souci the palace a few yards away from – if not exactly – where he killed Sans Souci the man. Coincidence and inadvertence seem quite improbable. More likely, the king was engaged in a transformative ritual to absorb his old enemy.[21]

Such practice was known in Dahomey. Dahoman oral history reports that the country was founded by Tacoodonou after a successful war against Da, the ruler of Abomey. Tacoodonou 'put Da to death by cutting open his belly, and placed his body under the foundation of a palace that he built in Abomey, as a memorial of his victory; which he called Dahomy, from Da the unfortunate victim, and Homy his belly: that is a house built in Da's belly' (Norris [1789] 1968:xiv).[22] The elements of the Sans Souci plot are there: the war, the killing, the building of a palace, and the naming of it after the dead enemy. Chances are that Christophe knew this story. He praised Dahomans as great warriors, and he bought or recruited four thousand blacks, many of whom were reportedly from Dahomey, to bolster his army. A hundred and fifty of his Royal-Dahomets, based at Sans Souci, formed his cherished cadet troop (Lacroix 1819:II,287; Leconte 1931:282). In light of these facts, the emphasis on Potsdam by non-Haitian historians, which deprives the colonel's death of any significance, is also an act of silencing.

The Defeat of the Barbarians (Part One)

For Haitians, the silencing is elsewhere. To start with, Potsdam is not even a matter of fact. When I raised the issue of the influence of the German palace on the construction of Sans Souci, most of my Haitian interlocutors acknowledged ignorance. Some historians conceded that they had 'heard of it.' But the connection was never taken seriously. In that sense, Haitian historians are playing by the rules of the Western guild: there is no irrefutable evidence of a connection between Milot and Potsdam. But for most Haitians (most urbanites at least), the silencing goes way beyond this mere matter of fact. The literate Haitians with whom I raised the Potsdam connection did not simply question the evidence. Rather, the attitude was that, even if proven, this 'fact' itself did not much matter, just as the colonel's name and murder – of which they are well aware – does not much matter.

For the Haitian urban elites, only Milot counts, and two of the faces of Sans Souci are ghosts that are best left undisturbed. The colonel is for them the epitome of the war within the war, an episode to which they have denied, until recently, any retrospective significance. This fratricide sequence is the only blemish in the glorious epic of their ancestors' victory against France, the only shameful page in the history of the sole successful slave revolution in the annals of humankind. Thus, understandably, it is the only page that they would have written otherwise if history depended only on the wish of the historian. And indeed, they tried to rewrite it as much as they could. For most writers sympathetic to the cause of freedom, Haitians and foreigners alike, the war within the war is an amalgam of unhappy incidents that pitted the black Jacobins, Creole slaves and freedmen alike, against hordes of uneducated 'Congos,' African-born slaves, Bossale men with strange surnames, such as Sans Souci, Makaya, Sylla, Mavougou, Lamour de la Rance, Petit-Noël Prieur (or Prière), Va-Malheureux, Macaque, Alaou, Coco, Sanglaou – slave names quite distinguishable from the French-sounding ones of Jean-Jacques Dessalines, Alexandre Pétion, Henry Christophe, Augustin Clervaux, and the like. That many of these Congos were early leaders of the 1791 uprising, that a few had become bona fide officers of Louverture's army, that all were staunch defenders of the cause of freedom, has been passed over. The military experience gathered in Africa during the Congo civil wars, which may have been crucial to the slave revolution (Thornton n.d.), was a non-issue in Haiti – not just because few Haitians are intimate with African history, but because Haitian historians (like everyone else) assumed that victorious strategies could only come from the Europeans or the most Europeanized slaves. Words such as 'Congo' and 'Bossale' carry negative connotations in the Caribbean today. Never mind that Haiti was born with a majority of Bossales. As the Auguste brothers have recently noted, no one wondered how the label 'Congo' came to describe a purported political minority at a time when the bulk of the population was certainly African-born and probably from the Congo region (Auguste and Auguste 1986).

Jean-Baptiste Sans Souci is the Congo par excellence. He was the most renowned of the African rebels, and probably the most effective from the point of view of both French and 'colonial' higher ranks. He is a ghost that most Haitian historians, urbanites, literate, French speakers as they all are, would rather lay to rest. 'Mulatto' historian Beaubrun Ardouin, who helped to launch Haitian historiography on a modern path and whose thousands of pages have been pruned, acclaimed, and contested, is known for his hatred of Christophe and his harsh criticism of the dark-skinned heroes of Haitian independence.[23] Yet, when it came to Sans Souci, Ardouin the 'mulatto' took the black Creole's side. Describing a meeting during the negotiations over the leadership, in which a 'courageous,' 'energetic,' 'distinguished,' 'intelligent,' and (suddenly) 'good-looking' Christophe used his legendary magnetism to influence Sans Souci, Ardouin writes:

[B]randishing his sword, [Christophe] moved toward [Sans Souci] and asked him to declare whether or not he did not acknowledge him as a *général,* his superior ... [S]ubjugated by the ascendance of a civilized man, and a former commander at that, the African told him: 'General, what do you want to do?' 'You are calling me *général* [replied Christophe]; then, you do acknowledge me as your chief, since you are not a general yourself.' Sans Souci did not dare reply ... The Barbarian was defeated. (Ardouin [1853–60] 1958:V,75)

The Barbarians Revisited

Sans Souci is also an inconvenience inasmuch as, from a Haitian viewpoint, the war within the war may prove to be a distraction from the *main* event of 1791–1804: the successful revolution against both slavery and colonialism. Here his silencing and that of Potsdam converge. They are silences of resistance, silences thrown against a superior silence.

The major silence is the one that Western historiography has produced around the revolution of Saint-Domingue/Haiti. That silence, ironically, originates in the significance of the revolution itself for its contemporaries and the generation immediately following. From the years 1791–1804 to the middle of the century, many Europeans and North Americans came to see that revolution as a litmus test for the black race, certainly for the capacities of Afro-Americans. Haitians did likewise (Nicholls 1988). Christophe's constructions, like the military efficiency of the former slaves, figured highly in these debates, as by-products of the revolution.[24] But if the revolution was significant for Haitians as Haitians, to most foreigners it was primarily a lucky argument in a larger issue. Thus apologists and detractors alike, abolitionists and avowed racists, liberal intellectuals, economists, and slave owners used the events of Saint-Domingue to make their case, irrelevant of Haitian history itself. In the earliest segment of the corpus that I have mentioned here one finds a businessman-Quaker, a white supremacist, a French pacifist in uniform, a prejudiced U.S. physician from New Hampshire, a British spy, a Cambridge technocrat-squire, and a few slave owners. Haiti mattered to all of them, but only as a pretext to talk about something else.

The silencing of Saint-Domingue/Haiti was strengthened by the fate of Haiti itself. Ostracized for the better part of the nineteenth century, the country declined both economically and politically, in part as a result of this ostracism (M.-R. Trouillot 1990). As Haiti faded, the revolution itself became for most Westerners a consequence of yellow fever, an effect of French miscalculations or British interference, if not a non-event. At best, some Western historiographers reluctantly recognize it as a mere side effect of the French Revolution. To wit, it does not figure in the *Penguin Encyclopedia of History*, which traces significant events and characters from 1789 on. To wit, British Marxist historian Eric Hobsbawm (1962:93) manages to write a book entitled *The Age of Revolutions*, in which the Haitian Revolution receives only a footnote, although Toussaint Louverture is acknowledged as 'the first independent revolutionary leader of stature' in the Americas. Saint-Domingue is mentioned in three sentences (once in its own right, once between parentheses, and once in a quotation about something else). U.S. historian Robert Stein (1985) acknowledges the fact of a revolution, but places most of the credit for the liberation of the slaves on a zealous French Jacobin, Léger Félicité Sonthonax, no doubt a revolutionary in his own right. Other writers tend to stay prudently away from the word 'revolution' itself, more often using terms such as 'insurgents,' 'rebels,' 'bands,' and so on (e.g., Cauna 1987; Geggus 1982).[25]

Yet since at least C.L.R. James's classic *The Black Jacobins* (but note the title), the demonstration has been well made to the guild that the Haitian Revolution is indeed a 'revolution' in its own right by any definition of the word.[26] Until the 1970s, however, the silence in significance was total within modern Western historiography. Then Eugene Genovese and more recently Robin Blackburn (1988) have suggested the centrality of the Haitian Revolution in understanding the overthrow of colonial slavery, but the majority of historians working on slavery and abolition still have to admit the point or even argue against it. In the context of this silencing, Potsdam remains a vague suggestion, and the colonel's death is a mere matter of fact, while the crumbling walls of Milot still stand as a last defence against oblivion.

NOTES

This paper was originally prepared for the Sixth International Roundtable in History and Anthropology, 'The Production of History: Silences and Commemorations,' in Bellagio, Italy, 29 August–2 September 1989. Hans Medick, Viranjini Munasinghe, Michèle Oriol-Spurmont, Hanan Sabea, John Thornton, Katherine Verdery, and the volume editors provided comments, tips, and assistance at various stages of the project. Special thanks are owed to Pierre Buteau, Lyonel Trouillot, and Drexel Woodson for doing the same and much more. Another version of this essay has been published as 'The Three Faces of Sans Souci: Glory and Silences in the Haitian Revolution,' chapter 2 of *Silencing the Past* (Boston: Beacon Press, 1996), 31–69.

1 I have not done fieldwork on the oral history of Sans Souci. I suspect that there is much more in the oral archives than this summary, which encapsulates only 'popular' knowledge in the area, as filtered through the routine performances of the guides.

2 There was a long-standing animosity between Christophe and Sans Souci, the cause of which remains unknown. The French intended to make full use of this personal conflict to set Christophe against Sans Souci, but Christophe disappointed them, showing little enthusiasm in this first campaign (Lacroix 1819:220–1).

3 French general Pamphile de Lacroix, a veteran of the Saint-Domingue expedition, later noted in his memoirs his surprise at Sans Souci's military effectiveness. Christophe himself came close to suggesting that if the colonial troops had used guerilla tactics similar to those of Sans Souci, they would not have lost the first phase of the war against the French (Lacroix 1819:219, 228).

4 These moments are separated here, in part to emphasize the processual character of historical production, in part as a rhetorical artifice. I wish to argue that the unequal control of the means of historical production obtains at various points of the process *even* if we relegate completely the issue of narrative intent (the historians qua historians' preferences, their unknown or acknowledged stakes) as a separate, post-factual moment. One could certainly suggest different ways of phasing the process or place additional phases between those that I noted here. One could also suggest, as I do below for some sources and documents, that in many cases the specific products of these moments appear simultaneously.

5 By 'archives' I do not mean only the libraries sponsored by states, foundations, or individuals, usually recognized as such, but any institution that sorts sources to organize facts, according to themes, into documents to be used and monuments to be seen. The creation of such institutions and the work that they do (the classification of 'facts,' the elevation of sources to the rank of documents, the imposition of a *thématique*, the redistribution of space, etc.) occurs also in oral transmission by way of similar mechanisms of exclusion. Chosen individuals become the living depositories of 'classified' knowledge (e.g., Price 1983).

De Certeau (1974:20–1) conflates 'sources' and 'documents,' which indeed can emerge simultaneously. My own insistence on two different moments has three purposes that will become clearer below. First, lest we dismiss too easily the issue of power and its consequences, we cannot discard the distinction between history and fiction, even though we need to recognize that it is not as solid as we used to think. Second, we need to keep in mind that uneven historical power obtains even *before* any work of classification by non-participants. Third, the fact that the kind of power used in the creation of sources is not necessarily the same as that which allows the creation of archives matters enormously to Third World countries with a colonial past (see note 8 for an example).

6 I leave aside as an unnecessary distraction at this point the much-debated issue of the nature of the historical fact, except to reject both the idealist proposition that it is created out of nothing (rather than produced) by the historian and the crude materialist proposition that it is a mirror of a 'thing,' if not the thing itself.

7 This is one reason why I find it useful to distinguish between the creation of facts and their collection, the creation of archives. And if we distinguish, as we may now, between the professional archivist and the professional historian, the latter's entry into historical production can be located more properly at the third moment.

8 The history of the Rochambeau Papers themselves is full of silences. They were bought by the University of Florida from Sotheby's, but how they came to the auction house remains a mystery: there is no record of provenance (Monti 1972:4). Some Haitians suggest that the appropriation of the papers by whomever Sotheby's was acting for could very well be a case study of the quite concrete effects of differential power in the international market for documents.

9 To claim otherwise would be to suggest that a 'source' can be 'the thing' itself, which is nonsense. Because facts are not things (they cannot be asserted only, if at all, on ontological grounds), sources are always *about* something *else*.

10 Silences of this kind show the limits of strategies that imply a more accurate reconstitution of the past, and therefore the production of a 'better' history, simply by an enlargement of its empirical base. Even scholars who can hardly be accused of empiricism sometimes come close to equating a 'new' history with a turn toward new objects defined primarily in terms of their content matter (e.g., Le Goff and Nora 1974–5). To be sure, the continuous enlargement of the physical boundaries of historical production is certainly useful and necessary. The turn toward hitherto neglected sources (e.g., diaries, images, bodies) and the emphasis on unused facts (e.g., facts of gender, facts of the life cycle, facts of resistance) are path-breaking developments. My point is that when these tactical gains are made to dictate strategy, they lead, at worst, to a neo-empiricist enterprise and at best to an unnecessary restriction of the battleground for historical power.

11 At one point during the war within the war, he told the French that he would surrender only if they expelled Christophe, a proposition which a French witness refers to as a 'pretext' (Lacroix 1819:220).

12 The constructivist position has roots in European literary theory (e.g., Propp, Barthes, Greimas). As most forcefully presented in North America, however, it rests in part on quite hasty misconceptions about 'scientific' discourse, projected as the counterpart of history. Its dichotomies are Eurocentric. Of course, history has no language of its own, but neither does nature. Of course, 'events' have no intrinsic claims to concrete existence, but neither does a molecule. That historical narratives use fictional tropes (Jauss 1987) is no more news to some anthropologists than that scientific discourse emplots its representations. The point is that the stated conventions about which the acceptability of a narrative as science, history, or fiction is actually debated vary and that one cannot easily dismiss these variations and their concrete results. On further comparisons of history and fiction, see de Certeau 1975:312–58; 1982. For recent critiques of constructivism, see Carr 1986 and Hobart 1989.

13 Most Haitians are illiterate and unilingual speakers of Haitian, a French-based Creole. The first published memoirs and histories of the revolution were written almost exclusively in French. So were most of the written traces (letters, proclamations, and so on) that have become primary documents. Currently, the vast majority of history books about Saint-Domingue/Haiti are written in French, with a substantial minority of those published in France itself. The first full-length history book (and for that matter the first non-fiction book) written in Haitian dates from 1977 (M.-R. Trouillot 1977).

14 The division between guild historians and amateurs is itself premised on a particular Western-dominated practice. In the Haitian case, few if any individuals make a living writing history. Haitian historians have included physicians, journalists, businessmen, bureaucrats and politicians, high school teachers, and clergymen. Status as historian is not conferred by an academic degree but by a mixture of publications that abide to a large extent by the Western standards and active participation in ongoing historical debates.

15 The suggestion is not far-fetched. That Christophe deemed himself one notch above most mortals was well known even in his lifetime. Further, his reliance on transformative rituals, and his desire to control both humans and death itself are epitomized in his last moments. Having engaged unsuccessfully in various rituals to restore his failing health, and knowing that he had lost the personal magnetism that made his contemporaries tremble at his sight, a paralysed Christophe shot himself, reportedly with a gold-cast bullet, before a growing crowd of insurgents reached Sans Souci. Whether that bullet was meant to save him from a Congo, as such, we do not know.

16 There are, in this story, instances of memory lapses, both collective and individual, both doubtful and genuine. William Harvey of Queens College (Cambridge), who served as Christophe's adviser during some months of residence in Haiti and wrote what may pass for the king's first biography, flatly states that the palace was named 'probably, from the manner in which it was defended by nature' (Harvey 1827:133). Whether Harvey, who moved extensively within the kingdom, heard about either the colonel or Potsdam is not clear. But he had the prudence that has come to characterize foreign consultants, and 'nature' may have looked to him as a perfect alibi. Similarly, one can tie the silence of some Haitian witnesses, such as de Vastey, to a desire to preserve a favourable image of Christophe.

17 The conversation mentioned, which occurred in the first phase of the war within the war, already suggests Christophe's wish to make of Sans Souci a non-object of discourse. In the course of the exchange, the French general bluntly challenged Christophe's claims to fame, hinting that if he was as popular and respected as he affirmed, he would have convinced the blacks to betray Sans Souci. (Note the pattern of induced betrayal.) As de Lacroix reports the exchange, Christophe dodged the issue of command and popularity. He called Sans Souci a 'brigand,' displacing into the field of Western tastefulness what was a serious competition for national leadership (Lacroix 1819:227).

18 We know, and Brown perhaps ignored, that Sans Souci was not an uncommon name for places or individuals. For example, there was in colonial times a coffee area within the parish of Vallières (between what is now Vallières and Mombin-Crochu) called Sans-Souci, more than forty kilometres southeast of Milot (Romain 1960).

19 'Here, at the foot of the Pic de la Ferrière, guarded by the fortress that he called Citadel-Henry, he built San-Souci, naming it out of admiration for Frederick the Great and despite the fact that it was also the name of the bitter enemy whom he had murdered' (Cole 1967:207).

20 For the record, Cole was often sympathetic to his subject. My point is that this sympathy pertains to a particular field of significance that characterizes treatments of the Haitian Revolution by Western historians.

21   A possible corroboration of this interpretation is an ephemeral change in the name of Grand
Pré itself. Sometime between the death of Sans Souci and 1827 the plantation was rebaptized
'La Victoire' (The Victory). Mackenzie's first volume opens with a picture of a plantation
entitled 'La Victorie, formerly Grand Pré, on the road to Sans Souci' (Mackenzie 1830:I,
frontispiece). Unfortunately, we do not know if the name change occurred during
Christophe's tenure or in the seven years between his death and Mackenzie's visit.

22   I am thankful to John Thornton for this reference and for reminding me of Christophe's
Dahoman connections.

23   On 'mulatto' historians and the Haitian past, see Nicholls 1988, chap. 3. On Ardouin in
particular, see H. Trouillot 1950. For a close reading of Ardouin, see Woodson 1990.

24   James Franklin ([1828] 1971:214–15), an avowed racist, after suggesting that Sans Souci and
Citadel Henry were 'old works of the French repaired,' concluded his diatribe in these words:
'unless Baron de Vastey can adduce other proofs of Haitian capacities, I must be excused if
I remain sceptical.'

25   The 'revolution' in Geggus's title is the *French* one. Note that Haitian urban historians use
the same dichotomy, but include much fewer individuals among the 'barbarians.' Only recently
have some Haitian intellectuals argued that contradictions within the revolutionary camp require
much more analysis than was previously thought and that the study of these contradictions in no
way diminishes the global achievements of the founders of Haiti and the retrospective
significance of the revolution (M.-R. Trouillot 1977, 1986; Auguste and Auguste 1986).

26   James's book was published in France by Gallimard, so French historians cannot claim an
accidental failure of transmission in this case. But old habits are die hard: even though his
subtitle contains the word 'revolution,' his Italian editor turned it into 'the first *revolt* against
the white man' (James 1968).

REFERENCES

Ardouin, A. Beaubrun
    [1853–60] 1958 Études sur l'histoire d'Haïti. Port-au-Prince: François Dalencourt.
Auguste, Claude B., and Marcel B. Auguste
    1986 L'expédition Leclerc, 1801–1803. Port-au-Prince: Imprimerie Henri Deschamps.
Blackburn, Robin
    1988 The Overthrow of Colonial Slavery. London and New York: Verso.
Brown, Jonathan
    1837 The History and Present Condition of St. Domingo. 2 vols. Philadelphia.
Candler, John
    1842 Brief Notices of Haiti: With Its Conditions, Resources, and Prospects. London: Thames
        Ward & Co.
Carpentier, Alejo
    [1949] 1983 The Kingdom of This World. New York: Alfred A. Knopf.
Carr, David
    1986 Time, Narrative, and History. Bloomington: University of Indiana Press.
Carr, David, W. Dray, T. Geraets, et al.
    1982 La philosophie de l'histoire et la pratique historienne aujourd'hui / Philosophy
        of History and Contemporary Historiography. Ottawa: University of Ottawa
        Press.
Cauna, Jacques
    1987 Au temps des isles à sucre. Paris: Karthala.

Certeau, Michel de
  1974 L'opération historique. *In* Faire de l'histoire, vol. 1, Nouveaux problèmes, Le Goff
      and Nora, eds. pp. 3–41. Paris: Gallimard.
  1975 L'écriture de l'histoire. Paris: Gallimard.
  1982 L'histoire, science et fiction. *In* La philosophie de l'histoire, Carr et al., eds. pp.19–39.
      Ottawa: University of Ottawa Press.
Césaire, Aimé
  [1963] 1970 La tragédie du roi Christophe. Paris: Présence Africaine.
Chesneaux, Jean
  1988 Le temps de la modernité. L'Homme et la société 22(90):105.
Cole, Hubert
  1967 Christophe, King of Haiti. New York: Viking.
Dray, W.H.
  1982 Narration, Reduction and the Uses of History. *In* La philosophie de l'histoire, Carr et
      al., eds. pp. 197–214. Ottawa: University of Ottawa Press.
Dumesle, Hérard
  1824 Voyage dans le Nord d'Hayti. Cayes: Imprimerie du gouvernement.
Foucault, Michel
  1969 L'archéologie du savoir. Paris: Gallimard.
Franklin, James
  [1828] 1971 The Present State of Hayti (Saint Domingo), with Remarks on Its Agriculture ...
      Reprint. London: Frank Cass.
Geggus, David P.
  1982 Slavery, War, and Revolution: The British Occupation of Saint Domingue, 1793–1798.
      Oxford: Clarendon Press; New York: Oxford University Press.
Harvey, William W.
  1827 Sketches of Hayti; from the Expulsion of the French to the Death of Christophe.
      London: L.B. Seeley and Son.
Hobart, Michael E.
  1989 The Paradox of Historical Constructionism. History and Theory 28(1):43–58.
Hobsbawm, Eric J.
  1962 The Age of Revolutions, 1789–1848. New York: New American Library.
James, C.L.R.
  [1938] 1962 The Black Jacobins. Toussaint Louverture and the San Domingo Revolution.
      New York: Viking.
  1968 Il Giacobinni neri. La prima rivolta contro l'uomo bianco. Milano: Feltrinelli.
Jauss, Hans-Robert
  1987 Expérience historique et fiction. *In* Certitudes et incertitudes de l'histoire, Gilbert
      Gadofrre, ed. pp. 117–32. Paris: Puf.
Lacroix, François Joseph Pamphile, vicomte de
  1819 Mémoires pour servir à l'histoire de la révolution de Saint-Domingue. 2 vols. Paris:
      Pillet Aîné.
Leconte, Vergniaud
  1931 Henri Christophe dans l'histoire d'Haïti. Paris: Berger-Levrault.
Le Goff, Jacques, and P. Nora, eds.
  1974–5 Faire de l'histoire. 3 vols. Paris: Gallimard.
Mackenzie, Charles
  1830 Notes on Haiti, Made during a Residence in That Republic. 2 vols. London: Henry
      Colburn and Richard Bentley.

Monti, Laura V.
    1972 A Calendar of the Rochambeau Papers of the University of Florida Libraries.
          Gainesville: University of Florida Libraries.
Nicholls, David
    1988 From Dessalines to Duvalier: Race, Colour, and National Independence in Haiti.
          London: MacMillan Caribbean.
Norris, Robert
    [1789] 1968 Memoirs of the Reign of Bossa Adahee, King of Dahomy ... London: Cass.
Phelipeau, René
    1786 Plan de la plaine du Cap François en l'isle Saint Domingue. Paris. Manuscript copy,
          Bibliothèque Nationale, Paris.
Prévost, Justin
    1819 Histoire du couronnement et du Sacre d'Henry I. Cap Henry.
Price, Richard
    1983 First-time: The Historical Vision of an Afro-American People. Baltimore: Johns
          Hopkins University Press.
Ritter, Karl
    1836 Naturhistorische Reise nach der westindischen Insel Hayti. Stuttgart: Hallberger'fche
          Berlagshandlung.
Romain, Jean-Baptiste
    1960 Noms de lieux d'époque coloniale en Haïti: Essai sur la toponymie du Nord à l'usage
          des étudiants. Revue de la Faculté d'ethnologie, no. 3. Port-au-Prince: Imprimerie de
          l'état.
Sanders, Prince, ed.
    1816 Haytian Papers: A Collection of the Very Interesting Proclamations ... London: Printed
          for W. Reed.
Stein, Robert
    1985 Léger Félicité Sonthonax: The Lost Sentinel of the Republic. Rutherford: Farleigh
          Dickinson.
Thibau, Jacques
    1989 Le temps de Saint-Domingue: L'Esclavage et la révolution française. J.C. Lattès.
Thornton, John
    n.d.   I am the Subject of the King of Kongo: African Political Ideology and the Haitian
          Revolution. ms.
Thornton, John K.
    1991 African Soldiers in the Haitian Revolution. Journal of Caribbean History 25:58–80.
Trouillot, Hénock
    1950 Beaubrun Ardouin, l'homme politique et l'historien. Comision de Historia. Mexico:
          Instituto Panamericano de Geografía e Historia.
    1953 La révolution de Saint-Domingue. In Catts Pressoir, Hénock Trouillot, and Ernst
          Trouillot, Historiographie d'Haïti. Comision de Historia, publicaciòn no. 168. Mexico:
          Instituto Panamericano de Geografía e Historia.
    1972 Le gouvernement du Roi Henri Christophe. Port-au-Prince: Imprimerie Centrale.
Trouillot, Michel-Rolph
    1977 Ti difé boulé sou istoua Ayiti. New York: Koleksion Lakansièl.
    1986 Les racines historiques de l'état duvaliérien. Port-au-Prince: Editions Henri Deschamps.
    1989 Haiti: State against Nation: The Origins and Legacies of Duvalierism. New York and
          London: Monthly Review.

1990 'Good Day, Columbus': Silences, Power, and Public History (1492–1892). Public Culture 3(1):1–24.

1992 The Inconvenience of Freedom: Free People of Color and the Aftermath of Slavery in Dominica and Saint-Domingue/Haiti. *In* The Meaning of Freedom: Economics, Politics and Culture after Slavery, F. McGlynn and S. Drescher, eds. pp. 147–82. Pittsburgh: University of Pittsburgh Press.

1995 Silencing the Past: Power and the Production of History. Boston: Beacon Press.

Vastey, Pompée Valentin, Baron de.

[1823] 1819 An Essay on the Causes of the Revolution and Civil Wars of Hayti. Exeter.

Veyne, Paul

[1971] 1978 Comment on écrit l'histoire. Paris: Seuil.

White, Hayden

1978 The Historical Text as Literary Artifact. *In* Tropics of Discourse. Baltimore: Johns Hopkins University Press.

1987 The Content of the Form. Narrative Discourse and Historical Representation. Baltimore: Johns Hopkins University Press.

Woodson, Drexel G.

1990 Tout mounn se mounn men tout mounn pa menm: Micro-level Sociocultural Aspects of Land Tenure in a Northern Haitian Locality. PhD diss., University of Chicago.

Against Experience: The Struggles for History, Tradition, and Hope among a Native American People

GERALD SIDER

Not man or men but the struggling, oppressed class itself is the depository of historical knowledge. In Marx it appears as the last enslaved class, as the avenger that completes the task of liberation in the name of the downtrodden. This conviction ... has always been objectionable to Social Democrats ... Social Democracy thought fit to assign to the working class the role of redeemer of future generations, in this way cutting the sinews of its greatest strength. This training made the working class forget both its hatred and its spirit of sacrifice, for both are nourished by the image of enslaved ancestors rather than that of liberated grandchildren.

Walter Benjamin, 'Theses on the Philosophy of History,' xii.

Any theory of culture must include the concept of the dialectical interaction between culture and something which is *not* culture. We must suppose the raw material of life experience to be at one pole, and all the infinitely complex human disciplines and systems ... which 'handle,' 'transmit' or distort this raw material to be at the other.

Edward Thompson, Review of R. Williams, *The Long Revolution*

I

As Edward Thompson and Raymond Williams taught us to see, from (and, we will add, against) 'experience' come both 'agency' and 'culture.' But experience is more than the raw material from which an active life is fashioned. It is, to begin, social and relational: a person who stands on an assembly line stamping out a hundred or so small brass fittings an hour does not have a hundred or so experiences of stamping fittings each hour, hour after hour, day after day.

What is experienced, rather, is a profusion of changing and repetitive conceptual and social *relationships*, between hurting knees and back and the smallness of the pay cheque and the pressures from the foreman to keep on working and the hope for and the dread of overtime and the satisfaction of knowing how to do one's job exceedingly well and the need to use the toilet and the need to wait for permission to leave the line – all this and, simultaneously, an inevitably changing, and thus necessarily continually tested, socially rooted sense of what can and cannot be claimed or done with and through these relationships, by oneself and by and with others. People do not simply 'have' experience: we also say they 'gain' it, and we can sense, if we cannot name, the costs. 'Experience' is not only socially formed and continually reshaped; it also names a major arena for the chosen and the unavoidable struggles of all forms and processes of differentiation – for example, class, gender, and ethnicity – for it is both from and against one's changing specificity that experiences are constructed.

When a building-services corporation advertises for a 'porter,' someone who, for the most part, spends his or her days removing garbage, and says in the advertisement, 'experience required,' and means it, we must ask ourselves: What kinds of 'experience,' with what kinds of outcomes, are being demanded? And how do we understand the gulf between the left belief that experience produces 'agency' and the corporate notion that such experiences make people less, not more, likely to protest significantly either the conditions or the rewards of such work? Are we on the left primarily referring to artisanal labour, where experience might well have a potential for engendering emancipatory confrontations, and the building-service corporation be referring to plain drudge work? Or, perhaps much more to the point, is the experience that produces agency[1] not simply what happens directly to you but, more significantly, to those you know and care about, so that what we call 'agency' becomes diffused through family and social life, rather than being contained, as it were, in the political economy (which may provide one component of the intensity and frequency of peasant revolts)? If what we call 'experience' names a domain of the social, how does it differ from what we call 'culture'?

Further, we may, following E.P. Thompson and, more generally, the British Marxist social history and cultural studies perspectives, find it useful to conceptualize both agency and culture as continually emerging from (and against) experience. This is, however, all the more reason *not* to conceptualize 'experience' as simply a historically inert ocean within which islands of history magically appear. We must, rather, understand experience to be also continually recreated and reshaped, but as what stands against both agency and culture. In this perspective, people hire 'experienced workers' not only for their task skills but also in order to get workers who have learned to go to work day after day, on good days and bad, and each day do more or less what must be done, give more or less of what is taken.[2] 'Experience,' in this perspective, is the *active and historically dynamic* opposite of agency: it names the changing outcomes of ongoing struggles over teaching and learning 'appropriate' behaviour within a complex field of obligations, in work and in daily life.

More generally, we should conceptualize 'agency' and 'experience' in ways that emphasize both the struggles that create each and the tensions between them. A brief illustration will help to clarify this point and set the stage for discussing the politics of socially constructed and enforced silences. In Lumberton, North Carolina, the county seat of Robeson County, which we shall soon describe in some detail, in the 1960s, young and middle-aged Indian and African-American women would walk along the sidewalks of the middle-class white neighbourhoods quite early in the morning, particularly around the holidays, and call out 'Any cleaning today? Maid? Cleaning?' The women of the house would open their doors and at times call back, 'Are you Indian?' To which the Indian women would respond, 'No, ma'am' – meaning, and sometimes saying, 'No, ma'am, I'm coloured.' (For a range of such incidents, see Blu 1980). The answer was probably more expected and desired than believed.

This is not agency, these ways of coping – on the one hand, to get a job or, on the other, to get a job done cheaply – but experience, and more is at issue than the experience of how and how not to hire or get hired. White people in this part of the south in the 1960s were more 'afraid' of Indians than of African Americans. They thought that Indians were 'meaner' and less deferential as workers, and they would tell stories of 'experiences' – their own or of people they knew, or just what they had heard – that purportedly demonstrated this view. The fact that both the question and the answer invoked 'experience' – a past – that was fantasy rather than reality made those experiences no less binding.

Walter Benjamin has taught us to see the deep connection between struggle and knowledge: how classes (and ethnic groups and genders as well) become the repositories of historical knowledge through struggle. At the same point in the construction of this perspective on class (cited in the epigraph above), he introduces the the importance of the 'image of enslaved ancestors.' More than one's hope for future generations, for Benjamin it is images of and from the past that stoke the passion for transformation. While each of the points is rather straightforward – the connection between struggle and knowledge, and the importance of images of the past in generating the commitment to struggle and sacrifice – these two points merge in very complex ways.

What Benjamin is telling us is that the 'experiences' that fuel the fires of struggle do not all happen directly to us. They may well be deeply personal: to take his example literally, it is *our* ancestors, *our* actual or symbolic grandparents, and not just anyone's, who matter most. But a great many people in this world seem to learn most from their grandparents (the most immediate ancestors) before they have ended their own second decade – before, that is, they have developed much ability to grasp the depth or the nuances of others' experiences. What they thus learn from their 'enslaved ancestors' may be more appropriately termed 'orientations' than experience: stories that, at best, point the senses and the emerging sensibilities in certain directions.

Further, neither we nor our ancestors have been free to choose the struggles that we find ourselves in, or whether or not we have to struggle. There is a substantial, and in some cases quite insightful, literature on 'experience' and the ways in which it becomes embedded in the 'construction of identity.' (see especially Joan Scott 1992) But the emphasis there is on the 'discursive construction of identity' and the point that people chose the meanings by which they interpret their experiences. Although the notion of 'discourse' can cover an extraordinarily large range of social interactions, sometimes quite productively, to call, say, a lynching 'the discursive construction of identity' would be to trivialize and, more, to misunderstand fundamentally what it means to be vulnerable to power. So would it be, more subtly, to claim that we can 'chose the meanings' that we attach to such events. There seems, rather, to be a very narrow range of *liveable* meanings, even including those that encourage confronting such brutality, and wending one's way through this narrow range of imposed, chosen, and deniable meanings in ways that enable survival is scarcely what we might realistically call 'choice.'

If knowledge is a product of struggle, the realization that we are not dealing with struggles that are always chosen and that the 'experience' which people bring to and from their struggles is not simply what has happened to them forces us to develop a more complex concept of 'necessary struggle.' Specifically, we must neither deny nor minimize but rather go far beyond the notion that socially *necessary* struggle comes almost entirely from the fundamental social polarities: class, 'race,' gender. A more developed and useful concept would fully include struggles *within* classes, ethnic groups, and genders.

To exemplify and clarify this point: lynchings were the context of an appallingly violent and destructive struggle by large numbers of Whites in an extensive area of the United States in order continually to force African-American people down. But they also became part of a very forceful, unavoidable struggles *within* Black families and neighbourhoods as, in changing circumstances, the boundaries of protest and acceptance, alliance and opposition, were continually and necessarily renegotiated. In this broader context of struggles that must be fought both between and within opposing groups (or socially imposed categories) we are also not fully free to choose the struggles we find ourselves in, and the issue here also is not simply what we learn from our struggles *but also what we must try not to learn*, what 'experiences' and what parts of our own histories and our own ways we must not only not take up but must set ourselves against.[3]

II

Robeson County is a large, now quite densely populated county on the swampy inland edge of the North Carolina coastal plain, along the border with South Carolina. In the context of eighteenth-century American political economy its social and physical geography made it a very special, if not unique, place on a coastal plain otherwise increasingly dominated by plantation agriculture. Its most salient characteristics then were land too swampy to be easily usable for market agriculture, multiple but not navigable rivers, and mostly very difficult terrain for road construction. During most of the eighteenth century it was an area claimed by both North and South Carolina and effectively governed by neither, an unusually isolated and 'remote' territory, but one that was far from the tumultuous western colonial frontiers and the intense pressures throughout the frontier regions to control Native peoples and their partly allied runaway slaves and escaped and former indentured servants. It was socially distant from the settled plantation economy but not dangerous to Native peoples in the way that the whole Appalachian frontier zone was, nor did it have the exterminatory Indian-slave raiding that characterized the piedmont region during the eighteenth century. (For an extended description of the historical political economy of Robeson County, see Sider 1993.)

Robeson County throughout the colonial period and on into the early nineteenth century was thus one of the major areas in the southeast where quite substantial numbers of Native peoples could settle and live, along with escaped slaves and indentured servants and many 'new' people, such as recently arrived, Gaelic-speaking highland Scots, too poor to purchase better farmland. In the isolated recesses of what is now Robeson County they could all farm the dry islands in the midst of their swamps, fish the teeming creeks, hunt, marry, and build. The relatively quite large area now called Robeson County became one of the major 'collecting points' for a substantial flow of Native peoples who had been pressed northward and southward along the coastal plain and piedmont, from central South Carolina to southern Virginia; joining with other migrating peoples, they all built small communities across this landscape.

During the early and mid nineteenth century the isolation was increasingly broken, and the peoples who had been living in the area were seriously impoverished but not destroyed. The rapid and substantial growth and consolidation of a White-dominated plantation economy in the nineteenth century, which intensified with the growing network of road and then railroad transportation during and after the 1830s, was further aided in the decade or more before the Civil War by a heightened control over an increasingly landless and impoverished population of 'free persons of colour' (in this area primarily Native Americans living as subsistence and small-market farmers). Their labour was used to drain the swamps and build a local network of railroads and roads and also to sustain a substantial naval-supplies industry in timber, turpentine, and pitch.

After the Civil War the farming population was in large part reduced to various forms of tenancy, although a quite substantial number of Native Americans, particularly in the very centre of the county, managed to continue as farm owners. As African-American people, particularly in the early twentieth century, moved out of agriculture and into the expanding county towns, a social demography was established that characterized the first three-quarters of the twentieth century: towns that were divided between Whites and African Americans – save one largely Indian town – and a countryside that, in the centre of the county, was very substantially Indian. Overall, the population of the county at mid-century was approximately one-third each White, Indian, and Black, with a rapidly growing Indian population, increasingly out-migrating Blacks, and an aging agrarian White elite just starting to be pushed aside by a combination of rising costs for farming and declining commodity prices, on the one hand, and increasing industrialization, on the other. The Indian population, recognized as Lumbee Indians by the state of North Carolina in 1953, were increasingly struggling to achieve full *federal* recognition of their rights and to use what federally based claims and ties they could muster, in conjunction with their local alliances and organizations, to develop their communities against the opposition of the local agrarian White economic and political 'power structure'.

By 1960 Robeson County was the second wealthiest rural county in the entire south by value of agricultural produce shipped and one of the one hundred poorest counties in the United States by average per capita income. A small handful of people did very well and a very large number of people lived very hard lives, and much was done both directly and indirectly to specific individuals, communities, groups, and categories of people to try to keep things just that way.

From the 1960s through the 1980s three 'movements' shook the county. The first was civil rights, here mobilizing both Blacks and Indians, politically cooperating for the first time since reconstruction to contest White domination. The second was a movement that in one of its manifestations called itself 'Red power' and was a complex, continually changing, continually combative Native American search for power, rights, justice, economic advancement, and local political control. At first it developed among the Lumbee, and then in the early 1970s, with the emergence of a sizeable faction of Lumbee who called themselves Tuscarora – some 3,000 Tuscarora out of a Lumbee population then about 35,000 – the Red power movement became a framework both for Native American assertiveness and for divisiveness. The third factor was a rapid and fundamental transformation of the county from agriculture to industry as the major economic activity and source of employment. In 1960 there were about 11,200 people working in agriculture and nearly 3,900 in manufacturing; in the 1970 census about 4,000 people were employed in agriculture and 9,600 in manufacturing.

Among the many outcomes of these transformations two are of special note. First, the local White, agrarian-based elite was losing both its political power and the economic basis of this power, particularly among the smaller operators, who had fewer resources for keeping up with the changes. Many became particularly ugly in their attempts to maintain their own status by increasingly squeezing their tenant farmers. Second, the small communities that dotted the county, each with its very local schools, churches, and stores, were becoming increasingly undermined by large-scale social and economic processes. Village schools were closing or being consolidated and integrated; farming and other forms of work within communities were rapidly ceasing to support anyone, even the poor, and those who could were driving substantial distances to factory work; local stores were closing under pressure from the new malls; even many village churches were in serious financial trouble, as local elites increasingly drove to 'prestige' churches with countywide parishes. Lumbee were splitting, with several Tuscarora factions emerging from within and quickly turning against the Lumbee and each other, provoked generally by this disintegration of community institutions and social relations as a framework for a reasonable and reproducible social life, and more specifically by intense and angry disagreements over how to handle the forced closing or integration of Indian schools, the possibility of full federal recognition of Indian status, and the advent and expenditure of rather substantial Indian 'poverty program' funds. This is the context for the following stories.

III

We start with a pair of stories from and about a Lumbee Indian woman called M. The first incident was designed to force me to stop trying to interfere further with their ongoing history, in part by confronting me with a 'celebration' of that history; the second, by way of an apology that was perhaps also an explanation for the pounding I took, revealed an opposite, ordinarily very silent experience.

The first incident: in the early 1980s I was asked to talk to a group of Lumbee Indians about economic development in the context of government programs then available for small and medium-sized business development. For a brief political moment then it looked as if a big development project, by Lumbee standards, could be started. The project would use a politically generated contract with the supplies-procurement branch of the army (a contract designed to evade charges of discrimination against 'people of colour' by doing something for Indians and continuing to disregard the needs of African Americans). The contract would be for several years' supply of army shirts, so many per month, and it could be used to secure a federal-government business-development loan to build a small factory – or more precisely, a sweatshop – to make these shirts. Since I had played a substantial role in establishing the Lumbee anti-poverty program a decade earlier, which was by then bringing more than a million dollars a year of federal government funds into the county, I was invited to talk with Indians active in this 'development.'

My grandmother had worked for years sewing shirts in a New York City sweatshop and had told me still-remembered, troubling stories about this experience when I was quite young. The factory in which she worked was next door to the Triangle Shirtwaist Company building, where 146 people, mostly women, were locked in and burned to death in 1911. I had briefly worked stamping brass handle clamps in a 'hard-run' small factory, one that assembled imitation-leather pocketbooks, where an old woman in a loose dress got her dress and then almost instantly her breast caught in an ancient industrial sewing machine, driven far too fast by low piece rates. These memories, together with my dismay at the increasingly intense class formation among Indians, gave me a far different agenda for my talk about 'developing' sewing factories than they expected or wanted.

My presentation included passionately argued warnings about the dangers of their potential 'economic development' project. I sought to explain that, the way things were likely to happen, light-skinned, relatively young Indian men would manage the plant, sitting in posh offices with telephones and secretaries and driving big cars to and from work, while dark-skinned Indian women worked the machines on the line at a nickel or dime more than the minimum wage, and the older and poorer or more vulnerable cleaned the toilets and swept the walks. My fears about the likelihood and the potential consequences of a tribal sweatshop, dressed up in the costume of 'progress,' were fuelled by the fact that the poverty program, which had been built with so many dreams and hopes, including my own, with so much work, and against so many fears and so much white-power opposition in that violent and difficult place, was already, a decade later, profiteering substantially from the day-care centres that it ran 'for' working Indian mothers, who were mostly factory workers. The day-care centres, all designed and managed by Indians, used mostly young Indian girls, whose wages were subsidized by a linked 'job-training' program, as childcare labour and charged Indian mothers or parents a substantial portion of what they earned on the production lines, the profits not going into private pockets but to subsidize future tribal projects. The fact that the money made was being held for such projects as building a tribal office building was sup-posed – by the men who designed the program – to justify what I regarded as fairly substantial price gouging of the parents, primarily mothers who worked in White-owned sweatshops at barely more than the minimum wage. I was, with every passion and reason I could muster, trying to urge the design of a project that would be more fully beneficial to the Indian people with the most intense needs.

I wanted in particular to talk directly about the issue of the increasing inequality among Indian people and to raise the point that it was one thing for Whites to dominate and exploit Indians and a very much different, in some ways even more destructive, thing for Indians to do it to each other. On this basis I suggested designing the project to include, for example, job rotation from the production line to foreman to management and back to the line, putting this proposal in the context of asking how an Indian or tribal develop-ment project ought to differ from one in the dominant society. I also argued strongly for the inclusion of subsidized van transportation from the more rural, 'swamp' areas of the county and special kinds of jobs for middle-aged and somewhat older folk. A particular concern, as I explained by way of conclu-sion, should be with these older people out in the county, who were being bypassed by all the forms of 'modern' development and who were increasingly unable to make a living at farming or farm labouring. They were stuck out in the recesses of the county, increasingly hard-pressed by the collapse of small-scale agriculture, living in broken-down houses that leaked when it rained and were draughty in winter, with no screens on the windows or doors in a land dense with flies, and any program that we developed had to include a lot of such folk, had to help them live an easier life.

At the end of my talk I was not so much directly attacked as very firmly pushed aside. The opening reply, from a wealthy and powerful Indian busi-nessman, was 'Where are *your* people from?' 'New York and before that eastern Europe.' Well, down here, [alien], we do things differently.' I got some support from one person, but it was all over fairly quickly. In less than five minutes my vision of egalitarian development and all my specific suggestions except the purchase of a van disappeared from the discussion. After the meeting ended, M, who I had expected to be the most effective local spokesperson for developing special programes for rural, marginal Indians and the strongest support for the position that I was advocating for the elderly, came over to me, extremely angry. Her grandparents, she very firmly told me, had lived in such a place as I described, a wood-plank house with no window or door screens; one of them still did, and it was a fine place to live. M had lived there when she was growing up, and I had no right at all to come in from the outside with my values and ways and criticize their ways and how they lived. Their ways of living were just fine, and if I did not appreciate them, I should not talk about it.

The second incident in this first pair of stories: a week later, by way of trying to make amends, I took M and her family out to dinner in a local Indian restaurant. In a quiet moment, when we had a chance to return to this still-open tension, she talked briefly about growing up in the grandparents' home. M said that the youngsters would 'steal' Clorox (a bleach; in Europe, Javel) from her grandmother's laundry supplies to put in the bathwater, trying to lighten their skin.

IV

Children of oppressed minorities are ordinarily far too vulnerable to struggle successfully against the brutalities of the dominant society. Indeed, their struggles often take the form of trying to join themselves to those ways, to have a better part in an ongoing history. Adults from such groups learn to claim their dignity and self-respect not just within but against the history of the dominant society. One can often find, among working people in the United States and among African Americans and Native Americans, a mixture of cynicism about one's choices, and a more or less subdued longing to both participate in and withdraw from the dominant society (often in both cases probably fuelled as much or more by economic pressure as by either envy or dismay), all enmeshed in a hard-won, if partial, cultural autonomy.

Such complex mixtures of orientations seem often to underlie the 'traditions' of minority and marginalized peoples. For an example, since 1971 the Lumbee have had an annual 'homecoming', on the July Fourth (Independence Day) weekend, which has always included among its main features 'beauty contests' for young women and six-year-old girls and a parade that also intensely mixes symbols of alliance and separation from the dominant society:

for instance, a very large banner with a picture of a brick house and underneath it the slogan 'THINK INDIAN.'

Eric Hobsbawm and T.O. Ranger's path-pointing work *The Invention of Tradition* focused almost entirely upon traditions that were invented by the dominant society – often the colonial elite – and foisted upon a populace. The essays scarcely paused to ask why ordinary people would be so receptive to such externally generated cultural constructions, which is one of the key issues here. At first it seemed to me that this analytical issue could be dealt with by rejoining what is called 'the invention of tradition' with the absent part of the process, the formation of class. This must be done, but a more complex conception of the social practices that come to be called 'tradition' is a precondition for incorporating an analysis of class formation.

'Tradition' names an extraordinarily large array of loosely related practices. Among these we can specify, and put aside as not relevant here, the nationalist and colonial ceremonies that are part of state-sanctioned attempts to engender cultural order in the midst of imposed social chaos, and we can also put aside those traditions that are part of a public presentation of a regional petty elite who are dependent upon the localization of class processes to maintain their small advantage (for example, the invented 'regional' costumes that Bavarian shopkeepers and middling bureaucrats use to decorate themselves and their historical pretences). The focus here is on the traditions of marginalized, dominated, rural people who, with and apart from their own local elites, must continually seek to build and rebuild a liveable social life, being ordinarily intensely buffeted by even small swings in larger economic and political processes. For such peoples, tradition is *not* part of their isolation from and self-sufficiency within these larger processes, but on the contrary, is embedded in and expressive of their intense vulnerability and the fragility of their situation.

For such peoples, and in such circumstances, 'tradition,' names processes of continuing cultural and social construction through which they seek to distance themselves from a dominant society and to build or claim for themselves frameworks of dignity and self-respect, while at the same time staying substantially within the dominant society's incorporative structures and institutions. The same process that we have learned to call 'the invention of tradition' can serve fundamentally different interests and needs. It can be both an arena for class formation and elite control and simultaneously a way of making distance from, and boundaries against, the ravages of class.

To make this issue clear we must realize that the order in which I heard the 'stories' from M – about the dignity of her grandmother's exceedingly poor home and about the Clorox – was the opposite of the way in which she experienced these incidents: first, the child realizes a life of continuing vulnerability through, as it were, the failure of the bleach to construct at least a skin-deep shield against racist assault, critique, and limitations; then, much later, comes the adult's intense and sincere claims for the dignity of the grandparents' lifeways, including their suffering.

This multi-layered transition – from bleach to dignity, as it were – should alert us to the ways that experience, formed and transformed in relative silence, becomes 'agency' but an agency that is transformative in ways that both are and are not emancipatory (and, in some contexts, potentially revolutionary). There is, I suggest, nothing special about the context of 'silence' that makes agency or experience different from what they would otherwise be. Rather, it is the *irreducible* ambivalence and ambiguities of silences that lead us to the project of rethinking how we understand concepts such as 'experience' and 'agency' and, it is hoped, to looking a little more at what actually happens to people as they gain 'experience'[4] and what kinds of actions might usefully be thought of as 'agency.'

V

The second story I have recounted before, but for a different analytical purpose. By the mid 1960s many of the smaller White farmers of Robeson County were in serious trouble. The costs of farming and of achieving modest 'middle-class' aspirations were outstripping the returns on the sale of the crop. One farmer in such circumstances had divided his farm, bringing in a second share-cropping family. To explain what this meant for him and for the sharecroppers, a few introductory points about the sharecropping system in the mid-twentieth-century south must first be made.

Sharecroppers ordinarily provide all the labour on a farm and all the tools and equipment as well. They pay for half the seed and half the fertilizer, and in the 1960s, when the crop was sold, they got a 'stated half' of the proceeds. A stated half – many times the farmers would take the crop to market, sell it, come back, and say (without showing receipts) both what it sold for and what would be deducted from the half due to the sharecropper to cover the costs of half the seed and fertilizer, and, in addition, the costs of the 'advances' – the credit extended from landlord to tenant for groceries, doctor's bills, and so on. Some tenants kept, or had their schoolchildren keep, their own records; most had to take whatever the landlord said. Whether landlords were truthful or not in their allocation of the proceeds, as the demand for sharecroppers and farm labourers declined precipitously by the early 1960s, the power of landlords to control the allocation of income increasingly became total.

In 1967 one farmer (among many who did so) administratively divided his farm. This farmer had a small farm, say, 110 acres, with one 'cropping family working it. After he brought in a second sharecropping family, each of the two families would be working approximately 55 acres, with more intense labour than was possible or necessary on a larger unit. With the extra labour the total output on the farm would go up, by perhaps 10 to 20 per cent from which increased output the landlord's 'half' would rise. The total income of the first family of sharecroppers would, of course, be something like 55 or 60 per cent of what it had been previously, and the second, new family would earn about the same amount.

Six months or so after the first harvest in this newly divided farm, in the early summer of 1968, the situation of the two sharecropping families was desperate. They were short of food: one of the two families I went to see had an opened loaf of bread, a half jar of jam, and some tea bags as the only food in the house. (I looked when I went to get a glass of water.) The other family were eating unripe pecans, and the children were having trouble controlling their bowels. An attempt was made, by a Black woman I worked with, to get these families food relief, in the form of what was then called 'surplus commodities,' from the county welfare department. In order for the families to get these provisions, the landlord would have had to sign a 'paper' stating that they had earned less than a certain amount – around $1,200 – the previous year. This he refused to do, chasing the woman away with a gun. *One of the families was White and one Indian.* What the landlord said when I took the paper out and asked him again to sign, and once more he refused, was 'If you give these niggers free food they won't work.' The people got nothing but what small and temporary help we could give: the landlords' signature was irreplaceable.

The landlord constructed for the sharecroppers, in the midst of that sentence, an active history, including a continuing, still-present past that cut deeply through actual skin colour and actual place of origin to the social- and cultural-relational core of the agrarian south, and also including a future, a future that demonstrated the claims that a declining agrarian capitalism could still make and enforce upon vulnerable people.

'If you give those niggers free food, they won't work.' That statement made children hungry before their parents' eyes and ears, and the parents could say nothing much to either the landlord or their children, not in those years of declining small-farm agriculture. If the parents were 'turned out' – fired and told to move – they would find it exceedingly difficult to get another chance to farm. The same statement thus makes us understand that the creation of culture is also, simultaneously and necessarily, the creation of silence, and that we can have no significant understanding of any culture unless we also know the silences that were *institutionally* created and guaranteed along with it. (On the institutional matrix of silence, see especially Smith in this volume.)

The drama of this specific confrontation should not lead us to narrow the point: the silence that I am delineating is far, far broader than what parents do and do not say to either their children or the landlord. For but one further form that such silences take, to illustrate their breadth: the same appalling violence that made those farm workers 'niggers' simultaneously made me White, and despite my having remained troubled by and thinking about this incident and that realization, it took a very long time for me to hear, in addition, how deeply I was implicated in the consequences of such actions – as a receiver not only of stolen labour but of stolen lives.

VI

Julia Swindells and Lisa Jardine (1990) have wrought a useful transformation in the cultural-struggle perspective of British Marxist historians. Focusing on an analysis of Raymond Williams and Edward Thompson, their critique develops within the Marxist analysis of culture, and it does so by a close attention not to gender but to women. The absence of women's voices in the central 'texts' of Marxist cultural analyses, they argue, has created a perspective that is fundamentally nostalgic, centred on late-nineteenth-century versions of industrial work and daily life and on the kinds of voices, largely literary, that emerged from that context and shaped a wider understanding of such experiences. They emphasize, rather, turning away from the notion of 'working-class culture' to address the tensions between working-class consciousness and 'culture' – culture that both belongs to and includes the working class, but that also seems distant, alien, intrusive, oppressive. What I find particularly useful here is not the distinction between consciousness and culture, but the point that people come to stand in partly hostile, distant, or antagonistic relations to their own culture.

'Silence' and 'experience' are best conceptualized as names for different aspects of this antagonism, this distance, between people and (substantial elements of) their 'own' culture. As I use the terms, 'silence' names the larger, social domain – for the crucial silences are those that are socially constructed and guaranteed – and 'experience' the local and the personal. Such definitional distinctions are always deeply problematic, but these problems fade to lesser importance when we restate the point in relational terms: the point before us is the struggle between experience and silence; between, on the one hand, what happens to people in fact and in their understanding and, on the other, what is and is not, can and can not be, discussed, negotiated, socially reconfigured.

VII

We are now at the point where we can bring the separate threads of the analysis together and foreground their consequences for Marxist political strategy. To begin: think about the anthropological concept of shared culture and then, by contrast, of young girls putting Clorox in their bathwater or of people trying to live in the face of a culture that claims 'If you give these niggers free food they won't work.' We have before us two fundamental tensions: between culture (even culture as a domain of struggle) and what people experience, between the experiences of people and the silences of their social world. What can we learn from these tensions that is strategically significant? I think, most usefully, that the 'weapons of the weak' (James Scott 1985) are not found in their more or less minor semi-confrontations with power, even in the aggregate, but in their relations to one another, including relations both of alliance and of antagonism.

So long as we are talking about foot dragging, false deference, insult, and minor, semi-hidden injury as the weapons of the weak,[5] we are defining a situation where, in our view, the weak can not possible make any effective claims upon history. The related notion that the weak or the oppressed can make effective claims on a 'moral economy' to alleviate their plight substitutes far too innocent fantasies about what morality ought to be (and occasionally is) for the 'morality' that actually exists in particular kinds of societies and for particular classes. So long as we call sporadic uprisings to lower the price of bread a 'moral economy' and give another name to either the commodity-futures traders who speculate in and profit from the price of staple goods, or to those who politically manipulate an increasing denial of adequate welfare payments; so long as we do not call it a 'moral economy' when states and families let women in childbirth or ill young girls die from easily preventable diseases – so long as we do all this, we will continue to trivialize an otherwise potentially powerful concept.

Further, and more to the point here, a narrow and utopian notion of what is a moral economy silences or denies the direct experiences of vulnerable and oppressed people, who witness the construction and reproduction of moral economies on their bodies and in their lives. They cannot avoid knowing, no matter how hard they try to shield their children and their own feelings from such knowledge, what is now again culturally central to the dominant society: 'If you give those niggers free food they won't work.' Not to recognize such statements as the reproduction of a moral economy is to make the mistake of thinking that the plight of these families could be remedied with a job-training program. Lastly, without a more realistic sense of what is a 'moral' economy, we miss or minimize the struggles *among* the vulnerable – within families and kin groups; within, indeed, one's sense of self and intimately connected others. Imagine what is very likely in a poor household, where things are continually mentally weighed, measured, and counted, better to plan their replacement. Imagine that the grandmother knew, in each protracted instance, that one of her granddaughters was stealing her Clorox and why, and out of respect for what the child was going through, or for the child's silence, chose not to intervene. Political-economic struggles are always also moral ones, both among the oppressed (and the oppressors) as well as between them, and it is precisely in the context of these double struggles that silence and experience become real – become social forces.

When we put aside our prior notions of what those who are dominated and exploited should or should not think by our standards of appropriate class or ethnic or gender consciousness; when we put aside our 'weapons of the weak' concern with whether or not 'they' are making themselves a nuisance to their middling or elite classes; when we put aside the issue of whether or not we have been silent about the oppressed in our writings for one another and instead look to the issue of their silences with each other, their voices to each other, and most of all, their relations of co-involvement with one another; then we might be able to participate more effectively in our necessarily conjoined struggles for liberation.

NOTES

The first draft of this paper was read at the conference at Bellagio and much benefited from the questions and comments of both the discussant, Robert Berdahl, and the members of the conference. Gavin Smith and Francine Egger-Sider provided key suggestions for the perspectives developed here, and important general issues about this engagement with history and anthropology were raised by Mario Bick, Kirk Dombrowski, and Shirley Lindenbaum.

1 Granting all the ambivalence and ambiguities built into our concepts of agency, as Perry Anderson pointed out (1980:chap 1), the issue is still how it takes on its transformative potential.

2 It might be claimed, in an alternative formulation, that this sense of experience is precisely the core of daily-life culture. To pose the analysis this way removes any significant historical dynamic from the domain of culture.

3 Smith 1989 is the key work on this point; Warman 1986 is also informative on how the state and the dominant classes insist upon perpetuating the struggles of the dominated – a continuing 'refresher course,' as it were, in the multiplicity of memory.

4 For an example of the very substantial difference that it makes to stop defining such key strategic concepts as 'class consciousness' completely in advance and then going out to see who fits our conceptual Procrustean bed, but rather spending some of our energies examining

the real political consciousness of actual segments of the working class – in sum, the importance and the difficulty of making our concepts empirically, as well as analytically, based - see Sider 1996.

5 In the 1950s, in the midst of the cultural tensions that surrounded the 'racial' integration of the U.S. armed forces, there were quite a few 'jokes' that circulated widely. One of the most often told has come, in my mind, to epitomize the need to critique the very popular 'weapons of the weak' model. The U.S. Navy was among the most offensively segregated; African Americans and 'Chinese' were used primarily as kitchen help. This particular joke concerned the physical and emotional tormenting of the 'Chinee' cook, to the point where he was physically injured. His tormentors went to the ship's hospital to apologize and mostly to promise they would never do it again. The cook, in imitation 'accent,' repeated several times their promises not to abuse him, being reassured each time, and then said in reply, 'Good. Very good. I no longer piss in your coffee pot.'

I think that we can very usefully delineate our sense of the political by, to begin with, thinking about whether or not we would want to call this 'pissing in the coffee pot' a political action. (In fairness to Scott, it is important to note that he deals with situations where the people who drink the coffee are led to suspect it at the time.) I am enough of an 'old left' sort to think that not only do such actions, known or unknown, have nothing to do with politics, but neither does setting fire to the ship. 'Weapons' (for example, bows and arrows) have to do more than annoy people; to be weapons rather than toys, or former weapons, they have to be capable of substantially changing the way things are. Social weapons have to have *continuing* social and/or political consequences to go on deserving the name. Once the dominant classes have adjusted to the 'weapons of the weak,' they cease to be politically relevant weapons, save as they reshape the ties of the weak to one another.

Further, it is no longer very 'political' to tell working people or the poor what they ought to believe and what they ought to do about it. The ultimate political issue for an analytical and participatory historical anthropology, I think, is rooted in understanding how oppressed people can form the kinds of relations to one another in their ordinary daily lives that make socially effective claims possible. For this task, the political potential of the terms 'experience' and 'silence' lies in the realization that they primarily name the changing relations exploited and oppressed people form with and against each other.

REFERENCES

Anderson, Perry
    1980 Arguments within English Marxism. London: New Left Books.
Benjamin, Walter
    1969 'Theses on the Philosophy of History.' *In* Illuminations, Hannah Arendt, ed. New York: Schocken.
Blu, Karen I.
    1980 The Lumbee Problem. Cambridge: Cambridge University Press.
Kaplan, Temma
    1977 Anarchists of Andalusia. Princeton: Princeton University Press.
Scott, James
    1985 Weapons of the Weak: Everyday Forms of Peasant Resistance. New Haven: Yale University Press.

Scott, Joan W.
    1992 Experience. *In* Feminists Theorize the Political, Judith Butler and Joan W. Scott, eds. New York: Routledge.
Sider, Gerald M.
    1993 Lumbee Indian Histories: Race, Ethnicity and Indian Identity in the Southern United States. New York: Cambridge University Press.
    1996 Cleansing History: Lawrence, Massachusetts, the Strike for Four Loaves of Bread and No Roses, and the Anthropology of Working-Class Consciousness. Radical History Review 65: 48–83.
Smith, Gavin
    1989 Livelihood and Resistance: Peasants and the Politics of Land in Peru. Berkeley: University of California Press.
Swindells, Julia, and Lisa Jardine
    1990 What's Left? Women in Culture and the Labour Movement. London: Routledge.
Thompson, Edward P.
    1961 Review of Raymond Williams, The Long Revolution. New Left Review 9 and 10.
Warman, Arturo
    1986 We Come to Object. Baltimore: Johns Hopkins University Press.

Pandora's History:[1] Central Peruvian Peasants and the Re-covering of the Past

GAVIN SMITH

It is well known that the English poet Siegfried Sassoon spent much of the First World War recuperating from his experiences in the trenches and writing bitterly about the carnage. It is perhaps less well known that it was the anthropologist William Rivers who made it his job to persuade Sassoon and other young soldiers like him to come to terms with the unspeakable horrors that they had witnessed.[2] I want to take this observation as the point of departure for exploring the extent to which all intellectual pursuits like anthropology and history are, in the end, attempts to help us come to terms with the unspeakable.

The reflections contained in this chapter are a response to a rich body of ethnography which celebrates the flirtation and, it is hoped, eventual marriage of social anthropology with social history, one in which ethnographic history writing and historically focused ethnography will become one. I am strongly in favour of a thoroughly historically informed anthropology, but the way that it is usually done can often conceal the profound difficulties that arise when intellectuals take up the history of subaltern peoples.[3]

As we noted in the introduction, it was a desire to bring to light popular experience that escaped orthodox social history which was the impetus behind Eric Hobsbawm's *Primitive Rebels*, published in 1959. It was an impetus that was to gather force with the publication of Raymond Williams's *The Long Revolution* in 1961 and E.P. Thompson's *The Making of the English Working Class* two years later. All three of these writers saw themselves as seeking to give voice to the silenced, and each in his different way was quite aware of his debt to anthropology.

Perhaps ironically, Thompson's work has called forth the use of 'thick description' among both anthropologists and historians as a means of reproducing everyday culture from the perspective of people themselves.[4] This approach is quite consistent with Thompson's stated project – to bring to light 'the values actually held by those who lived through the Industrial Revolution' (Thompson 1968:485–6) – to give voice to what was unspeakable. But disempowered people thread their memories through an intricately complex frame. The experience of W.R. Rivers and Siegfried Sassoon reminds us of the very complicated role that power played in coming to terms with the unspeakable. Perhaps in our concern with the way in which people's memories of the past can be silenced *externally* by powerful others, we have tended to avoid some of the ensuing effects among those people. And I am referring here to something like the opposite phenomenon (less celebratory) to James Scott's everyday forms of resistance in hidden transcripts (Scott 1990).

The Rivers-Sassoon case draws our attention to two more difficult features of subordination. To begin with, disempowered people themselves repress the unspeakable – just one of the many insidious effects of political repression is repression of the psychoanalytic kind (Rebel 1988–9). And second, in eventually finding a voice – in his poetry – Sassoon relied, albeit unwittingly, on official accounts of the war to give the touchstone of truth to what he wrote. It was the specific contours of power that eventually helped find a voice for what was hitherto unspeakable. This creates a much more complex dilemma for the historian or anthropologist. It means that simply assigning authenticity to *any* voice of the subaltern is perhaps naive.

Thompson himself spoke of judgments of value in two forms. Besides their concern with the values of those they study, he insisted that historians have to make 'some judgment of value upon the whole process entailed in the Industrial Revolution *of which we ourselves are an end-product*' (Thompson 1968:213; italics mine). This latter judgment of value that he made arose out of his *engagement with the present*. Anthropologists and historians who turn to the past as a means of fleeing from the moral complexity of the present run the risk of becoming blind to the way that the present affects this selection process – not just our own selection process as scribes; not even, most importantly, our own selection process: rather, *most importantly*, for the people we write about, as they live their everyday lives or engage in collective political action.

While Thompson's partisan historiography remains a model to be emulated, it nonetheless raises some difficult problems for the professional intellectual. These result from two fundamental characteristics of the intellectual having to do with distance, on the one hand – for the historian, distance between the present and the past; for the anthropologist, between the 'here' and the 'there' – and with our role in producing reports, on the other hand, referred to hereafter as *accounts*. There is always some distance between us and those we study. To believe that being an *organic intellectual* resolves this problem – a working-class historian of the working class, a gay anthropologist of gay culture – is to be misled, and Gramsci is quite clear about this (1976:12–16). Our being distinct, in turn, means that our project can never be identical with the people we study, and the fact that we are obliged, sooner or later, to produce accounts often serves to emphasise the differences.[5]

Here is an especially well honed *account* from Peru to start with. On 31 July 1983 the *New York Times Magazine* carried a long piece entitled 'Inquest in the Andes.' The article was by the Peruvian novelist Mario Vargas Llosa, and it was subsequently published in *Le Monde* and in Spain in *El Pais*. It came out in the English literary journal *Granta* under the title 'The Story of a Massacre.' 'Vargas Llosa described how eight journalists ... traveled to the highlands to investigate reports that comuneros of a small peasant community of Huaychao had killed seven "*terroristas*," members of ... Shining Path ... As narrated by Vargas Llosa, the eight journalists arrived at Uchuraccay ... en route to Huaychao. They had a dialogue with the local people, but then were suddenly and cruelly massacred with stones, sticks and axes. The journalists' bodies had been horribly mutilated and buried upside down, two to a grave, in shallow pits away from the village cemetery. Anthropological testimony described these mutilations and burial practices as typical of the way local people treat their enemies' (Mayer 1991:466).

One has to read this account very carefully to discover that it was produced as a result of the fact that the then-president of Peru had appointed Vargas Llosa, the country's world-famous novelist, to head a commission of inquiry into the deaths of the journalists. In effect, it was an account of an attempt to seek a satisfactory account (the commission's report) of the massacre of some people who themselves had been killed seeking, as journalists, to produce an account of apparently mysterious events, also involving a massacre. (It is not hard to see how tempting such a multi-layered plot must have been to Vargas Llosa.)

He ends the account with a vignette whose symbolism he cannot have missed. He paints a picture of himself – this intellectual seated on the hard ground of the village square, notebook in hand. Before him dances a withered old crone singing, in the high screech of much Andean chanting, a refrain in Quechua, a language that Vargas Llosa does not understand. This is a highly evocative image, a condensation of a whole series of things that he wants to say, or more accurately, wants us to hear. And I shall return in a moment to the tension between a writer's need to evoke images through literary devices and the rather different calls to memory felt by subaltern peoples themselves.

What is important for the moment is that Vargas Llosa consulted those whom he felt to be Peru's most eminent anthropologists. The picture that he carried in his head of Peruvian society, moreover, he claims to have taken directly from the country's greatest historian, Jorge Basadre: a Peru *profundo* set against 'official Peru.' 'That there is a real nation [Peru *profundo*] completely separate from the official nation is, of course, the great Peruvian problem. That people can simultaneously live in a country who participate in the 20th century and people like the comuneros of Uchuraccay ... who live in the 19th – if not to say the 18th century. This enormous distance which exists between the two Perus is behind the tragedy that we have investigated' (Vargas Llosa 1990:46; quoted in Mayer 1991:478).

Vargas Llosa's account, of course, gave great publicity to the events in Uchuraccay. But it also, as a by-product as it were, seemed to derive its authenticity from being thoroughly informed by professional anthropologists (and historians) and thereby provided – like it or not – an anthropological account of what was going on in the remote Andes. It was a caricature that was picked up and reproduced by the American Peruvianist anthropologist Orin Starn (1991), who published an article in *Cultural Anthropology* in which he accused anthropologists of inventing something called *lo andino*. More recently, Starn has written an article for *Current Anthropology* entitled 'Rethinking the Politics of Anthropology: The Case of the Andes,' in which he reiterates his perception that Andeanists have created an orientalist construction called *lo andino* (for an incisive critique and a call for more responsible scholarship, see Roseberry 1995).

While calling for what he terms 'a more emancipatory politics,' Starn eschews the greater ambitions of the Western intellectuals who came before him. Yet, despite his belief that his predecessors 'have not thought seriously enough about how our own personal political and theoretical agendas influence our depictions' (13), I wonder if he is any more sensitive to the contradictions of his role as an intellectual than Vargas Llosa. Part of Starn's solution to the problem of the intellectual's position is that we should produce accounts like Catherine Allen's *The Hold Life Has* and Scheper-Hughes's *Death without Weeping*, which use novelistic devices to bridge the gap between the anthropologist and the informants, on the one hand, and the author and her audience, on the other.

What does this example of a series of *accounts* tell us then? Well, it tells us something about one kind of effect that these accounts have once they are produced and thrown into circulation. There seem to be many layers to the onion already, but as we strip off each of them, we encounter still more onion. We have a novelist giving authenticity to *his* account by misrepresenting the work of anthropologists and historians. And since this novelist is far more widely read than those he cites, what we get is a widely shared understanding

of what anthropologists and historians do – not from reading what they produce, but from reading *an account* of what they do by Peru's foremost spinner
of fiction, an author, moreover, who firmly subscribes to notions of *andeanismo*.
Then we find an anthropologist, unhappy precisely with the way in which
orientalist-style *andeanismo* has positioned anthropologists vis-à-vis the people
who live in the Andes, advocating as a solution just the kind of evocative
accounting that makes Vargas llosa so widely read. And for the same reason:
to reach a wider audience.

Advocates of the evocative account as a form of intellectual engagement
usually wish to distinguish their position from 'romanticism.' The way that
they usually do so is by suggesting that such accounts allow for a multiplicity
of voices. Older accounts derived a major part of their authenticity, it is argued, from the authority of the author. Here authenticity is displaced at least in
part onto the people themselves, not simply by reproducing what the author
approves of, but rather by letting *all* the flowers bloom (Ortner 1995). Unfortunately, there are serious problems with accrediting authenticity to an account
simply because it is voiced by the subaltern (Comaroff and Comaroff 1992: 3–
48; Samuel 1992), and we are not much helped by calls to a political agenda as
vague as 'a more emancipatory politics.' This was certainly far from Thompson's
position. The dispositions that he gave voice to had a lot to do with his own
very deep involvement in making the English working class. An authentic
voice *could* sound more like Ian Jack, son of an Edwardian steam mechanic:
'The class conflict as I often heard it expressed was not so much between
classes as internal to each of them: it was "decent folk" versus the rest ... A
strict application of socialist theory would mean that our natural allies were the
Davidsons (crash, thump; "Where's ma fuckin' tea?") and that we would be
bound to them for life. And bound not only to the Davidsons but to another
heart of darkness in our family's past ... the chaos and poverty which my father
had caught the last whiff of as his family completed the last trek through the
volcanic industrialism of Victorian Scotland' (quoted in Joyce 1991:334). Ian
Jack then was engaged in a process of silencing the memories that might take
his father back into the heart of darkness. Thompson, on the other hand, as a
socialist historian was, like Rivers, engaged in getting people back into the
fight by confronting the unspeakable. In that sense he was working *against* the
willed memory of an Ian Jack. And we should not blind ourselves to this fact.

Thompson has been criticized by feminist historians for his blindness to the
role of women in the making of the English working class. His engagement
with the present was pre-eminently masculine – and white – and through these
lenses he selected from the past. As a result, there was a gap, a myopia not just
vis-à-vis women but also vis-à-vis the politics of everyday life beyond the

workplace, the spontaneous uprising, or the charivari ritual.[6] But many feminist historians would agree that the task is to work as much against the memory that experience produces as with it, for political repression is closely linked to more intimate kinds of repression.

Isabelle Bertaux-Wiame (1982), for example, has for a number of years been collecting life histories from older women who migrated to Paris from the provinces. She tells of how, as she started her work, she expected to find the most vivid memories of migration among the concierges and domestic workers whom she interviewed. Yet she gradually discovered that most of these people had no memory at all of their early days of insecurity and poverty. It was only when she turned to more upwardly mobile informants that she began to find quite vivid and often carefully reconstructed stories of their 'bad times.'

The different perspective of the engaged intellectual and the people with whom they try to be engaged is poignantly brought out in Bea Campbell's reflections in her book *Wigan Pier Revisited*:

I went home to the woman I'm staying with, a single parent with three children ... She doesn't get a newspaper and had to ask the social security for new shoes for the two children at school ... I arrived home at about teatime, we talked a bit, the children were charging around until about 7 pm, when they had their baths, and by 9 pm they were in bed. By then I was in front of the TV with tea and biscuits watching the news. That felt quite odd. I've noticed how rarely women watch the news. There were two major reports on the news, one showing mass rallies in Spain on the eve of the elections there ... and the other on the miners' ballot ... The woman I'm staying with comes from a mining family, and as I watched the news I heard the ironing board creaking in the kitchen. She was still working, doing the ironing at ten-o'clock at night. She missed the news. It had nothing to do with her anyway. (Quoted in Swindells and Jardine 1990:ix–x)

Articulating the silenced history of the past is not *just* a question of letting those silenced by others find a voice, then. It also requires a sensitivity to the institutions and practices – the social spaces like those around the ironing board in the kitchen – which serve to divert or to facilitate, first, the articulation of single voices and then the connecting up of those voices in a way that makes evident the link between that ironing board and the pithead. This process in turn means that the historian or anthropologist has to be especially aware not only of the forms of expression of those whom he or she studies, but of the forms of expression that we as communicators use. How much are subaltern people's glimpses into the past, occluded as they are by workaday pressures, at odds with the evocative techniques that we use to attract the attention of the reader? Think of how often we are tempted to begin our essays with a vignette, apparently strange, even a little exciting, later to use it as a window into the quotidian and normal.[7]

I want to reflect here, then, on why, in our desire to focus on the everyday of the ordinary person, we find ourselves using this particular stylistic device, one so strikingly at odds not only with the grindingly boring data of a more statistically oriented social history but also, it seems to me, at odds with the grinding routines of the workaday lives of our informants. And I want to do so by saying something about the capturability of certain elements of the past and the elusiveness of others. In so doing I want to switch from repressed to other kinds of silences and selectivity vis-à-vis the past, returning to my opening suggestion that the voice which Sassoon eventually found – possible with the help of Rivers – partook in some way of the official version and eventually became part of it.

My own case material suggests another reason, besides stylistic evocation in order to compel the reader's attention. While I was doing fieldwork with the people of a small highland area on the Huancavelica border in central Peru, they witnessed the successful conclusion of a campaign to regain their lands from neighbouring haciendas, when 40,000 hectares of ranch land were handed over to them by court order (Smith 1989). From the end of the Peruvian-Chilean war in the mid 1880s, when they had expropriated all the neighbouring haciendas and retained them for ten years, evidence of these people's resistance has been marked on the map of 'official' history through a series of apparently sporadic 'visible' incidents, in 1919, 1930, and 1948 and fairly continuously from 1963 until the success of the 1970s.

I found that as I talked to informants about their participation in this resistance, I would often refer to some event or other as I had read about it in the newspapers or in police reports: the burning of the hacienda, the massacre in Cañon Blanco, the removal of the police post from the area, and so on. And certainly to begin with, informants themselves took great delight in paying attention to these self-evident dramas. But it gradually dawned on me that the dramas themselves did not capture anything like the entirety of the resistance campaign. While one element in successful resistance was indeed to do with the balance between courage and discretion at these highly visible moments, another element, *a far more important element*, was that of sheer endurance: from week to week, year to year, decade to decade, through years of oppression to the capturing of the advantage of a correctly judged conjuncture, when the centre did not hold.

A river flows across limestone, at moments on the surface, there recorded on the maps, and at other moments plunging beneath the surface and flowing through underground caves to resurface once more downriver. What I was doing was insistently talking to informants about the springs and surface streams that were the common property of journalists, lawyers, and peasants alike. And inasmuch as non-peasants were familiar with these landmarks, so peasants found it relatively untaxing to talk about them. In a sense, the 'official' history of these people (that is, the history written and consumed beyond the immediate locality) is constituted by the chronological connecting of these visible dots: the land invasion, massacre, and then settlement of 1948; the massive invasions that followed after 1963; and the eventual destruction of the hacienda and the revindication of the claim to over 40,000 hectares of land.

Unlike the disappeared or disappearing world of many of the people whom we study, those whom I am talking about are not threatened by the obliteration of that history. True, in the course of time, it may disappear amidst the cacophany of noisier histories, like the recent one focused on Sendero Luminoso. But one would not really refer to this as a 'silence.' The silences reside in the moments that separate the dots on the map of the 'official' history. These silences are problematic in a number of senses, and I want to write about those senses now.

In fact, I want to discuss them in two ways – two ways that are made dangerously contradictory by my inquisitive interest in them. Perhaps what made me so enthralled by people's ways of remembering the past was an acute sense that the problem for people who are not at the helm of history is to find a way of connecting in some meaningful way the periods, always of unforeseeable duration, between their audible strikes on the bell of history. This 'connecting together' is a problem and a project *for them*.

For our part, we should not forget what is meant by the expression 'a wall of silence.' For us, the enquirers, as intellectuals, whether we like it or not, the 'connecting together' is of a different kind. It effectively celebrates the official version, while the blank spaces – which have to be explained – are symbolized by the imagery of the 'stoney-faced Indian' that so troubled Vargas Llosa, an image that suggests at once inaccessible silence and a passive deceit, which may or may not mask a real ignorance of a distant world:

Captured and taken to the island prison of El Fronton, Victor found himself brought in for questioning. On the opposite side of the table was an army officer. Beside the table was a man dressed like a lawyer. The officer began by accusing Victor of being an agitator and member of the outlawed party APRA. 'What was I to do?' reflected Victor as he recounted the event years later. 'I could not deny it. I was in prison with engineers, teachers and lawyers: Apristas. This man here was probably a lawyer from APRA. I had to go back into that cell. So I said, "Apra? Apra? What is apra? In my language *apra* means to be blind."' (Smith 1975)

Now, I know that we are all very aware of the danger of oversimplifying reality by presenting a binary pair with hegemonic history on the one hand and popular culture on the other. But my difficulty lies just a little bit to one side of such observations. For the people themselves, the official version is called up differently: in keeping alive through the long silences of terror and repression a spirit of opposition or, something less, merely an alternative vision of the world, powerless people call up the past. And the past most accessible to them is the audible moments when their political agency has been caught on the quicksilver of public history, even if with the most awful results. But, as I have said, these are the events that are taken over by History with a capital 'h': recorded in the papers, in the police records, and in extreme cases perhaps even in the history books. So, just as they talk to me, the intellectual, the need for some convenient common ground for communication pulls their version of the event toward my own, itself weighted by my reading of 'the official version.'[8]

And then again, attracted as I am to the texts of the accounts that I am studying, I have to remind myself that they are thoroughly embedded in the praxis of the present. Present purposes act as a significant organizing principle in talking about the past, yet the purposes of one participant vary from those of another, and in the intercourse of daily life this means an open-ended incompleteness – the past is never thoroughly accounted for, the book never closed.

Yet once members of the community of Huasicancha had assigned me the task of recording the history of their campaign to recover their land, from its inception in 'the darkest mists of time' to their present struggle, by reading newspaper accounts, hacienda correspondence, and police reports and by talking to a local lawyer, I was able to put together a fairly good account of what had happened in the immediately preceding confrontation, which occurred in 1948. It went something like this:

On New Year's Eve 1947 the entire community of Huasicanacha, including not only men, women, and children, but also every animal that could move, from guinea pigs to cattle, decamped from the village and occupied an area of Hacienda Tucle's land covering roughly two square miles. Though troops were brought in and there was considerable bloodshed in the neighbourhood, nobody from the village was hurt, chiefly because of well-disciplined leadership and group solidarity.

As a result of the refusal of people to remove themselves from the hacienda's land, the civil guard arrested a number of leaders, who were taken to prison, accused of membership in the outlawed APRA party. Meanwhile a legal hearing was underway, and despite the unwillingness of the authorities to take the side of the local people against the owner of the hacienda, their claim to the land was so indisputable that the court had to grant it to them. The barely visible remains of the ditch that you now see across that area of land represents the boundary which was settled at that time.

In talking to people from the area, I could quite easily elicit accounts that were more or less along these lines and in any event did not contradict any of the components of this account. Generally, a group of people would be standing around, perhaps sharing a drink, and I would ask a question such as 'Why did the troops leave peacefully here when they massacred so many people in Chongos Alto just moments before?' And someone would reply, 'Because here we have *unión*, and besides, Martin was here and he is a very cunning fellow.' 'Yes,' continued another, 'that's how it was. Victor went over and dealt with that officer. He sent them packing soon enough.' To which all would nod in concurrence.

Yet, having for many weeks enjoyed these rousing history lessons, I feel impelled this time to ask, 'But you said it was Martin who was the cunning one. And *you* said, Victor. Which then? Victor or Martin?'

'Victor, Martin, they were close friends,' comes the reply. 'Yes. And Antonio. He was a friend too.'

'Oh yes,' all agree, 'Antonio too.'

Without going into the details of my investigation (see Smith 1989:169ff), I will take a short cut. Despite the fact that local people did not significantly contradict the account that I had derived from written records, many months – indeed years – later and after many such talks, including men and women, old and young, residents and migrants, and after looking at records of village meetings and rather haphazardly drawn-up diaries (usually started in jail), I have to conclude that rather important components of this account are not merely inaccurate; they are logically inconsistent and, more striking, fly in the fact of real and present evidence.

For the fact is that the remains of the so-called boundary ditch do not carve out an area of recovered land anything like two square miles, and the records show that out-migration from the region after 1948 increased in a wave. There are no court records of this settlement in the Juzgado de Tierras archives (though a sale is recorded in the land registry office). And village records, as well as the aforementioned diaries, all suggest that there were strong differences of opinion about goals and tactics and that they were not resolved by New Year's Eve 1947. A number of sources, moreover, suggest that Martin was absent during this event, including his own account.

It seems then that the immediately preceding campaign to the one that I was witnessing had not been a great success. It netted very little land, and so disappointed were participants not only with the result but with prospects for future success that they had migrated in droves. Moreover, they had never succeeded in getting proper legal recognition of what little land they had acquired. The hacienda had agreed to a sale of a small piece of land,[9] payment for which was to take the form of digging a dividing ditch between the two properties. In the event, disappointed with the settlement and denuded of young men, the community never completed the ditch.

Now, all this is not especially surprising, and I do not expect anybody to raise his or her arms in startled wonderment and disappointment at the duplicity of (peasant) informants. I am not trying here to juxtapose against the oral histories that I have collected 'what really happened'. Not at all. In fact, we must remember that the version of events which I had originally constructed from other – 'official' – sources matches no better with what I have just recounted.

Instead, let me try to say something about the relationship between recordable, visible, communicable historical events and what seems to me to be almost their opposite. To begin with, there is the institution of recounting the past – the forum in which these accounts are given. What is spoken of here is not something of some small, but not spellbinding, concern. On the contrary, when the issue of the 1948 campaign is raised, it can be guaranteed to command the interest of those present. First one and then another recounts what happened, sometimes following one another, sometimes interrupting, sometimes backtracking, and so on: 'It was Martin. It was Victor. They were friends.'

We are dealing here, then, with two events: the one that occurred in 1948 and its recounting in 1972.[10] The two have somewhat different requirements. As to the second event, it was initiated by my reference to a version that I had heard and my request that some element of it be confirmed, denied, or elaborated upon. And the request was then taken up by a variety of people. At this point one of two things happened. I was seeking an answer. So if I remained the focus of attention, then that was what I was given. I could make a note and close my book on the matter. But if the focus of attention shifted to the account givers themselves, then closure was absolutely the last thing sought. It was precisely the open-ended inconclusiveness of the account that mattered. A resistance campaign was going on, and history still had to be settled.

Nevertheless, it was not just anything that could be discussed with such commitment and vigour. It was an especially visible moment of history when, for a brief period, the struggles of the Huasicanchinos and the awareness of the world came together. What to me is impressive is that, removed though these people were from the daily press or from a casual discussion with a lawyer or schoolteacher, their account of events is strikingly similar to the written accounts. It is broadly agreed that the people of this area are quite successful resistance fighters; that their skill is recognized not just by the local landlord but by the legal authorities, who, recognizing their de facto possession, wrote it into law; and that much of this strength comes from good leaders of united followers.

This is where I believe the danger lies. For I think that at least part of what we see here is an appropriation of the Huasicanchinos' visible moment of history in such a way that over time their own version loses its intra-community distinctivess. In part, this change has occurred because a characteristic of the official version is that it be communicable in a specific – written – record. Such a characteristic may not quite call for heroes and villains, but minimally it does call for subjects, actions, and objects, and the step then to placing responsibility on one or more 'leaders' is a small one.

Moreover, to be communicated it must begin at a certain moment; a series of events must then occur, often apparently causally linked (the Huasicanchinos have invaded the land of Hacienda Tucle; Hacienda Tucle suffers serious loss through fire; the local peasants have resorted to arson), and then there must be an end. The event disappears from the press and police reports. Yet I have used the imagery of a river flowing over limestone to illustrate that this public visibility is very partial. Indeed, for the participants themselves, the problem lies in capturing these visible moments of history in order to sustain themselves through the long periods of silence that lie between, thereby to feed a spirit which will surface once more; at the first opportunity, in the light of yet another 'visible moment.'

But it is at this point that communicability and what is to be communicated can be at odds. It is not enough that the heroic moments of 1948 be kept alive against those forces who would have them repressed. The *lesson* of 1948 also must be learned. And while the sharpness of structure and the drama of action make the official version well suited to communication, they may (intentionally or otherwise) teach misleading messages. My own view is that insofar as intellectuals set out to bridge the gap between a form of historical accounting satisfactory to themselves and their peers and the one operative around the village pump, they act as a force that tends to stress the narrative communicability of accounts over other possible characteristics of accounting performance.

Yet within the local community itself the manner of presentation can convey a message about the past too. We can see this process if we superimpose the heightened discussion, in 1972, of what happened in 1948 back onto those 1948 events. For in 1972 it is generally agreed that on one rainy night all the members of the community uprooted themselves and marched on to the hacienda land. Not a dissenting voice was heard, and this unanimity was, at least in part, because of the sagacious leadership of Martin and/or Victor. Yet as the account is being given, the agreement reached is essentially to carry on the impetus of the narrative, come what may. The tintinnabulation of so-called agreement – agreement to differ, that is – is almost deafening! Surely this state of affairs conveys something about the kind of agreement that fell upon those people as they made their way onto the hacienda land on New Year's Eve in 1947.

It seems to me that as long as people are able to continue engaging thus in refusing to close the book on the past, not only will the *memory* of those especially visible moments of their history be preserved, but also the far more complicated senses contained therein will be carried forward. And so long as people do so, their willing acceptance of the official version is in fact a most effective form of silence. For what is contained in each and every one of those official versions is the thorough incomprehensibility, not of peasants per se, but of peasants insofar as they choose to rebel. Yet for local consumption, if we give as much weight to the institutions through which presentations of an account occur as we do to its content, it is only in a limited way that we can conclude that the Huasicanchinos are silent about their internal disputatiousness in the midst of an externally directed struggle.

In summary, I think that there are very visible 'events' when, for a few moments, people take up the reins of history. Written accounts record these events. What they do not record are the subterranean passages that link up the events. Connecting the moments of visibility through the long silences of repression becomes the task of a certain kind of oral account giving. Two characteristics of this account giving are especially noteworthy: first, it is not immune to the charms of 'the official version,' and second, it is pre-eminently open-ended, an institutionalized practice in its own right. These two characteristics are potentially contradictory: the official version demands closure, while closure means death to an ongoing oral account, whose life depends on its incompleteness, its element of 'still-to-be-settledness.' Local people can handle this quality. Indeed, their acceptance at face value of the official version is a form of silence: they leave it as an uncontested domain whose principal feature is the abiding incomprehensibility of the peasantry.

When intellectuals seek to break open silences for unrestricted and, I would say, vicarious consumption, the act is not self-evidently a good thing. On the other hand, the earlier examples taken from Thompson and Bea Campbell remind us that there may indeed be moments when voicing repressed histories should be endorsed, sometimes even *against* the memory of those we study. The result is that we are called upon to make political judgments in every moment of our intellectual enterprise.

Anthropologists have increasingly become sensitive to their role in listening to the voice of the subaltern. In a sense, I suppose I am arguing that the orthodoxy in anthropology has shifted from the study of the *institutions* of other peoples, whose distinctive feature was that they were 'not like us,' to an interest in the *expression* of people whose distinctive feature is their subalternity. I have suggested that this approach was, at least in part, the project of the old New Left, and indeed, many anthropologists' interest in history has been mediated through the exemplary figure of E.P. Thompson. Yet, I have argued, Thompson saw history as part of a very self-conscious political program for the present. As a result, he was not *just* interested in reading the tombstones over silenced bodies. To my mind, this quality makes his work less duplicitous than the hearing of voices on the road to Damascus, which often constitutes the only touchstone of legitimacy for contemporary anthropologists.

This more clearsighted and thoroughly developed program for the present helps us to sort out the way we as intellectuals deal with history. Yet because Thompson is so forthright in his political stance, I have used his example to raise difficult questions about the role of *all* intellectuals vis-à-vis subaltern peoples, with particular attention to the production and repression of their histories. Not only are these difficult questions sidestepped if we confine our criticism of capitalism or modernism to ironic and playful engagements with its surface, cultural manifestations, but our focus on voice to the exclusion of the material and institutional bases of silence itself helps us to come to terms with the unspeakable.

Thus, in the first part of this essay I have argued that intellectuals are called upon to do more than simply listen to the voices of the subaltern; they may be required to work against the subaltern's own silences. But evidence from the second part suggests that willed repression is not the only issue here. Rather, the ability to express oneself and the form that expression takes are both profoundly linked to the institutions and practices that make expression (of all kinds) possible. For we found that certain institutionalized practices served to make the engagement with history open-ended, incomplete, and, I would add, *in the present.* This observation seems to suggest that we should attend to something inherent in intellectual practice itself: that our part in sorting out a story is also a way, whether we like it or not, of *putting things in the past* and thereby closing down the institutions through which unconcluded histories can be voiced, exchanged, modified, or held suspended in a noisy room for the moment when 'sounds offstage' suddenly turn collective reflection into collective practice.

NOTES

Emerging out of my conversations with Huasicanchinos, this paper has benefited from a subsequent wider conversation, first with the participants at the original history and anthropology conference in Bellagio, to which I was invited as a latecomer, especially the discussant of my paper there, Robert Berdahl, and then in discussions with Malcolm Blincow, Micaela di Leonardo, Philip Gulliver, Winnie Lem, Nicole Polier, William Roseberry, Marilyn Silverman, and Ignasi Terradas. I am very grateful to all of them for their help, but an especial thanks must go to Gerald Sider, who has been an inspirational companion as this paper has unfolded. Its limitations remain my own.

1 'Given a box that she was forbidden to open, Pandora disobeyed out of curiosity and released from it all the ills that beset man, leaving only hope within.' *Collins English Dictionary*.
2 The relationship between Rivers and Sassoon and the former's experiences of the First World War are the subject of Pat Barker's novels *Regeneration* (1993a) and *The Eye in the Door* (1993b). I should stress that my reading of Sassoon is not that of Barker, who wants to suggest that Sassoon's attitude to his war experience was quite different from the kinds of repression that characterized his other patients (1993a:25–6).
3 A great deal of literature has been produced recently along the fault line between ethnography and social history. I refer here specifically to projects which, either explicitly or by assumption, suggest that the 'thick description' of subordinated people's everyday practices *in and of itself* plays a positive role for them or for the history of subordinated peoples generally. The most widely read current is what might be called Geertzian history (see Darnton 1984; Davis 1987; Medick 1987; Corbin 1992; for an interesting discussion of these and similar approaches, see Samuel 1992). From a political point of view, a far more important strain is that represented by the History Workshop (see the journal of the same name), the subaltern studies group (Guha 1982, etc.; for critical comments, see also Sarkar in this volume; also Gupta 1985; O'Hanlon 1988), John and Jean Comaroff (Comaroff 1982; Comaroff and Comaroff 1992), and work such as that of Chatterjee (1986; 1993) and various feminist historians (for example, Swindells and Jardine 1990). It is to these latter, to my mind far more important, works that my comments are directed in this essay.
4 The irony is brought out in Smith (1998), in which I argue that issues of working-class *culture* were always discussed alongside problems of social *organization* in the works of Thompson, Hobsbawm, and even Williams.
5 Both Alain Touraine (1985) and Alberto Melucci (1989:198–201) claim to have evolved a method that addresses the issue of the role of the intellectual in the study of social movements. Both are strikingly naive about this issue of the role of their finished texts, however.
6 As for Natalie Zemon Davis (1981:272–3), so for Thompson, the attraction of anthropology arises 'in locating new problems, in seeking old problems in new ways, in an emphasis upon norms or value systems and *upon rituals*, in attention to *expressive functions* of forms of riot and disturbance, upon *symbolic expressions* of authority, control and hegemony' (1977:248; emphasis in original).
7 Sometimes this stylistic device, which I call 'the Magritte effect,' is used so successfully that the reader is unaware of what is happening; an especially self-conscious example might be used to illustrate. As the curtain rises on Tom Stoppard's *After Magritte*, the audience is faced with a plethora of strange juxtapositions, from a person being ironed on an ironing board to another hanging from the light in the ceiling. By the time the curtain falls, we find the same scene before us, but the action between the two moments has now made the entire scene 'normal.' Pursued almost to the same extreme, we find the device in Darnton's cat massacre (1984) and in Corbin's *Village of Cannibals* (1992). The device is used to far more subtle

effect in Geertz's famous piece on the Balinese cockfight (1973) and is frequently employed by anthropologists who would not otherwise endorse his form of 'accounting' (see especially Taussig 1980, 1987).

In fiction the Magritte effect is usually created by the strangeness of a fictional situation, and its function was described well by Victor Scholvsky in terms of *defamiliarization*: 'Habitualization devours objects, clothes, furniture, one's wife, and the fear of war. "If all the complex lives of many people go on unconsciously, then such lives are as if they had never been" ... The technique of art is to make things "unfamiliar" ... so as to increase the difficulty and duration of perception' (quoted in Scholes 1974:83–4). Noting how terrorists have displaced novelists, Don Delillo has remarked on the increased power of the device *if the strangeness of the situation is not generated within the fiction* but arises in *fact*. Hence the 'faction' novels of Delillo, Mailer, and others. Anthropologists are, of course, professionals in this regard – from the sex life of savages to the teachings of Don Juan. Its use as an extremely successful device *within* an account should not distract them, however, from its inevitable cavalier employment of people's ordinary lives for literary effect.

8 To overemphasize the extent to which I or anybody else was or is influenced by the written historical records would be to miss my point here. All I wish to stress at this stage is that I had used these sources as a preliminary way of establishing a chronology of events relating to rural resistance in the region.

9 The significance of this 'sale,' as opposed to legal recognition, is open to different interpretations. The sale or purchase of land by officially recognized Indian communities was illegal at the time. This would seem to suggest that the *hacendado* could renege on the sale at any time. But the community's lawyer at the time stated to me later that he felt that, insofar as the sale was not legitimate anyway, it would not interfere with any subsequent claims that the community might want to make against the hacienda.

10 And a third: my recounting herein. There could well be more. I am unhappy with the term 'event' given the sharp boundedness and conclusiveness that it implies. Even so we should not be too precious about these things: history may not be one damned thing after another, but bounded, conclusive events *are* necessary as the currency of history, however much intellectuals may earn a living through devaluing their worth by removing them from the gold standard of 'reality.'

REFERENCES

Barker, Pat
    1993a Regeneration. London: Plume [Penguin].
    1993b The Eye in the Door. London: Viking.
Bertaux-Wiame, Isabelle
    1982 The Life History Approach to the Study of Internal Migration: How Women and Men Came to Paris between the Wars. *In* Our Common History: The Transformation of Europe, Paul Thompson and Natasha Burchardt, eds. London: Pluto Press.
Chatterjee, Partha
    [1986] 1993a Nationalist Thought and the Colonial World: A Derivative Discourse. Minneapolis: University of Minnesota Press.
    1993b The Nation and Its Fragments: Colonial and Postcolonial Histories. Princeton: Princeton University Press.

Comaroff, John
    1982 Dialectical Systems, History, and Anthropology: Units of Study and Questions of
            Theory. Journal of Southern African Studies 8:143–72.
Comaroff, John, and Jean Comaroff
    1992 Ethnography and the Historical Imagination. Boulder, CO: Westview.
Corbin, Alain
    1992 The Village of Cannibals: Rage and Murder in France, 1870. Cambridge: Harvard
            University Press.
Darnton, Robert
    1984 The Great Cat Massacre and Other Episodes in French Cultural History. New York:
            Vintage Books.
Davis, Natalie Zemon
    1987 Society and Culture in Early Modern France. Oxford: Polity.
Geertz, Clifford
    1973 Deep Play: Notes on the Balinese Cockfight. In The Interpretion of Cultures. New
            York: Basic Books.
Guha, Ranajit, ed.
    1982–5 Subaltern Studies. 4 vols. New Delhi: Oxford University Press.
Gupta, Dipankar
    1985 On Altering the Ego in Peasant History: Paradoxes of the Ethnic Option. Peasants
            Studies 13:11–28.
Hobsbawm, Eric
    1959 Primitive Rebels: Studies in Archaic Forms of Social Movement in the 19th and 20th
            Centuries. Boston: Beacon Press.
Joyce, Partick
    1991 Visions of the People: Industrial England and the Question of Class. Cambridge:
            Cambridge University Press.
Mayer, Enrique
    1991 Peru in Deep Trouble: Mario Vargas Llosa's 'Inquest in the Andes' Reexamined.
            Cultural Anthropology 6:466–504.
Medick, Hans
    1987 'Missionaries in a Rowboat'? Ethnological Ways of Knowing as a Challenge to Social
            History. Comparative Studies in Society and History 29:76–98.
Melucci, Alberto
    1989 Nomads of the Present. Philadelphia: Temple University Press.
O'Hanlon, Rosalind
    1988 Recovering the Subject: Subaltern Studies and Histories of Resistance in Colonial South
            Asia. Modern Asian Studies 22:189–224.
Ortner, Sherry
    1995 Resistance and the Problem of Ethnographic Refusal. Comparative Studies in Society
            and History. 37:173–93.
Rebel, Hermann
    1988–9 Cultural Hegemony and Class Experience: A Critical Reading of Recent Ethnological-
            Historical Approaches. Parts 1 and 2. American Ethnologist 16:117–36, 350–65.
Roseberry, William
    1995 Latin American Peasant Studies in a 'Postcolonial' Era. Journal of Latin American
            Anthropology 1:150–77.

Samuel, Raphael
    1992 Reading the Signs: II. Fact-Grubbers and Mind-Readers. History Workshop Journal
        33:220–51.
Scholes, Robert
    1974 Structuralism in Literature. New Haven: Yale University Press.
Scott, James
    1990 Domination and the Arts of Resistance: Hidden Transcripts. New Haven: Yale
        University Press.
Smith, Gavin
    1975 The Account of Don Victor. Journal of Peasant Studies 2:113–17.
    1989 Livelihood and Resistance: Peasants and the Politics of Land in Peru. Berkeley, Los
        Angeles, Oxford: University of California Press.
    1998 Ethnographic Method and the Politics of Engaged Anthropology. In Otherwise
        Engaged: Essays in the Politics of Anthropology. Oxford: Berg.
Starn, Orin
    1991 Missing the Revolution: Anthropologists and the War in Peru. Cultural Anthropology
        6:63–91.
    1994 Rethinking the Politics of Anthropology: The Case of the Andes. Current Anthropology
        35:13–38.
Swindells, Julia, and Lisa Jardine
    1990 What's Left? Women in Culture and the Labour Movement. London, New York:
        Routledge.
Taussig, Michael
    1980 The Devil and Commodity Festishism in South America. Chapel Hill: University of
        North Carolina Press.
    1987 Shamanism, Colonialism and the Wild Man: A Study in Terror and Healing. Chicago:
        University of Chicago Press.
Thompson, E.P.
    1968 The Making of the English Working Class. Harmondsworth: Penguin.
    1979 Folklore, Anthropology and Social History. Brighton: John L. Noyce.
Touraine, Alain
    1985 An Introduction to the Study of Social Movements. Social Research 52:749–87.
Vargas Llosa, Mario
    1983 The Story of a Massacre. Granta 11:5–23.
    1990 Questions of Conquest. Harper's, December.
White, Hayden
    1985 Tropics of Discourse: Essays in Cultural Criticism. Baltimore: Johns Hopkins
        University Press.
Williams, Raymond
    1961 The Long Revolution. New York: Columbia University Press.

Renaissance and Kaliyuga: Time, Myth, and History in Colonial Bengal

SUMIT SARKAR

The youthful band of reformers who had been educated at the Hindoo College, like the tops of the Kanchenjungha were the first to catch and reflect the dawn.

>   Kishorichand Mitra 1861; quoted in Susobhan Sarkar 1970:121–2

A lot has been said about the benefits of English education, but no one has written about the evils it has brought ... blind imitation of the English has derailed social reform ... It would be no exaggeration to say that selfishness is synonymous with today's civilisation ... educated wives no longer perform their domestic duties diligently ... Europe has so much of commerce and industry: can *chakri* [clerical jobs] alone support so many *bhadralok* [respectable people]?

>   Rajnarayan Basu 1874, 1951:1, 81, 86, 66

See the course of *Kaliyuga, dharma*[1] has declined / Vedic ritual and customs have vanished, men and women become the same ... the Shudra will place his foot on the Brahman's head ... the son will disobey the father / the mother will be the servant of her daughter-in-law ... so many factories, impossible to list / King Kali is so powerful ... his commands so rigorous / no one can escape.

>   Aghorechandra Kavyatirtha, 1902:3, 7, 80

Kali comes after *Satya, Treta, Dwapar* / Blessed is *Kaliyuga*, say all Vaishnavas.

>   Tarakchandra Sarkar 1916, in a metrical biography of Harichand Thakur, founder of a low-caste (Namashudra) religious sect

Blessed, blessed, be this *Kali* age.

>   Rashsundari Devi 1868:77, in the first autobiography by a Bengali woman

I

In texts written and printed in colonial Bengal between 1861 and 1916, two well-known intellectuals of high-caste origin, an obscure Brahman school teacher-cum-playwright, a member of a low-caste religious sect, and a recently widowed housewife who is known only through the autobiography that she composed are all thinking about their times. They evaluate in distinct ways the changes that they have lived through, and sometimes the language they use to conceptualize time itself differs: a new 'dawn,' a 'Kaliyuga' about which it does not seem to matter whether one uses the past, the present continuous, or the future tense. Kishorichand Mitra and Rajnarayan Basu were both distinguished alumni of Hindu College in Calcutta, founded in 1817 as the first major institution for higher education on the Western model and in the English language in Bengal. They differ, clearly, in their estimates of what Western education and colonial rule have brought, but share a commonsensically 'modern' conception of time as the abstract, linear framework in which events happen.

The playwright who elsewhere describes himself as a 'poor Brahman,' the upper-caste housewife, and the Namashudra author of a metrical biography refer, in contrast, to a conceptual world familiar to Indologists and scholars of ancient India, but largely assumed to be irrelevant for understanding colonial or 'modern' India. This is the classical Hindu conception of cyclical time, in which Kaliyuga endlessly recurs as the last epoch in an eternally repeated four-*yuga* cycle, the epochs distinguished from each other by their moral qualities. For high-Hindu religion and philosophy, Kaliyuga normally is the most degenerate of times, when Shudras (low-castes) dominate over high-castes and hierarchies of gender and age are reversed: the woman and the Namashudra here have found it to be 'blessed.'

Texts such as these were evidently made possible by two major innovations brought in by colonial rule, clock time and print culture, which stimulated diverse ways of thinking about time and enabled even an otherwise obscure housewife to publish an autobiography. The facts here are familiar enough, but a general persistence of simplistic 'impact-response' frameworks in studies of indigenous culture under colonialism have often hindered historians from problematizing or exploring their implications. The unstated assumption has been of a quick, painless, and total transition from cyclical Kaliyuga to linear time, from 'myth' to modern 'history' on the Western model. The specific consequences of the equally belated and sudden entry of print culture have also remained unexplored.

Impact-response frameworks have been of two kinds: eulogistic and denunciatory. As my first extract indicates, Kishorichand's metaphor was being used a hundred years later to substantiate the model of a 'Bengal renaissance,' in which the rediscovery of ancient Hindu cultural achievements by European Orientalists and the inflow of modern Western ideas through English education were supposed to have sparked off a whole series of progressive changes amounting to an 'awakening' to modernity.[2] Rajnarayan's statement, in contrast, points towards alternative viewpoints that displaced acceptance of the 'civilizing' mission of the West by critiques of colonial domination from perspectives that could be traditionalistic, extreme nationalist, or radical left.[3] A variation of this second approach has recently acquired an international and interdisciplinary audience through the widespread influence of Edward Said's *Orientalism* and the consequent rise to prominence of 'colonial discourse analysis' in metropolitan academic centres. There are ample signs that this has become a counter-orthodoxy in metropolitan cultural studies, as well as in certain sectors of Indian history writing, literary theory, and feminist scholarship.[4]

Eulogy and denunciation can become mirror images, inversions of each other. What they have had in common here at times is an assumption of effective and total 'acculturation' that tends to eliminate the autonomy and agency of the colonial subject. This attitude is at its most blatant in some applications of the Saidian framework where the critique of colonial power-knowledge gets extended into an assumption of complete control or seamless cultural hegemony. The colonial middle class, it appears, is capable of not only 'derivative' discourses (Chatterji 1986).[5]

A series of self-validating homogenizations can follow from this basic assumption of total domination by post-Enlightenment rationalist power-knowledge (itself a highly simplified and overgeneralized construct). Domains less affected by it – the uncontaminated pre-colonial or 'popular' – cannot, perhaps, be really explored, as our sources would be overwhelmingly of colonialist or indigeneous Western-educated origin, and the tools and categories of today's historians likewise tainted by Enlightenment rationality. Circularity proves convenient, however; for a vague 'community consciousness' can now be postulated as relatively free of internal tensions or structures of oppression, an indigenism that can become extremely retrogressive in its political implications in today's India. More directly relevant for my argument here is the way in which such a framework, quite as much as in the 'Bengal renaissance' historiography that it repudiates, remains focused on the 'high' literati, as English education has been merely inverted from instrument of awakening to principal sign of subordination. Such a concentration on successful and prominent intellectuals, of course, tends to 'confirm' the basic premise of acculturation/ surrender.

My intention in this paper is to emphasize difference and variation, to break up some of these homogenized blocks, and here divergent perceptions of time, myth, and history can provide vital clues. The colonial introduction of clock time in Bengal, for a start, had certain very specific, yet seldom-noted features. Belated entry produced a remarkable telescoping of phases. Clocks and disciplinary time came more or less together here, whereas in western Europe the transition from medieval clocks showing hours alone, through watches ticking off minutes and seconds, to bureaucratic-industrial structures of the time took some five hundred years, a history, moreover, marked by a great deal of pain, resentment, and resistance (Thompson 1967). Colonial India had to undergo a similar process, and that under conditions of alien rule, within a couple of generations. The tensions and contradictions bred by such an abrupt and forced transition surely need to be explored.

For the educated middle-class *bhadralok*[6] of nineteenth-century Bengal, disciplinary time manifested itself primarily in the form of clerical jobs in British-controlled government or mercantile offices – the *chakri* about which Rajnarayan complained – along with, perhaps, the new educational institutions.[7] Studies of the colonial middle class have generally concentrated on its higher echelons, about whom information is so much more readily available: the reasonably successful English-educated religious and social reformers, writers, journalists, lawyers, doctors, teachers, or politicians. Among such people a sense of moving forward in harmony with time was sometimes noticeable, constituting elements that would later be put together into a 'renaissance' format, and Kaliyuga disappeared without much fuss or became a not very serious turn of phrase. Foreign rule had bestowed some benefits in the shape of modern culture, and there were hopes that it could be gradually reformed or even eliminated through the efforts of the patriotic *bhadralok*. A high premium was consequently placed on a variety of forms of predominantly male *bhadralok* activism: education, religious reform or revival, many-sided efforts to improve the conditions of women, philanthropy, nationalist politics. Yet even the narrative of high-*bhadralok* activism would be repeatedly punctuated by gaps, relapses into passivity and inward-turning moods, doubts, and mordant auto-critiques. Such dimensions become more prominent once we try to enter the world of the less-successful *bhadralok*: declining traditional literati who had failed to adapt to English education, graduates without jobs, college or high school drop-outs, hack writers, humble schoolteachers, clerks. Here the myth of Kaliyuga remained meaningful, indeed, proliferated through print culture, and took on significantly new dimensions.

The evils of Kaliyuga had always been associated with the reversal of proper caste and gender hierarchy, with insubordinate women and Shudras lording it over upper-caste men. But now, as we shall see, the woman on top came to be associated with the lure of money and commodification, while there emerged a totally new and obsessive focus on the harshness and humiliation of office work, or *chakri*. Kaliyuga thus became a language for expressing the anguish, frustration, and resentments of the less-successful high-caste educated men. It offers an entry point into a partially distinct, 'lower-middle-class' world ideal – typically embodied in the declining traditional rural literati and the city clerk (*kerani*), a milieu that has been neglected by historians virtually everywhere (Mayer 1975; Crossick 1977). The tonalities of Kaliyuga, however, could appeal at times also to the 'high' *bhadralok* in their darker moods, for colonial domination kept the self-image of the successful enterprising male always fragile, unstable, and open to racist humiliation. And so Rajnarayan Basu, too, complains about *chakri*, and the evils of modern times that he talks about have clear affinities with Aghorechandra's depiction of Kaliyuga.

I intend to use two entry points in this exploration of variation and difference. Print culture, as elsewhere, lessened the mnemonic advantages of verse, stimulated a flowering of vernacular prose, and enabled the incorporation into writing of a much larger range of everyday experience. Ample documentation consequently exists concerning the high-*bhadralok* oscillation between outward-looking activism and introspective moods. This fact is central to my argument questioning the unduly seamless representations of the colonial middle class that underly both canonization and debunking. Illustrative samples here will include some biographical material, ways of looking at history, and trends in *bhadralok* religious life, in particular the strange and significant appeal of Ramakrishna Paramhansa.

The principal evidence for the persistence-cum-modulation of Kaliyuga in nineteenth-century Bengal comes from a somewhat different, less well known corpus: a multitude of cheap tracts, stories, plays, and farces, to which a visual component was added by the prevalence of similar themes in the 'bazaar paintings' hawked outside temples such as Kalighat in Calcutta. As with the *bibliothèque bleu* of seventeenth- and eighteenth-century France, it is necessary here to avoid the identification of this 'low-life of literature' (Darnton 1971; Chartier 1987) with a culture that can be termed 'popular' in any unqualified sense. The consumers of the tracts and farces and the prints churned out from the Bat-tala quarter of north Calcutta did not necessarily exclude the most exalted among the *bhadralok*, while the surnames of their authors indicate most of them to have been upper-caste, indeed, very often Brahman. Literacy, even in Bengali, was both low and broadly homologous with caste hierarchy: only 39.9 per cent even among Brahmans in 1911 and going down to 4.9 per cent among Namashudras (S. Bandopadhyay 1985).

Cheap booklets and prints, peddled by hawkers as well as sold in bookshops, could, however, be read out to others besides the literate. Plays and farces had the potential for reaching even wider audiences in so far as they were actually staged. The Bengali theatre had at first been characterized by patronage, with performances in rich men's houses alone. But from the 1870s public theatres emerged in Calcutta, creating a ticket-paying audience that could span a wide range of social groups and include women as well as men. A fair number of printed plays seem to have been scripts for *jatras*, a 'folk' form of entertainment that did not use the Western-style proscenium stage, performed by wandering groups of players in villages and small towns as well as in cities. Unlike the *bibliothèque bleu*, produced by big Troyes firms and consisting in large part of abbreviated or simplified versions of extablished high-culture texts, nineteenth-century Bengali cheap printed literature came from a multitude of small publishers and seems to have been somewhat more distinctive in its subject matter.

Tarakchandra Sarkar and Rashsundari Devi, authors of the last two extracts with which we started, are reminders that the upper-caste male myth of Kaliyuga could on occasion develop interesting low-caste and feminine variants, but data here remain extremely scanty. The other very major problem with the material that I am using is that audience reception is difficult to gauge, for data about print runs and the specific social composition of readership is absent. We know next to nothing about the possibly differentiated ways in which texts were received, what meanings may have been read into them by various audiences, how – if at all – they were related to everyday life. It is in this context that I have found useful a pamphlet describing a most unusual incident in an East Bengal village in December 1904, for here elements of the Kaliyuga myth suddenly seemed to come alive, with consequences both unexpected and ultimately disastrous (Chaudhuri 1905).[8]

An upper-caste householder, Lalmohan Majumdar of Doyhata village (Munshiganj subdivision, Dacca district, East Bengal), had invited into his home a wandering poor Brahman *sadhu* (ascetic, religious mendicant, holy man), Kalikumar Chakrabarti, who called himself Kalachand. The *sadhu* claimed powers of miraculous healing and occasionally that he was Kalki-avatar, the tenth and last incarnation of Vishnu, supposed to come at the end of Kaliyuga to set the degenerate world in right order again and restore ideal caste and gender hierarchy. Kalachand was followed into the Majumdar household by two untouchable disciples, Prasanna, a Namashudra, and Ananda, a Bhuinmali. On the afternoon and night of 8 December 1904, Prasanna suddenly started enacting his own, extremely peculiar version of the end of Kaliyuga. He killed Ananda, apparently with the latter's consent and the complicity of Kalachand

and Lalmohan. This event was interpreted by Lalmohan as the killing of Yama, the god of death, which would end all death on earth. Prasanna, however, seems to have thought, and persuaded Ananda to believe, that the latter would be resurrected with a new 'divine body' by Kalachand, whose powers consequently would be recognized by all, even by the British.

Prasanna then set fire to neighbouring houses (he was burning 'Lanka,' he claimed) and insulted, stripped, and tore the sacred thread of several upper-caste gentlemen. The women of the Majumdar household had to take off their clothes, touch a (presumably sacred) fire, and do homage to Kalachand. Some had their pubic hair burnt, while Lalmohan's wife was ordered to kick her husband's forehead in an exact inversion of *pranam*, the Hindu ritual gesture of deference towards elders, social and gender superiors, and divinities alike. The general atmosphere was one of *yuga-pralay*, the cataclysmic end of an epoch. Everyone was remarkably compliant for hours, even though a police station lay only a quarter-mile away. Somehow, in the imagination of an enraged Namashudra, what had been associated in high-caste texts with the restoration of Brahman and male authority had suddenly come to mean the insulting of high-castes by an untouchable and of a husband by his wife. 'All the soldiers of Bharat [India] together will not be able to do anything to me,' Prasanna was defiantly shouting when he was at last overpowered and arrested early next morning.

He remained defiant and unrepentent in court, while Lalmohan abjectly begged for mercy and Kalachand sought to evade responsibility through an enigmatic silence. Prasanna, a Calcutta paper noted with surprise, seemed 'quite unconcerned with what is going on, commenting freely and gaily on the depositions of several witnesses' (*Bengalee*, 17 March 1905). The Dacca sessions court jury, consisting of local bhadralok, recommended surprisingly mild sentences, probably out of a desire to save the two upper-caste accused. The British judge disagreed, and the Calcutta High Court eventually awarded stiffer sentences for all three accused (Sumit Sarkar 1989). A local newspaper quickly made a pamphlet out of the Dacca court proceedings, thus creating our principal source. But Doyhata soon became one of those scandals that the *bhadralok* knew but were embarrassed to write about, and a local history of the Dacca region published in 1909 passed over the affair with a single, cryptic sentence (J. Gupta 1909).

Doyhata embodied a brief, explosive encounter between different, yet overlapping worlds: respectable high-caste householder belonging to a community exceptionally proud of its learning and culture; wandering poor Brahman mendicant of uncertain reputation, who might turn out to be charlatan or divine incarnation; despised, illiterate outcaste, normally never allowed inside a *bhadralok* home, who now virtually takes it over for one night. Here we touch the limits of Kaliyuga discourse, the point where it is appropriated by an untouchable and briefly turned on its head, making the incident itself unmentionable. Doyhata, then, is important despite, or indeed precisely because of, its evident atypicality. Lalmohan, Kalachand, and Prasanna may help us to go some distance beyond the sterile polarities that currently dominate the historiography of colonial middle-class Bengal.

II

Lalmohan Majumdar would have remained unknown to the historical record but for the Doyhata case, and not very much emerges even from the court depositions. With *prajas* (tenants) but not the guards or armed retainers that a big landlord (*zamindar*) would have had, he presumably belonged to a small *zamindar* or tenure-holding high-caste family of the Bikrampur region of East Bengal.[9] The family home seems to have been full of women relatives or dependents; most of the men possibly had jobs in Calcutta or elsewhere. Lalmohan, who had some English education and a smattering of Western medicine, stayed on, however, in Doyhata village. He was reputed to have been a good family man, made some extra money through dispensing medicine, did not take fees from poor people, and appears to have been a fairly typical do-gooding *bhadralok* – until the coming of Kalachand. The wandering poor Brahman *sadhu* initially attracted him, not through teachings or miracle-working claims, but by 'his face, it seemed like that of a boy, and *vatsalyabhava* [paternal feelings] were evoked in me.' Soon Lalmohan sank into a kind of passivity, lost interest in his medical practice, and 'spent much time in idleness ... saying, if asked about anything, "The *sadhu* will provide everything, there is nothing to worry about"' (depositions of Lalmohan and his wife, Rajlakshmi, Chaudhuri 1905:10, 46). This behaviour again was succeeded by a brief moment of ecstasy. Lalmohan danced and sang after the killing of Ananda, proclaiming that the *yuga-pralay* (cataclysmic end of an epoch) was at hand.

  The material is sparse, but interesting linkages and affiliations can be teased out from it. However obscure in himself, Lalmohan belonged to an extremely prominent social group, the Bikrampur *bhadralok*. As in much of East Bengal, the bulk of the population of the Bikrampur region consisted of Muslims or low-caste Hindu (quite often Namashudra) peasants, but above them towered a thick cluster of predominantly high-caste Hindu rentiers. Bikrampur was a land of small, fragmented *zamindaries* and intermediate tenures, rents from which needed to be supplemented by income from professional or clerical jobs in Calcutta or other towns. Western education, which had become the essential prerequisite for such jobs, came to be exceptionally well developed here, often through the private initiative of the *bhadralok* themselves. In 1909 the regional historian Jogendranath Gupta mentioned with pride the existence in Bikrampur of twenty-four high English schools at a time when the whole of the United Provinces outside the district headquarters had only fourteen. He provided a long list of *bhadralok* worthies born in the region, renowned for the kinds of reformist, philanthrophic, literary, scientific, or political activities which in twentieth-century retrospect would come together to constitute the 'renaissance' myth.

And yet it was precisely such an activist mileu which in colonial Bengal persistently created a recurrent undertow of introspection, nostalgia, and apparent passivity. Forward-looking male activism was frequently accompanied by a series of intermingled, if logically distinct, Others: past as contrasted to present, country versus city, a deliberate feminization as opposed to active masculinity, the attractive playfulness and irresponsibility of the child or the *pagal* (madman, or better, perhaps, holy folly, reminiscent sometimes of European conceptions of madness before Foucault's 'great confinement': McDaniel 1989) as against the goal-oriented instrumental rationality of the adult male. Such rationality, embodied in the multifarious projects and endeavours of the *bhadralok*, in any case seemed to end all too often in whimpers, as when the Brahmo religious reform movement petered out amidst internal squabbles, or Vidyasagar's bid to improve the lot of Hindu widows failed to change dominant social attitudes. The failures would have seemed particularly apparent during what I have elsewhere described as a late-nineteenth-century hiatus in *bhadralok* history – the years, roughly 1870–1905, during which the dream of improvement and reform under British tutelage turned sour, without as yet being replaced by an alternative viable patriotic myth of ending the country's ills through drastically modifying or ending foreign rule (Sumit Sarkar 1992).

It was during these years, more precisely from around the 1880s, that nostalgia about the countryside found enduring literary expression through the 'romantic' poetry about nature of Biharilal Chakrabarti and the early writings of Rabindranath Tagore. A significant shift had taken place here from the 'epic' style of Michael Madhusudan Dutta in the 1850s and 1860s, where nature had remained subsidiary to heroic action in defiance of overwhelming odds and in which traditional divinities and incarnations had been treated at times in a remarkably subversive manner.[10] Calcutta, more generally, which in twentieth-century retrospect would become the heart of a 'Bengal renaissance,' figured little in nineteenth-century literary representation, except in negative terms: it was certainly not conceived of as, say, a new Florence (T. Sarkar 1992). The colonial metropolis provided the *bhadralok* with education, culture, new luxuries and tastes and jobs. As the political and economic heart of Britain's Indian empire, with mills, firms, and offices controlled by Europeans or enterprising immigrants such as the Marwaris, it was at the same time a city that often appeared peculiarly beyond the control of the Bengali *bhadralok*. Here the less fortunate of the *bhadralok* eked out a living as *kerani* (clerk), and even the prosperous Bengali gentleman until well into the next century would normally refer to his Calcutta residence as a *basa* (lodging), reserving the more privileged term *bari* (home) for the ancestral village or small-town house.

What happened, usually, in personal life as well as in literary representation, was not a rupture or neat separation into activist and inward-turning groups, but a commingling of moods within the same text, movement, or personality. The oscillations of Lalmohan, apparently eccentric and insignificant, thus have wider affinities.

Better-known middle-class personal trajectories constitute one kind of evidence about such tensions and transitions. The Young Bengal (or 'Derozian') group, for instance, Hindu College students of the 1830s inspired by the brilliant young history teacher Henry Louis Vivian Derozio, who had introduced them to the ideas of eighteenth-century rationalism and the French Revolution, has been repeatedly hailed, or denounced, for its youthful, iconoclastic rejection of Hindu traditions. Actually most of its members made their peace with orthodox society fairly soon and came to hold respectable administrative or professional positions. Already by the 1840s some of them, in a significant turn towards 'history,' had started celebrating the cultural glory and military prowess of the Hindus in the past. They failed to develop any effective reform program: what remained, perhaps, was an inner agony of spirit that found expression through an epidemic of drinking that blighted many of their lives, as well as through occasional self-critical satire. Thus, in a play by Dinabandhu Mitra, Nimchand Dutta, a brilliant, cynical, and dissipated character thought by some to have been modelled on Michael Madhusudan, greets in a drunken stupor a policeman's lantern as Milton's 'Hail, Holy Light!' (Sumit Sarkar 1985). The surrender to colonial discourse even on the part of those often denounced then and later as denationalized Anglicists was perhaps less total and unambiguous than is often imagined today.[11]

A generation later, to take a second, very different example, a young man of intermediate-caste (Tili) origin started a school in his Central Bengal village (Kumarkhali, Nadia district) and then a vernacular journal explicitly designed to voice the sufferings of villagers at the hands of *zamindars*, British indigo planters, and local officials. Harinath Majumdar (1833–96), nicknamed 'Kangal' (destitute) Harinath, had to struggle against poverty all his life and incurred through his journalistic exposures the wrath of the local *zamindars* (the powerful and exceptionally cultured Tagores). The journal, *Grambartaprakashika*, which was started in 1863, folded in 1884 as a result of lack of funds. It had published in 1872 the first *bhadralok* account of Lalan Fakir, a major exponent of the Baul tradition of syncretistic folk religious song and ritual. After his journal collapsed, Harinath, who had had Brahmo (reformist Hindu) connections in his youth, turned towards more emotional and esoteric kinds of religion and even started writing Baul songs himself under the name of Fikirchand. The story has some interesting sequels. Rabindranath Tagore, son of the *zamindar* whose officials seem to have tormented Harinath, later contributed greatly towards making Baul poetry, and Lalan Fakir in particular, respectable – even prestigious – among the *bhadralok*. And Akshoy Maitra, an younger colleague of Harinath who had helped to run *Grambartaprakashika* in its last days, became in course of time a distinguished historian, dedicated to rediscovering the lost splendours of Bengal (Chakrabarti 1992; Bandopadhyay and Das 1943).

Patriotic history – writing, efforts to tap folk cultural resources, satirical theatre, introspective and emotional forms of religious devotion – such seem to have been some of the ways through which the inner tensions of the *bhadralok* found expression. In remarkable contrast to what would later become standard form in the renaissance myth, nineteenth-century middle-class cultural achievements were seldom eulogized by their own makers. Bankimchandra Chattopadhyay (1838–94), Bengal's first major novelist, for instance, explicitly used the European Renaissance analogy in 1880 to describe, not contemporary *bhadralok* activities (often the target of his merciless satire), but the religious, philosophical, and literary developments of fifteenth- and sixteenth-century Bengal (Chattopadhyay 1880).

Sekal-o-Ekal, the pamphlet from which I took my second extract, provides striking evidence about this tendency among English-educated worthies to be self-critical about contemporary life. It records a lecture delivered by Rajnarayan Basu (1826–99), distinguished Hindu College alumnus, friend of Michael Madhusudan, and moderate Brahmo reformer. The past (*sekal*) to Rajnarayan was not anything very distant, but childhood memories about elders, the dividing line being the introduction of higher education in English through Hindu College in 1817. The evils of the present for Rajnarayan begin with an alleged decline in male physical strength as a result of endless book learning in enclosed classrooms, followed by excessive, time-bound labour in clerical or professional jobs. The Bengali male who matters, then, is the educated *bhadralok* tied to *chakri*. Meanwhile, the traditional Brahman literati has fallen on evil days, as Sanskrit learning is no longer honoured. The new, educated *bhadralok* has become ensnared by European luxuries, and selfishness is corroding old norms of kinship behaviour and hospitality – except, Rajnarayan adds in a characterisitic conflation of spatial and temporal retrospect, in 'far-off villages' where 'mutual sympathy' still reigns. And women who have received a smattering of education are the worst: they prefer immoral novels to housework and are no longer properly obedient to their husbands. The themes, we shall see, are strikingly similar to the ones often listed under the rubric of Kaliyuga in a large number of near-contemporary plays, farces, and religious discourses, even though the term itself never occurs in Rajnarayan's text.

Shifts in religious forms, moods, and language constitute probably the most fruitful, if still somewhat underexplored, entry point into the tension-ridden, internally differentiated, unhappy consciousness of the nineteenth-century *bhadralok*. Taken as a whole, nineteenth-century *bhadralok* piety does give an impression of a thrust towards a novel, socially oriented, ameliorative activism. As elsewhere, however, the self-image of predominantly masculine rationalistic activity and self-confidence was often clouded over by introspective moods, self-conscious 'feminizations,' and 'retreats' from adult responsibility.

Such transitions are noticeable within both the major Hindu traditions in Bengal – the Vaishnava devotion to the incarnations of Vishnu (particularly Krishna) and the Shakta worship of the mother goddess Kali – as well as in the new reformist Brahmo sect founded by Rammohan Roy in the 1820s. The early Brahmos, for instance, like the Protestants on whom they had partially modelled themselves, usually stressed the fatherhood of their theoretically impersonal, formless godhead. In the 1860s their most active leader was Keshabchandra Sen, engrossed in an enormous variety of social-reform activities. By the next decade, however, partly through the influence of Ramakrishna, he had largely withdrawn from reformist activity and simultaneously begun to conceptualize divinity in material terms.

Rural retrospect, feminization, a turning away from social activism towards the attractive irresponsibility of the child and the *pagal* – all came together, in fact, in the extraordinary appeal of Ramakrishna (c. 1836–86). A near-illiterate temple priest given to spells of mystic ecstasy, he had lived for some thirty years in a suburb of Calcutta before suddenly becoming a major cult figure among the educated *bhadralok* in the late 1870s and early 1880s, the 'hiatus' years, again. Ramakrishna's early disciples, in addition, often had a clerical ambience: few among the wealthy or successful professional men initially came to him. The central message was one of quietistic, inward-turning *bhakti* (see note 10), and Ramakrishna was often openly scornful of socially activist, ameliorative projects, even of philanthrophy. He conveyed his ideas purely through conversation, in a rustic language full of earthy parables that seemed to bring back a rural world from which the city *bhadralok* now sometimes felt that they had unwisely uprooted themselves.

Devotees chronicled with respect and admiration Ramakrishna's lifelong fondness for women's roles, and they seemed to have found even more attractive his childlike surrender to the Shakta divine mother: 'Attaining *Ishwara* [the divine] makes you into a five-year old boy' (quotations from M. Gupta 1902, etc.; Sumit Sarkar 1992). Hagiographers loved to describe the *balak-bhava* of Ramakrishna behaving like a child, one of the acceptable ways of relating to divinity in Shakta traditions; this included lack of inhibitions about nudity and soiling himself in public. Upper-caste Hindu constructions of childhood, it has been pointed out, differ significantly from both puritannical discipline and romantic glorifications of pure, aesthetically pleasing natural growth. The child may have 'no personal time-table ... no rules of hygiene or cleanliness imposed from outside ... He seems to live by pure whim' (Biardieu 1989:33–4). The child model, in other words, could slide into the of the *pagal*, and partly through Ramakrishna's influence, the runaway, irresponsible, yet attractive male and the wandering *pagal*, often of poor Brahman origin, as embodiments of holy folly became long-lasting stereotypes of Bengali literature.

Attitudes such as these have deep cultural roots, and yet we cannot afford to ignore contextual specificities, which may help to explain why it was precisely the Western-educated who felt drawn to Ramakrishna, and that from a particular time. Colonialism had counterposed to European active, virile masculinity the stereotype of the conquered 'native' as effeminate, irritatingly childish, or at best pleasantly childlike. Direct references to colonial domination are extremely rare in Ramakrishna's conversation, but he subverted, in effect, the distinctions between male and female, adult and child, work and play, that the 'civilizing mission' of the West had made more rigid in nineteenth-century Bengal (Nandy 1983). The *bhadralok*, excluded anyway from the privileged male occupations of military and political command and successful independent entrepreneurship and relegated to dull and lowly clerical jobs, perhaps expressed a 'muffled defiance'[12] through a preference for feminization, childlike behaviour, and the irresponsibility of the *pagal*. Ramakrishna's message of *bhakti* could help to create an inner living space detached from the imposed world of formal routinized education and *chakri*.

Many dimensions of our strange Doyhata tale now begin to fall into broader patterns, though without losing idiosyncrasies of their own: Lalmohan's paternal feelings aroused by the boyish countenance of the *sadhu*, as a phenomenon rooted deep in the culture of *bhakti*, and described by him through the appropriate religious term (*vatsalyabhava*); his sudden withdrawal from responsible worldly activity; Kalachand, poor Brahman village schoolteacher who had become a kind of religious drop-out, a wandering *pagal* claiming miraculous powers of healing and eventually of world deliverance as Kalki-avatar. Kalki is an element of the Kaliyuga mythic corpus,[13] and it was through modulations of that age-old structure that a variety of nineteenth-century resentments and hopes found expression. 'Kaliyuga' was a term often on Ramakrishna's lips, and the motif emerged in some profusion in cheap paintings, tracts, plays, and farces the floodgates for which had been opened by the coming of print. It is time to take a closer look at what the late nineteenth century tried to make of Kaliyuga.

III

The many evils of Kaliyuga, a recurrent and powerful format for voicing a variety of high-caste male anxieties for some two thousand years, include disorders in nature, oppressive *mleccha* (impure, alien) kings, Brahmans corrupted by too much rationalistic argument, over-mighty Shudras expounding the scriptures and no longer serving the Brahmans, and women choosing their own partners, disobeying and deceiving their husbands, and having intercourse with menials, slaves, even animals. Kaliyuga was invariably located in the present and would end in a very distant future amidst universal fire and flood, or alternatively through the wars of Kalki, the last incarnation of Vishnu. Born in a 'Sambhalgram' Brahman family, he would in a conflation of Brahman and Kshatriya (royal or warrior) virtue destroy all *mleccha* kings and restore a Satyayuga in which purified Brahmans would be on top and Shudras and women once again duly subordinated. And then an identical four-*yuga* cycle would begin again, and so through eternity.[14]

Despite occasional apocalyptic language, Satyayuga was clearly very different from the millenarian dreams of equality and freedom that inspired so many heresies and plebeian rebellions in medieval and early-modern Europe. The apocalypse in any case lay far in the future, for Kaliyuga was to last for 432,000 years. The message was one of resignation, since the evils were inevitable; they could, however, be made more endurable through modifications in ritual practices. These were the Kali-varjya, things allowed earlier but now discovered to be no longer permissible by Brahman ritual experts – an interesting method of introducing a conservative kind of flexibility through which caste and gender discipline was tightened up from the twelfth to thirteenth centuries onwards. The high-Hindu ideal was not really the restoration of Satyayuga, which would degenerate again anyway, but a purely individual escape, *moksha*, from the chain of rebirth (*karma*) across endless cyclical time. Alternative ways (*marg*) were prescribed for this individual escape: asceticism, intellectual contemplation, ritual, and devotion (*bhakti*) (Eliade 1955:chap. 1, 2, 4; Kane 1973:III, chap. 24).

Shudras and women, the two social categories to be kept subordinate and excluded from the sacred Vedas by Brahmanical power-knowledge, normally constituted the major sources of degeneration in Kaliyuga texts. *Bhakti*, however, which in the medieval centuries at times inspired powerful movements with much participation, even leadership, of lower-castes and women, produced important modifications – indeed, near inversions – in the dominant image of Kaliyuga. The worst of ages, it also paradoxically became the best of times, for in it, much bhakti literature insisted, deliverance comes easily, and even mere recitation of the divine name may suffice. The paradox extended further, for women and Shudras, the two major sources of Kaliyuga corruption, could attain good simply through performing their duties to husbands and high-caste men. The humble constitute the ideal *bhakta* (devotee), and subalternity is privileged – provided, of course, that it remains properly subaltern. *Bhakti* and *tantra*[15] are repeatedly declared to be the two forms of religious practice peculiarly appropriate for Kaliyuga, and both are explicitly open to women and Shudras, unlike Brahmanical learning and ritual. *Bhakti* modulations of Kaliyuga thus created a richly ambiguous space for subordinate groups, offering opportunities that were profoundly attractive, at times almost rebellious, and yet always open to ultimate recuperation by dominant hierarchies of caste and gender (Sangari 1990; Beane 1977:237–9; Biardeu 1989:105).

Print culture broadens the potential audience for 'traditional' texts even while stimulating new genres and themes, and Kaliyuga, arguably, became better known than ever before precisely in the century that witnessed the entry of clock time and Enlightenment rationality.[16] Successful *zamindars* or professional men no longer bothered much about the myth. The reformers among them found its message of stricter caste hierarchy and subordination of women distasteful, while conservatives could content themselves with complacently reiterating the old theme of tighter regulations through Kali-varjva as sufficient for the new challenges. Very different, however, was the deployment of Kaliyuga in a mass of minor plays and farces, as well as in many Kalighat 'bazaar paintings.' Here moods of pessimism, self-doubt, and resentment werre expressed through black humour and satire. Among 505 plays published between 1858 and 1899 catalogued in a recent massive survey, 31 have 'Kali' in their titles, and a content analysis brings out many more references (Goswami 1974). Though mostly published from Calcutta, many were also performed by travelling theatre groups (*jatra* parties) in small towns and villages. The bazaar paintings, sold 'at a price ranging from a pice to an anna' near Kalighat temple, other pilgrimage centres, and village fairs, were produced by struggling artisans for whom, it has been said, 'the world was passing through a dark age, a *Kaliyuga*' (W.G. Archer 1953; M. Archer 1977:143; Paul 1983).

Nineteenth-century Kaliyuga literature and painting made few references to insubordinate Shudras; unlike Maharashtra, lower-caste protest movements were not of much account in Bengal prior to around the turn of the century. Women, as always, remained key targets, but no longer primarily for the sexual immorality that they supposedly embodied or provoked. The focus now was on the 'modern' wife, allegedly ill-treating her mother-in-law, enslaving her husband, neglecting household duties to read novels, and wasting money on luxuries for herself. Pictorial and verbal representation at times coincide here: a wife in a farce dresses up her husband in sheep's clothes, while in a couple of Kalighat paintings a woman leads a sheep with a human head and another boldly bestrides a prostrate man (Mukhopadhyay 1876: Archer 1953:70). The 'modern' wife, in fact, has become emblematic of a perceived threat to kinship obligations and ties through the spread of market values. The crucial innovation in a multitude of late-nineteenth-century farces and tracts is a totally new, obsessive focus upon the miseries of *chakri*, and the close interrelationship that is assumed to exist between the disorderly wife, the 'modern' craze for money and luxuries, and the clerical job that the husband is forced to take up to please the one and get the other. Ramakrishna's conversation repeatedly associated the evils of *kamini* (the woman who evokes lust) and *kanchan* (gold, wealth) with the *dasatya* of *chakri* (bondage of an office job), and the triad recures endlessly in late-nineteenth-century plays and farces as the hallmark of Kaliyuga.

What made *chakri* appear intolerable at this specific conjuncture was its connotation of impersonal cash nexus and authority, embodied in a new work discipline regulated by abruptly introduced clock time and enforced by foreign bosses through an imperfectly understood, alien language of command. The luxuries were foreign importations; 'modern' wives could be plausibly represented as particularly tempted by them; *chakri* was usually in British-controlled offices. Thus a patriotic subtext could emerge fairly easily at this point. In Harishchandra Bandopadhyay's *Kaler Bau* (Calcutta, 1880), for instance, subordination to wives gets conflated with political subjection to the 'sons of the London queen,' and thus the figure of the suffering mother, neglected by her sons who have been entrapped by the wiles of the 'modern' wife, becomes a metaphor for the enslaved 'motherland.' Unable as yet to resist foreign bosses or alien rule effectively, the clerks, or rather the middle- or lower-middle-class writers and audiences empathizing with them, displaced part of their resentment on to 'their' womenfolk. Emergent nationalist consciousness thus became intertwined with a strengthening of patriarchal assumptions.

Interesting modulations can be noticed also in the alternative, *bhakti*-inspired, more positive version of Kaliyuga. In many plays from the mid-1880s onwards, the pure women (usually wives) start going beyond the model of exemplary suffering typified by Sita in the Ramayana and traditionally idealized as a subalternity that is peculiarly privileged. They now intervene in ways that are assertive and effective, while remaining deferential. Within a continued traditional idiom, a new content is emerging, where the ideal woman's role goes beyond noble endurance of suffering to include the prospect of a change of heart brought about by such endurance and fortitude. The women are helped at times by old-world servants, representing the good Shudra, and so a sub-theme extolling simple peasant virtues starts entering this literature (Ghosh 1889; S. Chattopadhyay 1901, 1904). Women and Shudras are thus given a positive role in defending and re-establishing a structure within which they would once again be deferential, but to husbands and social superiors who have been reformed and purified by the efforts of subordinate groups. Such paradoxical ascription of agency is often associated also with inspiration and guidance from wandering poor Brahmans. 'Mad' (*pagal*) to the conventional world, they are holy madmen who have opted out of the rat race for money and worldly success, and emancipated themselves from the world of clock time and office space, and so can purvey divine truth in simple, earthy language. The plays of Girishchandra Ghosh, which dominated Calcutta theatre for a generation from the 1880s, have a whole gallery of such figures, some of them clearly modelled on Ramakrishna, whose devotee the author had become.

The transitions within the Kaliyuga format are epitomized most clearly in Aghorechandra Kavyatirthas's *Kalir Abasan, ba Kalki-avatar Geetabhinoy* (The end of Kali, or the coming of Kalki-avatar, 1902). The playwright describes himself as a 'poor Brahman' from Central Bengal, now teaching in a Calcutta school, and claims that this play has served as a script for *jatra* performances in many district towns and villages – a fact of some importance for us, for it then becomes not beyond the realm of historical possibility that some of our Doyhata protagonists had seen *Kalir Abasan*: at the Nangalbandh bathing festival, perhaps, where Prasanna first met Kalachand. Developed print culture had by now introduced a premium on textual fidelity, and Aghorechandra tries to be faithful to Kalki-purana, thereby highlighting the occasional self-conscious departures. The evils of Kaliyuga are squarely located in an association of the 'new' insubordinate educated woman with money, and as we have seen in the extract quoted at the beginning of this essay, there is a reference also to *karkhanas* (factories) with a peculiarly oppressive discipline. The most striking innovation, however, is the situating of Kalki himself, both in a recognizably contemporary Bengal setting (and not aeons away in the future) and in a poor

Brahman context. Kalki's elder brother almost dies of hunger, but is saved by Govin-Pagla, a figure of divine folly who goes around preaching the simple *bhakti* of Hari-nama (reciting the name of the god). The traditional long account of Kalki's many wars is dramatically compressed into a few lines. From embodiment of Kshatriya virtue, Kalki, in other words, has been relocated in a totally new context of poor Brahmans, wandering folly, and *bhakti*, with which is immediately conjoined the figure of a deferentially assertive woman, Kalki's mother, Sumati. A stronger personality than her husband, she is able to dissuade the latter from killing himself when poverty appears unbearable. But Sumati still reiterates that she is 'only a servant ... the chief *dharma* of womenkind is to serve their husbands' (Kavyatirtha 1902:78).

From a dystopia of privileged Brahmans expounded in Sanskrit (the sacred language that women and Shudras were generally forbidden to know), Kaliyuga in colonial Bengal had thus moved to a milieu subordinated to foreign rule and often downwardly mobile, being now written about entirely in the vernacular, by and for fairly humble, if still predominantly high-caste, *bhadralok*. Print culture facilitated its occasional appropriation also by more subordinate groups. The obscure housewife Rashsundari Devi and the Namashudra hagiographer Tarakchandra Sarkar, who hailed Kaliyuga as 'blessed,' were not just uttering a platitude common to many *bhakti* modulations of Kaliyuga. Rashsundari's autobiography chronicles her painful efforts to learn to read and write in secret, an endeavour that went against the grain of the entire Kaliyuga depiction of the educated woman as depraved (T. Sarkar 1993). Tarakchandra composed the biography of Harichand Thakur (c. 1812–78), founder of the plebeian Vaishnava Matua sect among the Namashudras (once known by the contemptuous label of Chandal) of south-central Bengal: untouchable poor peasants, agricultural labourers, fishermen, and boatmen, from whose ranks came Prasanna, the central figure of our Doyhata tale. The Matua sect in course of time became the core of a powerful Namashudra caste movement. For Tarakchandra, Kaliyuga is glorious not just because salvation becomes easy and open for subalterns who behave properly: in it even divine incarnations seek affiliation with, or come from, downtrodden groups. The text lays unusual emphasis on Krishna's cowherd (Gop) origins, makes a passing reference to the 'Muslim weaver Kuber' (presumably Kabir, the radically iconoclastic medieval *bhakti* saint of Benaras), and hails the Buddha, standard figure of abuse in much Kaliyuga literature.

In the Balarami sect of the Meherpur region of Nadia, confined entirely to lower-castes, we come across a more radical, though much more marginal, world where the *yuga*-cycle framework itself is deliberately subverted. Balarami oral traditions invariably express hostility towards high-caste landlords. A member of the sect was beaten up, we are told, for refusing to perform the ritual gesture of obeisance (*pranam*) while passing a *zamindar*. Interestingly, such defiance was taken to be an indication of *ghor kali* (the depths of Kaliyuga) by the *zamindar*'s companions. Balaram Hadi (c. 1780–1850), the founder of the sect, imagined a *divya-yuga* (divine age) superior to the four *yugas* of Brahmanical orthodoxy, over which presided the supreme and sole deity, Hadiram. A note of plebeian materialism is struck here through the caste name of Balaram's untouchable group. *Hadi* resembles *had*, which means the bones of the human body, and escape from the *yuga*-cycle meant for the Balaramis not spiritual *moksha*, but an explicitly *physical* immortality (Chakrabarti 1988; Chatterji 1989). We shall encounter startling traces of not dissimilar conceptions soon at Doyhata.

I have been dealing, in the main, with literary representations, and what meanings readers or audiences drew out of these texts remain a difficult, possibly intractable, problem. Doyhata, I have suggested, may be of some help here, through its striking pattern of affinities and distinctions. Kalachand was a figure reminiscent in many ways of the numerous poor Brahman wandering *pagals*, who are so ubiquitous in contemporary plays. A schoolteacher in a Faridpur village, not too far from Doyhata, he had become a *ganja* (hemp) addict and slipped away from his family as a religious mendicant, with disciples at first only from low-castes. Lalmohan, hearing about him from a low-caste tenant of his, invited Kalachand into his household, for 'a Brahman's son should not stay with a Chandal.' The precise teachings of Kalachand remain utterly obscure, for British justice, unfortunately for us, was quite uninterested in finding out more about them. The one undisputed aspect seems to be the openness of Kalachand's message to multiple meanings, even wholesale inversion by a Namashudra and his Bhuinmali adjutant-cum-victim. Prasanna, then, becomes the central figure in the concluding part of our story.

IV

With his uninhibited behaviour at Doyhata and in the courtroom, Prasanna offers us a glimpse into lower depths that remains brief, tantalizing, and full of mystery. Locating Lalmohan and Kalachand meaningfully within *bhadralok* society has not proved too difficult, even though they had been far more reticent in court. The problem with Prasanna lies precisely in such contextualization, for his was an eruption from a largely unrecorded oral culture, about which official and literate Indian testimony alike are silent, confined to bare statistics, or immersed in stereotypes. Scantiness of background material makes an exploration through the actions and words of an evidently unrepresentative figure extremely hazardous; paradoxically, it also adds to the interest and importance of Prasanna through sheer lack of alternative material about lower-caste perceptions.

At the most obvious level, Prasanna embodied the fury of a Chandal unleashed. A newcomer to the village, he could have had no personal grudge against the Doyhata gentlefolk; his presumably was an elementary caste-cum-class anger, the settling of scores for a lifetime of humiliation. It needs to be noted, however, that his entry into the Doyhata scene had been made possible by the *bhadralok* themselves, and that the anger was largely articulated through a rearrangement, *bricoleur*-fashion, of fragments of high culture. Assumptions of complete subaltern autonomy, of over-sharp distinctions of cultural 'levels' or 'domains,' do not seem very helpful here. A man such as Prasanna would normally never have been allowed into a bhadralok's home, far less permitted to share a pipe (*kalke*) with its master, for the touch of a Chandal is supposed to pollute a high-caste. Prasanna could enter because he had become a 'Chandal *sadhu*,' a disciple of a Brahman guru. At first he merely performed the properly subaltern duty of preparing the *ganja* for Kalachand and Lalmohan. He attracted notice, however, because he 'talked so fast that it was difficult to follow him' (Chaudhuri 1905:2; *Bengalee*, 17 March 1905), not a trivial detail, for a man like him would be expected to remain deferentially silent in high-caste company. Incessant talk then became abuse of superiors and finally erupted into explosive violence.

And yet even at the most violent moments a sense of limits was retained. There is not the faintest hint of rape, robbery, or attempts to kill anyone apart from the ritual murder of Ananda. More significant, there were traces of an underlying structure, derived in large part from selective appropriations of bits and pieces of high-caste culture. Prasanna called Lalmohan 'Dronarcharya,' described the fire he started as an '*yajna*,' brandished a bow (like Ekalavya, perhaps, the tribal youth who had made Drona his guru in the Mahabharata), called himself Hanuman, and termed the Doyhata that he was burning 'Lanka,' mixing together with a fine lack of discrimination elements also from that other great epic, the Ramayana. What remained consistently absent was the motif of deference, repeatedly emphasized in the standard version of stories about Ekalavya or Hanuman. Other conflations are also noticeable; thus the cult founded by Kalachand presumably had Vaishnava affiliations, and Prasanna always called his guru '*gossain*,' preceptor in a tradition that abhorrs blood sacrifices. And yet the sacrifice of Ananda seems to point towards elements associated more with the alternative, Shakta mode of Hindu devotion.[17]

Doyhata, however, was more than a *bricolage* of well-known fragments of high culture, more, even, than a pattern of ritual inversions of the kind that many anthropologists have loved to analyse. Prasanna's actions did involve a whole series of inversions: most fundamentally, a Shudra had taken over bits and pieces from mythic traditions that had exalted proper caste and gender hierarchies, and used them to humiliate upper-castes and make a woman kick her husband. What he had achieved for one night was indeed a kind of double inversion. The Kaliyuga dystopia had been of an inverted world with Shudras and women on top, which the Kalki-avatar would set right side up again. Prasanna had burst into a re-enactment of this myth by a Brahman *sadhu* and his *bhadralok* disciple, and had appropriated it to terrorize the Doyhata gentry. Unlike ritual inversions with ultimate 'safety valve' functions, again, Prasanna was not acting out any established ritual, but maybe groping towards something new.

The open-ended nature of that Doyhata night was further enhanced by the inclusion of a real and startling innovation: the association of *yuga*-pralay with *physical* immortality. For Kalachand and Lalmohan, it seems, Ananda was Yama, the god of death, brought deliberately into the house by the *sadhu* as Kalki-avatar. And after his killing 'there would be no more death in this world.' The two low-caste disciples, we have seen, had a slightly different perception, and Prasanna had promised Ananda a *divya-deha* (divine body); both versions, however, share an emphasis upon bodily immortality or resurrection totally absent in the Kaliyuga-Kalki mythic corpus. The roots of this peculiar stress are impossible to determine with any certainty. But the *divya-deha* promised by Prasanna is a synonym of *divya-tanu* (both refer to a divine and immortal body), and the latter is a technical term in use among tantrics. *Divya-tanu* in tantrism is associated with *jivan-mukti*, which could imply physical immortality as distinct from the *moksha* of the soul (*atman*).

The underlying theme of *dehavad*, the human body as principal seat of religious practice, is in fact nearly ubiquitous in many medieval and later 'obscure religious cults,' largely plebeian in membership, in Bengal and elsewhere. We have already encountered one such group, active in the nineteenth century in a district not very far from Dacca: the Balaramis of Nadia. More directly relevant could be the Nathpanthis – influential for centuries among plebeian groups in East Bengal, including Muslims – whose beliefs and legends combined attainment of bodily immortality with a special hostility towards Yama, the god of death (Dumont 1970; D. Chattopadhyay 1950: chap. 5; Surendranath Dasgupta 1961; Bhattacharya 1982; Sashibhushan Dasgupta 1946). But all such beliefs had been 'esoteric,' with rituals conducted in secret away from everyday household life and therefore not too difficult to reconcile with outward maintenance of due forms. Doyhata was shocking and transgressive through their public importation into a *bhadralok* home.

The embarrassments did not end here. Trial proceedings revealed the *bhadralok* menfolk in an uniformly unflattering light, as complicit in or complaisant about the humiliation of the women of the household. And the women, too, refused to fit into any of the pigeon-holes constructed for them by conventional dominant male discourses. Lalmohan's wife, kicking her husband in the head at the orders of Prasanna, was hardly the disorderly woman-on-top, but neither was she the self-sacrificing, deferentially assertive wife. The proceedings also indicated that the women on the whole had been far more sceptical about Kalachand's claims than their menfolk, thus undermining yet another stereotype, that of being congenitally more 'superstitious' or 'pious.' The general *bhadralok* silence about Doyhata, despite its potential as salacious scandal, is thus quite understandable.

A pattern of purification through degradation seems to have characterized the actions of Prasanna that night. Upper-caste men and women were forcible dragged 'downwards' in both social and physical terms through abuse, nudity, having their sacred thread torn, being urinated upon, and so on – and by a Chandal or under his orders. Analogies with Bakhtin's well-known analysis of carnivalesque degradation/renewal in medieval and Renaissance popular culture through movement downwards into the 'grotesque realism' of the 'material bodily lower stratum' are tempting, but not perhaps entirely helpful. Cross-cultural comparisons are tricky things: official Christian and high-Hindu attitudes towards the body are far from identical, for instance, and the implications of their inverted forms are also likely to be different. Inversions reminiscent of the carnivalesque do surface occasionally at nodal points of seasonal cycles: Holi, most notably, as well as in the Carak festival before the Bengali New Year.[18] Where Doyhata differed quite fundamentally was in the absence of any community dimension: it had nothing to do with any open community action by Chandals or Bhuinmalis as a whole. and almost certainly the 'Sanskritizing' upwardly mobile offshoots of the Matua sect would have been as embarrassed by it as the *bhadralok* themselves. Prasanna remained an individual with a self-assigned special function, performing in public actions that retained a mysterious, esoteric character reminiscent of tantric rituals. The joyous abandon of community festivals such as Holi was conspicuously absent at Doyhata.

The affinity-distinction pattern can be extended further: in formal terms, though obviously not in content or consequences, Doyhata fleetingly brings to mind the movements premised upon rumours of sudden, total, miraculous change that were not uncommon in late-colonial India. Birsa Munda's tribal rebellion in south Bihar (1899–1900), for instance, was accompanied by 'rumours of miraculous cures and the resuscitation of dead men,' and much was made of a 'Satyayuga-Kaliyuga' contrast in which Satyayuga was obviously very different from the orthodox conception of restored ideal caste hierarchy (Guha 1983:267, 294–5). Such movements were particularly common in the early years of the Gandhian era, and in them cyclical concepts of time, myths about past golden ages under just kings or benevolent zamindars, intermingled with future-oriented impulses.

'Millenarian' hopes such as these invariably coalesced around leaders with a reputation for sanctity: Gandhi himself or wandering religious mendicants. Degradation through reduction to the 'material bodily lower stratum' can also be occasionally glimpsed in such collective, plebeian manifestations, as when rumours circulated in the Gorakhpur region in 1921 that respectable upper-caste people disobeying Gandhi's commands ran the risk of finding themselves covered with excreta. Rough, bawdy jokes often enhanced morale at moments of acute confrontation with authority. It is in such collective protests, and not a Doyhata, that we can expect to find elements of the Bakhtinian carnivalesque (Amin 1984; Sarkar 1987).

Yet newspapers noticed the strange cheerfulness of Prasanna in court, 'commenting freely and gaily on the depositions of several witnesses,' making sarcastic remarks aout the other accused, judges, and the jury (*Bengalee*, 17 March 1905). This could not be the rollicking, triumphant, 'Rabelaisian' laughter celebrated by Bakhtin as allegedly characteristic of the culture of the market place in late-medieval and Renaissance towns, nor could Prasanna's sarcasm and gaiety compare with the well-known genre of gallows speeches in eighteenth-century England or France, with its 'aspect of the Carnival, in which rules were inverted, authority mocked, and criminals transformed into heroes' (Foucault 1979:57-69). The essential component of a plebeian audience was missing in the *bhadralok*-dominated courtroom. Prasanna's could only be the wry, resigned, yet defiant smile of the isolated plebeian, caught in the machinery of bhadralok-administered colonial power-knowledge and aware that no one in court was really interested in finding out what he had meant by his actions, what inspiration and meanings he had derived from the teachings of his *gossain*.

The most 'populist' of historians is unlikely to make a hero out of Prasanna, whose actions merely brought death to a man of even humbler caste, a night of agony for some innocent women, and a purely temporary humiliation for a few *bhadralok*. Doyhata might be a reminder for us of lower-caste fires underground, but it is also a warning against tendencies towards valorizing all more or less autonomous plebeian or subaltern action. The carnivalesque is not necessarily a realm of pure freedom emancipated from cruelty and oppression. In twentieth-century India, and most recently at Babri Masjid and in the countrywide riots that followed in the winter of 1992–3, elements reminiscent of the

Bakhtinian carnivalesque have manifested themselves also in fratricidal conflicts between Hindus, Muslims, and Sikhs.

And yet precisely through his 'laughter,' Prasanna did attain a certain dignity in court, even – if we like to read it that way – a fleeting acuteness of perception. When Lalmohan was abjectly trying to wriggle out of all responsibility, the Chandal interjected, 'No, he did nothing, he just had three or four *kalkes* [pipes] of *ganja* with us.' Asked then by the judge to sign a statement taking full responsibility for what had happened, Prasanna replied, 'If I had known how to write, why, then, I would have become a judge and earned five to seven hundred rupees' (Chaudhuri 1905:74). Superb sarcasm, which allows us to rejoin the problematic with which we had begun. Education had been at the heart of the entire 'renaissance' enterprise of the *bhadralok*, and its meagre fruits in the shape of subordinate *chakri* had fuelled resentments expressed through a renewed Kaliyuga mood. Beyond this dichotomy lie caste and class dimensions, deeply affected by colonialism but extending before and after it – dimensions often elided in models of 'renaissance' awakening and critiques of colonial acculturation. Prasanna's last comment, with which he departs from the historical record for ever, points towards that little-explored and ambiguous world.

NOTES

1 Kali is the last and the most degenerate of four *yugas* (eras; the preceding are Satya, Treta, and Dwapar) which recur endlessly in the traditional high-Hindu conception of cyclical time. In Kaliyuga, dharma (right ritual and conduct; from the nineteenth century, often taken to be the equivalent of the Western notion of 'religion') is at its lowest ebb. As the rest of this passage indicates, in it low-castes (Shudras) dominate over Brahmans and other high-castes, and hierarchies of gender and age are also reversed.

2 Susobhan Sarkar 1970, from which I have taken the statement of Kishorichand Mitra, probably represents this approach at its best. See also A.C. Gupta 1958 and Kopf 1969. The 'Hindu' focus throughout my essay requires some explanation, as half or more of the Bengali-speaking population are Muslims, in particular the great majority of the peasants of East Bengal (the Bangladesh of today). The bulk of the colonial intelligentsia were high-caste Hindus, and Muslims do not figure also in the part-plebeian Doyhata tale I am going to recount.

3 Gandhi once declared in a very controversial statement that Rammohan Roy, the first major social and religious reformer in nineteenth-century Bengal, was a 'pigmy' compared to what he might have been but for Western education. For left critiques of the 'renaissance' model written some twenty years back, see the essays of Asok Sen, Barun De, and Sumit Sarkar in Joshi 1975, Sen 1977, and Sumit Sarkar 1985.

4 The deep impact of Said on studies of colonial India can be gauged from Chatterji 1986 and 1994 and a number of articles in recent volumes of Guha 1982-9, as well as from parts of Sangari and Vaid 1989 and Svati Joshi 1991. See also Viswanathan 1990. For a recent powerful critique of Said and his epigones, see Ahmad 1991, 1992.

5 It is tempting, incidentally, to pursue and analogy here with the acculturation thesis developed by some French historians of early-modern European popular culture, notably Robert Muchembled in 1978 (the year that *Orientalism* was published). An affinity across otherwise unrelated fields of scholarship can be suggested, perhaps, in terms of the withering away of the hopes of radical transformation aroused by Vietnam or May 1968, contributing to an insistence on the all-pervasive hegemony of power structures. For an elaboration of this argument, see Sumit Sarkar 1994.

6 This much-used term refers to gentlefolk, usually of upper-caste (Brahman, Kayastha, Vaidya) origin and marked out from the nineteenth century onwards also by Western education.

7 Industrial growth was slow in colonial Bengal and in any case controlled overwhelmingly by British (and later, immigrant Marwari) capital; the emergent working class, too, was largely recruited from non-Bengali up-country immigrants. There were no signs of capitalistic methods in agricultural production, and few *bhadralok* were recruited into the army. The material base for the overwhelmingly upper-caste Hindu educated *bhadralok* was provided by the vast proliferation of rentier interests under the Permanent Settlement of land revenue under Cornwallis in 1793. Many of these rentier incomes were fairly small and needed to be supplemented by professional or clerical jobs, for which at least a smattering of Western education had become essential.

8 Madhusudan Chaudhuri's *Kalki-avatarer Mokaddama* gives copious extracts from the Doyhata court proceedings and constitutes my principal source for this strange affair. For a more detailed analysis of the Doyhata incident considered in terms of its varied representations, see Sumit Sarkar 1989.

9 Under the Permanent Settlement, the revenue that *zaminders* had to pay to the state was fixed in perpetuity, but no limits were at first imposed on what these landlords could extract as rent from the peasants. (Subsequently, the tenancy laws of 1859 and 1885 passed under peasant pressure did impose some restrictions.) One consequence was a kind of sub-feudalization, with a large number of intermediate tenure-holding rentier interests emerging between the *zamindar* and the actual cultivators. These provided a principal social base for the *bhadralok*. Bikrampur was the indigeneous name for a region in East Bengal that in British administrative terms comprised Dacca district and the Madaripur subdivision of Faridpur district.

10 Madhusudan openly declared that 'he despised Ram and his rabble,' and his greatest work, *Meghnadbadh Kavya* (1861), an epic in pioneering blank verse, radically inverted the ancient Ramayana myth about Ram's war against Ravana, demon-king of Lanka. Ram had become the central icon of much of medieval Hindu *bhakti* (devotion: the cultivation of an internal emotional relationship between the devotee and his or her chosen deity, rather than the alternative religious ways of asceticism, knowledge, or ritual).

11 For an alternative view, see, for instance, the recent argument of Ranajit Guha: 'most of the nineteenth-century beneficiaries of [English] education imbibed from it ... unquestioning servility to the ruling power' through a 'superficial Anglicism' (Guha 1988).

12 I am borrowing this term from Mikhail Bakhtin's analysis of the St Petersburg clerk in *Poor Folk* (Bakhtin, 1984:205, 210).

13 In some texts about Kaliyuga, that dark age would end with the coming of Kalki, the tenth and last incarnation (*avatar*) of Vishnu, who as a kind of messiah would destroy all evil kings and restore Satyayuga.

14 Mahabharata, Vanaparva, sections 187–90 of the Markandya-samasya, is a principal *locus classicus* of the Kaliyuga myth. I am using an English prose translation (Pratap Chandra Roy n.d.), along with the authoritatitive nineteenth-century Bengali translation by Kaliprasanna Sinha (reprinted in 1974) and, for later versions of the myth, Hazra 1963.

15 Tantric traditions systematically inverted many orthodox purity-pollution rules, and some have found in them traces, though much appropriated by high-castes, of plebeian materialism (D. Chattopadhyay 1950: chap. 5; Bhattacharji 1982: chap. 5).

16 Thus Bengali translations of the Kalki-purana, the late-medieval Sanskrit text in which the myth attained its fullest exposition, came out in 1886, 1899, and 1908, and the 1899 version that I am using had gone into its tenth edition by 1982. Throughout the nineteenth century, Orientalist scholars, reformers, and conservatives showed equal enthusiasm for printing and translating ancient texts. In the case of the Vedas, orally preserved texts were actually being written down for the first time.

17 For the Doyhata details the central reference remains Chaudhuri 1905. *Yajna* is the sacrificial fire, central to ancient Vedic ritual and still retained in modern Hindu rituals such as weddings. In the Mahabharata, Ekalavya was a tribal youth who had become a master of archery superior even to the epic hero Arjuna, by practising before an image of Dronacharya, the military teacher to the Kaurava and Pandava princes. Dronacharya eventually gave Ekalavya his blessing, in return for the sacrifice of his forefinger, thus ending the threat to the Kshatriyas. In the Ramayana, Ram recovered his abducted wife, Sita, by destroying Lanka, the capital of the demon-king Ravana, helped greatly by Hanuman the monkey. Both Ekalavya and Hanuman are usually taken to exemplify subaltern devotion and loyalty.

18 Holi replaces 'separation by communion and interdiction by license' (Dumont 1970:51). For an account of Carak, see G. Chattopadhyay 1961.

REFERENCES

Ahmad, Aijaz
    1991 Between Orientalism and Historicism: Anthropological Knowledge of India. Studies in History 7.
    1992 In Theory: Classes, Nations, Literatures, chap. 5. London: Verso.
Amin, Shahid.
    1984 Gandhi as Mahatma: Gorakhpur District, Eastern U.P., 1921–22.' *In* Subaltern Studies, vol. 3, Ranajit Guha, ed. Delhi: Oxford University Press.
Archer, Mildred
    1977 Indian Popular Paintings in the India Office Library. London.
Archer, W.G.
    1953 Bazar Paintings of Calcutta. London.
Bakhtin, Mikhail
    1984 Problems of Dostoevski's Poetics. Manchester.
Bandopadhyay, Brojendranath, and Sajanikanta Das
    1943 Sahitya-Sadhak-Caritmala, volume 3. Calcutta.
Bandopadhyay, Sekhar
    1985 Social Mobility in Bengal in the Late-19th and Early 20th Century. Unpublished thesis, Calcutta University.
Basu, Rajnarayan
    [1874] 1951 Sekal-o-Ekal. Calcutta.
Beane, W.C.
    1977 Myth, Cult, and Symbol in Shakta Hinduism. London.
Bhattacharji, N.N.
    1982 History of the Tantric Religion. Delhi: Manohar.

Biardieu, Madeleine
  1989 Hinduism: The Anthropology of a Civilisation. Delhi: Oxford University Press.
Chakrabarti, Sudhir
  1988 Balahadi Sampraday Tader Gan. Calcutta
  1992 Bratya Lokayat Lalan. Calcutta: Pustak Bipani.
Chartier, Roger
  1987 Cultural Uses of Print in Early Modern France. Princeton: Princeton University Press.
Chatterji, Partha
  1986 Nationalist Thought and the Colonial World: A Derivative Discourse? Delhi: Oxford
         University Press.
  1989 Caste and Subaltern Consciousness. In Subaltern Studies vol. 6, Ranajit Guha, ed.
         Delhi: Oxford University Press.
  1994 The Nation and Its Fragments: Colonial and Post-Colonial Histories. Delhi: Oxford
         University Press.
Chattopadhyay, Bankimchandra
  1880 Banglar Itihas Sambandhay Kayekti Katha. Reprinted in Bankim Rachanabali, vol. 2,
         J.C. Bagal, ed. Calcutta: Sahitya Sansad, 1954, 1969.
Chattopadhyay, Debiprasad
  1950 Lokayata. Bombay: People's Publishing House.
Chattopadhyay, Gauranga.
  1961 Carak Festival in a West Bengal Village. In Aspects of Religion in Indain Society,
         L.P. Vidyarthi, ed. Meerut.
Chattopadhyay, Satischandra.
  1901 Chandiram. Calcutta
  1904 Annapurna. Calcutta
Chaudhuri, Madhusudan.
  1905 Kalki-avatarer Mokaddama / Bikrampure Bhishan Byabhicara. Dacca.
Crossick, G., ed.
  1977 The Lower Middle Class in Britain. London.
Darnton, Robert
  1971 The High Enlightenment and the Low-Life of Literature in Pre-Revolutionary France.
         Past and Present 51.
Dasgupta, Sashibhusan
  1946 Obscure Religious Cults. Calcutta.
Dasgupta, Surendranath
  1961 History of Indian Philosophy, vol. 3. Cambridge: Cambridge University Press.
Devi, Rashsundari
  1868 Atmakatha. Reprint, ed. N. Jana. Calcutta, 1981.
Dumont, Louis
  1970 World Renunciation in Indain Religions. In Religion / Politics and History. Paris,
         Hague: Mouton.
Eliade, Mircea
  1955 The Myth of the Eternal Return. London.
Foucault, Michel
  1979 Discipline and Punish. Harmondsworth: Peregrine.
Ghosh, Girishchandra
  1889 Prafulla. Calcutta.

Goswami, Jayanta
  1974 Samajchitre Unabingsha Satabdir Bangla Prahasan. Calcutta.
Guha, Ranjit, ed.
  1982–9 Subaltern Studies, vols. 1–6. Delhi: Oxford University Press.
  1983 Elementary Aspects of Peasant Insurgency in Colonial India. Delhi: Oxford University Press.
  1988 An Indian Historiography of India: A Nineteenth-Century Agenda and Its Implications. Calcutta: K.P. Bagchi.
Gupta, A.C.
  1958 Studies in the Bengal Renaissance. Calcutta: National Council of Education.
Gupta, Jogendranath
  1909 Bikrampurer Itihas. Calcutta.
Gupta, Mahendranath ('M')
  1902–32 Ramakrishna-Kathamrita. Calcutta.
Hazra, R.C.
  1963 Studies in the Upapuranas. Calcutta.
Joshi, Svati, ed.
  1991 Rethinking English. New Delhi: Trianka.
Joshi, V.C., ed.
  1975 Rammohan Roy and the Process of Modernisation in India. Delhi: Vikas.
Kane, P.V.
  1973 History of the Dharmashastras. Vol. 3, chapter 25. Poona.
Kavyatirtha, Aghorechandra
  1902 Kalir Abasan, ba Kalki-avatar Geetabhinoy. Calcutta.
Kopf, David
  1969 British Orientalism and the Bengal Renaissance. Berkeley, CA.
McDaniel, June
  1989 The Madness of the Saints. Chicago: University of Chicago Press.
Mayer, Arno
  1975 The Lower Middle Class as a Historical Problem. Journal of Modern History 47.
Mukhopadhyay Bholanath
  1876 Bhyalare mor bap. Calcutta.
Nandy, Ashis
  1983 The Intimate Enemy: Loss and Recovery of Self under Colonialism. Delhi: Oxford University Press.
Paul, Ashit, ed.
  1983 Woodcut Prints of Nineteenth Century Calcutta. Calcutta: Seagull Books.
Sangari, Kumkum
  1990 Mirabai and the Spiritual Economy of Bhakti. Economic and Political Weekly 25:27-8.
Sangari, Kumkum, and Sudesh Vaid, eds.
  1989 Recasting Women: Essays in Colonial History. New Delhi: Kali for Women.
Sarkar, Sumit
  1985 Complexities of Young Bengal. In A Critique of Colonial India. Calcutta: Papyrus.
  1989 The Kalki-avatar of Bikrampur: A Village Scandal in Early Twentieth-Century Bengal. In Subaltern Studies, Vol. 6, Ranajit Guha, ed. Delhi: Oxford University Press.
  1992 Kaliyuga, Chakri and Bhakti: Ramakrishna and His Times. Economic and Political Weekly 27:29.

1994 Orientalism Revisited: Saidian Frameworks in the Writing of Modern Indian History, Oxford Literary Review 16:1–2.

Sarkar, Susobhan

1970 Bengal Renaissance and Other Essays. New Delhi: People's Publishing House.

Sarkar, Tanika

1987 Bengal 1928–34: The Politics of Protest. Delhi: Oxford University Press.

1992 The Hindu Wife and the Hindu Nation: Studies in Domesticity and Nationalism in Nineteenth-Century Bengal. Studies in History 8:2.

1993 A Book of Her Own, A Life of Her Own: Autobiography of a Nineteenth-Century Woman. History Workshop Journal 36.

Sen, Asok

1977 Iswarchandra Vidyasagar and His Elusive Milestones. Calcutta.

Thompson, E.P.

1967 Time, Work-Discipline and Industrial Capitalism. Past and Present, 38.

Viswanathan, Gauri

1990 The Masks of Conquest: Literary Study and British Rule in India. London.

The 'Day of National Mourning' in Germany

KARIN HAUSEN

The death of individuals has always caused survivors to search for collective cultural forms, in neighbourhoods and religious communities, in order to overcome these threatening experiences of insecurity, loss, and separation. Again and again, historical change has forced societies to reformulate their forms of cultural dominion over death and mourning. In the industrial societies of the nineteenth and twentieth centuries ever more specialized agencies became dedicated to the task of elaborating commemoration and the celebration of the dead according to their respective societal needs and economic possibilities. Increased mobility, advanced urbanization, and a universal acceptance of market relationships created the prerequisites for cemetery administrators, undertakers, gravestone cutters, nurseries, haberdashers, and others to work together to accommodate the business of mourning to rapidly and fundamentally changing social relations; to bring mourning into harmony with fashions and a highly prized individual autonomy. Parallel to these developments, efforts in socialized medicine were geared towards limiting death as an unpredictable force of destiny and banishing it to the end of as long a life as possible.

At the same time, these efforts to socialize death in new ways and even eliminate it as much as possible were undermined by these very industrial societies, producing as they did unknown possibilities and occasions for wholesale slaughter in the name of national states. It was above all the First World War that forced this novel experience of death on millions of people. Since the French Revolution and the revolutionary wars that followed, people were mobilized in the name of the nation and for the defence of national values against an external enemy; military courage for killing and dying was required from every patriotic male citizen. Accordingly, the creation of a new meaning was necessary in order to allow the personal destiny of each soldier to be subsumed and revalued under the destiny of the nation and to justify to their families the temporary or permanent loss of a son or husband in war. In Germany the national rhetoric of killing and being killed in war was developed in the 1813–15 wars of liberation against Napoleon. The fundamental pattern of this legitimation continued to be relevant in the world wars of the twentieth century.

The First World War brought death to around eight to ten million people. Direct action in battle, as well as hunger, exhaustion, and the wounds that soldiers brought back from the front, created this abundant harvest for death. Imperial Germany sent thirteen million soldiers into war, from which more than two million did not return (Kirsten et al. 1965:172–3). The fact that the war was not won by the Germans made it more difficult to justify to family members the death of two million men destroyed by machine-gun fire and poison gas. Still, it was not merely a question of justification. It was also a matter of mourning. All nations that participated in the war were convinced that the work of mourning ought not to remain the private responsibility of particular families. They considered the memory and mourning for the millions of dead soldiers to be a national duty. The desire to elaborate mourning and remembrance as a collective task, however, forced them to find appropriate national forms and to make collective commemoration a political matter.[1]

Mourning as politics is the theme of the following exposition. I consider how and why personal mourning by individuals and families, for their particular men who were killed as soldiers, was taken over by annual public spectacles in the name of collective national commemoration. I will investigate these questions through the example of the German nation state. In 1918 Germany emerged from the First World War defeated; a revolution was attempted and a republic set up out of the fragments of the former empire. From the beginning, the political experiment was subject to constant struggle, and it finally collapsed in 1933 when Hitler took power. I will concentrate my investigation on the origin and elaboration of the Volkstrauertag (Day of National Mourning), which even today is celebrated in the Federal Republic and since reunification likewise in the territory of the former Democratic Republic. The Volkstrauertag was established against resistance during the Weimar Republic as an annual ceremony for the remembrance of the fallen soldiers of the war. It was supposed to be a memorial day for the 'victims on the altar of the fatherland,' a phrase stemming from the nineteenth century (Zimmer 1971). It was intended to invigorate and support the cult around new and old memorials by mobilizing the public in thousands of localities for ceremonial celebration.

I will analyse the history and meaning of the Volkstrauertag in four stages. The first deals with the 'war experience' and its later collective working through, and recalls the enormous differences between men and women in experience, disappointment, mourning, and the unbridgeable separation between existence at the front and at home which continued into peacetime. A second stage leads back into the nineteenth century. We have to consider why the collective memorial of the dead that had been celebrated annually for decades was no longer considered an adequate form for the collective remembrance of fallen soldiers, including those killed in the First World War. In the main part of my exposition I deal with the Volkstrauertag: how it was conceived, advertised, and supported by the newly founded Volksbund für Kriegsgräberfürsorge (People's Union for the Care of German War Graves) and how it was celebrated up to the end of the Weimar Republic in ever more official form. My report on the phenomenon of collective mourning in Germany ends with a view towards the reconfiguration of the Volkstrauertag in 1934, to the Heldengedenktag (heroes' memorial day) by the Nazis, and the surprisingly quick resurrection of the Volkstrauertag after the Second World War in West Germany.

Times of Peace and the Experience of War

As for England and France, so for the German empire: the war began in a mood of optimism and victory and with the conviction that the fatherland was to be protected from attack by the aggressor. Perhaps the description of universal 'war enthusiasm' that is presented by historians has preserved the overdrawn picture of war propaganda even until today. But quite clearly, at least in 1914–15 and especially in good middle-class families, many young men hurried to the front. It may not only have been the infection, slowly fed by nationalistic fever, which motivated these young men; George Mosse has offered us a possibility for understanding the situation which has far-reaching implications. It is well worth considering: 'War was an invitation to manliness' (Mosse 1985:144). In this context, men's problem was to cope with the shock that the new war generated. New technologies and chemicals made soldiers' deaths wholesale and isolated and gave individual soldiers little chance to live out heroic manliness in a demonstrative way.[2] In neither Germany, England, nor France during or after the war was the 'invitation to manliness' answered simply by disappointment because its anticipation had not been fulfilled. In fact, rather the opposite: some of the returning young men, grown old on the battlefield, persisted in the invitation. They continued to cultivate and vicariously celebrate the hope for military manliness in the name of the 'front soldiers.'

The phases of the literary celebration of these war experiences are well known.[3] During the war, short prose texts and war poems were especially popular. In 1916 *Der beiden Wanderer zwischen Welten* (*The Traveller between*

Two Worlds), by Walter Flex, appeared in Germany and quickly became a cult book of the youth movement, selling 250,000 copies by 1925 and 984,000 by 1949. Whether fallen or surviving, the hardened soldier in *In Stahlgewittern* (*The Storm of Steel*, 1920), by Ernst Jünger, manifested his manliness through the halo of a kind of primitive creature, through the male life-force, as well as the steadfast comradeship of the trenches, which levelled all differences of rank and class. The heroism of these men was supposed to urge the male gender on and do away with all banalities. Between 1918 and 1928 such literature comprised around a hundred prose texts published by officers in Germany. That pattern changed after the latter year. Between 1928 and 1933 the German book market offered over two hundred new world-war novels, which revised and explained the 'war adventure' in light of post-war experiences. Significant political controversies developed around these books. Erich Maria Remarque, who was born in 1898, wrote in the foreword to his 1928 best-seller, *All Quiet on the Western Front*: 'This book should be neither an accusation nor a confession. It should only attempt to report on a generation which was destroyed by the war even when they escaped its granades.' The novel was translated into thirty-two languages, sold eight million copies, and was made into a film in 1930 (Muller 1986:53, 60)

Most likely it was not just the men who had experienced the front who read the book. Those whose irredeemable fault it was to have remained civilians (since they were born too late to have experienced the front) surely were also looking for the collective masculine experiences of First World War soldiers in these novels. Perhaps wives, daughters, and sisters too hoped to understand more about the war adventures of their own men. For such experiences were exclusively those of men; women inevitably remained shut out. Nevertheless, in daily life women had to share, physically, psychologically, materially, and ideally, the burden of those experiences – experiences which, despite being made 'heroic,' were actually destructive for civilian life, even if their men returned from the front alive and with uninjured bodies.[4]

Women's sharing in the experiences of war and its consequences was seldom mentioned in the war literature. They remained excluded whenever the crucial experiences of the First World War were worked through publicly in literary and artistic creation and as such material was received. Whatever conclusions were drawn from the novels – whether pacifist or militarist, analytically critical or palliative, descriptive or glorifying – taken together the novels intensified a newly fashioned individual and political discussion about the war and at the same time concentrated public attention on those individual and collective experiences that had occurred to men and among men. In the world of the trenches the presence of women was reduced to longings from a distant perspective. At best, the closed military society opened up temporarily in order to allow the entry of women by depicting them, however figuratively, as eternal mother, mother earth, or mother homeland in need of protection, or as nurse, prostitute, or perhaps a woman in enemy territory who was subjected to rape.

It was not just the literary treatment of the war that brought male experiences and the closed community of men to centre stage. The same process occurred in the elaboration of public memorial events for honouring fallen soldiers, even during the war. In civilian life, where remembrance of the dead is established in ritual, the actions of women, alongside those of priests, have a crucial importance for the collective mourning ceremony. Women are the ones who wash and clothe a cadaver, who wail, and who care for the grave over the years. They carry out palpable work of mourning and give visible expression to its pain. In contrast to these practices, women were distanced from dying and death at the front; they embodied home. And the stylization of military hospital nurses as angels is part of this process of distancing. With the separation of front and home, trust in the practices of everyday mourning ritual apparently disappeared. As soon as it was a question of dealing with the extreme situation of a war, the military community of males closed around the fallen soldier and stylized every one killed from its own ranks as a hero; it obligated those who continued to live to make further sacrifices in the names of the fallen. In military death and mourning rituals, women receive, if at all, a place only on the sidelines as the mourning *pietà* who sacrifices her son, or as the disadvantaged one who is left behind. How this reformulation of collective mourning rituals took place can be demonstrated by the long prehistory of the Volkstrauertag.

All Souls' Day and Memorial Sunday

The collective remembrance of all the dead on one particular day in the year has a long tradition in Germany (Franke 1898; Graff 1905–6). In the Catholic church All Souls' Day was celebrated for centuries as an annual memorial day. In Protestant churches this tradition was at first given up, but from the beginning of the nineteenth century, despite inner church resistance, it was gradually reintroduced. Even today in Germany, Catholics visit cemeteries each year on All Souls' Day, and Protestants attend on Memorial Sunday in October or November in order to decorate the graves of their family members with wreaths and flowers bought from florists.

The return of the Protestant church to the commemoration of Memorial Sunday appears to have been closely tied up with the wars of liberation against

Napoleon. For the first time in 1816 the Prussian king Wilhelm III provided regulations for church celebration of a remembrance Sunday. He thereby apparently fulfilled an expressed need in parish churches. During the national uprising against Napoleon between 1813 and 1815, patriotic preparation for a war of liberation had been incited, legitimated, and blessed from the pulpits of the churches as a holy war against the power of evil (Dann 1976; Wittram 1949). Although the victory was won, the mobilized patriots saw their high-flown constitutional and national hopes bitterly disappointed by the decrees of the Vienna Congress. In this context, Memorial Sunday, as it was established by the king, gave mourning and commemoration a prominent public place and provided an occasion for urgently needed collections for the widows and children of fallen and invalid soldiers. In this post-war period it became usual to connect the commemoration of soldiers who had fallen in war with the collective remembrance of victorious battles. In order that both of these commemorations be elaborated patriotically, decisions about time, place, and supporters were less and less often left to the church alone. Increasingly, the direction of the more or less secularized commemorations came into the hands of numerous veterans' associations. They finally took the occasion of church memorial days, of All Souls' Day, and Memorial Sunday, to represent themselves, to deposit wreaths on war memorials, and to hold festive parades with flags, marching music, and speeches. There were already veterans' associations before 1848, but only after the foundation of the German empire did their numbers grow rapidly so that in the end there were more men organized in veterans' groups than in all other national associations and unions. The number of members rose from around 900,000 in 1888 to 2.8 million in 1913 (Düding 1986:101; Saul 1969; Trox 1990). The associations dedicated themselves providing charitable support for needy family members of deceased comrades and above all to maintaining comradeship and tradition.

In general, however, it appears that militarism and the cult of the nation in the long period of peace between 1871 and 1914 pushed the national remembrance of fallen soldiers into the background. Certainly, there continued to be plaques with the names of the dead from the years 1813–15 in or on churches and public buildings, and those who fell in later wars were remembered with monuments. But after the foundation of the Reich in 1871, the German middle class, which was nationalistic and faithful to the emperor, expressed its national unity and identity tangibly through elaborate national monuments, national places of commemoration, and Bismarck and Emperor Wilhelm towers. The cult of nationality left little room for the collective commemoration of the dead (Nipperdey 1968; Siemann 1988; Koselleck and Jeismann 1994).

This situation was soon to change in the first months of the First World War. When, by August 1914, family after family received more than one death announcement, a revival of the traditional collective celebration of the dead no longer appeared sufficient to rescue the courage of battle from mourning and lamentation. In October 1914 it was still remembered that during the war of 1870–1, localities and communities had set up monuments and memorial plaques in order to commemorate fallen soldiers. A little later the search began for new forms of expression in order to give a dignified structure to national mourning. Warrior memorials, halls of honour, hero grottoes, and honour cemeteries were proposed as new forms of remembrance. In 1916 great exhibitions in Berlin, Königsberg, Leipzig, and Cologne were concerned with the artistic arrangement of warrior graves and places of commemoration (VDB 1916:127–8, 139, 152, 174–5). For Memorial Sunday of 1914 the journal of the association of the Prussian war veterans offered the following inspiration:

The German people must sacrifice its dearest and truest blood on the altar of the fatherland ... The sacrificial death of the heroes of the fatherland transfigures those who have suffered it and those who lament over it. If we let our tears flow, we bow in humility to the unfathomable will of God ... On Memorial Sunday our dead say to us, admonishing and inspiring, that the sacrifice which they have brought us with their lives should not be in vain ... Through the night of death to the light of life! After the victorious peace of honour, a celebration of life shall follow that of mourning in a more beautiful and still-blossoming Germany, increasing in power, size, and morality. (Parole 1914:916)

After the war was lost, what could be rescued from the pronouncements on Memorial Sunday 1915, which declared that the German people had become 'a heroic people through the period of war' and that therefore 'for our people the celebration of mourning has become a spring festival of resurrection' (Parole 1914:926)? The search for meaning became even more urgent, since in the last years of the war a great silence over the senseless wholesale slaughter at the front shrouded the homeland. By 1916 and quite clearly in 1917 and 1918, All Souls' Day and Memorial Sunday were no longer occasions to glorify the death of heroes.

Day of National Mourning

The German population lived through the long-hoped-for ending of the war in 1918–19 with the accompanying conditions of defeat, armistice, and revolution. This was a difficult situation for the establishment of the first German republic, and until the end of 1923 its very existence was in question. Attempts to overthrow it from the right and worker rebellions combined with inflation and open conflicts over territorial boundaries and national sovereignty to define everyday political life. In this tension-filled period the questions repeated since the summer of 1919 – whether and how the national commemoration of fallen soldiers in the world war could be fittingly established – became a controversial political issue and challenge to the republic. But the state proved only its inability to provide a satisfactory answer. While the allied powers, victorious since 1919, honoured their dead soldiers by celebrating Armistice Day, 11 November, as the national memorial day, its right-wing critics argued that Germany showed 'the mark of German strife, disorder, and lack of discipline' so long as it did not succeed in introducing an official day of national commemoration and mourning (KrieFü 1925:10).

By the summer of 1919 in the constituent national assembly, in a countermove to the resolution to recognize 1 May as a national holiday, the right demanded a national day of mourning and in the following months repeatedly sought it by petition. In November 1920 the liberal parties in the Reichstag and members of the government attempted to celebrate the day of the signing of the Versailles treaty, 28 June, as a mourning day. But this attempt failed, as did the following initiatives on the part of the Reichstag and the government. The politically controversial project remained unresolved right to the end of the Weimar Republic, since the agreement between the central government, the governments of particular states, and the churches that was necessary on constitutional grounds could not be reached (Lurz 1985–7:IV; Schellack 1990; Schneider 1991).

Under these circumstances, however, the movement for the establishment of a day of national commemoration got started outside parliament through cooperation with governments and administrations. The Volksbund for the care of German war graves acted as a propaganda and organizational centre. Soldiers' associations, composed of the monarchist union of soldiers' organizations, Kyffhäuser, and the *völkisch* union of front soldiers, Stahlhelm, which were continually active after 1918, supported, along with organizations of war victims and many other associations, the development of a Volkstrauertag on a Sunday in spring which would be celebrated annually everywhere in the country.

The Volksbund für Kriegsgräberfürsorge had been founded in November 1919 'in the recognition that a cult of the dead and the feeling of obligation of the German people necessitates the quick establishment of care for war graves.'[5] Its chief task was to support the work of the Central Information Office for War Casualties and War Graves, which had been created during the war and since 1919 was attached to the Imperial Ministry of the Interior. Continuity for the work was embodied in Dr Siegfried Enno Eulen, who was the business manager of the Volksbund from 1919 to 1944 and who in 1917–18, on contract from the Prussian War Ministry, had had the care of German war graves first in Galicia and then in Turkey (KrieFü 1929:166–9). From 1933 Eulen wrote enthusiastic national-socialist observations in the association's monthly journal.

The Volksbund, which is still active today, developed only hesitatingly until the end of the inflation period in 1923, but it thereafter progressed rapidly. In the first years it acted above all as an information agency by providing members with research into those relatives killed or missing in action. Later the Volksbund took over with increasing display the care of soldiers' graves, including those in military cemeteries outside the German boundaries, which were developed with escalating monumentality. The expenditures for building such 'places of honour' increased from around 48,000 Reichsmarks in 1925 to 864,000 Reichsmarks in 1933 and to almost 6.5 million three years later (KrieFü passim). To finance and carry out its tasks, individuals and communities were sought as members, local groups founded, cemetery 'spade brigades' appointed, and street and house collections organized. The number of members rose from 72,000 in 1924 to 130,000 in 1929, to 295,000 in 1937, and to almost 2 million by 1944; it reached 500,000 by 1953. In 1929 the Volksbund was organized into forty-four associations with 1,315 groups. Its monthly journal, *Kriegsgräberfürsorge* (War graves care: information and reports of the People's Union for the Care of War Graves), which appeared from 1921, distributed 7,000 copies in 1924, 50,000 in 1929, 92,000 in 1937, 537,000 in 1940, and 150,000 in 1953 (KrieFü annual reports).

In November 1920, right after the failure of the anti-republican Kapp putsch and the first huge demonstration of the No-More-War Movement on 1 August,[6] the Volksbund pledged itself to the idea of establishing a national day of mourning outside political and confessional party wranglings as a 'unifying day for the whole people.' Spring was proposed for the holiday, with the justification 'Winter calls attention to the passing of everything human, while spring awakens new hope in us again, and we are a people in need. Our fallen should be a symbol for us that after the winter which we have had to endure, a new spring is coming' (ADW, protocol of the extraordinary meeting of the representatives Berlin, 12 November 1920:9)

Parallel to this initiative in the Volksbund, the soldiers' associations mobilized the honouring of heroes with increased feeling from 1920. The Kyffhäuser union directed all of its 30,000-member soldiers' associations in October 1920 to participate on All Souls' Day or Memorial Sunday in 'dignified commemoration ceremonies' and to pursue 'the idea of the introduction of a day of remembrance for the great deeds of our army.' In November that year the Kyffhäuser journal for the first time drew attention to the German 'heroes' on its title-page under the famous motto 'Invictis victi victuri' (To the undefeated the defeated who will conquer): 'to you we bow our knees and raise our hands and hearts in divine thanksgiving.' The object was to prevent 'that infinitely painful word "for nothing"' from standing 'over your death.' In 1920, in defiance of this 'for nothing,' the Kyffhäuser union entered the Berlin cathedral on the evening of Memorial Sunday with crepe-covered flags and banners to hold a memorial service (KrZ 1920: Beilage 15, 86–88, 197–9).

The next year the soldiers' associations declared 6 March, the Saturday before Easter, the German day of mourning. In October they characterized neglect as infidelity and ingratitude and warned, 'We should build the monument to the memory of those who fell in the war in our own hearts.' In order to make certain of this, they demanded an annual mourning day to supplement the silent commemoration of the dead with grottoes, monuments, and plaques. 'For it is not sufficient to establish a symbol in any form and then to let it lie in silence. Rather, it should be a *speaking monument*, since it must say to us and especially to our youth: "Stand still on this spot and be silent; here is holy ground. Meditate on those who died for you, honour them, and follow them when it is necessary' (KrZ 1921: Beilage 21). In 1922 the soldiers' associations agreed more explicitly than in 1920 that as 'soldiers of the unconquered army,' they could not allow the sacrifice of health and life by the heroes to have been made 'for nothing.' Therefore fidelity, fulfillment of duty, and readiness for 'peaceful battle' had to grow again out of the 'holy spirit of comradeship.' 'Through German energy, German fidelity, German work, we desire to smash the peace treaty of Versailles.' The 'spirit of readiness to sacrifice,' not 'conflict and disunity,' should rule. Everyone should see to it that 'a new, holy, pure feeling for the family enters you' so that homeland and family could be rescued (KrZ 1922:181–2, 61–2).

With these words, the right-wing war veterans formulated at the end of 1922 what became elaborated in the Volkstrauertag during the following years. The common national commemoration was to bind the nation in fidelity and gratitude to the dead soldiers. They were called heroes because they had died at the front. Their 'heroic death' could not be permitted to appear 'for nothing.' Providing meaning for the living in terms of an obligatory fidelity and trust was linked with increased urgency to the greater war defeat, the Versailles 'shameful peace,' and the threat of fraternal war let the death of two million soldiers appear meaningless and their heroic death doubtful. It must not happen that death on the battlefield, which was always supposed to have elevated the military man to hero status, now in post-war period should devalue the soldiers as absurd, tragic figures. Resisting such devaluation appeared a task that bound men together, that linked fathers with sons and adult men with growing male youth. Therefore it was necessary to erect in every heart a 'speaking monument,' for which a national commemoration would offer the means. It was supposed to move and bind hearts together in a cult of secular martyrdom. Honouring war heroes was to rekindle the flame of inner national unity and offer every man a place in the nation again.

In 1924, the year of stability, the Volksbund organized a kind of trial run for the celebration of the Volsktrauertag everywhere in Germany. The following year a mobilization for the so-called first German Volkstrauertag took place in great style on 1 March (KrieFü 1929:167–8). In subsequent years the Volksbund successfully saw to it that the Volkstrauertag, as was stated in looking back at its accomplishments from 1929, 'was born from the depths of the German temper' and attained validity as a 'lovely German custom.' Although not the government but rather the 'movement' for the Volkstrauertag had achieved the commemoration of the dead in the spring, the government nevertheless was now expected to provide proper protection against 'profanation and desecration' for this day (Jb 1925–6:112).

After 1922 a special committee for the establishment of the Volkstrauertag was formed (Jb 1925–6:111–2). The chairman of the Volksbund presided over the committee. Its members were recruited in 1924 from the Protestant, Catholic, and Jewish communities, the church welfare associations, the women's associations, the Red Cross, the Kyffhäuser union, and the Central Union for German War Wounded in 1925. The committee circulated 'directions for the preparation of the Volkstrauertag.' It was unable to establish a legal date, but did usually succeed in getting flags flown at half mast on public buildings and securing the official participation of the army and navy in local events. The organization of the day was the responsibility of local branches of the Volksbund. They were supposed to ensure the greatest possible uniformity of celebration, 'so that the festivities on the Volkstrauertag in particular cities and communities would, in their totality, produce a dignity and emotion which would render testimony to the importance of this day.' They were to work through church officials to see that religious services referred to the national commemoration and that at noon all the bells rang for a quarter-hour. Schools were to be let out before noon. On the Volkstrauertag, the local Volksbund groups were to organize public morning or afternoon ceremonies with musical accompaniment, the laying of wreaths on soldier cemeteries, publicity for the care of war graves, and street collections. Everywhere, from the beginning, in the celebration of the Volkstrauertag appeared the symbol of the Volksbund: five raised crosses.

Also, from this time on the staging of the day of national mourning ensured that the ceremonies would have their centre in Berlin, the capital both of the German Reich and of the Prussian state since 1926; the central Berlin ceremony was broadcast over the radio and later documented in the journal of the Volksbund with the printing of the commemoration address, together with a report and photographs. In order to stress the quasi-official character of the ceremonies each year, the participation of the president and other representatives of the Reich and the Prussian state and of civil and clerical officials was reported.

Until 1932 the location of the Berlin event was the plenary chamber of the Reichstag. Flowers, wreaths, and flags decorated the room, and towering over the lectern in the background was the symbol of the five crosses. The commemoration address was given by the chairman of the Volksbund. At the end of the ceremony, the song 'I had a comrade' was sung by everyone. For the first time in 1927 and again in 1928 and 1929, the Berlin student corporations ceremoniously bore the old flags of the Berlin regiment into the room. In 1930 and in the two following years, the event was open to the public. The Reich president marched in front of the honour company before the door of the Reichstag. In 1933 the Berlin State Opera provided the setting for the event, and the parade of the honour company was supplemented by formations of the regular army.

Up to the end of the Weimar Republic, the representatives of central state authority had not been able to develop an official memorial ceremony under their own responsibility. Instead, over the years, the so-called movement for the Volkstrauertag increased its influence, with growing support from the *völkisch*-national camp. In Berlin, the focus of the central memorial event, political turmoil erupted especially violently. In March 1930, with the fall of the last Social Democratic chancellor of the Reich, Hermann Müller, who was not in favour of the Volkstrauertag, the political dismantling of the Weimar Republic, which was driven from the right, quickly began to take place. Prussia, the largest of the imperial states and a democratic bastion which at first kept its Social Democratic government, was brought to an end by the *coup d'état* of Reich chancellor von Papen on 20 July 1932.[7]

From 1929 on there had been an increased willingness among the public to substitute demonstrative activism and militarism for any mourning over the experiences of loss from the war. An impressive episode throws a spotlight on this politically directed strategy of substitution. In 1930 the American Lewis Milestone had filmed *All Quiet on the Western Front*. Against the showing of this film at the beginning of December, the National Socialists mobilized protests with street riots, white mice in the theatre and stink bombs. The *völkisch* camp attached the film as offensive and an incitement, and demanded its withdrawal. The film censor was called upon. Against unequivocal commentary in

the democratic and social democratic press, but supported by appropriate opinion from the Army Ministry and the Foreign Office, the Ministry of the Interior
prohibited its showing on the grounds that the film endangered the German
reputation abroad and disparaged the German army (Müller 1986:79–80).

From the Volkstrauertag to the Heldengedenktag (Heroes Memorial Day) and Back to the Volkstrauertag

In 1934 the Volkstrauertag was raised by Hitler to a legal holiday and at the
same time renamed Heldengedenktag (Heroes Memorial Day). Responsibility
for the day now lay with the army, although the Volksbund continued to offer
necessary assistance. In 1935, after the Saar territory was rejoined to the Reich
on 13 January and universal conscription was announced on 16 January, military memorial ceremonies were regulated on 17 March in every garrison of the
army. In the same year the central Berlin memorial ceremonies were further
militarized. Now they took place in and in front of the Berlin State Opera. The
memorial address was given by the Reich minister of war. Behind the lectern,
the curtain no longer bore the five raised crosses but two enormous swastikas
and two iron crosses. The parade of the honour company became more important. The tenor of the celebration was no longer as a symbol of mourning but of
pride and the glorification of the heroic life. On the first Heldengedenktag after
the beginning of the Second World War, the central ceremony took place in the
courtyard of the armoury, and Hitler himself gave the ceremonial address and
called all Germans to prepare for sacrifice so that the German people would
show themselves worthy of the sacrifice of the fallen heroes.

During the Third Reich the Volksbund experienced an enormous upswing.
It concentrated its 'cultural work' on creating dignified monuments for the
army of dead and on developing soldiers' cemeteries all around the Reich into
'consecrated memorial.' They were to surround the Reich 'like an enormous
ring that will always protect the homeland' (KrieFü 1929:168). By 1921 the
image of 'heroes' who 'with their lives have constructed an impenetrable wall
around our beloved fatherland' (BadKrZ 1921:184) was now translated into
monumental buildings and parks. In the Volksbund journal the long-time business manager Eulen celebrated the National Socialists' triumph before a 'hero's
death' finally caught even him in 1944. As late as 1944 and without any break,
the 'heroic life view' still defined the terms of discourse. An example is Eulen's
New Year's address in 1941 (KrieFü 1941:1): 'The Führer has unified the
German people and in a wonderful series of victories set before it new, great
tasks. The precious seed of our dead from the world war and the post-war

period has ripened. The "for nothing," in which holders of power hostile to the people and to the race tried to falsify the sacrifice of our best sons, has been changed into a glowing testimony for the glorification of this effort.'

It is therefore startling that in the newly founded Federal Republic of Germany the Volksbund journal could appear again as early as October 1949 under its old title. Already by 1946 the Volksbund had begun to work itself out of the wreckage of the Third Reich (Petersen n.d.). But the reconstruction of the organization only succeeded in West Germany, where in late 1952 even the first president of the Federal Republic, the liberal Theodor Heuss, offered his patronage to the Volksbund. Just as after the First World War, the organization made itself indispensable as an efficient information source for anyone who undertook to find the whereabouts of sons, husbands, fathers, and other family members. The extent to which the old ideas were resuscitated, along with the people who built the organization back up again, was demonstrated in the introduction to the first number of the journal in October 1949, in which the discussion was of the hope 'that the Volksbund will be again what it once was: a union of the whole German people, who hold the memory of the victims of the war in fidelity and reverence and as warning for eternal peace.' Enno Eulen was recalled with thanks, and even the miracle of national resurrection after the First World War was remembered.

On 3 March 1950, in the plenary room of the Federal Parliament, the Volksbund staged the first central celebration of the Volkstrauertag after the war. Already in September 1949 the right-wing parties in the Federal Parliament had presented a motion for the reintroduction of the day. In 1951 after thorough research into the problems of constitutional procedure, the interior ministers of the federal states agreed to allow its official celebration on a Sunday, not in the spring, but in the fall. This agreement was passed by the Federal Parliament in 1952. The Volksbund again sought for uniformity and decorum for the celebration everywhere. As a result, in the following years there were continuous negotiations with the churches, the army, and the individual state governments. What had already been established since 1950 was the central celebration in the plenary room of the Federal Parliament, which directly continued the Weimar tradition under the symbol of the five crosses and with the closing song 'I had a comrade.'

Just as in the rituals, so also in its commentaries and addresses, the Volksbund carried out a suitable management of the recent past. In 1950 it justified the resurrection of the Volkstrauertag with the following reflections (KrieFü 1950:11): 'When a people in one of the greatest and most horrible wars in history has fought for its life for six long years, when millions of soldiers fell on all fronts, millions of women and children at home and on the flight from the east – then it is spiritually impossible for this people to go right back to everyday work and pleasure as if nothing of importance had happened.' The millions of people who were killed by the Germans were not mentioned at all. That made it easier to mobilize the unity of all Germans. 'In this year our will is: back to the old Volkstrauertag as a ceremony of death and life of the whole united people, united in its present and past generations, bound in unconquerable love with those outside who have fallen in the highest honour for their homeland.'

The only contrast to earlier years was that now the fallen soldiers were no longer described as heroes; it was accepted that their death was 'in vain,' and peace was the political perspective offered at the Volkstrauertag. At the same time, however, the commemorative celebration was regarded and used as an opportunity to restore the soldiers' honour. They were presented as men who were ready to sacrifice themselves in fulfillment of their patriotic duty and at the same time as victims who had been tragically misled by the inhuman, totalitarian National Socialist system. These public efforts to restore the soldiers' honour were part of the political campaign for rearmament in the Federal Republic of Germany, which at that time still was highly controversial and ardently disputed.

Even more significant for the political culture in West Germany during the fifties is the fact that for many years the victims of National Socialist violence were not thought of at all on the Volkstrauertag. In 1953, for example, the Volksbund invited the German people to commemorate 'the war deaths, the comrades fallen at the front outside and inside Germany, all men, women, and children who died in the nights of bombardment and chaos, and those killed for their convictions' (KrieFü 1953;163). Not until the late sixties, when the debate on the Third Reich became more critical and included hitherto carefully suppressed discussion about the far-reaching involvement of the German population in general and the army in particular in National Socialist politics, as well as in anti-Semitic and racist persecutions and exterminations, was the public consciousness and political sensibility sharpened and the scope of national commemoration and mourning broadened. Now the victims of National Socialist persecutions were explicitly referred to. But in the eighties, children, women, and men from all nations who had fallen and were yet to fall victims to war, violence, and terror were included in the commemorative program of the Volkstrauertag. Thus the memorial day was adapted to the current political situation, but in an extremely questionable manner, since it did away with confrontation with the specific German national and National Socialist past.

NOTES

I am grateful to David Sabean for the original translation of my article into English.

1 Recent publications on war memorials and commemorations are Gärtner and Rosenberger
   1991; Gillis 1994; Hutt et al. 1990; Koselleck 1979; Koselleck and Jeismann 1994; Lurz 1985–
   7; Mosse 1979, 1990; Prost 1977; Schneider 1991.
2 See, on war enthusiasm and war experiences, Adams 1990; Berliner Geschichtswerkstatt 1989;
   Bessel 1988; Hirschfeld et al. 1993; Knoch 1989; Leed 1979; Linden and Mergner 1991;
   Winter 1988. Letters from the front have been collected and published in great number. The
   more recent editions do not any longer serve propagandistic purposes, as did most of the earlier
   ones.
3 See Fussell 1977; Hüppauf 1985; Müller 1986; Theweleit 1987–9; Vondung 1980; Wohl 1979.
4 See Hausen 1994; Higonnet et al. 1987; Kundrus 1995; Thébaud 1992; Wall and Winter 1988;
   Whalen 1984.
5 See ADW, p.5, for the founding session on 22 September 1919 in the Reich Ministry of the
   Interior. Reminiscences of the Volksbund are given in Dollinger 1983; Petersen n.d.; Soltau
   1982; for critical accounts, see Lurz 1985–7:IV; Schellack 1990; Schneider 1991.
6 See ADW, p.6, for a report of the extraordinary meeting of the representatives in Berlin on
   12 November 1920. On August 1920 the pacifist No-More-War Movement organized its first
   demonstration at Berlin; in 1921 more than 100,000 people were mobilized in Berlin and more
   than 50,000 in other towns; in the following years the movement was split by inner troubles;
   and in 1924 the demonstration came under the pressure of the ten-year commemoration of
   war mobilization in 1914, which was officially celebrated by the central government. After
   1924 the yearly demonstration lost its attraction; see Lütgemeier-Davin 1981; Riesenberger
   1985:124–42.
7 Since 1929 the Social Democratic Prussian prime minister, Otto Braun, had pushed the
   reconstruction of the famous Neue Wache as a place of memorial for the fallen soldiers. The
   architect, Heinrich von Tessenow, finished his work in 1931, and the opening ceremony took
   place in June that year. But the old military elite did not accept the invitation to the event; see
   Demps 1988:103–32.

REFERENCES

Primary Sources

ADW
   Archiv des Diakonischen Werkes: AI c 15, vol.1, Akten betr. Deutsche Kriegsgräberfürsorge.
BadKrZ
   Badische Krieger-Zeitung.
Jb 1925–6
   Jahrbuch des Volksbundes Deutsche Kriegsgräberfürsorge E.V. 1925–6, ed. E. Eulen.
KrZ
   Krieger-Zeitung: Amtliches Blatt des Deutschen Reichskriegerbundes 'Kyffhäuser' der
       deutschen Krieger-Wohlfahrtsgemeinschaft und des Preußischen
       Landes-Kriegerverbandes 1920.

KrieFü
 Kriegsgräberfürsorge: Mitteilungen und Berichte vom Volksbund Deutsche
   Kriegsgräberfürsorge E.V.
Parole.
 Deutsche Krieger-Zeitung. Amtliche Zeitung des Deutschen Kriegerbundes.
VDB
 Verbandszeitung Deutscher Blumengeschäftsinhaber

Secondary Sources

Adams, Michael C.C.
 1990 The Great Adventure: Male Desire and the Coming of World War I. Bloomington:
   Indiana University Press.
Berliner Geschichtswerkstatt
 1989 August 1914: Ein Volk zieht in den Krieg. Berlin.
Bessel, Richard
 1988 The Great War in German Memory: The Soldiers of the First World War: Demobiliza-
   tion and Weimar Political Culture. German History 6:20–34.
Dann, Otto
 1976 Vernunftfrieden und nationaler Krieg: Der Umbruch im Friedensverhalten des
   deutschen Bürgertums zu Beginn des 19. Jahrhunderts. *In* Kirche zwischen Krieg und
   Frieden: Studien zur Geschichte des deutschen Protestantismus, Wolfgang Huber and
   Joachim Schwerdtfeger, eds., pp.160–224. Stuttgart: Klett Verlag.
Demps, Laurenz
 1988 Die Neue Wache: Entstehung und Geschichte eines Bauwerkes. Berlin: Militärverlag.
Dollinger, Hans
 1983 Kain, wo ist dein Bruder? München.
Düding, Dieter
 1986 Die Kriegervereine im wilhelminischen Reich und ihr Beitrag zur Militarisierung der
   deutschen Gesellschaft. *In* Bereit zum Krieg: Kriegsmentalität im wilhelminischen
   Deutschland 1890–1914, Jost Dülffor and Karl Holl, eds. pp.99–121. Göttingen:
   Vandenhoeck & Ruprecht.
Franke, R.
 1898 Zur Geschichte und Beurteilung des Totensonntag. Halte was du hast: Zeitschrift für
   Pastoraltheologie 22:14–28, 66–81.
Fussell, Paul
 1977 The Great War and Modern Memory. London: Oxford University Press.
Gärtner, Reinhold, and Sieglinde Rosenberger.
 1991 Kriegerdenkmäler. Innsbruck: Österreichischer Studienverlag.
Gillis, John R. ed.
 1994 Commemorations: The Politics of National Identity. Princeton: Princeton University Press.
Graff, P.
 ˙1905–6 Beiträge zur Geschichte des Totenfestes. Monatsschrift für Pastoraltheologie 2:62–76.
Hausen, Karin
 1994 Die Sorge der Nation für ihre 'Kriegsopfer': Ein Bereich der Geschlechterpolitik
   während der Weimarer Republik. *In* Von der Arbeiterbewegung zum modernen
   Sozialstaat: Festschrift für Gerhard A. Ritter, Jürgen Kocka et al., eds. pp.719–39.
   München: K.G. Sauer Verlag.

144   Karin Hausen

Higonnet, Margaret R., et al., eds.
  1987 Behind the Lines: Gender and the Two World Wars. New Haven, London: Yale
     University Press.
Hirschfeld, Gerhard, et al., eds.
  1993 'Keiner fühlt sich mehr als Mensch ...': Erlebnis und Wirkung des Ersten Weltkrieges.
     Essen: Klartext Verlag.
Hüppauf, Bernd., ed.
  1985 Ansichten vom Krieg: Vergleichende Studien zum Ersten Weltkrieg in Literatur und
     Gesellschaft. Königstein: Forum Academicum
Hütt, Michael, et al., eds.
  1990 Unglücklich das Land, das Helden nötig hat: Leiden und Sterben in den
     Kriegsdenkmälern des Ersten und Zweiten Weltkrieges. Marburg: Jonas Verlag.
Kirsten, Erich, et al.
  1965 Bevölkerung und Raum in Neuerer und Neuester Zeit, 3d ed. Würzburg: Plötz
     Verlag.
Knoch, Peter, ed.
  1989 Kriegsalltag. Stuttgart: Klett Verlag.
Koselleck, Reinhard
  1979 Kriegerdenkmale als Identitätsstiftung der Überlebenden. In Identität. Otto Marquard
     and Karl-Heinz Stierle, eds., pp. 255–76. München: Wilhelm Fink Verlag.
Koselleck, Reinhard, and Michael Jeismann, eds.
  1994 Der politische Totenkult: Kriegerdenkmäler in der Moderne, München: Wilhelm Fink
     Verlag.
Kundrus, Birthe
  1995 Familienpolitik und Geschlechterverhältnisse im Ersten und Zweiten Weltkrieg.
     Hamburg: Christians.
Leed, Eric
  1979 No Man's Land: Combat and Identity in World War I. New York: Cambrige University
     Press.
Linden, Marcel van der, and Gottfried Mergner, eds.
  1991 Kriegsbegeisterung und mentale Kriegsvorbereitung. Interdisziplinäre Studien. Berlin:
     Duncker & Humblot.
Lurz, Meinolf
  1985–7 Kriegerdenkmäler in Deutschland. 6 vols. Heidelberg: Esprint Verlag.
Lütgemeier-Davin, Reinhold
  1981 Basismobilisierung gegen den Krieg: Die Nie-Wider-Krieg-Bewegung in der Weimarer
     Republik. In Pazifismus in der Weimarer Republik, Karl Holl and Wolfram Wette, eds.
     pp.47–76. Paderborn: Schönigh Verlag.
Mosse, George L.
  1979 National Cemetries and National Revival: The Cult of Fallen Soldiers in Germany.
     Journal of Contemporory History 14:1–20.
  1988 Nationalism and Sexuality. Madison: University of Wisconsin Press.
  1990 Fallen Soldiers: Reshaping the Memory of the World. New York: Oxford University
     Press.
Müller, Hans-Harald
  1986 Der Krieg und die Schriftsteller: Der Kriegsroman der Weimarer Republik. Stuttgart:
     Metzler Verlag.

Nipperdey, Thomas
1968 Nationalidee und Nationaldenkmal in Deutschland im 19. Jahrhundert. Historische
Zeitschrift 206:529–85.
Petersen, Thomas-Peter
n.d. Die Geschichte des Volkstrauertages. Kassel:Volksbund Deutsche Kriegsgräberfürsorge
E.V.
Prost, Antoine
1977 Les anciennes combattants et la société française, 1914–1939, 3 vols. Paris: Presse de la
Fondation des Sciences Politiques.
Riesenberger, Dieter
1985 Geschichte der Friedensbewegung in Deutschland: Von den Anfängen bis 1933.
Göttingen: Vandenhoeck & Ruprecht.
Saul, Klaus
1969 Der 'Deutsche Kriegerbund': Zur innenpolitischen Funktion eines 'nationalen'
Verbandes im Kaiserlichen Deutschland. Militärgeschichtliche Mitteilungen
2:95–159.
Schellack, Fritz
1990 Nationalfeiertage in Deutschland von 1871 bis 1945, Frankfurt, Main: Lang Verlag.
Schneider, Gerhard
1991 '... nicht umsonst gefallen?' Kriegerdenkmäler und Kriegstotenkult in Hannover.
Special issue of Hannoversche Geschichtsblätter. Hannover.
Siemann, Wolfram
1988 Krieg und Frieden in historischen Gedenkfeiern des Jahres
1913 In Öffentliche Festkultur: Politische Feste in Deutschland von der Aufklärung bis
zum Ersten Weltkrieg, Dieter Düding et al., eds. pp.298–320. Reinbek: Rowohlt
Verlag.
Soltau, Hans
1982 Volksbund Deutsche Kriegsgräberfürsorge: Sein Werden und Wirken. 3d ed. Kassel.
Thébaud, Françoise
1992 La grande guerre: Le triomphe de la division sexuelle. In Histoire des femmes: Le XXe
siècle, Georges Duby and Michelle Perrot, eds. pp.31–74. Paris: Plon.
Theweleit, Klaus
1987–9 Male Fantasies. 2 vols. Minneapolis: University of Minnesota Press
Trox, Eckhard
1990 Militärischer Konservatismus: Kriegervereine und Militärpartei in Preußen zwischen
1815 und 1848/49. Stuttgart: Steiner Verlag.
Vondung, Klaus, ed.
1980 Kriegserlebnis: Der Erste Weltkrieg in der literarischen Gestaltung und symbolischen
Deutung der Nation, Göttingen: Vandenhoeck & Ruprecht.
Wall, Richard and Jay M. Winter, eds.
1988 The Upheaval of War: Family, Work and Welfare in Europe, 1914–1918, Cambridge:
Cambridge University Press.
Whalen, R.W.
1984 Bitter Wounds: German Victims of the Great War, 1914–1939. London: Cornell
University Press.
Winter, Jay M.
1988 The Experience of World War I, London: MacMillan.

Wittram, Reinhold
   1949 Nationalismus und Säkularisation: Beiträge zur Geschichte und Problematik des
         Nationalgeistes, Lüneburg.
Wohl, Robert
   1979 The Generation of 1914. Cambridge: Harvard University Press.
Zimmer, Hasko
   1971 Auf dem Altar des Vaterlandes: Religion und Patriotismus in der deutschen Kriegslyrik
         des 19. Jahrhunderts. Frankfurt, Main: Thesen Verlag.

PART II:
SILENCES AND COMMEMORATIONS

Histories of Mourning: Flowers and Stones for the War Dead, Confusion for the Living – Vignettes from East and West Germany

ALF LÜDTKE

On 27 January 1993 the German federal government decided to set up in Berlin a national memorial to 'those killed through war and violence' during the Second World War.[1] The choice of site clearly referred back to a previous memorial, the 'new guard house' (Neue Wache) in the centre of the nation's capital, Berlin. This modest classicist building of the 1830s[2] had been dedicated to a similar purpose in 1931. At that time, more than ten years after the end of the First World War, the Prussian state government had proposed erecting a memorial and called for a public debate on its proper form. The most unheroic and unsentimental plan was chosen. The architect Tessenow's design avoided any reference to 'grand' historical or political meanings of death in war. Subsequently, the Nazi government transformed the Neue Wache into a shrine celebrating the 'undefeated heros' of the Second World War whom the Nazi movement claimed as their own immediate ancestors. In 1945 the Soviet administration closed the hall but prevented its destruction by East German authorities. And in the 1950s the East German government no longer ignored the symbolic capital invested in the site. It was here that the German Democratic Republic presented a symbol of its claim to be the 'better part' of German

---

Author's note: The notes contain that dimension of the story which is rendered by the archival material. They provide a parallel text and appear therefore as footnotes to make them available during the reading without turning pages.

1 On 13 November 1993, the annual Day of National Mourning, Chancellor Kohl dedicated the memorial, although this project of his had encountered harsh criticism; see the *New York Times* of 15 November and also below.
2 Its classic Greek-temple style is owing to the architect, Friedrich Schinkel, who in the 1820s and 1830s reshaped the appearance of central sites of downtown Berlin with his buildings of Empire-style and 'classicist' design.

history, linking that past with the glorious present and the promised future of socialism. The Neue Wache was turned into the state's central memorial 'To the victims of militarism and fascism.'[3]

In the democratic period of the late 1920s, public discussion of the issue of how to commemorate the dead had been intense, and official figures participated. But in 1993, in another democratic age of German history, the federal government kept its decision secret. It was not until the committee of finances of the Federal Parliament became involved that public interest was aroused. Politicians from the opposition informed the press about the importance of the issue. A furious outcry was the first response of the media, and this reaction has not yet diminished. One of the most prominent critics of the plan, the historian Reinhart Koselleck, noted sarcastically that 'our society not only *feels* patronized: it truly *is* patronized.'[4]

It is not the site so much as the chosen icon and intended symbolism that have aroused debate. The government's proposal revolves around the notion of 'victims.' To this end, one of the most intimate and private works of Käthe Kollwitz, showing an aged mother cradling her dead son, was to be enlarged from one foot high in the original to three feet high – turned into 'the' public *pietà*. Even more vigorous protests have been stirred by the inscription. It reads 'To the victims of war and violence.'[5] Critics point out that this text erases the fundamental difference between (overwhelmingly German) perpetrators and their accomplices and those people and peoples throughout Europe whom they made victims of destruction, genocide, and murder. German soldiers and civilians suffered and were killed too; but with a few exceptions, these people acted in support of the war effort. The critics hold that in the public arena these

---

3 The reconstruction started in 1951 but was not completed until 1957; the inscription was added three years later; see Dieckmann 1993.

4 Koselleck 1993; this article reviews the issue and puts particular emphasis on the view of the opponents to the government's decision. Koselleck has triggered historical research on commemorations of war dead and, in particular, on the differences in national 'styles' for the design of memorials. He suggests increasing 'democratization' of commemoration: less and less the individual hero and rather the dead 'everybody' is commemorated; see his piece of 1979. On the controversy about the Neue Wache, see also Stölzl 1993; Akademie der Künste Berlin 1993; Buchten and Frey 1993; Hoss 1994.

    Of course, commemoration of the war and the Holocaust is cutting across national boundaries; see Young 1993; Friedlander 1992.

5 In German the term that is rendered here as 'violence' is *Gewaltherrschaft;* it explicitly refers to brute force but connects the latter with *Herrschaft,* thereby invoking legitimacy. In other words, the German term *Gewaltherrschaft* euphemizes the range and fury of extermination that it meant to the victims.

victims cannot be put on an equal footing with the targets of the German machinery of war and destructions.

This debate mirrors both the long-standing silences and the well-established politics of mourning in the two German states from 1945–9 to 1989. In this paper I will try to uncover some of their layers and show how they are, in contradictory ways, interconnected. My essay cannot, however, present a coherent picture. Rather than claiming to tell a consistent story, my attempt is to represent the fractured reality of private and public claims and practices in a series of 'vignettes.' Hereby I will follow a meandering path into this landscape of mourning and commemorating, of remembering and forgetting.

The first site, the cemetery at Halbe, reflects official attitudes in former East Germany as to both the necessities and the limits of commemorating dead German soldiers of the Second World War. From this vantage point I depict individuals who care for flowers and graveyards differently, or, as it were, the memory of the dead. In addition, I refer to ways of coping with official and individual claims on the dead in what was then West Germany. At the centre of this piece are, however, the practices in and by which individuals appropriate sites and rites of mourning.

I

It was a sunny day in April 1989. The place was the small country town of Halbe in East Germany. Together with a colleague from the East German Academy of Sciences, I concluded a field trip to graves and memorials for war dead. This trip was very different from ethnographic research as it had become common in western Europe: I had had to apply months in advance to the East German bureaucracy. I made use of a new treaty on mutual academic research programs between the two Germanies. Under this umbrella it seemed possible to ask my East German partners to get a clearance for travelling and visiting cemeteries. But even that meant venturing into new terrain. For until the late 1980s West Germans were denied any social (and ethnographic) research in East Germany. But even after I had received my visa, I was not sure whether it included permission to visit those graves and memorials. Even so, upon arrival in East Berlin I was informed that the approval had been granted. Moreover, colleagues from East Berlin had already prepared a detailed route. During the next three days we managed to see all of the proposed sites except for the largest cemetery of German soldiers in East Germany, the one located at Halbe.

We had difficulty finding this cemetery. At the entrance to the village, fifty kilometres south east of Berlin, we found only a very small sign pointing to the 'Central Cemetery.' When we had asked people for directions, they had given us rather vague instructions which, at least in one case, led directly to the gate of a military training area of the East German army and the Red Army. However, when we turned around, we realized that the training area for today's soldiers was directly adjacent to the cemetery for the dead soldiers of 1945.

The cemetery covered several acres and stretched under the firs of that part of the forest which was designated as a cemetery. Long rows of greyish sandstone markers, each about thirty centimetres square demarcated the place where about 22,000 bodies had been (re)buried. The victims had been killed between 22 and 30 April 1945, in the last days of the war. The Soviet armies were about to encircle Berlin, while south of the German capital (beyond Hitler's refuge) dispersed German units continued to resist. These units were crushed by the Soviet troops, and an unknown number of soldiers and fleeing civilians were killed during the fighting.

On some of the stones we could read the names and sometimes the dates of birth and death. A number of those who had died were fifteen or sixteen years of age; others were in their seventies or eighties. On some of the stones that had names we found flowers, and when we walked a little way up the hill we reached a sandstone stela about four metres high. The inscription at the base reads,' 'The dead exhort us to live for peace.'[6]

A little further down we encountered a group of four women: the workers who cared for the place. Their task was to clear the leaves and pine needles from the cemetery and to weed around the stones. They pointed out how tiresome this labour was: 'You are always on your knees. You have to bend down all the time. Your hands get dirty. Your nails get damaged.' The pay was obviously low, but at least as important: for over a year 'the man' who had previously been in charge of the group had not been replaced (the former foreman had been given his pension). In a matter-of-fact way the women mentioned that his wage (which apparently was more than theirs) was not distributed among them or given to the person who acted as his deputy. Instead, they were furious that they had to carry heavy loads and to do other chores which clearly 'the man' had taken care of before.

I asked when the cemetery had been established. The answer was somewhat vague, not dissimilar to the one that we later received from the mayor: 'around

---

6 The stela was erected in 1960. The local pastor, Ernst Teichmann, however, requested that a wooden cross also be put up. When the prominent pastor and president of one of the West German churches, Martin Niemöller, visited Halbe in July 1961, Teichmann used the opportunity to elicit his support for the request. But in October the same year the 'council of district' decided that there was 'no need' for a cross, especially since a monument already existed in the cemetery. See letters of 12 October and 11 November 1961, in *Kreisarchiv Königs Wusterhausen*, No. 517; see also Pietsch, Potratz and Stark 1995.

1950.' Yes, pastors of the area and the local church had taken the initiative.[7]
They had started to organize the digging up and transporting of the remains to
this site. At Halbe most of the bodies, the overwhelming majority of whom
were unidentified, had been reburied in common and mass graves. To these
women it was proper and 'natural' that in due course the state and the community had taken over.

However, the women did not conceal their mixed feelings about recent
interventions by the community in general and the local mayor in particular.
The mayor, who had taken office only a year before, had issued new regulations for the cemetery. The major issue, at least for these women, was that
from then on nobody was allowed to put flowers on a single stone anywhere in
the cemetery. All flowers and wreaths had to be presented at one central point,
the stela. The women were furious: 'How can you dare to forbid people to put
flowers on the graves of their own beloved?' one almost shouted, and the
others nodded approvingly. Of course, we asked why the mayor had given this
order or, at least what he had given as justification. 'He told us that everybody

---

7 In fact, it had been one person, a Protestant pastor, who considered the proper burial of the
remains of the dead from the battle of Halbe his personal 'calling.' Ernst Teichmann had been
a soldier during the war. After the war he several times spent his vacations at Halbe; in 1948
or 1949 he requested to be transferred from his home church, the 'state church'
(*Landeskirche*) of Sachsen-Anhalt, and the parish at the village of Schierke to the state church
of Berlin-Brandenburg and its parish of Halbe (interview with his widow on 11 September
1992). The church of this small town had been abandoned in the nineteenth century; since
then Halbe had belonged to the parish of Märkisch Buchholz, a village about three kilometres
away. Teichmann, however, lobbied successfully for Halbe to be made a parish of its own
and for him to be appointed the local pastor. The church of Halbe was consecrated anew on
12 April 1953.
   On 5 April 1950 the bishop of the Protestant church of Berlin-Brandenburg, Otto Dibelius,
had approached the Ministry of the Interior of the state of Brandenburg to demand the
foundation of a 'central cemetery' at Halbe. In this letter the bishop referred to the 'consent'
of the Soviet military administration to the churches' responsibility for soldiers' graves in the
eastern zone (since 1949 the churches in the Soviet zone had established a special branch for
the 'care for war graves'; see Gemeinsames Archiv Bund – EKU – VELK [GA], Best. 1, No.
8275, 12 Dezember 1960). Dibelius indicated that the church wanted to take care of the
whole operation; intended was a 'most simple last resting place without regard to the
confession or nationality of the dead.' The bishop underlined that 'the public, the press, and
the people around' should be kept out and that the church asked for support as to the
workforce and means of transportation (GA, Best. 70, No. 61, fol 1–4).
   More than a year later Propst Grüber, who then was in charge of relations between
Protestant churches and the government of East Germany (the government having been
established in October 1949) urgently wrote to the prime minister of the state of Brandenburg
on the same issue. Obviously the digging up and transport of remains had begun. Grüber
stated, however, that it was 'undertaken in an irreverent manner'; in addition, nobody would
care for the identification of the dead. In order to convey all the information available to their

should be treated equally. All the deceased had suffered more or less equally, so they should be treated equally now.' But one of the women added, 'Well, we just don't obey this order. Or can you remove flowers from the place where someone feels he is closest to his beloved?'

As we approached the stela, we had seen at its base several flowers and wreaths with ribbons bearing inscriptions. The names of local schools and factories were printed on them. When we mentioned these wreaths to the women who worked in the cemetery, they told us that associations from the area, such as sports clubs, school classes, and 'work brigades,' came and brought flowers. Clearly these people did not restrict their activity to particular dates, but showed up all through the year. West Germans would visit on the

---

relatives, he demanded that as much attention as possible be paid to this task. In his last sentence he also directly hinted at public and political implications: the Western press 'takes our efforts under harrassing fire' (GA, Best. 70 No. 61, fol 5f).

In his response of 11 December 1951 the prime minister of Brandenburg, R. Jahn, denied these accusations of irreverence and disinterest in the identification of the dead. Axes and hoes had to be used because many remains were found under horse cadavers or among tree roots. He also pointed out that contrary to previous estimates of the church, there were neither 60–70,000 nor 10–15,000 dead. 'Up to now the remains of about 5,000 have been collected and reburied.' And 'several hundred may still be found, but that completes the number'; he thereby indicated that the efforts would soon be stopped (GA, Best. 70, No. 61, fol 16f). Teichmann wrote directly to Jahn in January of 1952 a single-spaced four-page letter arguing intensely for the necessity of pursuing the task (GA, Best. 70 No. 61, fol 19–22).

In April 1953 a representative of the central board of the German Protestant churches (EKD) and its *Berliner Stelle* visited the 'war cemetery' and noted the 'slightly deplorable appearance of the cemetery with the clay plaques on top of the graves; however, the installation can be developed' (GA, Best. 1, No. 827, Bd. I, 21. 4. 1953). In the late 1950s the state took over responsibility. The clay plaques were then replaced by small sandstone markers.

Bishop Dibelius, then the head of the church of Berlin-Brandenburg, including both West and East Berlin and the state of Brandenburg, was an outspoken and rigorous if not stubborn critic of 'the Communists.' While he lived in West Berlin, Propst Grüber lived in the east. In a letter to Dibelius of 26 October 1955 he rather resignedly pointed out that 'most people [who complain about the Soviets and their refusal to allow any search for the graves or remains of German soldiers in the USSR] do not accept that they did the Russian people injustice in following the orders of the German leaders.' In Grüber's view also, the theological aspect should be considered, because the prevalent invocations of the Germans' 'sin before God' would simplify the issue and make it less burdensome to most people than 'to feel guilty for other people and peoples.' He added that 'it is unjust to try to compensate for guilt with [one's own] suffering' (GA, Best. 70, No. 134). On developments since the mid-1950s, especially the unofficial ties that the East German churches had established with the West German semi-official institution designed to take care of graves and cemeteries of (German) war dead, the Volksbund Deutsche Kriegsgräberfürsorge, see Reuth 1992.

World Day of Peace, the first Sunday in September. Then an official delegation laid a wreath.[8]

Only very few of those who suffered in the battle of Halbe in 1945 were local people. Most of the soldiers belonged to scattered units who, one might say, came from everywhere and nowhere. Among them, to be sure, were reserve units who were more or less from the area, the so-called Volkssturm units. But there were also large numbers of refugees who were on the road from the eastern provinces and were fleeing the Red Army. If local people nowadays visit the graves of those who were killed in April 1945, they can be pretty certain that those who are 'unknown' are, to a large extent, not from 'their' area.

II

The scene was the mayor's office at Halbe, after my colleague and I had visited the cemetery. Both of us had simply shown up, without any appointment, at the door of his tiny room. I introduced myself as a historian from West Germany who was writing a study on war memorials, and I asked for an interview.

Though we had not told the mayor that we were coming, he was surprisingly accessible. He answered our questions without hesitation: the cemetery had been established in the 'early 1950s' and would contain about 22,000 bodies of German soldiers and civilians. The majority of the bodies had been collected from the surrounding forests and villages and placed in common graves. However, if particular individuals had been able to trace their relatives or if someone had answered the calls of the research unit of the International Committee of the Red Cross, the administration had put up a plaque giving the name and date of the respective person on an individual tombstone. The mayor concluded his statement by emphasizing that, in his view, the East German state – 'my state' – had 'solved' the problem of commemorating the deceased

---

8   The East German authorities granted permission to visit the cemetery only to a very limited number of people from the west during the 1950s and 1960s. At the same time, Teichmann continually approached the mayor and council of Halbe, the authorities of the county and the district, and also the central authorities. He strongly advocated a more open or 'humane' attitude towards applications from, in particular, West Germans to visit the cemetery. At the same time, he also tried to call attention to the grief of East Germans who were not allowed to visit close relatives who lived in the west, in particular, their parents before their death; see *Kreisarchiv Königs Wusterhausen,* no. 504 and 517. At my visit in September 1990, that is, after the opening of the Wall, one of my informants, Frau Kühn, mentioned explicitly that the Stasi (shorthand for Ministerium für Staatssicherheit, the East German internal and external spy network) cut off the streamers of the West German wreaths after only a few days. Rumours were that anonymous people did this, but Frau Kühn was sure that it was the Stasi.

soldiers of the 'Hitler army': 'In Berlin we have erected a central memorial. It is dedicated to all victims of fascism and militarism.'[9]

I asked whether he, the mayor, was sure that all the soldiers who died could be subsumed under the inscription on the central memorial in Berlin, which read: 'To the victims of fascism and militarism.' Did he mean that the soldiers who had perpetrated fascism – or contributed to sustaining its regime – should also to be considered 'victims'? The mayor gave me a strange look but did not reply. Instead, he said that on every Totensonntag (Memorial Sunday) the West German ambassador appears and presents an official wreath from the Federal Republic.

III

The East Berlin 'memorial to the victims of fascism and militarism' was located in the centre of the city, in a modest but distinguished building on Unter den Linden. This boulevard has been one of the most prominent loci of the conspicuous display of state power in the Prusso-German capital since the days of Frederick II and his troops in the later eighteenth century. The building that housed the memorial resonated with the military character of Prussian statehood. Until 1945 this 'new guardhouse' had once a week seen a military display: the changing of the guard.

After having been shut down by the Soviet authorities in 1945, the building had remained vacant for several years. However, in the mid-1950s the East German authorities used the site to enshrine its reading of recent German history. The interior was completely changed. As one entered the building, low light created an aura of solemnity. On the floor there was a permanent flame, and on the wall the inscription read: 'To the victims of fascism and militarism.' At the side several wreaths were displayed. Official ceremonies took place on the Day of Liberation 9 May and on Anti-War Day (1 September), when huge wreaths from the head of the ruling party, the Socialist Unity Party (SED), or other high-ranking officials were laid by soldiers of East Germany's Nationale Volksarmee (NVA).

A permanent militarization had been reinstituted in late 1964. In front of the six columns that dominate the street side of the building two soldiers were

---

9 Only around 1970 were the burial places of war dead from Western countries systematically registered. Before that only the graves of dead from the 'socialist countries' had been registered and were officially cared for. This was one step in the context of the GDR's preparation for membership in international organizations, especially the United Nations; in this case at stake were Red Cross conventions of 1949; see letter of Dr Dieter Krüger, Neubrandenburg, 22 October 1992.

posted to act as ceremonial guards. Passers-by, predominantly tourists, viewed the soldiers as a 'special' object for photos to take home. Every Wednesday morning at 11:30 a crowd would gather. People loved to watch the 'changing of the guard' with its Prussian-style marching order, the hammering of jack-boots, the drum-beat, and the brassy sound of military music.[10]

This spectacle was but one symptom of the strong efforts by the NVA to evoke German military traditions. The cut and colour of the NVA uniforms was scarcely distinguishable from those of the Hitler Deutsche Wehrmacht, which in turn were almost identical to the 'Feldgrau,' which had been introduced in 1914. 'German' were the badges of rank, as was the goose-step at parades. The forms of representation did not break with, but pursued, the distinctive tradition of the German military. The implicit appeal of 'Germans don't shoot Germans' referred, strangely enough, to symbols of that military formation which had been the backbone of Nazi warfare and Nazi dominations.

In order to distance their efforts from such allusions, the East German authorities claimed the NVA would draw upon the 'best aspects' of 'our national military heritage' and refer to 'truly patriotic' features of German military history.[11] Pivotal to this account was the Prusso-Russian alliance against Napoleon in 1812. Invoking the 'hard core' of reactionary Prussianism might, however, legitimize anti-Western political alignments. Thus other references had to balance the presumed dangers of this specific allusion. Fitting was the other prominent thread of the web of military 'heritage' (a term employed purposefully) spun from the lore about proletarian soldiering. Accordingly, models should be, first, the revolutionary sailors of November 1918 and sec-

---

10 In fall of 1963 the (East) Berlin daily *Berliner Zeitung* had carried letters calling for a more conspicuous military display, that is, the changing of the guard, at this site; see Lücke 1990.

11 On the justification for these uniforms, their colour, and their badges, see the elaborate reference to the 'history of the armed forces of our people' given in an unsigned text, presumably of a speech dating from early 1956, in the papers of the then prime minister of the GDR, Otto Grotewohl, in Stiftung Archiv der Parteien und Massenorganisationen der DDR im Bundesarchiv (SAPMO), NL 90/449, fol. 136ff. The author emphasized the fundamental difference between a 'people's army' as designed in the GDR and what had been started in West Germany: 'an army of mercenaries.' On this issue, see earlier Walter Ulbricht, the first secretary of the SED, in his speech at the 2d party conference, 9 July 1952, in Herausgeberkollektiv 1989: 117. Weeks before, Fred Oelssner, a leading party functionary, had started a re-evaluation of the Prussian and German military; on this and the lines of propaganda until the early 1960s, see Azaryahu 1991:135ff. The 'positive' recognition of the uniform of the NVA by citizens is reported in one of the regular trade union *Informationsberichte* compiled from local and regional reports: SAPMO, FDGB-Buvo A 2672, *Informationsbericht,* no. 6, 10 February 1956, p.5. On the development since the 1960s, see the account of an ex-officer of the NVA, Hanisch 1992:255–68.

ond, the German members of the International Brigades in republican Spain from 1936 to 1939. To be sure, at the same time the NVA rigorously enforced disciplinary standards that followed closely the code of order and unlimited obedience practised in the Prusso-German armies since the eighteenth century. In other words, the public (re)presentation of the NVA directly reflected its obsession with upholding a seemingly untainted military 'tradition.'

IV

For the West German visitor, the appearance of the East German soldiers underlined both differences and similarities between the two German armies. In the Federal Republic, the military had been re-established in November 1955, although preparations dated back to 1950 – to the years of the intensifying Cold War and its becoming 'hot' in Korea. In turn, the East German version of history stressed that East Germany had acted out of self-defence when it drew up an army two months later, on 18 January 1956.[12] In the west the political and military leaders claimed to have broken away from German military traditions altogether.[13] Here a small core of advisers pressed hard for a more 'civilian tone' inside the barracks. But did drafted soldiers and, more important, NCOs and officers really abandon the military's traditional preference for viewing society, polity, and history in terms of 'fighting'? While the social and political attitudes of the troops remained difficult to assess, there

---

12 This was the very date of the proclamation of the German empire at Versailles in 1871. The first West German soldiers had been sworn in on 11 November 1955, the birthday of Scharnhorst, one of the leading Prussian generals of the anti-Napoleonic rebuilding of the Prussian army and the wars of liberation in 1807–14 (Scharnhorst remained a historic figure whom not only the West Germans claimed: the most distinguished military decoration of East Germany became the Order of Scharnhorst). In fact, in East Germany paramilitary units (Hauptverwaltung Ausbildung) had been established in 1946–7. In West Germany similar efforts at the federal level were completed in the fall of 1950, in the wake of the war in Korea.

13 In 1945 the four Allied powers considered Prusso-German 'militarism' as one of the most decisive features of German society for the breeding of fascism. Accordingly, the destruction of militarism was at the heart of their re-education efforts. When, in the course of the Korean War, the Western allies unanimously decided to reconstruct a (West) German military, a number of German officials strove very hard for an army with a distinctively 'new' structure and outlook. As a guideline of this new 'federal army' these officials, most of them having been officers before 1945, proposed the 'citizen in uniform.' Accordingly, the principle of *Innere Führung* emphasized 'civilian' conduct also within the military. The proponents of this line wanted to rule out unconditional obedience. Instead, subordinates should follow their leaders by consent and conviction; see Meyer 1993; see also Abenheim 1988 and Bald 1994, chaps. 2 and 3.

was no doubt that appearances had changed. The goose-step was banned from the very beginning, and the uniforms look purposefully 'non-German.' American designs had impressed the tailors – or at least they had influenced those officials who decided on uniforms. Above all, a new colour was introduced, stirring much comment in the papers and at parties during the mid-1950s. Resemblance to the previous army was minimized by removing any green; thus slate grey became the hallmark of the reformed, 'democratic' army in West Germany.

Over the years the uniforms of the West German army were reshaped: the (short) 'Eisenhower jacket' was abandoned; in addition, badges and decorations were changed or added, bringing them back to the ones in use previous to 1945 or 1933. The colour of the uniforms was changed too, but the combination of light and dark grey that was introduced in the 1960s is even more different from pre-1945 colours than those of 1955. In general, however, the West German military kept a very low profile in public. At state ceremonies, officers and troops remained on the margins. Even more striking was the break with tradition regarding the dress of soldiers off duty. In the west civilian clothes were allowed, and the vast majority preferred these (especially those who had been drafted).

The rituals and colours of the East and West German armies displayed difference. However, by demonstratively referring to difference, these non-verbal symbols of western and eastern armed statehood constantly invoked the non-present other. Observing one of them necessarily would remind the observer of the 'other' dimension of the German military legacy.

V

In April 1989 I was a visitor from West Germany. My views on commemorating the soldiers of the Deutsche Wehrmacht related to West German experiences: since 1945 West German state and municipal authorities alike claimed that those who had in fact sustained the Nazi regime should be regarded as among its true victims. According to this view, the overwhelming majority of German soldiers had only been obeying orders, even if they had fought until the 'very last shot' was fired (and even later). But this equating of soldiers and victims of German warfare and genocide was increasingly contested. It was the so-called 'celebration of reconciliation' at Bitburg cemetery in April 1985 that triggered public criticism of the constant neglect of the difference between accomplices (or perpetrators) and victims. At Bitburg the West German chancellor, Helmut Kohl, and the U.S. president, Ronald Reagan, jointly commemorated Allied and German soldiers at a cemetery where members of the

Waffen-SS were also buried. Kohl had proposed and agitated for this demonstrative act. Reagan, obviously in order to calm public criticism in both countries, expanded his program and paid tribute to the victims of the Holocaust by visiting the memorial and the site of the concentration camp at Bergen-Belsen before going to Bitburg.[14]

In the wake of the bitter controversy over Bitburg, an undercurrent of political debate that had been silenced in the established media and by politicians gained momentum. However, at the *Stammtische*, in pubs, voices about a seemingly 'never-ending penance' of Germany and 'the Germans' had never been mute. Now such views were aired with increasing vigour; even more important, such attitudes were reflected in statements by politicians. It was in this context that in 1986 even professional historians questioned the 'singularity' of the Holocaust. The philosopher Jürgen Habermas sharply denounced such revisionism.[15] His intervention triggered a furious debate which also involved the role of the German army.[16] Finally, at least one of the ministers of the federal government, Norbert Blüm, conceded during that debate: 'As long as the eastern front did not crack, the SS could continue its murderous task at Auschwitz.'

The Bitburg incident revealed to the international public what had been commonplace in West Germany since the early 1950s: each year Volkstrauertag (Day of National Mourning) has been celebrated in public.[17] At the national

---

14 See the collection of documents and essays in Hartman 1986.

15 See the comprehensive discussion by Geoff Eley (1988); on Habermas's role, see 178ff.

16 Hillgruber 1986; according to Hillgruber, historians would have 'to identify themselves with the fate of the German civilian population in the east and with the desparate and self-sacrificing struggles of the German armies at the eastern front' in order 'to understand the end of fascism' (24–5).

17 Bitburg, however, occurred at a different season; Volkstrauertag is always the first Sunday of November. This date had been chosen in 1952 in a determined move to distance the renewal of this day from the Nazis 'Heroes' Memorial Day which had been celebrated on the second Sunday of March (the same day in March had already been designated the Day of National Mourning in the Weimar Republic. See the meticulous case study on the various commemorations and their changes from the early nineteenth century to the 1960s in the city of Hanover by Gerhard Schneider (1991); on the reinvention of Volkstrauertag and the official (re)inauguration in 1952, see 310ff; the (unsuccessful) efforts of anti-fascist groups to establish an official day to commemorate the victims of fascism are described on 284ff. After the opening of the Wall, old and neo-Nazi groups of East and West Germany tried to 'seize' the occasion: at the Volkstrauertag of 1989 26 November, only two weeks after 9 November, when 'the Wall came down,' several hundred hard-core (neo-)Nazis gathered at the Halbe cemetery. On an even larger scale they staged their 'heroes' day' at this site in 1990 and 1991. The following year, however, the state authorities successfully banned any public gathering at Halbe.

level the commemoration takes place at a special session of the Federal Parliament. At the same time, however, local authorities organize similar events at hundreds of local war memorials. The celebrations regularly include a speech by a community spokesman and the placing of wreaths; in most cases the scenario is completed by a small unit of the Bundeswehr, the federal army. The line has not changed over the years: the dead soldiers are presented as the principal (if not sole) victims of Nazi terror. Whether they were volunteers or draftees, they just fulfilled their duties in the army. Had these poor fellows not paid 'their price' to the 'brown terror' regime? To be sure, the audiences have become smaller over the years. Mostly, it is family members who gather; but representatives of local associations and parties often participate as well.

The Bitburg incident underlined something else: in West Germany there is no 'central' memorial to those who were the true victims of Nazism. There is no memorial either to the Holocaust or to the hundreds of thousands of individuals who were tortured and killed by German fascism and fascists. It was not until 1985–6 that small groups in Berlin started to demand immediate action by politicians. These were mostly liberal and leftist intellectuals who drew attention to the embarrassing fact that there was no central German memorial to the Jewish victims;[18] they called for a Holocaust memorial. In fact, these people reacted to construction plans for the Prinz-Albrecht-Strasse (then

---

18 At the same time, in the summer of 1985, members of the Jewish community of Frankfurt am Main started to protest publicly against the plans of the Frankfurt theatre to perform a play by Rainer W. Fassbinder, the author and film director. The protesters claimed that Fassbinder in his play *Der Müll, die Stadt und der Tod* dwelt on the same anti-Semitic prejudices, especially the stereotype of the 'scrupulous Jewish capitalist,' that the Nazis had used. The dispute that followed revolved mostly around the issue of freedom of speech and of the arts. The protest included direct action: protesters several times occupied the stage and blocked rehearsals. After several weeks the theatre withdrew the play.

It was certainly not accidental that in the following year intellectuals and 'left' political activists from Frankfurt started to rally for the preservation of remnants of the Jewish ghetto in the city. During construction work on a central public administration building, these remains had been uncovered again (they had been determinedly buried under a main traffic throughway in 1954, in the context of the first reconstruction of the bombed city after 1945). Finally, and after the site had been occupied by protesters in August 1987, the city council decided to incorporate the remnants into the administration building by using glass for those walls that would 'face' the remains. Thus the building was still erected on top of the former ghetto; this past of the city was, however, now replaced by a museum-like display. Ironically enough, the windows that should offer a view on the remnants were built too high above the ground: even standing on tiptoe did not allow people to have a look; see *Frankfurter Rundschau*, 11 September 1990, p.11. Meanwhile this situation has been changed; see Bartetzko 1992.

close to the Wall): this was the site of the former Gestapo headquarters.[19] For the left and liberal intellectuals, the very spot where the perpetrators had administered their killing plans called for both a demonstrative gesture and a permanent sign of remembrance.

In contrast to the total absence of 'central' memorials, local memorials were to be found in almost every village and town in West Germany. Take the example of Göttingen, a medium-sized university town in central Germany.[20] As in most other German towns and villages, there is a memorial that commemorates the 'glorious warriors' of the war against France in 1870–1. In the 1950s, however, its huge stone eagle was removed and put in the yard of the city's building department. Interestingly enough, it was reinstalled in the late 1980s. However, its place was no longer in the public arena but physically sealed off from criticism or attacks by graffiti sprayers: the local authorities had accepted an invitation from the local military and put the eagle inside the military precinct of the Göttingen barracks.[21] Another memorial in Göttingen featured the imperial eagle striking down some disloyal subjects (it was intended to recall the slaughter of the native Herreros in 1904 in South-West Africa, then a German colony). To the outrage of many respectable citizens, this iron bird was stolen in 1978. Accusations aired in the papers and local rumours held students of the 'radical left' responsible. Since then the pedestal has remained empty.[22]

---

19 In November 1989 a private initiative inspired by the proposal of a television producer, Lea Rosh from Berlin, started to call for support of a German Holocaust memorial that would be erected at or close to the former Gestapo headquarters at Prinz-Albrecht-Strasse. In April 1992 the federal government and the Berlin state government gave their consent and provided part of the cost (including the land). The proposal to build a place to commemorate the millions of individual Jews who had been murdered led also to a rather bitter debate as to whether it would deliberately exclude gypsies (and should be changed in order to include other victims). The core group supporting the Holocaust memorial initiative insisted on its aim to offer a site for memorializing the murdered Jews; on the fissures and agonies of this debate, see Ross 1992, Kraft 1992, and Endlich 1992.

   Not in organizational terms but substantially related to the project of a national Holocaust memorial is the plan for a Berlin Jewish museum; a competition for an architect was decided in June 1989, and after extended delays, construction according to a plan by Daniel Libeskind started in 1992. The commemoration of the 1938 pogrom stimulated many activities, among them private and state agencies of Berlin that invited artists to propose memorials for two local sites of the Holocaust in Berlin; see Gedenken und Denkmal 1988.

20 Gottschalk 1992.

21 See the anonymous newspaper article in the *Göttinger Tageblatt*, 2 July 1993, p.17.

22 In the Soviet zone of occupied Germany, the military authorities in June 1946 ordered destroyed all those inscriptions on any public monuments (including those in church cemeteries) and comparable street names which celebrated war heroism or displayed other

However, one memorial has attracted particular public attention. It is the stone erected by the association of the survivors from the infantry regiment which had its base in Göttingen. Its inscription does not celebrate previous wars but the 'fallen comrades' of 1939–45. This is the site where the bereaved and their dependents on each Volkstrauertag are invited to commemorate their beloved. The mayor is present, as are representatives of local associations and political parties and, not least, a delegation of the federal army in full ceremonial gear. Here the army's wreath is laid. Since the mid-1980s, each year some dozen people have tried to prevent the gathering, but of course police pushed them aside. These critics demand a memorial to the deserters, to those who refused to fight for the German army and, in turn, for German fascism.[23]

Inscriptions on memorials in Göttingen, as well as at other places, explicitly refer to 'violence' as the cause of death of those who are commemorated. However, this 'domination of violence' remains totally abstract and anonymous. In particular, no individual perpetrators are named or referred to. Thus these inscriptions convey a twofold message: neither the specifics of violence nor the individualities of both victims and perpetrators matter. Individuals or groups – not to mention the 'criminal organizations' such as the SS and Waffen-SS – do not figure in these inscriptions. The *shared complicity* of hundreds and thousands of Germans (and of their collaborators) remains 'out of sight' at these sites of commemoration.

'militaristic' features; also destroyed should be the monuments themselves if their design showed such characteristics. On the Soviet orders and the respective reports of the German local authorities, see *Landeshauptarchiv Potsdam,* Rep. 230 Oberlandratsamt Cottbus, no. 66. On the emphasis of the Soviet authorities on the 'anti-fascist' struggle against 'remnants' of the old order, see Tjulpanov 1987: 165–79; Tjulpanov was then a colonel and in charge of cultural and ideological affairs in the Soviet zone.

23   This initiative was successful: on 1 September 1990 Göttingen was the first (West) German city officially to inaugurate a memorial to the deserters of the Second World War. The lord mayor of Göttingen, social democrat Arthur Levi (who had been in exile during the war), presented the granite plaque to the public. It displays by its very structure a broken swastika, and across it the artist has chiselled a cherry branch. Below that he added a quotation from the renowned author Alfred Andersch on desertion, Andersch himself having been a deserter: 'Not for fear of death but in order to live!' The conflicting opinions and fierce debate about the legitimacy of such public and even official acclamation of desertion was vividly demonstrated, however, at the very occasion of the plaque's inauguration: what appeared to have been one public ceremony was in fact two. Most of the about two dozen people who attended the occasion also observed the second part, which consisted of a short address by the sculptor and a talk by a member of the group Reserve Soldiers Resisting War Service. Sponsored by the local council of the trade unions, only this second ceremony addressed the actuality of deserting and questions about continuity or discontinuity between war service during Nazism and military service today.

VI

Most of the German soldiers who were killed during the war were buried in foreign countries. The increasing numbers of war dead who were killed in Allied air raids after 1940 were mostly civilians. However, it was not until 1945 that the land war reached its place of origin. Now it was also German soldiers who filled the burial grounds in Germany or who were buried somewhere in the fields and forests of their homeland – if their surviving comrades had time or still cared. These were the corpses of men who, despite a broad range of practices of 'getting by,' still marched and shot even when defeat was obvious, as it was in 1945.

However, the range of feelings and needs, of interests and longings, amongst the soldiers varied immensely, especially in 1945. Some had volunteered, but most had been drafted. Large numbers had been in service since the Blitzkrieg, while others had been thrown into these battles and killings on 'German soil' only weeks or even days before. Some formed 'regular' reserve units; others found themselves by January or March of 1945 in the militia (Volkssturm), mobilized as the very last reserve. Genuine adherence to Nazism had mostly vanished. It was only amongst those youngsters who had been 'called' to the 'defence of the Reich' (for many of them, this meant 'their folks') that the illusion sprang up that 'miracle' weapons and Hitler's genius would still turn the tide. Most of the soldiers who had experienced fighting, used rather distanced ways of 'getting by,' together with the desperate wish not to get killed in these last days of a war that, as far as they were concerned, was 'finished anyway.' But nonetheless, almost all of them stayed with their units, that is, with their immediate comrades.

Thus, one might say that the forging of the masses into an army was rather successful, even at the end of the war. Hundreds of thousands of men were still transformed into 'fighters,' practising military discipline. And in addition to the feeling of belonging to 'their folks,' most still seem to have felt bound by the oath they had taken, which called for personal sacrifice to Hitler. Most of them struck to this oath to the Führer; to them it comprised a personal tie to the state and simultaneously to a person who appeared time and again to be exempt from the mistakes of all the others, the generals, ministers, and Nazi leaders alike.

VII

My visit to the Halbe cemetery completed a trip of several days to explore burial places of German soldiers killed in the last weeks of the Second World

War. On the East German side two colleagues whom I had not met before, a military historian working at a regional museum and a European ethnologist from Humboldt University in East Berlin, had set up the agenda. The route led us to the areas of battle in late March and in April of 1945, in particular to the north and east of Berlin.

We started north of Berlin. Among the first sites we saw was a single grave dominating a peasant's large garden. This well-kept grave and the huge stone were quite visible from the road. The inscription read 'To the memory of our beloved son.' My guide pointed out that in March 1945 the inhabitants had found their own son among the corpses of dead soldiers lying around their house.

Further on, in a village on the west bank of the river Oder, we met a woman who cared for the graves of twenty-three soldiers killed in March 1945. That was in the period when the Soviet army was preparing to cross the river with artillery shellings and air raids on German trenches on the river's west bank before launching its final attack on Berlin. The woman told us that it was the inhabitants who had collected the corpses when they returned to their villages after the Soviets had carried out their assault in late April or early May of 1945. Among the villagers was this woman, then about twenty years old. The people in her village knew (and they had told one of my companions and guides) that she was acquainted with one of the soldiers who had been killed and 'perhaps she had fallen in love with him?' Over the years this woman had been engaged in setting up twenty-two other graves and tombstones in addition to that of this man. Since May 1945 she had put almost all her energy into creating a 'decent' cemetery out of the sandy ground.

In a small village some kilometres to the south, a medium-sized irregular block dominates the (modest) village square. Facing the street a black stone plaque has been set up; the gold letters of its inscription read 'The dead remind.' In front of the block one could see in the grass a small stone whose weather-worn inscription shows the years 1914–18, and an almost unreadable text refers to the fallen of that war. Passers-by could not explain this memorial. But an elderly woman told me that in the 1920s the bigger stone had been encircled by a number of smaller ones, all of them carrying names of dead soldiers from this village. After the Second World War the smaller stones were taken away. One of my companions had mentioned that the stone plaque had not been changed after 1945 but had simply been turned around. This woman, however, shrugged her shoulders; she never heard this story.

Another site: a tiny village close to the small town of Prenzlau, also northeast of Berlin. Just one grave lay next to the church. When we approached this place, an old woman opened the door of one of the houses nearby. She hastily came over, but relaxed when she recognized one of my two companions. Immediately she started to explain: 'Well, at this place four unknown German soldiers were buried in April 1945. I lost two sons on the eastern front during the war. And I must take care of this grave. I am pretty sure that someone has done the same for my sons in Russia.' Without pausing she turned to immediate concerns. She angrily complained, 'Young folk sit on the fence that I put up around the grave, and they throw their cigarettes on the grave and they rip off the flowers.' But some of her anger was aroused by small animals; in particular, rabbits liked the flowers. So she had added a wire fence, which made it almost impossible for the rabbits to reach the flowers.

VIII

One of my companions was working at a regional museum. But that was not the whole story: he also was a retired officer of the NVA, the East German army. During our trip he pointed time and again to the graves. 'A couple of years ago you could find helmets on top of the graves. But now most of them have gone.' These were helmets from the war days. At several places we still found some; at others these helmets had either been taken away or they had almost disappeared among the flowers or greenery that grew around them.

When we met, I asked this companion about the development of the state care for war cemeteries and single graves of German soldiers and about war memorials. According to the data that he had collected, things developed very slowly after 1945. In the first weeks the Soviet military authorities took the initiative. They ordered German people and the newly established German authorities to bury the bodies. In particular, military physicians pressed for proceeding rapidly: bodies decayed very quickly in the hot weather of those days, and so there was imminent danger of epidemic disease.

According to the retired officer, the Germans who had to do the work figured in the recollections of local people primarily as body strippers. However, in the later months of 1945 and the following year local pastors became more and more active. They took responsibility for collecting the bodies from the fields and the places where they had been buried 'on the spot.' In a forested area, a couple of kilometres north of Halbe, a woman who had then been about ten years old recalled that the local pastor had offered one mark (cash) to everybody who pointed out a burial place among the trees which had not been recognized properly. And she remembered that she and her peers took pride in caring for some of these burial sites.

When, in 1949 and 1950, the church and state authorities in this area systematically collected the bodies in order to bring them to Halbe, these children lost something that had become very special to them – 'their graves.' Here they could put up flowers and arrange them the way they wanted. Simultaneously, it was these independent activities that received applause from adults. The public sites of these graves provided both recognition and a space 'of their own' for the children.

IX

State authorities entered this field about 1947 or 1948. As Herr N. recalled, it was in the process of establishing German administrative agencies for the whole of the Soviet zone that the burial places of the war dead were registered and filed in a proper administrative fashion. He was not sure whether the Deutsche Verwaltung des Innern, the predecessor of the Ministry of the Interior, had organized a central filing system, but the middle level of the administrative hierarchy had centralized all the available information for their respective districts.

From then on nothing of note happened.[24] But around 1970 a new and final development occurred. At this time, East Germany was trying very hard to obtain international recognition and ultimately to become a member of the United Nations. According to the Fourth Protocol of the Geneva Treaties, one of the long lists of conditions that had to be fulfilled in order for it to join the UN was the proper care of war memorials and burial places of war dead.

---

24 In their emphasis on their 'anti-fascist' stance, the East German authorities cared for other cemeteries and memorials. They focused on sites where those victims of fascism were buried whom the party considered dead heroes of the labour movement, in particular, members of the Communist Party from the 1920s and 1930s. Before the foundation of the East German state, one of the leaders of the communist movement in Germany and then the co-chairman of the Socialist Unity Party, Wilhelm Pieck, began his efforts to change and rebuild the memorial and cemetery of the 'old socialists' at Friedrichsfelde (located in the eastern part of Berlin). In February 1949 he approached the lord mayor of East Berlin, Friedrich Ebert (the son of the president of the Weimar Republic) and proposed in detail changes and enlargements of the whole site. In the months to follow he time and again pressed for these changes. The site should become a memorial to the victims of terrorism against socialists and communists not only during the Nazi period but also during the Weimar Republic. At the centre should be reconstructed what the Nazis had destroyed: the graves of Rosa Luxembury and Karl Liebknecht and other victims of the slayings of January 1919 (see SAPMO, NL 36/611 fol. 57 ff). The personal involvement of Pieck reflected both the party's effort to (re)produce a heroic tradition and his personal attachment to leading figures of early communism in Germany. He had been among those who had suggested and encouraged the building of the monument to the dead of 1919 which had been completed in 1928. Here he had commemorated his comrades several times before 1933. And here he again took up this tradition in January 1951.

Consequently, the registration of graves was carried out once more or at least checked. At the same time, the state organized care for these sites at the local level. As we heard in another village, this meant that a payment of between one and two hundred marks per year was available for the person who took care of the four, six, or, for that matter, twenty-three graves in a certain village or cemetery. The money was to be used for flowers.

X

Several years before, in June 1985, I had already visited a spot close to the village of Kunersdorf, on the west bank of the river Oder about forty or fifty kilometres south of the area we toured in 1989. This was where one of the main attacks of the Red Army had been launched in April 1945. The director of a local museum nearby, who took us on a tour, referred to estimates that about 20,000 soldiers and members of the Volkssturm were killed during those days. But only about 1,500 were listed as having been buried in the local cemeteries. The director added that the owner of the adjacent Friedland estate had founded a cemetery in March 1945 at the top of a hill overlooking the Oder meadows. Here several dozen corpses were buried immediately after the fighting in April.

Yet this was the burial place of those who had been killed by artillery shells or bombs before the offensive of the Red Army started. Thus, in the fields about 18,000 bodies (or part of bodies) were not buried properly. Even now, as the museum official pointed out, one sometimes stumbled over them. Or, as the retired officer recalled during the trip of 1989, once when he set out for a walk in one of the neighbouring forests to collect some mushrooms and picked up a branch that he found on the ground, he later discovered that it was not a branch but a bone. The great difference between the presumed number of dead and the actual number of buried corpses points to people's comments and discussions when once again bones have appeared in the fields or in the woods: what happens if nobody lays the remains to proper rest?

In 1985 the museum director had talked about the memory of '45,' that is, the memory of the battles of March and April 1945, among the local villagers. According to his report, these memories revolved around a prohibition against putting up tombstones or name plaques on graves of German soldiers. In contrast, the remains of soldiers of the Red Army and its allies had been buried in common graves in the area, and each had been given a memorial. In other words, it stuck in the recollections of the local people that the new authorities had not offered a place to pay one's respects to the deceased Germans. The director said that in the early 1980s, during preparations for the celebration of forty years' 'liberation from fascism,' the local authorities of the SED (the Socialist Unity Party) had allowed a small-scale oral history project. People of the area were asked how they had experience the days of March and April 1945. This process stirred up memories of anxiety – of fear but also of the hope of survival – and of the desire not to become a victim of those who were the liberators. Immediately after 9 May 1985, however, the SED authorities had told the people who had started the oral history project that now the date had passed and nobody needed any of this effort any longer. Memories and reflections on one's own past were not part of the regional plan for further developing 'cultural activities' in the area.

When we had driven from the cemetery on the hilltop (which was then in rather bad shape) down into the Oder meadows in 1985, we encountered another cemetery (still in the vicinity of Kunersdorf). It was a very small, but extremely well kept place, where almost every single plant seemed to be well tended. Here we were on the grounds of the Friedland estate. The cemetery consisted of a row of about ten graves. The first stone was from the eighteenth century; the last dated from August 1914. This latter was the grave of a second lieutenant in one of the Royal Guard regiments. The cemetery had been privately financed and organized. The contrast was stark: in the surrounding fields thousands of corpses had never been buried, and so the fields simultaneously concealed and referred to layers of silent and silenced memories, while on this spot one could not avoid the conspicuous signs of those who not only had been killed but also had participated as officers in an imperialist war.

XI

Just a few kilometres to the south of Kunersdorf one reaches the small town of Seelow. If one approaches it from the river bank, the most impressive, in fact the only, landmark is a large statue of a soldier in full gear. As one gets closer, the statue turns out to be a colossal figure about eight metres high. The Seelow memorial celebrates one of the most dramatic battles in the bridging of the Oder and pursuit of the attack on Berlin. The Red Army suffered huge losses: apparently over 33,000 soldiers were killed. The memorial was inaugurated as early as 27 November 1945. The statue was commissioned by Marshal Shukov, then the commander-in-chief of the armies approaching Berlin. In 1972, on the fiftieth anniversary of the USSR, the memorial was rebuilt, and a museum and display of guns and tanks was added. In 1985, on the fortieth anniversary of the offensive against Berlin, the German and Soviet authorities expanded the display so that it included a reconstruction of Shukov's command post of 1945.[25]

The director of the local museum and I visited the place late one cold afternoon: people were gone, but a wreath documented their gathering. Most of the flowers and wreaths bore Russian inscriptions, but we recognized German and Polish wreaths as well. In appearance, the memorial was like that to the victims of the concentration camp at Ravensbrück. It differed from Halbe, where flowers from local companies and schools had been laid. In Seelow, by contrast, as at Ravensbrück, the German wreaths came from groups of the SED or the youth organizations FDJ and from official state organizations.[26]

The Seelow memorial is just one among several conspicuous memorials to the deceased of the Red Army in the countryside around Berlin.[27] These dead soldiers, more numerous than the German military and civilian dead, were buried in common graves. The burial places lay at the edges of settlements or in the open fields. As at Seelow, they contained erect stone monuments. Generally these were field stones; only at central sites has a reddish marble been used instead of field stones. Most were erected in the first months after the victory; some were put up in the late 1940s. The texts refer to the 'heroes of

---

25 See Gedenkstätte der Befreiung auf den Seelower Höhen 1985, especially 50ff. and 56ff., on the usage for military ceremonies by the Soviet, East German, and Polish armies. At a visit to the museum on 10 September 1990 I found an inscription showing the figures of visitors up to 31 December 1989: 287,774 from the Soviet Union, 24,381 from Poland, 8,951 from West Germany, and 2,255 from West Berlin, as well as small numbers from other countries; the figures for visitors from East Germany were not given. It was then that some exhibits for the first time also pointed to the German side of the battles. On the display was a photograph showing graves close to Lietzen in the Oderbruch. The caption said that German soldiers were buried by German troops, and grave markers in the form of an iron cross were shown in the picture.

26 After 1989–90 Seelow became the site of a counter-memorial: in April 1991, close to the Soviet monument, the prime minister of the state of Brandenburg, Manfred Stolpe, jointly with Soviet and Polish generals planted trees designed to form a 'forest of peace.' This alternative monument was to symbolize the necessity of developing an alternative to war and death, as Stolpe put it at the time; see the anonymous report in *Die Kirche,* 28 April 1991, p.8.

27 The most monumental Soviet memorial in Germany, however, was erected in 1947–9 in a park in the southeastern district of Berlin, Treptow. This park had been a traditional location for working-class demonstrations and outings since the late nineteenth century. Here on 1 May 1946 a small memorial stone had already been put up by German trade-union members and anti-fascists.The big memorial was constructed between 1947 and May 1949; among other materials the architects used marble from Hitler's former New Chancellery. On 8 May 1949, the fourth anniversary of the end of the war and the liberation, the memorial was officially opened; see Köpstein and Köpstein 1987. The site became a standard topic in

the great patriotic war,' to their struggle and endurance, and to the 'perennial glory' of the dead.

These *kurgans* (to use the Russian words) were and still are visible from quite a distance. They reshape the landscape. They reorganize visual fields, enforcing their imprint upon those who were or are busy in their fields or those who pass(ed) by. To be sure, some graves carried names and dates, and here the tombstones often had plaques with pictures of the deceased, a Russian and not a German custom. But overwhelmingly these are common graves that simply refer to the numbers of the dead.

The Soviet authorities had strictly ordered their troops to bury only their own dead. In the village of Wartin, 150 kilometres to the northeast of Berlin, the retired officer had heard people talking about a common grave below the *kurgan* that had been erected close to the village. This meant that German and Soviet dead were lying side by side. When I looked around in 1990, I found graves of German war dead at the parish cemetery. They were as well kept as the surrounding ones. At this time, which was after the opening of the Wall in November 1989, the circle of flowers and wreaths around the stone at the centre of the *kurgan* that we had seen in April 1989 had disappeared. The entire site looked utterly neglected. An older woman from a peasant's house nearby said, 'There seems to be no more money for *that* kind of thing now!' As to the common grave, she just shrugged her shoulders. Had they dug it up, or had it just been a myth anyway? I did not dare insist on questioning her further.

During our trip in April 1989 my guides and companions several times mentioned the 'Russian custom' of burying people. They were 'pretty sure,' but explicitly stated that they did not have confirmation, that 'in Russia' mass graves are most common. 'Isn't it just that the Russians don't care about individuals?' one of my guides asked. Not only my guides but the local people of this area generally had a different image of what constituted the 'proper' burial of war dead. Graves of dead soldiers and civilians, of the 'fallen' of the war, had to carry names and crosses, and as for soldiers, steel helmets should be put on top.

---

textbooks and children's books; see, for example, a children's book describing a tour through East Berlin: Dänhardt 1979–81. One of the thirty-one locations that are mentioned is the Ehrenmal für die gefallenen Helden der Sowjetunion; the author explains that this is the 'central memorial for the fallen heroes of the Soviet Union.' Another site mentioned is the 'memorial for the victims of fascism and militarism,' the Neue Wache (68). Since the Wall came down, the cemeteries of the war dead of the Red Army have become a focus of right-wing youth gangs and neo-Nazi groups; for instance, the *Berliner Zeitung* reported three cases from the vicinity of Berlin for the weekend of 29–30 May 1993; see its edition of Tuesday, 1 June 1993, p.4.

XII

What the people on the spot did not point to (or even hint at) was that between 1941 and 1945 about three million captured Soviet soldiers were starved to death in the prisoner-of-war camps.[28] The dead were buried in mass graves. No name plaques or signs were erected. As for our small team, all of us seemed to assume that we all 'knew.' So one of my guides, the retired officer, mentioned only in passing that he had requested from local East German authorities, in a private initiative, a 'proper' burial place or at least some kind of memorial for one of those burial places near the town of Neubrandenburg. However, he had run into enormous difficulties: the ground belonged to the state and was now part of a military site. The NVA had told him that any memorial or sign would interfere with the military routine, and so he should refrain from pursuing his request further.[29]

On hearing this, I asked him, 'Why are you so involved in searching for burial places? Why do you want to get in touch with the people who take care of them?' he turned to me: 'Well, I was an active officer. I took it seriously. Of course, you cannot escape the question – what would happen to you if there was war? One of my strongest feelings was that I want to be buried properly. And if I have this wish, and if I imagine the misery and hardship of those guys who were in the front line, then I feel very close to these poor creatures who suffered and were killed, in particular in the very last days of this bloody war.'

XIII

From these vignettes no conclusion can be drawn, yet the contours of a fundamentally fractured picture begin to emerge. What comes across is, above all, the paradox of commemoration. The situations that I have described encapsulate the contradictions of public ritual and private mourning. They bring out the simultaneities of negating and appropriating public and private grief; the interaction of personal history *and* history as a grand or menacing 'force.' Yet these paradoxes are produced and created anew in and by the practices of the people who clean the graveyards or place flowers, as well as by those who participate in public ceremonies.

---

28   Streit 1988.
29   See Krüger 1990a.

1   The Historical Specificities of Commemoration

(a)

There was a striking similarity between the ceremonial displays and the rhetoric of commemoration in West and East Germany.

In West Germany the official phrases referred to the 'Nazis.' These interpretations blame Hitler and some fanatics. And though contested, such interpretations have some support among academic historians as well. According this view, a gang of criminals manipulated and terrorized not only peoples throughout Europe and beyond, but also their own people, the Germans themselves. This reading denies two fundamental facts: first, the social and societal configurations that made the domination of Hitler (and the 'polycracy' of the leaders of the state and party, as of the military and of industry) possible, and, second, the complicity of millions who coped with German fascism or, for that matter, with Nazism in a way that 'let it happen' and, finally, helped to sustain it.

In East Germany public terminology and public ceremonies were different, but also more monotonous. Inscriptions and visual representations insisted that 'fascism' caused horrendous sufferings, that 'the fascists' bear responsibility for war and thus for the killings and for the dead.[30] At the same time, orators underline how fiercely 'fascism' had been erased 'by its roots' in East Germany after 1945. They present as evidence the expropriation of larger private properties, in particular, in industry and agriculture, and also the dismissal of almost all officials who had belonged to the Nazi Party. Thus they claim that the structures which bred fascism were completely and permanently altered. However, there is no mention of the fact that 'the fascists' consisted of thousands if not hundreds of thousands of German men and women who actively pursued their occupations in a 'Nazi spirit' and who also – if occasionally – avoided or boycotted a Jewish shop, or during the war hit a *Fremdarbeiter,* one of the enforced and concentration-camp labourers, or reported one of his or her 'crimes' to the authorities.

---

30   Of course, the terminology and accentuation referred to the type of analysis that was confirmed by the Komintern at its conference in 1935. Here the leaders of the Stalin-dominated communist movement stated that fascism was a 'terrorist' political movement that reflected and resembled the most reactionary forces of capitalism. Called forth was the notion of the overwhelming force of socio-historical processes. The involvement of individuals, whether in terms of villainy or complicity, was considered merely a matter for apology, if not simply 'below the standard' of historical analysis.

In both German states, perceptions of German fascism have been fostered consistently which deny this common history by selectively silencing different but related dimensions. In the West, the suffering and dying of Germans at the fronts 'out there' and 'at home' was and still is stressed and commemorated. Totally neglected, however, are both complicity with the fascist leaders among Germans and the suffering of those who had been attacked by the German armies. In the east the suffering of the victims of German warfare was commemorated. However, it was not individual suffering and grief but military and political victory that was presented at memorials and in ceremonies. Common to both views is the erasure of the Germans themselves. But it was the Germans who perpetrated fascism and made it 'Nazism.' They were not the victims but the agents of 'their' wars of extermination and of the Holocaust.

(b)
Commemorations at the same time stimulate and conceal anti-commemorations. Obviously, the ceremonies at memorials in West German towns have raised public protests and calls for honouring those who were hitherto effaced from public memory (such as runaways and deserters during the war).

However, the very displays of the military are imbued with contradictions of their own. Certainly, the ritual of performance in front of the memorial was accentuated differently in west and east. But the 'stately' behaviour of soldiers and military units in public, indeed, the very dramaturgy of celebrations, resembles the military order and thus recalls the military purpose of killing – which at the same time is being condemned in the commemoration speeches. To put it another way: the display of troops constantly contradicts the declared purpose of their presence. 'Proper' dress and 'proper' marching order certainly accord with images of seriousness, as well as of the responsibility 'of the state.'[31] However, the weapons and, even more, the parading of these troops – in particular, their goose-stepping (as with the NVA in East Germany) – invoked (and invokes) images of action that are images both of treating others brutally and of being treated brutally oneself.

2   The Private within the Public; the Public within the Private

(a)
Public commemoration can elicit and support private needs, as with the money for flowers. Even more, public action may be the only means of sustaining

---

31 In addition, the associations may include the social-democratic rhetoric of the Kaiserreich, which to a large extent is taken by East German authorities to be the predecessor of the SED. 'Revolutionary *armies*' or 'the *march* of the revolution' as well as 'revolutionary *battles*' figured prominently in the thinking (and talking) of many of the party leaders and writers.

some 'space' for private needs. Here again we might think of the local-level funding or of the state assumption of care for the graves if local people give up, as is likely to happen, for example, when the woman with the rabbits dies. But at the same time, they can assault and mock private needs ('You must put your flowers at the stela').

(b)
Private needs can be expressed in public display, such as in caring for public graves. Here we might think of the children who created and clung to their own space, even when the persons buried there were completely unknown to them. Indeed, public display may open up the only 'space' for private needs. One may think of the woman who created the cemetery for the twenty-three dead soldiers, including the one whom she had perhaps loved. Or we might think of the retired officer. He seemed to be driven by anxieties and perhaps by horror (he had been among those who had dug up the remains). To him the preservation and creation of graves and, for that matter, of memorials was a deep and serious concern that he could 'express' only in permanently caring for the places and the people around them.

(c)
It is this effort of individuals to seize 'space of their own' that rendered possible the use by the state of their concern about and care for the remnants of the dead.

3   Silences Are Embedded in Commemoration

(a)
The lack of a date – a publicly admitted or stated date – for the foundation of the large memorial cemetery at Halbe was part of a public silencing of what the cemetery contains, whom it contains, and how the remains got there. The mayor's admonition – better focus on the central memorial at Berlin – was the other side of the East German approach to commemorating and mourning the German war dead. This type of private mourning should be kept strictly private; it should never be possible to turn it into public commemoration.

(b)
The silencing of the history of the cemetery and the solemn display of long rows of stones disguise the fact that the surface does not cover orderly rows of corpses but rather conceals a mass grave assembled from bones picked up from the woods and fields. The long rows of stones recall the internationally approved iconology of war cemeteries. One might read it as an appeal to the

'victimhood' of all dead soldiers. On this view, the cemetery tries to claim a minimum of solidarity among human beings who, in the end, had nothing in common but misery and death. However, the horror of their actual miseries and sufferings is totally denied. At the same time, these horrors may constitute the only similarity to those people who were made victims of German fascism in a much more comprehensive sense, especially the inmates of the concentration camps.

Still another layer of the past was silenced. After the opening of the Wall the memory of other dead has surfaced. In one sector of the Halbe cemetery several hundred, if not thousand, corpses were reburied from the camp of Ketschendorf, one of the five 'internment' camps for presumed Nazi perpetrators which the Soviet authorities had installed in their zone in 1945.[32]

However, denials and silences are not simply a 'lie.' The very scenery at the cemetery, in its strictly preserved and thus artificial order, conveys hints of what is 'underneath.' Arrangements of order and ritual at the same time disguise, silence, and refer to the horrors of dying. It is this simultaneity of disclosure and concealment that (re)creates the site as a necessity for both state claims and private needs.

(c)
Ultimately, the witnesses to the commemorations, the workers on the site, the people who come and lay their wreaths or flowers (and are told to put them at the central stela), the officials and the soldiers who attend and perform at official ceremonies – in one respect, all are in the same position as those who have been killed and whose remains lie under the feet of the witnesses. In contrast to those who were explicitly designated as 'victims' by the fascists, the dead as well as contemporary mourners or workers aimed (or aim) at connecting space 'of their own' with loyalty to the demands of state.

At the very same moment the difference is total: witnesses, workers, and officials are alive; those whom they commemorate or mourn are dead. History, or more precisely, the past as a force that finally, when it comes to life and death, intervenes from 'the outside,' silences the histories of those who have been killed. For the dead, acceptance of the state's demand did not 'pay.' They paid with their lives. If their remains are buried, the site of their graves is granted forever by the state. But it is only the survivors and those who come

---

32 On the wide range of people who were brought here for various and often quite unclear reasons and their suffering, see the case studies on two other camps in Krüger 1990a, b; Krüger and Kuhlbach 1991; Kilian 1992. As for the graves of the dead from Ketschendorf at Halbe, see Flocken, Klonovsky, and Münter 1990.

later who can recognize this permanence (if such it is). To them, it is a place for remembering and mourning and for ceremony. Ordinary graves differ from memorials. The latter demand specific attitudes and behaviour: disciplined mourning, if not ceremonialized respect. Yet even here the living may permeate the official history with their histories and practices, which claim and at the same time conceal these histories.

However, the differences remain limited in another sense: both graves and memorials symbolize the dangers and horrors of connecting two distinct aspirations. Both stand for the impossibility of achieving individual fulfilment and at the same time being 'loyal' to authorities who claim 'grand' goals and 'total' responsibility. Graves and memorials represent the outcome of such efforts, which millions had to face and did not survive: serial death.

NOTE

I am particulary grateful to Dr Dieter Krueger of Neubrandenburg and Herbert Pietsch of Berlin, who in April 1989 opened my eyes to the traces of war and the remnants of war dead in the fields north and east of Berlin. Both made every effort to help me get in touch with individuals who cared for graves and tried to preserve the memory of the horrors of war in what was then the German Democratic Republic (GDR). However, this exploration also owes much to Professor Dr Wolfgang Jacobeit and Dr Sigrid Jacobeit (both of Fuerstenberg a.d.H.) and Dr Diether Schmoock of Fuerstenwalde, who alerted me during a previous visit to the GDR to the continued presence of memories of the war dead in the countryside along the river Oder east of Berlin. I would not have developed my impressions into this paper if Gerald M. Sider of New York, friend, colleague, and partner for a long time, had not challenged me and stimulated my thoughts on its production and meaning.

REFERENCES

Abenheim, Donald
    1988 Reforging the Iron Cross. Princeton: Princeton University Press.
Akademie der Künste Berlin, ed.
    1993 Streit um die Neue Wache: Zur Gestaltung einer zentralen Gedenkstätte. Berlin:
          Akademie der Künste.
Azaryahu, Moaz
    1991 Vom Wilhelmplatz zum Thälmannplatz: Politische Symbole im öffentlichen Leben der
          DDR. Gerlingen: Bleicher.
Bald, Detlef
    1994 Militär und Gesellschaft 1945–1990: Die Bundeswehr der Bonner Republik.
          Baden-Baden: Nomos.
Bartetzko, Dieter
    1992 Die Angst vor der Geschichte: Zur Eröffnung des Museums Judengasse. Frankfurter
          Rundschau, 27 November, 27.

Büchten, Daniela, and Anja Frey, eds.
1993 Im Irrgarten deutscher Geschichte: Die Neue Wache 1818–1993. Berlin: Aktives
Museum Faschismus und Widerstand.
Dänhardt
1979–81 Alex, Spree und Ehrenmal. Berlin.
Dieckmann, Friedrich
1993 Schinkels Wache als nationales Mahnmal. Neue Zeit 154 6 (July):12.
Eley, Geoff
1988 Nazism, Politics and the Image of the Past: Thoughts on the West German
Historikerstreit 1986–1987. Past and Present 121:171–208.
Endlich, Stefanie.
1992 Ereigniswege zum Holocaust? Gedenkstätten-Rundbrief 52:1–2.
Flocken, Jan Van, Michael Klonovsky, and Christian Münter
1990 Halbe mahnt! Denkschrift für Frieden, Freiheit und Völkerverständigung. Halbe.
Friedlander, Saul, ed.
1992 Probing the Limits of Representation: Nazism and the 'Final Solution.' Cambridge,
London: Harvard University Press.
Gedenken und Denkmal
1988 Entwürfe zur Erinnerung an die Deportation und Vernichtung der jüdischen
Bevölkerung Berlins. Berlin: Berlinische Galerie / Der Senator für Bau- und
Wohnungswesen.
Gedenkstätte der Befreiung auf den Seelower Höhen
1985 Seelower Höhen: Gedenkstätte der Befreiung. Seelow: Bewag Berlin.
Gottschalk, Carola, ed.
1992 Verewigt und Vergessen: Kriegerdenkmäler, Mahnmale und Gedenksteine in Göttingen.
Hanisch, Wilfried
1992 In der Tradition von Müntzer, Scharnhorst, Engels und Thälmann? Zum
Traditionsverständnis und zur Traditionspflege in der NVA. *In* NVA: Ein Rückblick für
die Zukunft, Manfred Backerra, ed. pp.255–68. Cologne.
Hartman, Geoffrey H., ed.
1986 Bitburg: In Moral and Political Perspective. Bloomington: Indiana University Press.
Herausgeberkollektiv
1989 Die Militär- und Sicherheitspolitik der SED 1945–1988. Berlin: Dietz.
Hillgruber, Andreas
1986 Zweierlei Untergang: Die Zerschlagung des deutschen Reiches und das Ende der
europäischen Judentums. Berlin: Siedler.
Hoss, Christiane
1994 Nach einem Jahr: Rückblick auf die Auseinandersetzungen um die Neue Wache.
Gedenkstätten-Rundbrief 3:1–5.
Kilian, Achim
1992 Einzuweisen zur völligen Isolierung: NKWD-Speziallager Mühlberg/Elbe, 1945–1948.
Leipzig: Forum
Köpstein, Horst, and Helga Köpstein
1987 Das Treptower Ehrenmal: Geschichte und Gegenwart des Ehrenmals für die gefallenen
sowjetischen Helden in Berlin. Berlin: Staatsverlag.
Koselleck, Reinhart
1979 Kriegerdenkmale als Identitätsstiftung der Überlebenden. *In* Identität, Odo Marquard and
Karlheinz Stierle, eds pp.255–76. Munich: Fink.

1993 Stellen uns die Toten einen Termin? Die vorgesehene Gestaltung der Neuen Wache wird denen nicht gerecht, deren es zu gedenken gilt. Frankfurter Allgemeine Zeitung, 23 August, 29.

Kraft, Rudolf
1992 In trennendem Gedenken. Die Zeit, 24 July, 53.

Krüger, Dieter
1990a '... doch sie liebten das Leben': Gefangenenlager in Neubrandenburg, 1939 bis 1945. Neubrandenburg: Regionalmuseum.
1990b Briefe Betroffener und Hinterbliebener: Fünfeichen 1945–1948. Neubrandenburg: Regionalmuseum.

Krüger, Dieter, and Egon Kühlbach
1991 Schicksal Fünfeichen, Part 1: Gefangene im NKWD/MWD-Lager Fünfeichen, 1945 bis 1948: Versuch einer Ermittlung. Neubrandenburg: Regionalmuseum.

Lücke, Detlev.
1990 VVVVVVOOORR! Sonntag 35:11.

Meyer, Georg
1993 Zur inneren Entwicklung der Bundeswehr 1960/61. In Anfänge westdeutscher Sicherheitspolitik 1945–1956, vol. 3, Militärgeschichtliches Forschungsamt, ed. pp.851–1162. Munich: Oldenbourg.

Pietsch, Reinhard, Rainer Potratz, and Meinhard Stark
1995 Nun hängen die Schreie mir an ... Halbe: Ein Friedhof und seine Toten. Berlin: Edition Hentrich.

Reuth, Ralf Georg
1992 Volksbund Deutsche Kriegsgräberfürsorge: Noch fehlt vielen Soldaten ein würdiges Grab. Frankfurter Allgemeine Zeitung, 16 November, 4.

Ross, Jan
1992 Singulär: Mahnmal in Berlin. Frankfurter Allgemeine Zeitung, 25 July.

Schneider, Gerhard
1991 '... nicht umsonst gefallen'? Kriegerdenkmäler und Kriegstotenkult in Hannover. Hanover: Hahnsche Buchhandlung.

Stölzl, Christoph, ed.
1993 Die Neue Wache unter der Linden: Ein deutsches Denkmal im Wandel der Geschichte. Berlin: Koehler & Amelang.

Streit, Christian
1988 Keine Kameraden. Stuttgart: DVA.

Tjulpanov, Sergej
1987 Deutschland nach dem Kriege (1945–1949). Trans. G. Grossing; ed. L. Jäger and Stefan Doernberg. Berlin.

Young, James E.
1993 The Texture of Memory: Holocaust Memorials and Meaning. New Haven, London: Yale University Press.

Silences of the Living, Orations of the Dead: The Struggle in Kenya for S.M. Otieno's Body, 20 December 1986 to 23 May 1987

DAVID WILLIAM COHEN AND E.S. ATIENO ODHIAMBO

On Saturday, 20 December 1986, Silvanus Melea Otieno, a prominent Nairobi lawyer, aged fifty-five, fell ill at his farm at Ngong near Nairobi. At 6 p.m. he was declared dead at Nairobi Hospital. Within a few days, Voice of Kenya radio carried the widow's announcement that the body of S.M. Otieno would be buried at their Ngong farm on Saturday, 3 January 1987. But then on the same day the VOK carried Otieno's brother's message that the burial would take place at Nyamila village in Siaya district, western Kenya. Nyamila, Otieno's birthplace, and Ngong, his residence for a number of years, are some four hundred kilometres apart.

The *Daily Nation* of Nairobi quickly reported that a dispute had developed over the plans for removing Otieno's body from the city mortuary for a public viewing and for the burial. The dispute pitted the widow, Virginia Wambui Waiyaki Otieno, whom the Kenyan press sometimes referred to as a 'Kikuyu lady' – her brother is Dr Munyua Waiyaki, a former minister of foreign affairs – against Joash Ochieng' Ougo, the deceased's brother, and Omolo Siranga, head of the Umira Kager clan, which joined Joash in claiming the corpse of their Luo kinsman as one of their own and as their rightful property. On 29 December the *Daily Nation* reported that announcements of plans for Otieno's burial had been halted by the Voice of Kenya. In the days that followed, court orders and injunctions blocked the plans of the widow and the brother for their respective ceremonies on 3 January 1987.

The contest for control of the remains of SM – his friends knew him that way during his life and at death – moved through seven legal settings over the next months. The struggles within the court were accompanied by large demonstrations in the streets of Nairobi, calls by one side and the other to take the body by force from the city mortuary, and an avalanche of correspondence and commentary in the national press. The legal struggles for SM's remains were also widely reported in the overseas press, which tended to view the litigation as either a contest between 'tribes' (Wambui, the Kikuyu widow, versus Ochieng', the Luo brother) or as a struggle between 'modernism' and 'traditionalism' (occasionally read 'tribalism'), missing the crucial role of the courtroom contest in the very constitution of ideas concerning the 'modern' and the 'traditional' in Kenyan life.¹ And during the trial the Kenya press at times reflected this same reading of the case as a reconvening of old, persisting struggles between Luo and Kikuyu in Kenyan national life, misreading the complex interests and intentions on both sides of the case.

The fate of S.M. Otieno's body, the rights of the disputants, and the prospective reverberations of the various possible outcomes became subjects for serious comment at funerals held throughout the country during the litigation. Although the president of Kenya, Daniel Arap Moi, did not speak publicly on the case during the period in which it was before the courts, a number of his ministers, members of Parliament, and important public figures positioned themselves on one side or the other. The struggle was concluded only by a final judgment for Joash Ochieng', handed down by the Court of Appeal, Kenya's highest tribunal. Otieno was finally buried by court order, not on his Ngong farm in the Nairobi suburbs, but rather in the land of his kinsmen at Nyamila village in Siaya on 23 May 1987, just a few days more than five months after his death.

From the end of December through May, the question of who would bury the body of S.M. Otieno and where that burial would be produced an immense public debate in Kenya – within the courts, in the streets, in clubs and bars, and in scholarly seminars – concerning the risks and liabilities of 'intermarriage between tribes'; the nature of the body as material property; the appropriate authority of 'custom' and 'tradition'; the relative standing of statutory, customary, and common law; the meaning and force of bonds of intimacy between husband and wife; the worth and legitimacy of 'modern' social practice; the rights of women within marriage, as widows, and before the law; the meanings of death and the purposes of interment; and the idea of 'home' as the only appropriate site of burial for a Luo individual. Within the struggles for SM's body, powerful texts on Luo and Kenyan culture and past were produced and invoked by witnesses, jurists, and the public. Political networks were realigned amidst public valorizations of 'tradition' and the 'modern marriage.' Ideas about culture and the past were openly debated as to their veracity, appropriateness, and meaning. History and anthropology, as largely scholarly ventures in knowing and representing the past and culture, were convened as open fields, defined now through deeply interested debate within the examination of witnesses and the arguments of jurists.

Although some observers of the Otieno case, overwhelmed as the public was with news and gossip, would hardly imagine that there could have been any *silences* constituted or sustained within and around the case, there were silences of great significance, including the exclusion from the judicial case itself of Wambui's political agenda. There was no direct address to the place of wealth and privilege in the dispute, though the courtroom testimonies constitute a source on the meanings and force of social status in contemporary Kenyan life. Likewise, however powerfully advanced in the courtroom and in the streets, the arguments in respect to claims to 'tradition' and 'custom' were profoundly constricted both within and outside the courtroom.

That the contest for SM's body became the site and the moment for a great national debate over the meaning of culture, and over the place of national and customary law within the intimate lives of Kenyans, is not to assert that this was the first such struggle, the first such vigorous national experience centring on a corpse. The sudden deaths by apparent assassination of Pio Pinto, Tom Mboya and M. Kariuki in the 1960s and 1970s unleashed enormous public demonstrations focused on the funerals of the victims, anticipating the mass and heavily politicized funerals of fallen revolutionaries in South Africa in the 1980s.[2] While contested funerals could animate enormous public energy anywhere in Africa, such events could, as in the Otieno instance, generate both public *and* private and intimate upheavals. Anthony Appiah has recently narrated an account of such a conflict in Ghana over the disposition of his own father's remains (Appiah 1992:181–92).

This is clearly not a phenomenon of twentieth-century Africa, for we know that across the pre-colonial continent the funerals of kings were moments of immense contestation over the past and future of kingdoms. And beyond Africa, while the authors were developing their treatment of the S.M. Otieno case, numerous examples of struggles over bodies of the dead were brought to their attention or were prominent in the news – from a contest in the state of Washington among several parties to establish authority over the ashes of the late transsexual jazz pianist Billy Tipton to the threat by Imelda Marcos to spread her husband's ashes across the Hawaiian landscape if his still-living body was not permitted to be returned to Manila; from the initiatives to remove Lenin's remains to a normal grave to the recent celebration of the reburial of heroes of the 1956 uprising in Hungary.

It is possible to see the production of history and culture on each side of the Otieno case. The conflict is indeed a site in which we can observe 'the production of history,' an expression that encompasses 'conventions and paradigms in the formation of historical knowledge and historical texts, the patterns and forces underlying interpretation, the contentions and struggles which evoke and produce texts, or particular classes of texts along with sometimes powerfully nuanced vocabularies, as well as the structuring of frames of record-keeping' (Cohen 1994-5).[3] Within such litigious settings, one may see critical junctures, fissures, and contradictions located in the interstices between popular and expert representations of culture and history, as knowledge is transferred and remade while moving within argument, across debate, and between academic and popular discourse. Here we have taken a position different from Parkin (1978). Where he observed, or argued, that the Luo of Kenya are marked and affected by the overarching condition of 'stifled cultural debate,' in our study of the Luo of Siaya and in other 'Siaya locations' in Kenya, including Parkin's Kaloleni site in Nairobi, the present authors have observed that 'the struggles over knowledge of past and over ordering culture and society are exceedingly rich' (1989:7). The challenge here is not to claim that it is a 'stifled' cultural debate or a rich one, but to examine the ways in which such a debate over the nature, authority, and meaning of culture proceeds as a complex event.[4]

Within the contest over S.M. Otieno's body, the productions of history and culture on both sides of the litigation may be seen as organized in social practice. There is the opportunity to relate the close reading of text -- now built out of literary criticism into art in certain branches of historical and anthropological scholarship – to an analysis of the social relations of the actors or producers of text. The Otieno debate brought to the surface the practices of experts and publics in constituting new or reworked values in Kenyan national life, in this case, constructing national culture in the struggle over a single body. The case presents an opportunity to take up Sally Falk Moore's challenge to find ways of studying 'historical changes as they happen' (1987:727–36).[5]

The living S.M. Otieno was widely recognized as one of Kenya's leading legal practitioners. He had been called to serve on a number of national boards and commissions and maintained a substantial private practice to his death. Remarkably, he left his survivors no written instructions concerning the disposition of his remains. But during his last years SM had, according to a number of witnesses, given considerable voice to the question of his own burial. He had, as the record of litigation reveals, given many individuals a clear sense of his intentions and desires – only he had given distinctly different 'instructions' to various relatives and acquaintances.

Questions regarding SM's intentions as to the disposition of his body at death and of the import of his alleged instructions constitute the first layer of the open courtroom struggle over the control of his remains. The statements of only three individuals among a considerable parade of witnesses, suggest the rhetorical and dramaturgical range of these recollected or alleged instructions. On the one side, in testimony before the High Court of Kenya, Wambui Otieno, the widow, recalled that her husband had once announced, in her presence, 'If I died and you pass Westlands [in Nairobi] on the way to Nyamila, I will kick the coffin open, come out and beat up all those in the convoy and go back into my coffin' (Egan 1987:22).[6]

The Nairobi advocate Timan Njugi was presented as a witness before the same High Court proceeding. He recalled how, as counsel to the Miller Commission of Inquiry into the conduct of former attorney general of Kenya Charles Njonjo, he had worked closely with S.M. Otieno, who was serving as a consultant to the commission. Njugi recollected that one day in early 1984, he and several others were seated in a Nairobi office awaiting Otieno's arrival. Otieno entered the office, greeted his friends, and according to Njugi, announced: 'Mussajjah, I've bought a piece of land in Kiserian (Ngong) [a short distance to the west of Nairobi] ... I shall be buried at Kiserian and I have made this plainly clear to all parties that might be interested in my funeral. I shall be buried at Kiserian' (Egan 1987:40).

On the other side, the High Court of Kenya heard from Albert Ong'ang'o, an elderly gravedigger and mason from Siaya district,[7] that a few years earlier, when he was completing the preparation of a grave at Nyamila in Siaya, Mr S.M. Otieno, the distinguished Nairobi criminal lawyer, had stooped over the edge of the grave and called down to him: 'Albert, Albert, you have prepared my brother's grave. In case I die, you will also prepare mine next to my father's' (Egan 1987:83).[8]

These simple gambits concerning SM's intentions opened into a far larger and more complex struggle over the essential nature of Otieno's entire life, as if the character of his life, as constructed through witnesses and examination, held its own declaration of his intent. For the widow, a considerable number of witnesses, including Wambui Otieno herself, offered stories and episodes that presented SM as a 'modern' individual, a devout Christian, a person of the city rather than of the countryside, oblivious to the activities of his clan and hardly ever attending funerals in the Siaya. His life was accounted for by the books that he was said to have read, the conversations that he was said to have had, the friends whom he kept. Piece by piece, an image of an almost whole person was constructed through day after day of witnesses, examination, cross-examination, and summary argument.

For the brother and the clan, their witnesses presented an alternative view. SM could not, according to their construction of the man, throw off the traditions, responsibilities, and laws of his birthright. Though he had married not a Luo but a Kikuyu, though he had not built himself a *dala* (residence) in the countryside, his home was at Nyamila, where his placenta was buried at the time of his birth (Cohen and Odhiambo 1987:269–86; 1989: chap.2). The witnesses and counsel for the brother and the clan argued that as SM had not asked his father to perform the rites that would have established for him a home at a site other than his birthplace; regardless of his having houses and property elsewhere, his home and therefore his place to be buried was nowhere else but Nyamila in Siaya.

It is in the tension, within statements and cross-examination, over these simple and fundamental words 'home' and 'house' that one sees most clearly the *work* of counsel upon the production of texts in the litigation. In cross-examination, John Khaminwa, lawyer for Wambui Otieno, appears to have sought to force a slip, an admission, even inadvertent, on the part of one of his adversary's witnesses that S.M. Otieno's residence in Nairobi was his, or even a 'home.' Likewise, Richard Otieno Kwach, counsel for the brother and the clan, appears to have made his witnesses exceedingly sensitive to this tactic. This constructed and imposed tension is further reminder of the particular quality of a court transcript in which composed and tactical speech is rendered more powerful by such naturalization. The point here is not that court testimony is thereby unreliable because of its extensive 'scripting.' Rather, one may recognize the modes of production of historical text – court testimony and other – the veiling of which is part of the process of production.

Subtleties lay within the various testimony on S.M. Otieno's life, and the arguments of counsel and witnesses were in considerable disagreement over the meanings and intentions of a vast number of things that SM was reported to have said and done during his life. For example, counsel for the widow, Wambui Otieno, asserted that Albert Ong'ang'o, the gravedigger, had simply lied about the incident or, being elderly and also well down in the grave from where SM spoke, did not hear him correctly, given that SM had made clear to so many of his Nairobi friends and to members of his immediate family that he wished to be buried at his Ngong residence.

But counsel for the brother and the clan said that the point of SM's statement at the graveside was not that he wanted to have his body buried at Nyamila – there could not have been in his mind any alternative to Nyamila – but simply that he wanted Ong'ang'o to know that he should be the one to prepare the grave. And for the brother's counsel, SM's alleged declarations to his friends, children, and wife were either the fabrications of the witnesses or just the kind of joking about things that goes on in everyday conversation among friends.

Around the events in the courts there was occasional discussion of whether SM was a party to the case or its subject. At the conclusion of the litigation toward the end of May 1987, the law correspondent of the *Nation* newspaper in Nairobi noted that SM had died before letting the Law Society of Kenya know what paper, if any, he was to present in response to their invitation to give one before their 1987 annual meeting. The journalist wrote, 'Did SM probably wish to write a paper like "Of the laws of Kenya and burials and all that?" We do not know. What we do know ... is that it is no simple topic to discuss ... In his death and during the hearing of the dispute, in the final submissions by counsel and in the judgment of the honourable judge, SM has written his paper worth reading and analysing' (Egan 1987:183).

Through the contests over the accuracy and meaning of practically every detail offered up concerning SM's life, an extraordinarily conflicted person – or is it a 'transcript' of a life? – is resurrected from the body lying in a fully embalmed state in the Nairobi city mortuary. One is alerted, through the relating of episodes by witnesses and their cross-examination, to the simultaneous fragility and power of memory. The struggle was, at one level, over the very nature of the person who could be resurrected or constituted in testimony and through memory, but also, at another level, over the authority to inscribe S.M. Otieno's 'transcript.' As each side attempted to anticipate and also establish the logic through which the justices would hear and read their argumentation, one sees memory shaped and organized into testimony.

The key to the power of the body of Otieno in this struggle for the remains was that he, S.M. Otieno, was both party to and absent from the litigation. A whole life was created in the court proceedings. Meanings and emotions could be attached to the body in death and associated with it, retrospectively, in life. His interests and intentions could be located, cited, and relayed through the attributions, inferences, and declarations appropriated to his corpse – 'the orations of the dead,' as the title of this paper conveys. SM's life, with its multiple voices and intentions, could be thickly and conflictually inscribed in death in ways that it could not in life.

The immense public notice of the case throughout Kenya provides another challenge in the comprehension and dissonance between the courts of Kenya, with their self-confirming authority, and their meaning to and reception by Kenyans at large. The work of Carlo Ginzburg on the formulations and reformulations produced and articulated by the miller Menocchio (1980) invites a close examination of the ground lying between a formal and self-presented legal system and all its apparatus, on the one side, and it popularly received and reformulated constitution as constructed in public discourse, on the other.

The case for SM's body brought into an organized dispute setting the entire moral ground of Luo beliefs about death and Luo funeral practices. Witnesses for the brother and the clan were brought into the court to unveil the meanings of death and the purposes of burial for the Luo. Under cross-examination by John Khaminwa, the chief counsel to Wambui Otieno, Mrs Idalia Awino Odongo put forward the view that 'If Luo adults die and are buried outside Luoland, everybody in his family, including children, will be in problems ... evil spirits will follow even us who are married. The whole family will be affected ... Even in the Bible, there is a parable of the demons which descended upon swines and they went and drowned in the river' (Egan 1987:76–7).

For the brother and the clan, countryside burial sustained ancient and core values of being Luo and supported the Luo person in life and also in death. The funerals of SM's forebears, among many other Luo 'rich and famous,' were recalled as substantiation of the countryside burial tradition. In his summation, the counsel for the brother and the clan, Richard Otieno Kwach, argued that

it is my submission that my clients are not a group of cannibals. They want to carry out a time-honoured custom which we believe in. The witnesses called have testified about these customs. Their belief in them and what would happen if they did not carry them out. Professor Oruka has told us that if a child named after a person who has died falls sick, *manyasi* is prepared to cure him or her. This consists of some soil from the grave of the person who the child is named after. My lord, it would be a long distance from Siaya to upper Matasia if there is a need to save a life in this manner ... My lord, my learned friend asked you to strike down as repugnant some Luo customs. That would be a draconian measure and will offend the tribe. My lord, you need evidence of atrocity before you can strike them down as being repugnant to justice and morality (Egan 1987:97).

Witnesses and counsel for the widow sought to bring attention to the numerous burials of Luo corpses, including some of SM's own late kin, that had been organized far from countryside homes. And they sought to present Luo funeral practices as archaic and outside the fold of Christian belief. In his summation John Khaminwa, for the widow, argued:

It has been emphasized to your lordship that Luos are never buried outside Luoland so that Umira Kager clan can have an opportunity to exercise these rituals to remove fears of being haunted because death can destroy them. My lord, this is not what a court of law should enforce. It is contrary to public policy and Christian beliefs. Your lordship is fully aware that whoever causes death by witchcraft must face the consequences. Witchcraft is no defence. The fact that the Umira Kager clan believes in ghosts, spirits and demons and that they fear that their son will kill them or that their wives will be unable to give birth is not sufficient to warrant this court to give them the body of S.M. Otieno for burial. It is neither here nor there. In my submission, it would be outrageous that such myths should be given a legal basis in our courts. (Egan 1987:88)

Within the litigation an ethnography of Luo death beliefs and rituals was constituted through the statements of counsel and witnesses. Yet also, in testimony, through cross-examination, and by summary argument, Luo burial practices were deconstructed. Luo core values were problematized. Implicit and hidden meanings were exposed and challenged. Concepts of 'modern,' 'tradition,' and 'Christianity' were constituted within the examination and cross-examination of witnesses.

Expert witnesses were invited to the court by both sides to participate in this intensive scrutiny of Luo culture, and more than forty published authorities were referenced in argument. The Bible was quoted as authority by both sides throughout the court proceedings. The cross-examination of experts, as well as the challenging of expert texts and the juxtaposition of expert and non-expert testimony, raised questions for the jurists and for observers concerning the relevance and authority of 'modern' academic expertise in the representation and reproduction of 'traditional' cultural practice. Expertise – ethnographic, historical, and legal – was continually invoked, yet also continually challenged. Indeed, in their final opinion the judges of the Court of Appeal admonished John Khaminwa, the widow's counsel, who, they said, 'confessed before us that he did not really understand the Luo customary law. Needless to say, it was his professional duty to carefully study and understand the Luo customary law and, if he thought it was in the appellant's interest, to call evidence' (Egan 198:178).

Curiously, two days after the judges of the Court of Appeal had issued the final ruling on the fate of S.M. Otieno's body, with its admonishment of Khaminwa, Robert Stevens, then president of Haverford College in Pennsylvania, presented a degree of doctor of laws *honoris causa* to (in the words of Stephen G. Cary, who presented Khaminwa for the degree) 'John Mugalasinga Khaminwa ... Distinguished lawyer, spokesman for human rights, articulate scholar educated on three continents, you have come far indeed from your modest Quaker roots in rural Kenya. In your achievements, you do honor to your parents and your teachers, who gave you knowledge, and through their example, illumined the values that now guide your life.'[9]

The honorary degree was awarded without reference to Khaminwthe's role as Wambui Otieno's counsel, but was intended to bring attention to lawyer's courage during seventeen months of detention without trial in Kenya and to human-rights concerns in Kenya more generally. On 19 March 1988 President Moi of Kenya raised the subject of the Haverford degree with a visiting group of Kenyan scholars: 'I cannot understand some people instead of rewarding someone like Mr. Kwach who has defended our culture I hear that they have now honoured the other person.' The president shortly thereafter rewarded Richard Kwach by appointing him to the High Court.

The layering of assertions and arguments concerning expert knowledge opened to view some of the complexity of cultural debate within and around the Otieno case. Juridical practice and the social constitution of argument among people in the streets, clubs, bars, law chambers and courtrooms unearthed and mediated but also silenced the discussion of certain critical issues. For example, the court contest appears to have constructed a grand silence around lowly voiced, yet heavily conflicted ideas concerning community and equity among Kenyan Luo.

But neither side was interested in disclosing and centring the explosive tension emergent in Kenya between relatively wealthy urban residents and their poorer urban and rural affines and kin. There appears to have been an effort, beginning with leaders of the Umira Kager clan but also extending out among other Luo leaders, to silence the voice and opinion of Oginga Odinga at gatherings, meetings and funerals in which support for the position of the brother and clan in the litigation was developing. Odinga, the great patriot if not the living patriarch of the 'Luo nation' of Kenya, expressed strong support for long-time comrade Wambui Otieno in her ordeal (Cohen and Odhiambo 1992:53–5). Wambui Otieno's counsel clearly saw no value in an argument concerning the importance to many urban citizens, such as the Otienos, of protecting their hard-won wealth from the claims of country cousins.[10] One could and did speak of the morality of immense expenditures on funerals in Kenya, but the counsel of neither side chose to consider such an expenditure as essentially a transaction between those of wealth and those of poverty, nor did either counsel bring into view the lowly voiced ambivalence among many Luo concerning the relative priorities given to programs of collective and private expenditure in education, development, and business and the great cultural project of countryside burial.

A further silence concerned the history of Luo burial practices. The counsel for the brother and the clan, with witnesses, sought to construct Luo beliefs concerning death and practices of burial as ancient, perduring, and authentic. In so doing, they produced an ethnography both normative and static. John Khaminwa, the counsel for Wambui Otieno, sought to portray such Luo beliefs and practices as antiquated, out of touch with the realities of the 'modern Kenya nation.' He referenced anthropological monographs to argue that these monographs – during the trials he referred specifically to quite a number of works, including ones by Leakey, Wagner, Hobley, Ochola-Ayayo, Snell, Hollis, Peristiany, Kipkorir, Welbourn, and Massam[11] – presented a passing way of life not chosen or shared by S.M. Otieno. 'The Luos cannot continue with customs that tend to isolate them from the rest of the country. There are a lot of books written by people – anthropologists – on burials. In respect to these books, they refer to a society of the old order and do not refer to contemporary society at all. Some of the things said in these books – we are living in a modern Kenya – and we would find them unacceptable and not in keeping with us ... The literature by anthropologists is no longer applicable in contemporary Kenya' (Egan 1987:89).

The static and normative portrayal of 'Luo custom' was jointly enacted by the opposing camps, and this ethnography from the court excluded knowledge of substantial change in burial and belief in this century: for example, knowledge from a 1905 source, which held that Luo corpses were buried in a sitting-up position within their houses, to a later practice that Luo were buried in a reclined position with the head facing in a specific direction, to the growing use of coffins more recently and the early reactions to coffins, among some Luo, that 'they tended to suffocate the ghosts of our people.' The counsel for the brother and the clan saw it in their interest to present Luo beliefs and practices as relatively unchanging, of having value and power because of their antiquity. The counsel for Wambui would find no value in revealing to the court that Luo beliefs about death and burial practices were flexibly changing to adapt to new circumstances. This is not to claim that there was an organized suppression of knowledge on the part of counsel and witnesses. It may be that they actually were poorly informed on earlier Luo practices and beliefs. Needless to say, the model of 'unchanging African tradition,' whether accorded great value or subjected to intense criticism, holds great power in Kenya and elsewhere, even when everyday knowledge and common sense provide alternative perspectives on the past and on change.

While substantial portions of the witnesses' testimony concerning the nature of Luo burial rites read as normative and static, the trial transcripts are also thickly illustrated with detailed information about the social organization of funeral practices, including the ways in which individuals, families, clans, and associations undertake the practical arrangements of transport, mourning, and burial. One recognizes how the ritual of Luo death and burial rests profoundly upon carefully organized and orchestrated activities – activities albeit, in, a conflicted field. The cultural architecture of a funeral is not a handed-down or simply a given tradition but rather a complex social construction. One sees in the Otieno case resonances with Geertz's treatment of a Javanese funeral (1959), in which he attempts to situate a heavily conflicted burial rite between what is held to be the correct mode of burial by Javanese tradition and what is held to be possible, given the specific form of the political and social field in which the funeral was worked out as rite.

The court was only slightly exposed to the deep contests and struggles located within the Luo political community of Kenya and of the play of this case as an effort to restore unity to the Luo house. Oginga Odinga, the Luo and Kenyan leader of the left, whose writings on the core values of Kenyan Luo culture were clearly a centrepiece in the case for countryside burial, was notably absent from the proceedings in court. He was heard to have voiced in a number of settings the view that 'it was only since the 1940s that all this attention to burial in the countryside began ... that before 1940 people were buried pretty much where they died ... that somehow the present Luo interest in funerals is related to the accumulation of wealth in the cities.'[12] It is only with the legal capacity and financial enthusiasm of Luo for the purchase of property that the issue of where to bury a corpse would arise.

That Odinga, the leader of the great chronicle of Luo political, cultural, and social movements in the twentieth century and the supreme authority on Luo political values, was to be separated from this movement introduced a range of contradictions into the political agenda of the Umira Kager clan. The fate of Odinga's voice leads one to consider how the battle for Otieno's body transgressed old, well-established boundaries of solidarity and established a significant new ground for the constitution and invocation of broader political and social thought concerning both local and national culture and both given and produced history. Odinga explained his situation to a friend, Odinga Odera, in these terms: 'There is no need for the Luo to be struggling for the body of S.M. Otieno. Otieno was lost a long time ago – *nene olal choon!* So you people are trying to rehabilitate a lost cause' (Atieno Odhiambo, personal communication).

The case and the debates around it have been seen by some as a next phase in the elaboration of an idea of a strong Luo nation within the Kenya nation, advancing its interest into every sector of life while defending itself against the oppressions and inequalities of a larger society.[13] That the contest for SM's body was also a struggle between a Luo clan and a 'Kikuyu lady' was somehow confirmation to many observers, particularly the foreign press, that once again ethnic or tribal conflict had lifted its ugly head in Africa.

But the case, with Luo witnesses on both sides, and its subtleties, which the foreign press failed to capture, has the potential of revealing much about the various 'republics of free discourse' within the 'Luo nation.' Great silences concerning wealth and privilege among Luo families, the levelling yet also impoverishing functions of vast expenditures on funerals, and the source and purposes of extraordinary pressures upon successful Luo in Kenya 'to build a *dala*' (residence) in the countryside – these great silences actually themselves invite attention to the differences in condition, status, opportunity, and interest among Luo in Kenya, whether in the city or the countryside. Was the Umira Kager clan's case for SM's body empowered by these differences as various parties struggled for interpretative power among several possible positions? Or did its source and power lie in the recurrent experiences of ethnic consolidation in which the signs of the various and conflicting 'republics of free discourse' are suppressed?

It is quite clear that 'Luo ethnicity' was centrally involved in this case, but the introduction of this move in the contest over SM's body reveals a great deal of complexity within Luo ethnic politics. One approach might be to see the problem of his body as initially one for the Umira Kager clan, of which SM was member number eighteen and then only secondarily as a problem for the entire Luo speech community, of which the Umira Kager clan was only one corporate entity among many that served Luo constituencies in Nairobi and Mombasa. But there was more to this issue than one clan or lineage among many; the Umira Kager clan, in its experience over the past hundred years, has most clearly exemplified a sub-hegemonic process in western Kenya of continuous expansion into and increasing control over once Bantu-speaking areas along the Luo-Luhya speech boundary. Umira Kager carried a heightened sense (as against other Luo congeries) of ethnic solidarity and considerable experience in operationalizing it, and this process was extended to the neighbourhoods of Nairobi as large numbers of Luo speakers travelled and settled in Kenya's capital. In the growing tension between the voiced positions of Umira Kager and those of Oginga Odinga, one may see a paradox in which the informed historical sensibility brings Odinga to an inflexible position at odds with his own historical and political community, while the experience of extraordinary change, coupled with an historical discourse, promotes a more flexible interpretation of history and culture on the part of Umira Kager and drives the formation of a new political constituency, far broader than the clan. One view is that in this shift the Luo were for the first time 'liberated' from the working-class ethos and radical agenda of Odinga, and thereby became more acceptable to the core of power in Kenya constituted in the president's office and the person of Daniel Arap Moi and in the interests and resources of a national bourgeoisie (and thus more accessible to the entitlement of cooperation than ever were the legions and rabble of Odinga).

Still another powerful layer of debate rose to the surface amidst the open discussion of the moral ground of Luo burial; this concerned the rights of women within marriage in Kenya and within the Kenyan nation. For some Luo women, Wambui Otieno's case offered a chance for their assertion as individuals and as spouses. But for others, her claim to SM's corpse was perceived as ultimately threatening to the woman's fragile security in her countryside household. The various voiced positions of Wambui Otieno, the widow, seen moving along a continuum, reveal much about the challenges faced by women within litigation in Kenya. She first announced that she was burying her husband at their farm. When this decision was blocked, she – or her counsel before the court – asserted that she was following her husband's wish to be buried at the farm. Again, when this simple position was answered, she and her counsel were forced to reposition their case in terms of a more complex argument – but one which at first appeared not so difficult to mount – that her husband had lived outside the locus of operation of Luo customary law. Challenges to this argument led Wambui Otieno, her counsel, and her witnesses to develop an elaborate argument that the Otienos lived and raised a family within a 'modern marriage' which gave her absolute rights to her husband's property, including his physical remains, both within Kenyan statutory law and in broader English common law (which has continued to have some standing in Kenyan courts since independence).

The day after the Court of Appeal had made its final decision against her claim, Wambui Otieno, the widow, changed her position again, angrily announcing that she and her children would not attend the burial in Siaya: 'As far as I am concerned, that is the end of the road. I have now discovered that women are discriminated against in Kenya. There is discrimination in Kenya, contrary to the United Nations Convention for the Elimination of the Discrimination Against Women which Kenya ratified in 1984 ... The judgement was very bad. I have been denied the right to bury my husband. I will take the matter to the International Court abroad' (Egan 1987:181).[14]

Wambui's several positions, constituting a continuum, suggest an economy of constraint that women confront before the law in Kenya, as well as within marriage.[15] Most profoundly, neither counsel saw it useful to relate that Wambui Otieno was respected as one of the leaders among Kenyan women – through the National Council of the Women of Kenya – as well as one who carried the credentials of a vigorous and radical fighter for national independence in the 1950s. Nor did they relate that her marriage to S.M. Otieno had been the stuff of national mythology, given her record of participation in protest movements and union organization, a year of detention served in Lamu Prison, and their wedding shortly after she left prison in January 1961. Eight years before S.M. Otieno's death, Wambui related her thoughts on her own 'intermarriage' to Chelagat Mutai (Mutai 1979:10–12).

I was not bothered by his tribe, though this very issue was to cost me much in later life. I cared only for an assurance from him that I was free to continue my public activities. He has given me, as he did then, wonderful love and support and I do not mind telling you that in the 1969 election he spent ten thousand pounds on my bid for the Langata seat ... I had not realized at first that inter-tribal marriages are so detested, especially ones between a Kikuyu and a Luo. It amazed me because this was the only thing that made me lose the 1969 election. In 1974 I knew the score; I had not divorced my husband, so I could expect nothing from the electors ... If two people have a basic affection, and a willingness to understand each other's shortcomings and the patience to work out solutions, any marriage can work, be it inter-racial or intertribal. Personally I do not stand many ceremonies of my husband's people which I regard as archaic, but apart from that our attitudes are the same ... Kenyans must practice what they preach: that we are all united as one people, that we are above petty belief in tribe and custom, that we shall give leadership to those of ability. I should dearly love to see such a Kenya.[16]

Wambui Otieno had campaigned for Parliament and served as treasurer of the 1985 International Women's Conference less than two years before the Otieno litigation. She had been active in national women's organizations in Kenya for a number of years, while maintaning close ties with prominent feminists in other countries. All this personal history was excluded from the litigation.

Both within and outside the court process and throughout the duration of the case, the intimate relations of SM and Wambui Otieno within their marriage were exposed to public view, as one side sought to impugn Wambui Otieno as a witness and as the other sought to enhance her status as a 'modern wife' duty-bound to organize the rites as her husband (or she herself) would have wanted. As the contest spread out from the courtroom to streets, bars, clubs, and residences, a 'whole' family history was exposed to public and became centred in public debate, including the issue of her sexuality.[17]

Her social and political capital rendered nil, Wambui Otieno came to recognize the complexity of organizing, as a woman and in respect to the rights of women, in legal contests in Kenya. One might imagine that she, in parallel with Umira Kager (Luo) support for the clan, could draw on Kikuyu crowds and popular opinion, and also women across Kenya, to support her position. At one point in the public remonstrations concerning her husband's body she said that she could bring out her legions just as Umira Kager were producing theirs. In fact, Wambui Otieno largely failed to do so. Politicians such as Grace Ogot, a novelist and elected member of Parliament, moved away from early support of Wambui Otieno, as an expression of women's solidarity toward a position more in consonance with her own Luo constituency in Gem, Siaya. More demonstrably, after the Court of Appeal ruling in May 1987, a number of Kenyan women went to court and, arguing from the Otieno precedent, got judges to enjoin their husbands by 'traditional marriage' from taking new wives in civil union -- hardly the outcome of the modernizing agenda that Wambui Otieno and her counsel had sought within the litigation.

The silencing of the 'transcript' of Wambui Otieno, the disappearance of her person behind the litigation – accompanying the constitution of the person of S.M. Otieno out of his corpse in the Nairobi mortuary – was, it could be argued, jointly transacted by both parties to the case, their counsels, and their witnesses. Within the production of the case, Wambui Otieno was immobilized by the very positions that the anticipated juridical discourse (the good wife, the good husband, the good marriage, the modern family) imposed upon the practices of counsel and witnesses. As her husband's dead body was invested with life, so in pressing her claim for his remains, she was faced with the prospect of becoming socially dead.

NOTES

This paper was originally prepared for and presented to the Sixth Roundtable in Anthropology and History – The Production of History: Silences and Commemorations – held at Bellagio, Italy on 29 August to 2 September 1989. It and other writings by the two authors developed into a book-length treatment (Cohen and Odhiambo 1992). We are grateful for the many questions and comments raised by those present at Bellagio and in other settings. We are especially indebted to David Anderson, James Currey, Garrey Dennie, Louis Galambos, Ivan Karp, John Lonsdale, Shula Marks, Elijah Oduor Ogutu, Jonathan Sadowsky, Gabrielle Spiegel, Ed Steinhart, Lynn Thomas, and Katherine Verdery. James Currey and Luise White contributed to and helped inspire this project. We acknowledge the assistance of Patricia Stamp, with whom we exchanged views about the conflict over S.M. Otieno's burial, and the commentaries and critiques of Peter Amuka, Martin Chanock, Michael M.J. Fischer, Corinne Kratz, John Lonsdale, and Sally Falk Moore, whose responses to the book-length manuscript were included as an afterpiece to the 1992 book.

196   David William Cohen and E.S. Atieno Odhiambo

The authors acknowledge the support provided by the Max-Planck-Institut für Geschichte
(Göttingen), John Hopkins University, Northwestern University, and Rice University, which
supported their collaboration.

1 See *New York Times*, 25 February 1987, and *Washington Post*, 14 February 1987.
2 See the research on the politics of mourning ritual in South Africa undertaken by Garrey
   Dennie (1997).
3 Drawing upon Cohen 1986, but also see Cohen and Odhiambo 1992:20. 'The Production of
   History' was, of course, the concern of the Fifth and Sixth International Roundtables in
   Anthropology and History, the first in Paris in July 1986, convened by the Maison des
   Sciences de l'Homme, and the second held at Bellagio, Italy, in August and September 1989.
   A first definition of 'the production of history' was advanced in the position paper prepared
   and circulated in advance of the 1986 round table (Cohen 1986).
4 See also Cohen and Odhiambo 1992:20.
5 In this call for attention to 'current history,' 'process,' and 'change-in-the-making,' Moore
   argues for a recognition of the important distinction between the practice, now quite
   developed in anthropology, of reading system out of a closely observed and described event
   and a more recently emergent practice of seeing within events the 'struggles to construct
   orders and the actions that undo them' (Moore 1987:735).
6 The court transcripts are provided in Egan 1987. The Egan volume presents the case record
   with a number of additional reports from the *Daily Nation* (Nairobi). Catherine Gicheru and
   Paul Muhoho are credited as reporters for the entire publication. The case was discussed at a
   special seminar organized by the Faculty of Law of the University of Nairobi on 18 July
   1987. A number of papers were presented to this seminar. The daily and weekly Kenyan press
   contains an extraordinary reservoir of correspondence and commentary on the case. The
   authors also have in hand a good deal of private correspondence with Kenyans concerning the
   case.
7 The court removed itself to Westlands Cottage Hospital, Nairobi, for the purpose of taking
   testimony from Mr Ong'ang'o, who was a patient there following surgery.
8 Albert Ong'ang'o reported that the grave in Nyamila was being dug for the remains of
   Mr Simon (Simeon) Odhiambo, who had died in Nairobi Hospital. Simon Odhiambo was a
   brother of SM.
9 We are grateful to Linda Gerstein, Haverford College, and especially to Hogie Hansen,
   secretary of the college at the time that the award was made, for assistance with the terms of
   this honorary degree.
10 Some observers of and participants in the litigation saw the struggle as one over the
   inheritance of S.M. Otieno's property and have variously interpreted the different positions
   taken as gambits to grasp control of that property. For example, the datum that Wambui
   locked the gates to their farm immediately upon hearing of SM's death is read as a ploy to
   give her time to remove some of his property from access and the view of visitors and, in one
   variant, to give herself time to find and destroy his will so that she could, in an intestate
   situation, impose her wishes upon the disposition of his remains and personal property.
11 For a list of works cited in court, see Cohen and Odhiambo 1992:141–2.
12 E.S. Atieno Odhiambo, from personal reminiscence.
13 Some guides to the evidently broader resonance of the Otieno case in Kenya are to be drawn
   from work by E.S. Atieno Odhiambo, Bruce Berman, and John Lonsdale on the debates –
   both popular and expert – concerning the nature and meaning of Mau Mau in Kenya and in
   the academic guilds more generally; work on political culture in post-colonial Kenya by
   Angelique Haugerud, among others; evocative studies of comparable experience such as E.M.

Simmonds-Duke (1987) on debates in eastern Europe over the meaning and interpretation of revolution, in which the expositions of several historians are peeled away layer by layer to reveal critical silences and hidden and low-voiced argument, along with the broad forces and resonances that surround the productions of history within and alongside the academy; and such studies as Carolyn Hamilton's examination (1989) of the production of history in South Africa through the 'lens' of struggles for control and meaning of history, culture, and politics in the production and reception of the Shaka Zulu television series.

14 To the best of our knowledge, she has not actually done so. She did announce that she had become a 'reborn Christian' immediately after her defeat in court (Cohen and Odhiambo 1992:30–1); this development is not necessarily to be read as a retreat from the politics of women in Kenya, for the new churches of 'reborn Christians' there are now seen as an important arena for the expression of opposition to some state policies in a setting in which free expression is otherwise felt to be impossible. Wambui Otieno is currently finishing a book about the experience.

15 From a more polemical feminist position, Patricia Stamp of York University has examined the embattled situation of Wambui Otieno both before the court and before her critics (Stamp 1991:808–45). Stamp's perspective joins and extends the view taken by the present writers (Cohen and Odhiambo 1992:30–6) of the structural, political, juridical, and rhetorical constraints on the constitution of a feminist position in Kenya in the 1980s.

16 We are grateful to Lynn Thomas for bringing this interview to our attention.

17 Patricia Stamp (1991) has detailed this assault on Wambui Otieno's credit during and after the litigation. For a broader treatment of women before the law in Kenya in the 1960 and 1970s, see Thomas 1989.

REFERENCES

Appiah, Kwame A.
    1992 In My Father's House. New York: Oxford University Press.
Clifford, James
    1988 Identity in Mashpee. In The Predicament of Culture: Twentieth-Century Ethnography, Literature, and Art, pp.277–346. Cambridge: Harvard University Press.
Cohen, David William
    1986 The Production of History. Position Paper prepared for the Fifth International Roundtable in Anthropology and History, Paris. Unpublished.
    1994 The Combing of History. Chicago: University of Chicago Press.
Cohen, David William, and E.S. Atieno Odhiambo
    1987 Ayany, Malo and Ogot: Historians in Search of Luo Nation. Cahiers d'études africaines 27:107–8, 269–86.
    1989 Siaya: The Historical Anthropology of an African Landscape. London: James Currey.
    1992 Burying SM: The Politics of Knowledge and the Sociology of Power in Africa. Portsmouth, NH: Heinemann.
Dennie, Garrey
    1997 The Politics of Funerals in South Africa. PhD dissertation, Johns Hopkins University.
Egan, Sean, ed.
    1987 S.M. Otieno: Kenya's Unique Burial Saga. Nairobi: Nation Newspapers.
Geertz, Clifford
    1959 Ritual and Social Change: A Javanese Example. American Anthropologist 61:–991–1012.

Ginzburg, Carlo
   1980 The Cheese and the Worms: The Cosmos of a Sixteenth-Century Miller. Baltimore:
         Johns Hopkins University Press.
Hamilton, Carolyn
   1989 A Positional Gambit: Shaka Zulu and the Conflict in South Africa. Radical History
         Review, spring, 5–31.
Moore, Sally Falk
   1987 Explaining the Present: Theoretical Dilemmas in Processual Ethnography. American
         Ethnologist 14:727–36.
Mutai, Chelagat
   1979 Still Committed to the Struggle. Viva, April, 10–12.
Ojwang, J.B., and J.N.K. Mugambi, eds.
   1989 The S.M. Otieno Case: Death and Burial in Modern Kenya. Nairobi: Nairobi University
         Press.
Parkin, David
   1978 Cultural Definition of Political Response: Lineage Destiny among the Luo. London:
         Academic Press.
Simmonds-Duke, E.M.
   1987 Was the Peasant Uprising a Revolution? The Meanings of a Struggle over the Past.
         Eastern European Politics and Societies 1: 187–224.
Stamp, Patricia
   1991 Burying Otieno: The Politics of Gender and Ethnicity in Kenya. Signs 16: 808–45.
Thomas, Lynn
   1989 Contestation, Construction, and Reconstitution: Public Debates over Marriage Law and
         Women's Status in Kenya, 1964–1979. MA thesis, Johns Hopkins University.

Lords Ask, Peasants Answer: Making Traditions in Late-Medieval Village Assemblies

GADI ALGAZI

In the western parts of late-medieval Germany, subject peasants were invested with the authority to tell the local law (*weisen*). Sworn representatives of peasant communities declared the law at least once a year in the assembly, attended usually by all male full members of the community in question. The norms, rights, and rules that they expounded were claimed to have been handed down to them from their ancestors. As a rule, these norms were not read out from some record but reconstructed orally in a complex ceremonial dialogue between lords and peasant jurors. The lord or his representative put the questions; the peasant jurors were to give binding answers.[1]

The lord summoned the assembly on traditional dates, often three times a year. On the evening prior to the assembly he arrived at the village and received food and lodging from the peasants. The assembly was ceremoniously opened the following morning, a privilege space was marked off from its surroundings, and a special peace was proclaimed. The peasant jurors, often called *Schöffen*, formed a circle in the middle, along with the chairman of the court, usually the lord or his local representative. After the presence of all the peasants obliged to appear in court had been verified, the laws were related by the peasant jurors, a practice known in German as *Weisung*. The specific contents of the *Weisung* differed from one lordship to another; it almost invariably included the lord's main claims vis-à-vis his peasants – labour dues and rents – and enumerated the peasants' collective obligations.[2] A typical *Weisung* might also comprise descriptions of fines and penalties, regulations concerning rights of common, rules pertaining to modes of inheritance, stipulations on the local land market, weights and measures, and so on. The declaration could also address village affairs and sometimes also some peasant counter-claims vis-à-vis the lord. Peasant *Weisung* encompassed yet more than rights and claims pertaining to the inner workings of the rural lordship. Peasant jurors often proclaimed who the lord of the community in question was and in what capacity he was ruling; they reported the rightful claims of the territorial prince and how powers of jurisdiction were to be allocated among different lordships represented in the village; they also provided minute descriptions of the boundaries of lordships and communities.

What happened after the *Weisung* was not so strictly regulated. If the date of the assembly coincided with that of the delivery of peasant dues, the lord might then demand them from his subjects. He might ask whether anyone knew of any encroachments on his rights in the village, or whether anyone had any charges to bring; this query would open the court session. Peasants were under obligation to inform the lordship of infractions of the law; judgment was given by peasant jurors, the lord's role being largely confined to presiding over the court, enforcing its decisions if necessary, and collecting the fines paid. Fines from jurisdiction were in fact an important source of revenue for lords, yet occasionally the jurors or the whole community had a share, especially in the smaller fines. Many of the fines were immediately paid during the assembly with wine and bread, which were distributed among the assembled, and the whole event was often sealed off with a meal, sometimes served only to the jurors, at the lord's expense. Court records were seldom kept in medieval Germany, whereas written documents related to the *Weisung*, the most formal part of the assembly, have survived in growing numbers from the twelfth century onwards, reaching a peak in the fifteenth and sixteenth centuries.

That peasant communities were governed according to a body of 'customary' law 'found' by local jurors was not exceptional in late-medieval western Europe; west German peasant communities seem to have differed in that this body of norms did not remain implicitly embedded in the practice of local courts or merely alluded to occasionally to support some unusual decision, but was explicitly reconstructed in a special ceremony at the opening of rural assemblies, the *Weisung*. More important, the fragmentation of political authority in western Germany and the peculiar form assumed by processes of state formation in the early-modern period lent unusual weight to peasant *Weisung*. Peasant declarations of law were extensively used by rival lords – territorial rulers included – who elicited such statements from their peasants in order to present them in courts to corroborate their claims, thereby enhancing for a while peasant legal authority.

The same process also played a crucial role in shaping the written evidence of rural legal traditions. *Weistümer* – written documents related to *Weisung* events – often owed their production to attempts to export the products of local normative traditions into more-remote legal markets by having them written down. *Weistümer* did not survive in such quantities simply by virtue of having once been written down. To survive, they had to be recorded, committed to archives, constantly transcribed and summarized, cited, and refuted. It was rather the special position that they assumed within the changing legal landscape of late-medieval and early-modern western Germany, circulating between courts and quoted by diligent scribes, which accounts for their survival. This was thus not a simple derivative of written documents' material properties but a relational outcome of a complex social process, involving practices of conservation and modification. The profusion of written *Weistümer* is an effect of a specific social, political, and legal configuration, which enhanced temporarily the value of allegedly oral rural traditions, before the further consolidation of legal systems and the advancing monopolization of legal authority by learned jurists relegated them to the newly reconstituted realm of folklore and 'tradition' – only to be rediscovered there almost immediately by nineteenth-century folklorists and historians.

In the fifteenth century, however, these processes, which were to transform the notions of both law and tradition, were still incipient. In the following discussion I shall neglect these wider contexts of peasant *Weisung* and the varying combinations of oral and written representations to which they gave rise, and focus on the local implications of this practice. A further limitation results to a large extent from the kind of sources available. Since few court records have survived from late-medieval Germany, litigation and justice, arguably the more important part of their dealings in the local context, cannot be adequately analysed.[3] In their absence, the role of *Weisung* in the context of local peasant society remains perforce unilluminated and leaves a whole series of important questions unanswered. How effective was the apparent exclusion of women from full participation in the assembly and what did it imply for gender-related notions of normativity and authority?[4] In what ways did the recitation of particular claims and rights in the assembly allude obliquely to local alliances and conflicting interests within villages? Similar difficulties arise when we try to assess the jurors' behaviour in the context of rural society. Most seem to have been village dignitaries of some kind; yet the extent to which they were able, for instance, to use their position in court to influence community affairs can seldom be assessed. It is, however, important to point out their ambiguous position between the lords and the rest of the villagers.[5] Although they owed their authority partly to nomination and recognition by the lords,[6] they had to rely on community support and assent in declaring the law. Unlike their late-medieval urban counterparts, members of a German village elite could not establish a formal monopoly over their positions of authority and legal competence. The social career of this group was often arrested by the presence of lordship and their necessary reliance on village support.

Some of these constraints can be discerned in the *Weisung* itself. The spokesman for the jurors, stepping forward to pronounce the answer in the face of a demanding, potentially menacing lord, remained under the eyes of the whole assembly (*Umstand*). The assembled peasants were more than spectators exercising passive censorship over the jurors' performance; although one usually expected the jurors to declare the *Weisung*, legal knowledge was assumed to reside among all members of the community, a fact underscored by jurors regularly retreating to 'consult the community' in order to return with an authorized answer,[7] or at times by peasants interfering in the dialogue between lord and jurors in order to correct their statement of the law. In the middle of the fifteenth century, for instance, the jurors of Bruttig, a wine-growing village on the Mosel river, were publicly contradicted by community members and hastily revised their statement.[8] I can say very little, though, about the inner divisions of village society which might have been the cause for such conflicts.

Because we have to rely on accounts of the *Weisung* as a body of norms without the records of particular decisions and detailed knowledge of local conditions, hidden edges and subtle modes of collaboration are bound to escape our notice. Instead, the *Weistümer* foster an image of a frontal encounter between lords and peasants in the assembly. They offer, however, some possibilities to explore the making of traditions as shaped by continuous dialogues between unequals and the specific representation of the past embedded in such a practice.

Being involved in the making of tradition had serious implications for peasants. In the case of the *Weisung*, 'tradition' did not stand for the unofficial refuge of subjects excluded from the making of 'real' law: it was itself the law, and peasants took an active part in transmitting and reshaping it. In this respect, peasant participation in the work of tradition was a resource that at least some of them could deploy and an important constraint on the lords' freedom of action, a point stressed notably by Max Weber.[9] He seems to have overlooked, however, the darker side of peasant participation in the making of legal tradition. His analysis of the implications of lay participation in law-finding in different medieval settings remained too formal: a given institutional arrangement might have contradictory implications in different social contexts. Regular participation in law-finding may have represented an important asset for nobles attending feudal assemblies, but its consequences for subject peasants remained deeply ambiguous. For them, telling the law was both a resource and a burden, since in the *Weisung* they were taking part in the legitimation of their own subjection by publicly recognizing their manifold obligations. A typical *Weisung* from the mouth of peasant jurors was mostly about peasant obligations: rents to be paid, labour dues to be performed, and various fines to be paid for not attending the assembly, poaching in the woods, or not asking for the lord's permission when alienating land. Ascribed authority weighed even more heavily on peasants having to recite publicly the disabilities of serfdom. But even innocent stipulations might contain a hidden edge. In wine-growing regions, for instance, jurors were routinely proclaiming the prohibition to begin the vintage until a lord's agent arrived in the village and gave the signal, a typical measure intended to prevent peasants from depriving lords from their due share in the produce. It did so, however, by impairing the labour process and thereby endangering the vintage itself.[10] Giving authoritative answers in the assembly could have dangerous implications for the speakers themselves, as later court protocols show. In Kesten the *Weisung* was followed in 1592 by a court session. After having recognized in the *Weisung* the penalty for wine-growers who persistently failed to keep their vineyards in good condition, one of the jurors, Peter Schenneten, was himself denounced for the very same infraction.[11]

Lords or their representatives came to villages, as a recurrent formula had it, in order to listen to peasants tell the law; jurors' answers had, however, undeclared addressees, since they were actually reminding themselves and the assembled peasants who they were and what obligations they had. To the extent that lords' claims upon subject peasants were represented in the *Weisung* as handed down from the past and hence legitimate, peasants were sharing with their lords the work of transforming again and again the past of lordship into the seeming lordship of the past.

Questions and Responses

In the case of the *Weisung*, 'tradition' did not form a fixed body of norms or a pre-given, bounded text handed down, for both did not exist independently of the encounters between lords and peasants in the assembly. In principle, no single encounter could be held to be an exhaustive embodiment of the local law; new questions might be posed, and answers could vary. Tradition might better be provisionally understood as the ongoing *process* of shaping legal norms, rules, claims, and obligations in dialogues between the lordship and its subjects.

How misleading a hypostatized notion of tradition can be becomes more evident when we ask: Where would 'tradition' in the sense of a body of norms be thought to be 'located'? It was not believed to reside in peasants alone, whose declarations were considered valid only when given publicly as answers to lords' questions; neither did it officially reside in lords' archives. Seigniorial officials might possess notes with lists of common questions and expected answers (Ringholz 1904:205); still, in order to be considered 'traditional,' that is, legitimate, the answers had to be declared in the assembly by peasants. Their answers, in turn, were shaped by lords' questions. Hence, instead of abstracting a body of norms from their interactions and confrontations, I suggest that we look at the whole assembly as a contradictory *inscription system*, whose actual working can be provisionally termed 'tradition.' No single actors could be considered 'bearers' of authorized versions of the local law; their social configuration could. The visible interactions between lords and peasants were bringing forth publicly recognized, binding, and transient versions of the past; they were shaped by an underlying institutional framework and a common repertoire of accepted moves and countermoves; both the game and the moves were embedded in the social organization of lordship, constraining and enabling the production of the legal past. The *Weisung* thus presents a good case of the dialogic production of the past under lordship.

Modifying Halbwachs's broad concept of 'collective memory,' Roger Bastide has proposed to apply the term only to those cases in which the structure of a group itself functions as a memory structure (Bastide 1970, 1978; Douglas 1986). Without adopting Bastide's terminology or committing myself to his actual findings, I use his model in order to bring out by way of comparison and contrast the distinctive features of the *Weisung*. Studying the transformations of African religions in Brazil, he has depicted their rites as symbolic enactments of group structure. Social roles and activities were reproduced in the articulation of roles assumed by participants in religious ceremony. Bastide has suggested that 'collective memory' could be usefully understood as 'a memory of a scenario, of links between roles,' so that 'it is the structure of the group which furnishes the frameworks of collective memory, defined not as collective consciousness, but as a system of interrelations between individual memories' (1970:92, 94). In his account, forgetting is also shaped by the structure that he portrays. As the Brazilian descendants of African slaves tried to reconstitute the ceremonial ensemble after the dislocations brought about by slavery, omissions and gaps emerged. The absence of participants as a result of death or dispersion did not entail, however, 'total forgetting,' because it was felt as a missing part in a structure of coordinated actions and expectations created by the scenario (ibid.:96). Bastide can thus show how structured silences and bounded forgetting can be conceived as specific effects of a social practice.

The *Weisung* was likewise not a monological text; it was an orchestrated performance, in which peasants were not mere spectators but active participants. The mutual dependency of participants in the ceremony was expressed in the formal allocation of roles in the dialogue, with lords posing questions and peasants giving answers. To obtain a valid declaration of their rights and claims, lords had to have community representatives tell it; to tell the law legitimately, peasant jurors had to be properly asked by their lord. Dialogue roles, however, were neither exchangeable nor symmetrical. Speaking turns in the *Weisung* were allocated according to a fixed scheme. The jurors spoke only when spoken to and were expected to give relevant answers. The distribution of legitimate speech was controlled quantitatively and qualitatively by the lord posing the questions. It was his right and privilege to ask, while peasants were under obligation to answer. They could seldom pose counter-questions to their lord. Moreover, the obligation to answer extended beyond the jurors alone to include the whole community, formally required to help to tell the law and to confer with the jurors.[12]

Posing questions in the assembly also had political and symbolic dimensions. It was an attribute of lordship, so that when disputes arose between lords over rights of lordship in villages, parties often adduced evidence to prove that they were holding assemblies and posing questions regularly.[13] More generally, being questioned was also closely associated with peasants' experience of lordship, because for both church authorities and secular lords, questioning their subjects was an important aspect of exercising power. On the other hand, situating the question-and-answer form in the context of the existing 'repertoire of available interrogative strategies' (Goody 1978a:5) also brings out the differences between the *Weisung* and the interrogation of individuals by worldly lords or the examination of Christian believers by their church superiors. Lords were held to respect customary procedures when posing questions in the *Weisung*, and only occasionally could they attempt – with varying success – to go beyond the set of received questions. Peasants, for their part, could make use of a repertoire of legitimate countermoves and strategies. Thus, depending on local circumstances and the temporary balance of power, questions put by lords' representatives could sound like anything from a cautious request for an answer to a penetrating interrogation.

If the lord was the one who put questions, then the one who put questions could be presumed to be the lord. Accordingly, since the right to ask was an attribute of lordship, peasants' willingness to be asked implied recognizing that lordship. Such recognition was implied in answering questions (Toch 1986:667–8), in obeying the bells summoning the assembly, and in attending it – in fact, already in accommodating the lord when he arrived in the village and providing for his needs. This principle is well indicated by cases of resistance and rebellion, signalled by peasants not attending the assembly. Thus, as in the rites studied by Bastide, the ceremony of *Weisung* itself constituted an act of the commemoration of the lord's authority, the explicit declaration of law comparable to the myth accompanying a rite. By participating in the assembly, peasants were reminding themselves who they were, that is, to whom they were subjected.

On the other hand, in contrast to what Bastide's model implies (1978:245), no simple correspondence existed between the social organization of the group in question and the image of relationships projected by the ceremony. The *Weisung* was a carefully controlled inversion of the everyday visage of lord-ship, since lords were ascribing legal authority to their subjects. Peasants could perhaps be made to say what lords wanted to hear, but for their answer to be considered representative and authoritative, they had at least to appear to be speaking freely and uncoerced, especially when scribes were present.[14] In order to elicit effects of legitimacy from rural assemblies, lords had to work their way through a host of ritual constraints. The *Weisung* was therefore not a transparent projection of existing social relations onto the gathering, but a transfiguration of existing power. It remains to be seen whether it was also accompanied by the kind of collective belief on the part of participants which Bastide seems to surmise for the rites that he has studied.

A central aspect of the transfiguration of lordship in the *Weisung* consisted in backgrounding the threat of violence and the means of coercion at lords' disposal.[15] A strict demarcation of the assembly as the setting for the declaration of law was maintained by a series of ritualized opening questions and a special peace proclaimed for its duration (Burchard 1893; Feigl 1974). Within the *Weisung*, lords had to translate their power into discursive resources that would allow them to control its course. The right to put questions was foremost among these. It permitted lords to elicit answers, to direct attention, and to control to a large extent the making of issues and non-issues (Goody 1978b:17–43). Asking questions was essential to the organization of social bias in the assembly. But it was not enough to secure a proper *Weisung*, for lords were still dependent on obtaining the 'right' answers.

The ritualization of the process of *Weisung* also served to control the behaviour of peasant jurors in a setting that excluded the use of unconcealed threats by lords. Lords were not formally confined to putting only customary questions, though peasants could claim they did not know the answer to novel ones. Peasant jurors, however, were bound to answer in ways consistent with their previous declarations. Lords could therefore insist on 'traditionality' and refer recalcitrant peasant law-finders to their own or their predecessors' past recognitions.[16] Accordingly, many a *Weisung* was itself about the customary course of *Weisung*, as peasants were asked not to cite their ancestors but themselves citing their ancestors, that is, to remember how they usually 're-membered.'[17] This strategy reduced to a degree the risk of wild interpretations and uncontrolled production of the past by peasants. Ascribing to them the authority to produce binding versions of the legal past restricted to a degree the lords' ability to argue directly against peasants by adducing their own version; thus not the remembered past itself, but past 'remembering' was used to constrain peasant *Weisung*. Peasants would thus be confronted with their own past statements, and the lord's power over the living could assume the form of the lordship of the past. It is important to see how a specific representation of the past, of 'tradition' and 'traditionality' – indeed, 'traditionality in the second degree' – was not a feature of some peasant culture but a specific effect of an institutionalized practice in a given social context. When actually confronted with lords or their legal counsellors waving written documents in the assembly, peasants were not facing some disembodied 'power of the written word' but their past acts of recognition noted down, extracted, and cited in order to shape their recitation of the law.

Still, controlling the ceremony and even supervising the words spoken did not ensure the lords' full control over the production of tradition, as long as the relevant interpretative community consisted of peasants. Symbolic gestures embodying legal claims, for instance, were liable to be given contradictory interpretations by lords and peasants.[18] Peasants' 'wild interpretations' could not be easily discarded by lords because legal competence was ascribed to peasants by the very same gesture that sought to install lords' archives in their 'memory.' The case of the Brauweiler monks and the villagers of Klotten in the electorate of Trier is especially revealing in this respect. The Brauweiler peasants in Klotten were allowed to intermarry with subjects of a small lordship in Klotten, whose patron was St Peter; they were thus permitted to marry 'the people of St Peter.' In 1501 the Brauweiler chronicle noted that some peasants from Klotten had married 'foreign women.' The peasants cited the local *Weisung* in support of their claim that they were entitled to marry any 'man of St Peter,' that is, any subject of the territorial principality governed by the archbishop of Trier, whose patron saint was also St Peter. This interpretation would amount to making the imposed marriage limitation practically void. The Brauweiler lordship forced the peasants publicly to renounce their heretic interpretation of the local *Weisung* and to pay the marriage fines; it also seems to have taken measures in order to incorporate the 'proper' interpretation more clearly in the *Weisung* of 1511.[19] Yet by 1652 the peasants of Klotten enjoyed the right of marriage earlier denied to them.[20]

· Besides the peasants remembering their own past 'remembrance,' there was a further central act of remembering involved in the *Weisung* which may be easily overlooked. Opening the *Weisung* session, the lord's representative usually reminded (*[er]mahnt*, a loaded term that also means 'admonished' or 'warned') the jurors and the community of their oath of allegiance and asked them to declare the law. Thus the appeal to peasants' memory within the *Weisung* was itself embedded within the lords' reminding them of their status as subjects owing allegiance. This was a way of introducing pre-existing power relations into the circumscribed setting of the *Weisung* without laying bare device. Before peasants were to assume their formal personae as law-finders, the imprint of lordship on their peasant selves was evoked by reminding them of their oath. As far as lords were concerned, the peasants would be expected to speak as freely and authoritatively as their ritualized role as jurors would demand, but also as faithfully and loyally as their social subjection implied. Different dimensions of peasants' social identity were thus evoked and played against each other. Such evocations could also be deployed during a *Weisung*, as in Fankel on the Mosel river in 1422. Taken aback by the statement of the unruly jurors, who omitted the rights of his lord, the Count of Sponheim, from their *Weisung*, the agent of the count reminded them that they were his lord's jurors and had sworn by the saints to declare the law only when admonished on their oath and asked to do so.[21] Then the jurors gave a proper *Weisung* 'as it was handed down to them from their forefathers,' as the lord's agent reported with satisfaction. Yet resistance did not subside, and in 1438 some Fankel peasants were still refusing to do homage to the count and were arrested.[22]

Lords' power was thus backgrounded but never wholly missing from the scene of the *Weisung*; the interaction was constructed as a carefully framed setting in which participants might point beyond it to its enclosing frames. The presence of the lords' following is a further case in point. The lord's right to accommodation by his subjects had an obvious economic importance. The number of followers whom he was allowed to bring with him was often specified in *Weistümer*, and some lords had the *Weistümer* describe in great length the food and drinks to be served and the bed and lodging required, not omitting bread for their dogs and fodder for their horses. Leaving aside the issue of the onerous proximity of lords intruding as guests into peasant milieu and maintaining the focus on the *Weisung*, we should note that lords' followers were not only *representing* lordly lifestyle in the village; their actual presence as armed retainers affected the interaction. Thus within the ceremony their presence was a component of lordly representation, a symbolic attribute of lordship; at the same time, it tacitly pointed to their role beyond the ceremony as part of the means of coercion at the lords' disposal;[23] finally, in written accounts of the *Weisung* the followers were often listed only in the concluding section as witnesses authenticating the document. Written documentation hence neutralized the effects of their presence, but variations between declarations of law given by the same communities within a short span of time can be plausibly accounted for by shifts in the immediate balance of power generated by the presence of lords' armed retainers at the assembly. Thus in the 1422 case of the Fankel jurors, it seems that it was not the Sponheim agent's admonition alone that made jurors 'remember' the proper *Weisung*, but the actual presence of 'friends' of the Count of Sponheim at the scene of the assembly.[24]

Lordship, transfigured, underlay the *Weisung* event. The *Weisung* owed its form to the social organization of the seigniory mediated through self-concealing strategies and an accepted repertoire of moves and countermoves by lords and peasants. 'Remembering' was not a straightforward derivative of group structure but the social effect of a series of reminders exchanged between and unequal parties. Whereas in Bastide's model 'memories are articulated together with the memories of others in the well-ordered interplay of reciprocal images' (1978:247), such could hardly be expected in the strained articulation of the *Weisung*. Such well-ordered interplay existed on paper in scenarios for proper *Weisung* produced by scribes for the use of lords' bailiffs. In actual *Weisung*, questions were not necessarily followed by answers, and the images of the past projected by lords' questions were not always met by transparent peasant consciousness reflecting it back and lending it authority. That such was the case can be shown if the relationship between lords' questions and peasants' answers is examined more closely.

The subject matter of a question is partly determined by the answer.[25] It was therefore not enough for lords to be entitled to put questions in order to determine completely the topic of the interchange in the assembly. An attempt by peasants radically to redefine the subject would clearly be perceived as an open challenge to the lords' position. This was what the Fankel jurors actually did in the *Weisung* referred to above. Asked about the rights of the Count of Sponheim, they responded by declaring the rights of his rival, the prince-elector of Trier. The count's angry official insisted that 'no one asked them about that *Weistum*' and that what they did was unlawful. The peasants' ability to redefine questions did have its limits, but these were limits to be explored and pushed further as the occasion arose. Jurors could evade a question[26] or append a peasant complaint[27] or a counter-claim[28] to a required recognition of lord's rights.

A limiting case consists in answering a question with a question and trying thereby to take control of the course of the conversation.[29] Consider the case of the peasants of Ensheim near modern Saarbrücken, subjects of the monastery of Wadgassen. In 1511 and 1520 they were recorded as responding to the ritual question opening the *Weisung* – 'whether it is the right day and hour to hold the lord's yearly assembly' – with the routine answer, 'When it seems to my lord of Wadgassen that it is the right day and hour, then this is the time.'[30] In

1538, however, the speaker for the jurors posed a counter-question: he wished to know 'whether my lord the abbot of Wadgassen is willing to leave the jurors and the court to their old customs and usage; to which the [lord's] provost gave them this answer: My lord the abbot of Wadgassen is not of the wish or of the intention to deprive you of some old rights, usages and customs or to diminish them, but to keep them rightfully to the best of his ability.' Only then did the jurors give the expected answer, allowing the assembly to resume its course.[31] Here peasants seem to have left the realm of ritualized exchange and entered open negotiations with their lord, probably taking advantage of some favourable constellation. It is tempting to see the occasion as a local repercussion of the German Peasant Revolt (1524–6) intervening between the earlier *Weisung* and this one. Indeed many villages of Wadgassen took part in the revolt, but Ensheim apparently did not; it may, however, have benefited from the revolt by refraining from participating, since the abbot is reported to have favourably considered the list of grievances that the peasants submitted in 1525.[32]

Not only were peasants' responses not necessarily followed by the answers that lords expected, but a lord's question could be pending in the air for a while before it was answered. Jurors would sometimes retreat and confer among themselves or with members of the community before returning to the circle to pronounce their reply. They could deploy this right in order to gain time before pronouncing an answer likely to irritate the lord facing them, as the jurors of Fankel did in the 1422 *Weisung* cited above.[33] Also, by leaving the court and 'conferring with the community,' peasant jurors could turn attention to their official mask, their role as representatives and mediators between lord and community, moving in a space carved out between their personal status as subjects and their institutionalized role as jurors in the assembly. However, it is worth pointing out that the room for such strategies was partly opened up by the lords themselves, whose scribes often emphasized that peasants' favourable answers were given 'after due deliberation' in order to lend them special weight.[34]

The time span separating a question from an answer could be stretched even more when jurors claimed that they did not know the *Weisung* and needed a recess to think it over.[35] This was a recognized move and could sometimes end up with the lords' question not being answered at all.[36] Asked about the obligations and liabilities of serfdom, the jurors of Gersheim claimed that they did not know the answer and were given a month to think it over (*gemude*). In reply, the representative of the lordship, the monastery of Herbitzheim, confronted them with a rather unconventional question: What happens when jurors take time to consider an answer and do not give one within the set term – who pays the costs? In response, the jurors asked for a month to consider this question, and presumably also its implications for themselves.[37]

Differential Silences

Cases in which the ceremonial exchange between lords and peasants turned into an actual dialogue bring to the surface the tensions that the usual ritualized flow of the ceremony may conceal. This does not discard the ceremony as mere form, but points to the efforts and the risks involved in keeping up appearances and the specific strategies that they gave rise to. Instead of the almost mechanical reciprocal mirroring of shared visions postulated by Bastide, we find in the *Weisung* a strained refraction of conflicting images of the past, with peasants being reminded by their lords of what they were supposed to remember and seeking to counter this ascribed remembrance by reshaping the questions put to them or by claiming ignorance.

Claiming ignorance can be considered the only recognized form of peasant silence within the *Weisung* situation, whereas remaining completely silent, ignoring the lord speaking, would be a direct affront. Besides formally claiming ignorance, one could try to pass upon an issue in silence, evade the question, or misunderstand it. Since the *Weisung* was a structured event, a ritualized dialogue, silences were articulated as omissions where answers were expected. Peasants' attempts to pass over certain issues in silence are therefore easily noticed as issues raised by lords' questions and avoided by peasants. In contrast, lords' unformulated questions, the issues that lords preferred not to raise at all, such as their obligations towards the peasant community, are easily overheard; they are non-issues. Even in those cases in which peasant jurors managed to make lords promise to respect peasant customary rights, such rights were summarily referred to and did not become the subject matter of a detailed *Weisung*, because lords could not be made to put the necessary questions.[38] Hence, whereas peasants' silence emerges easily to the surface of preserved texts, lords' strategic evasion and suppression of potential questions are not felt to be missing. This is another aspect of the inequality structuring the encounter: lords' and peasants' silences were not equally audible. Note that this mode of organizing social bias is a feature proper to the oral event, not to mention the further effects of silence generated by the written record.

Peasant silence as a discursive strategy within the *Weisung* can be contrasted with a much more radical kind of silence when a whole community defied its lord by failing to show up at the assembly. Such silence was eloquent enough. But it was again only a relative one, for it referred only to the occasion at hand, namely, the encounter with the lord: a lot of peasant talk could be expected to happen somewhere else, in autonomous peasants' assemblies, a major form of organization of medieval peasant rebellions.[39] Suppressing peasant rebellion, as in Germany after the Peasant Revolt involved rechannelling peasant public speech to assemblies held under the aegis of lordship and a strict prohibition of gathering without lords' permission and without the presence of their agents (Stockmann 1975:320–2).

Still, the radical challenge posed to lordship by collectively not attending the assembly should not be wholly severed from everyday infractions and conflicts making up the workings of *Herrschaft*. There were some recognized grounds for excusing individual peasants who failed to attend the assembly;[40] repeated non-attendance, however, would be taken as an indication of defiance and punished accordingly.[41] In Bruttig for non-attendance villagers paid the 'small fine' (ten pfennig), which was immediately consumed by the peasants attending the assembly, a provision paralleled by common stipulations in neighbouring villages, where the fine for individual non-attendance was paid as a *sester* or a bottle of wine, to be distributed among the villagers present. A peasant considered defiantly absent, however, would be punished by the lord at his will.[42] It seems that peasant could usually be trusted to implicate themselves in the daily practice of *Herrschaft* by denouncing those absent, pronouncing judgment, and consuming the fines. This changed, however, once a certain threshold had been crossed and non-attendance assumed a new meaning. Collective absence seems to have been a much less ambiguous matter than individual evasion.

On this level as well, differential meanings are ascribed to silences. For although one needed both lords and peasants for the ceremony to take its course, lords' absence had a different implication. They were not under obligation to appear; failing to hold a *Weisung* for an extended period of time, however, entailed the danger that lordship, or at least some of its essential claims, would sink into oblivion.[43] The need to counter 'forgetting' of this sort constituted a major stake in the *Weisung*. As in the case of peasants' non-attendance, lords' repeated absences mattered. By failing to claim his rights, a lord was risking the possibility of custom turning from ally into enemy, since silence and non-presence would acquire normative power by prescription. Here the differences with Bastide's account of forgetting as a result of participants' absences from the ceremony is telling: in both cases, 'forgetting' is structured by the scenario, felt and shaped by the articulation of complementary roles. But the differential effects of lords' and peasants' absence show the *Weisung* to be not a simple collective ceremony but an imposed structure intended to instil 'memory.' The formal mutual dependency of question and answer may conceal from us the fact that peasants could very well do without lords asking them questions. As a community of producers and neighbours they seem to have regulated their use rights without a similar question-and-answer ritual. Through the *Weisung*, lords were actually trying to insert themselves into the process of tradition,[44] yet peasant populations endowed with communal institutions had no difficulty imagining themselves doing well without lords.[45] One could see here a parallel with late-medieval lords' attempts to control potentially independent peasant household production. Indeed, it has been suggested that the emergence of the *Weisung* institution may be related to west German lords' gradual retreat from direct involvement in production on their domains in the High Middle Ages, so that *Weisung* was to bind peasants to lordship as its grip on their labour power was loosened (Patzelt 1924).

Wine and Memory

Not only words and texts circulated in the *Weisung*. In order for us to grasp the system at work, the material flow at the assembly should be at least summarily considered. Food and wine were not only jurors' and peasants' reward for attending the assembly and helping to recite the *Weisung*; law-finders' recurring insistence on their proper distribution suggests that their material importance should not be underestimated. Wine and memory were intricately bound together. In some villages white bread was given out at the assembly 'as a token,' 'for remembrance.'[46] More generally, according to a widely prevalent legal practice, by drinking 'testimonial wine' (*vinum testimoniale*) one was bound to retain things said and done. This custom should be borne in mind when we consider the role of food and wine in village assemblies. Avoiding the concluding meal or the wine shared after some public legal proceeding could indicate dissent and refusal to be committed in the future to its outcome.[47] Hence by consuming food and wine given out by their lord, peasants were actually committing themselves to serve as vessels of legal acts performed in the assembly,[48] their position analogous to that of jurors formally required to retain a testimony in their memory after having consumed 'testimonial wine' (Beyerle 1934:258–60; Erler 1971).

The circulation of wine and food was, however, more intricate than this account might suggest. During the assembly, wine circulated also among the villagers, as peasants' small infractions were brought forward and commuted to fines paid on the spot, often in wine (or beer) or bread. Different circuits of wine intersected in the assembly, and the flow of wine among community members, channelled through the court, also furnished lords' agents with valuable information and assisted their control of village life. The ambiguities involved can be gleaned from the proceedings in Unterneudorf in 1457, where the fine for not attending the assembly customarily consisted in paying for a round of drinks for all the villagers assembled. The lord's interest in compulsory attendance at the assembly was thus linked to the communal enjoyment of the fines for failing to attend it; this linkage could be expected to encourage reciprocal denouncements and intensify divisions within the community. The lord's bailiff was faced, however, with repeated cases of peasants refusing to drink this wine and donating the fine back to the villager found guilty; he therefore insisted that if they refused to drink the fine, it would nevertheless have to be paid, but directly to the lord (Krebs 1903:225–8).

Such acts of refusal seem to have been an exception. The amounts of wine usually consumed during assemblies can be gauged from occasional complaints about excessive drinking.[49] The Brauweiler abbot complained that his jurors in Klotten used to drink so much that they were able neither to keep their mouths shut during the ceremony nor to declare the law properly.[50] A fourteenth-century document has a peasant concluding a *Weisung* declaration by saying: 'Aultres choses ne vous raporte pour le présent for que Dieu vous doint bonne vie et allons boire, je vous en prie.'[51] Drinking wine in the assembly might have served to soothe local animosities, but it also provided ample occasions for new quarrels to break out, resulting in further fines to be paid by the parties for breach of the assembly's special peace and thus feeding the interaction further. Wine was flowing through the assembly especially in autumn, when many lords were entitled to impel their subjects to buy a certain quantity of lords' wine (*Bannwein*). In order to give a full account of the intricate flow of wine and the material exchanges in the assembly, one could also have to juxtapose peasants' meals at the lord's expense with the hospitality accorded to the lord and his followers when they came to the village. Finally, in wine-growing regions peasants were often paying their dues in kind, so that to the flow of wine downwards and upwards, from lords and among villagers through the court, one should add the presentations of wine to lords, some of which was solemnly tasted and evaluated in the assemblies.[52] The whole gathering took place amidst an intensive flow of wine and talk; villagers were eating and memorizing, denouncing and drinking, settling petty accounts with their neighbours or resolving quarrels with them.

The late-medieval *Weisung* can thus be pictured as a contradictory inscription system. German peasants were required to perform for and with their lords a particular kind of 'labour of memory,' governed by a complex and unequal division of labour. Rural assemblies were the actual sites of production for traditions, linking lords, peasants, armed followers and scribes, questions and answers, wine, bread and presentations in kind, scribbled notes, notarial documents, and expanding seigniorial archives, and operating according to locally variable sets of ceremonial rules and recognized repertoires of moves and countermoves.

The Shapes of the Past

A contradictory system for the production of the past under lordship, the *Weisung* entailed a specific mode of shaping the past. The binding, publicly produced, and jurally usable past was not a finished product but always at stake in the repeated, yet not fully repeatable, encounters between lords and peasant subjects. Hence, lords' interactional resources and their control of the situational dynamics impinged greatly on the long-term process of shaping local law. Lords' rights could easily sink into oblivion, at least as far as peasants were concerned. A medieval lord would like to hear the things that his peasants would like to forget – or rather, 'forget to tell.' That is the reason why he put the questions.

Putting questions, however, was not only a means to thematize existing norms and obligations or to make a selection regarding transmitted law; it was also a way of producing norms. Only when certain questions were posed were some norms and rights elicited, given form and binding force: 'Before someone asks you a question, you often do not know what you think' (Elias Canetti). By being formulated, declared as answers to questions posed in the required setting, accustomed practices could be transformed into customary ones and sometimes into prescriptive rights. Such attempts are best observed when they fail; otherwise they efface their own traces since the norms elicited and successfully turned 'traditional' cannot be distinguished from 'more traditional' ones.[53]

Lords needed their peasants in order to catapult present practices beyond the proximate temporal horizon and present them as having existed 'since time immemorial.' In this sense, the *Weisung* was usually not about things past, but about the past in the present, that is, those 'segments' of the present which, under the existing balance of power and with due respect for customary forms, could be successfully projected onto the past. The past typically produced by *Weisung* was shallow, an extension of the present.

The nature of 'remembering' involved can be further illuminated by considering the apparently special case of newcomers joining the lordship. Some *Weistümer* stipulate that at the assembly, newcomers should first take a public oath of allegiance to the lords in order to be able to join immediately afterwards with the rest of the peasants in reciting the law. Such a stipulation makes clear that when peasants were said to be looking backwards and citing their ancestors, they were often actually looking sideways and listening to their neighbours, learning by participating what they had always 'remembered.' This kind of 'memory' could only be ascribed to the group, not to each individual peasant; it came about by listening, mumbling, and joining in the recitation. It did not apply to things *passé*, but referred obliquely to present concensus forged in the community under the watchful eye of lordship.[54]

This process seems familiar enough from common accounts of 'traditional societies'; it also suits well-entrenched images of the 'traditional peasant'[55] and can easily be made to fit with common representation of 'oral culture.' Such accounts tend to ignore the specific social constraints on 'structural amnesia' and the struggles over 'forgetting' discussed above. Moreover, in the case of *Weisung*, 'tradition' itself was not simply a given of medieval 'culture' or 'mentality,' but the outcome of a specific social configuration: in the context of lords-peasants relations in late-medieval Germany, 'tradition' functioned as a mode of legitimation in a historical configuration in which lords and peasants could not resort to alternative sources of legitimation (such as common interest) in order to justify basic social arrangements.[56] More specifically, as I have tried to show above, in our case 'traditionality' was not an expression of some peasant 'mentality' but a strategy embedded in the practice of rural *Weisung* and occasionally used to control peasant declarations.

Peasants were indeed authorized to tell the law; but in any given moment they were held to tell it in the same way as they had done before: when speaking, they were always held to be citing. The moment in which peasants could make an authorized and free statement of the law was entrapped in infinite regression, constantly projected by the *Weisung* and constantly receding into the past, always re-enacted. It was allowed to be present only as a representation; yet so transformed, it could serve to lend legitimacy to lordship. In the *Weisung* a counter-factual state of affairs was enacted recurrently, carefully framed and controlled. A mode of legitimation by consent was actually embedded in the *Weisung* as a form of customary law-making. Unlike other modes of constantly deferring original consent, here consent was constantly receding into the past. You had to be your own dead ancestor in order to elude the restraints imposed by the presence of lordship on the production of the past.

The deep ambivalence of custom was well captured by the sixteenth-century German jurist Ulrich Zasius. He repeated the common learned opinion that both custom and prescription (i.e., a right arising out of uninterrupted usage) derive their normative power from the assumption that they embody implicit past consent to a given state of affairs, the difference being, he wrote, that prescription always works in favour of the people whose past practice serves as evidence for its observance, whereas custom may work against them.[57]

The projected moment of consent, however, was not receding by itself, as a side effect of a pre-given 'traditionality.' Lords had to see to it that it was pushed back against a countervailing tendency by peasants to endow it with reality, to take hold of the vanishing moment projected by the *Weisung*. They were seldom able to do so. To the extent that lords' power seemed secure and incontestable, peasants acquiesced and contributed to the process of legitimation, exacting from lords what they could for their cooperation. But that outcome was not all that they could think of. It is therefore essential to round out an account of the *Weisung* in the context of lordship by considering what peasants did when they had a choice.

'Self-forgetting' and Projected *Vorzeiten*

Constructing traditions in the assembly cannot be accounted for by referring to the available technologies of communication and transmission; it was inextricably related to the practice of seigniorial lordship. Late-medieval German lords were not unfamiliar with techniques of record-keeping; when records were damaged, they could hold a special inquiry and question their peasants. This special measure, known also in other parts of late-medieval Europe, is not to be confused with the regular practice of *Weisung*, which German lords retained even when in possession of functioning chancelleries. Peasants were rather to serve as extensions of these archives, a living *conservatoire* (Bourdieu 1980:chap. 4). In order properly to consider the social role of the *Weisung*, one has to place it in the context of the inherent difficulties of reproducing late-medieval lordship over peasants and reconstruct the contemporary discourse about 'forgetting' and the dangers that it spelled for lordship and the existing social order.

Here the crucial fact is German lords' exclusion from the production process, their growing reliance since the central Middle Ages on increasingly autonomous production by peasant households and on social organization provided by peasant communities.[58] This structure of production impinged directly on the reproduction of rural lordship. As far as economic relations were concerned, late-medieval German lordship faced the constant danger of being 'forgotten'; not only was a social order from which lordship would be absent imaginable, but many believed that it actually existed in the Swiss confederation. 'Custom' or 'traditionality' could not be trusted to countervail this tendency. In order to do so, German lords indeed resorted to 'extra-economic coercion.' Such coercion, however, is often conceived of as naked and direct violence, the kind used by each lord against his peasants. Also, it evokes images of manifest coercion and diverts attention from potential violence, underlying social relations, and structuring expectations. In my view, 'extra-economic coercion' should more usefully be applied to lordship's attempts to inscribe itself onto peasant subjects by means of traditional violence and of the violence of tradition.

The subtle violence of tradition is exemplified in the *Weisung*; it is the one embedded in uneasy questions, induced remembering, obligatory drinking, and forced hospitality. Traditional violence, however, was at least equally essential. Its major manifestation was the feudal 'private war' (*Fehde*). 'Feudal anarchy' – noble feuds and petty raids – did not necessarily undermine the social structure but was to a certain extent one of its foundations. It was a form of the social production of violence, that is, the uncoordinated production by the lords of the need for protection. Lordship would not sink into oblivion as long as the need for lords was constantly reproduced. German lords' insistence on their right to wage 'private wars' among themselves betrays how important this practice was for the social production of violence. They did not need consciously to cooperate in order to subdue peasants; it was exactly the uncoordinated nature of the social production of violence as an unintended consequence of lords' pursuing their particular interests and defending their honour through feuds which allowed it to produce its own ideological effects, setting up individual lords as protectors from external threat while simultaneously revealing and concealing their role in its production.[59] In fact, both violence and tradition were explicitly represented by some fifteenth-century authors as the means to make peasants 'remember who they were,' to work against their deeply ingrained 'forgetfulness': both violence and tradition were expected to (re)form proper peasant subjects (Algazi 1993).

In order to break with lordship, peasants had to break away from the past of lordship, indeed, to break with themselves as entangled in its production, whereas lords for their part could turn peasants' ascribed authority against them. Peasants' tendency to 'forget' lords' claims was to be constrained in the *Weisung*. More significantly, in the late Middle Ages, peasant rebellion itself was termed an act of 'self-forgetting.' This was the expression used by members of the estates who convened in the diet of Speyer in 1526 to discuss the urgent concerns of the Holy Roman Empire, after the suppression of the Peasant Revolt: the rebels, they said, 'have quite severely forgotten themselves' (Koch 1745:II,274). Consequently, it was necessary to remind them of their duties once the rebellion was over (Friedensburg 1887:537 [appendix VII]). The use of this term may give us an idea of socially determined contemporary notions of both 'forgetting' and 'self.' By rebelling, the peasants were 'forgetting' society within themselves, their socially ascribed 'self' as a locus of obligations. When they were said to 'have forgotten themselves,' not a momentary, involuntary, individual state of mind was intended; 'self-forgetting' denoted in this context collective, organized social action, just as 'remembrance' in the

Weisung was not an act of solitary rumination but a structured interaction. To 'remember' in the *Weisung*, peasants had to be reminded by their lords; the same held for the practice of violently 'reminding peasants who they really were.' By 'self-forgetting' they were misrecognizing themselves; they were trying to assume an improper social identity. Their 'real self' was socially ascribed and was to be violently reinscribed if 'forgotten.'[60] In a *Weisung*, peasants were to recognize their true figure in a mirror held out by their lords.[61]

What lords termed and treated as criminal 'self-forgetting,' peasants could consider a radical 'recollection' of lost rights and freedoms. Reconstructing the kind of past repressed by the *Weisung's* tradition-making is essential for grasping its function. In reply to lords' attempts to curb those few peasant rights that were actually included in *Weisung*, peasants could try to refer to those rights in their answers. Yet in order to question lordship more radically when deeply implicated in the production of the past of lordship, they had to find a province of the 'past' beyond the reach of lordship, a surface on which they could project their views of what was lawful and right. The *Weisung's* past was typically an extension of present lordship. In a sense, statements in the *Weisung* were actually about the present, about the way things are and 'always' have been 'as far as one can remember'; they were not about the way things had been before. Peasant thus often assigned their claims to the time 'before,' to *vor zeiten* ('former times' or 'times ago').

The term, denoting in modern German 'ancient times' or, in the singular 'prehistory,' appears to be a temporal expression, but actually denoted a structural property attributed to some aspects of the past in contrast with present ones. Both lords and peasants were familiar with claims located *vor zeiten*. Lords were occasionally referring to *vor zeiten* when they tried to revive an extinct practice or pressed a right that they claimed to have found documented in their archives. In such cases, they sometimes preferred to resurrect worn-out documents by having peasants lend their living voices to them.[62]

In contrast, peasants' *vor zeiten* were usually not enshrined in a *Weisung*. Therefore, whereas lords were often able to project successfully their archive-based claims onto peasant 'memory,' peasant claims would seem in comparison wild and inarticulate, emerging out of nowhere. At times, however, we catch a glimpse of other sites of tradition-making, of assemblies held beyond the reach of lordship and therefore seldom documented; one can surmise that the notions of lawfulness upheld in such assemblies surfaced in times of conflict and open rebellion. Take, for example, the monks of Brauweiler, lords of the village of Klotten, who launched an elaborate memory policy to inscribe their claims in the consciousness of their peasants. They had their official *Weisung* under control; but they seem to have been anxious to lay hold of the villagers' other assembly, held on St Valerius' Day. However, to judge by the extant evidence, only once did they actually procure a report on its course. In at least one documented case, collective action against the lordship of Brauweiler in a struggle over the nearby woods appears to have begun in this gathering regularly held on St Valerius' Day.[63]

The *Weisung* was thus not the ultimate embodiment of public village tradition; at times it was a contested site of tradition-making, standing somewhere between lords' archives and some other sites of norm-making lying further away. Still, one of the important weaknesses of peasants' reliance on claims located *vor zeiten* was that they were not properly embodied in public statements or written documents. It was accordingly not uncommon for peasant rebels to demand that lords produce withheld documents in which peasants believed their freedoms and privileges were recorded.[64] German peasants' recourse to the 'old law' to justify their claims during the Peasant Revolt of 1524–6 has usually been seen as evidence of their 'traditionality'; indeed, it has even been claimed that they relied on *Weistümer* to substantiate their claims.[65] It has been overlooked that peasants' notion of 'old' in the context of rebellion might have differed from the notion of 'old law' and the image of the past embedded in institutions such as the *Weisung*. 'Old' could designate a time before the era under the tight grip of lordship or, more generally, a time in which a set of alternative social arrangements had existed.[66] During the Reformation, in a complex process that I cannot properly deal with here, German peasants came to find the charter of this past in the Bible. The vanishing moment projected by the *Weisung* thus turned into flesh. It was, however, a reference to the 'old law' that implied a *rejection* of custom, since 'bad custom' is how original subjection sought to transfigure itself into lawful lordship. Why should peasants have some attitude to 'the past,' a learned construct, a massive abstraction? Instead of ascribing to medieval peasants some attitude to an undifferentiated 'past,' to argue about 'traditionality' or its absence, we should see how – to adopt a hypostatized language – different 'segments' of the past were differently controlled and shaped. We need to see the different regularities governing the production of such 'segments' of 'the past.'

This statement is still too unrefined to stand. In the late Middle Ages, *vor zeiten* did not denote a 'time' but rather was used as an adverb denoting things past.[67] Claims and norms said to have existed *vor zeiten* were not necessarily assumed to have existed at the same 'time,' that is, to have formed a part of some historical 'whole,' a 'past.' We may thus be dealing not with a peasant image of 'the past,' but rather with fragmented 'former times,' in which various practices and norms could be located without necessarily having to be interrelated or to form part of an image of a former time. Only in a complex process did perhaps variously located images of *vor zeiten* begin to crystalize into a former time (*Vorzeit*), a real 'first time.'

To a significant extent, the segment of past produced by officially recognized systems for 'tradition-making' such as the *Weisung* was a mode of inscribing lordship in peasants. Most of this past was neither of the peasants' own making nor wholly in their lords' image and likeness. In the *Weisung*, lords called upon peasants to find within themselves that which the lords were anxious to hear. Lordship was taking part in the making of peasant selves, since the strategies that peasants used to disengage themselves from full involvement in the production of the past – ignorance, forgetting, and silence – could themselves inform peasants' make-up. Would the practice of feigned ignorance in the face of lordship fail to leave some mark on peasants' image of themselves? Could peasants regularly participate in the *Weisung* and try to outmanoeuvre their bailiffs without implicating themselves even further in the workings of lordship? The boundaries between cooperation and collaboration traversed peasants' subjects because they formed a part of an externalized memory structure, incorporating both lords and their subjects. The contradictions of the *Weisung* practice, of authority ascribed and power withheld, may partly explain why German peasants are seldom known to have protested when disinvested of the authority to tell the law. Thus the reconfiguration of the legal field not only robbed them of a voice in legal affairs, turning their normative traditions into legal folklore, but it also freed them from the burden of tradition.

NOTES

I had the occasion to benefit from comments and criticisms by participants in the Bellagio History and Anthropology workshop, the peasant studies group (Oxford), and the graduate seminar on medieval history (Birmingham). I am especially indebted to Peter Baumann, Peter Blickle, Michaela Hohkamp, Clif Hubby, Peter Kriedte, Alf Lüdtke, Hans Medick, Zvi Razi, David Sabean, Jürgen Schlumbohm, Gerald Sider, Gavin Smith, and Heide Wunder, who commented on previous versions of this paper.

1 Most of the examples discussed below are drawn from a small group of villages in western Germany, mostly on the Rhein and Mosel rivers, between 1350 and 1550, though occasionally material from other villages will be introduced for comparison and illustration. The main collections of sources used are Grimm 1840–78; Weizsäcker 1957–73; Krämer and Spiess 1986. A useful introduction is Blickle 1978, to which one should add the instructive introduction by Spiess to Krämer and Spiess 1986. Research until the 1970s is summarized in Werkmüller 1972. Two important monographs are Eder 1978 and Hinsberger 1989. Some of the argument prefigure my forthcoming book *Herrschaft der Tradition: Weistümerstudien* and

are presented here in compressed form without all the supporting evidence. In the discussion
that follows, references to sources usually begin with the name of the village or the seigniory
in question, followed by the document's date if available and the usual references to printed
editions.

2 I am generally confining myself in this essay to the practice of *Weisung* in rural lordships
(whose written version is often called *Hofweistum*); laws were similarly recited by jurors in
non-seignorial rural courts (*Gerichtsweistum*) and in parish assemblies (*Sendweistum*). There
were numerous local variations.

3 For the difficulties involved in combining the records of particular lordships in order to
reconstruct demographic patterns, economic relations, and social structures in medieval
German rural communities, see Sabean 1972.

4 See, however, Vanja 1986.

5 For similar observations on England, see Razi 1987:273. See also the discussion of a juror's
position according to the Kesten court protocol cited below.

6 Modes of nomination, the scope for jurors' co-optation, and the degree of community
participation varied greatly (Wunder 1985). I use the term 'jurors' (in German *Schöffen* or
Urteiler) to designate members of a peasant collegium declaring the law, giving judgment,
and sometimes also running community affairs; they should not be confused with members of
an English jury.

7 In a text from Schweppenhausen (1407), villagers' authority is especially underscored: 'wen
sie hielden vnd erkenten vor einen obirstn heren zu Schweppenhausen in dem gerichte? Da
gingen die scheffenne vnd dinglute mit einander vβ, want als die scheffenne besaden, so
hatten die dinglute vff den tag moge vnd auch recht zu straffen vnd zu erkennen, als die
scheffene, vnd beryeden sich vnd qwamen da wiedervmb an die gerechtstait vor dem
scholtheiβen' (Grimm 1840–78:II,184).

8 Bruttig 1461–4 (Krämer and Spiess 1986:40, no. 11); the case was retold in 1468 (ibid.:50,
no. 13).

9 Weber 1972:438–9. Weber's account is still superior to most recent attempts to conceptualize
the *Weisung* institution (cf. the opening chapters of Weitzel 1985).

10 See the list of grievances submitted to the diet of 1526 (Franz 1963:594–5, no. 209).

11 It is not clear whether Schenneten was formally a 'juror,' but he is said to have answered the
first question, probably as a speaker for the small community (about thirty-five inhabitants).
Note that although the incriminating question was addressed specifically to him and to one
Georg Hansen, Schenneten is not explicitly mentioned as having answered it, which may
imply sudden silence on his part. His important position in the village may explain, however,
why among the five men formally denounced in court for the same offence, only he was
granted an extension. For the text, see Laufner 1957:42–4.

12 The point is explicitly insisted upon in a *Weisung* about a *Weisung* from the Mosel region:
'Everyone belonging to this lordship and paying rent, must come and pay the rent and assist
the lord to do a *Weisung* of the law and to hold the assembly.' Later on it is specified that
villagers are 'obliged to confer with the jurors in order to do a *Weisung* of the lords' rights'
('alle die ghene, die dair gehorich synt off zynss gelden, dat sy komen und betzalen den zynss
und helpen ouch dem heren recht und gedynge zo wysen und zo behalden; schuldich, myt den
scheffen zo beraden, omb der heren heyrlicheyt zo wysen'). Brauweiler court in Cochem,
1507 (Krämer and Spiess 1986:103, no. 25).

13 See, for instance, the attempts by the monastery of Herbitzheim to elicit from the peasants of
Gersheim (1508) recognition of its exclusive right to pose questions (Weizsäcker 1957–
73:625–31).

14 See, for example, Weiden 1478 (Grimm 1840–78:II,137–8); Vehihe 1395 (ibid.:II,688–90). Note the ironies of peasants' alleged freedom from coercion in Wahlhausen, 1419 (ibid.:III,338–9).

15 See, though, a jurors' appeal not to be chastised if they have been found to have made mistakes in their *Weisung* in Tettingen (undated, Grimm 1840–78:II,46–7).

16 See Gillenbeuren 1564 (Krämer and Spiess 1986:no. 9); Klotten 1446 (ibid.:no. 57).

17 Bruttig 1468 (Krämer and Spiess 1986:no. 13).

18 In a contest between rival lords over their rights in Bruttig, it turned out to be important whether the pail of wine given was locally named *Vogteimerwein* or *Raucheimerwein*, which could have had different legal implications (Bruttig 1469: Krämer and Spiess 1986:68, no. 17). Yet by far the most intense conflicts arose over the legal meaning attributed to peasants furnishing hens to lords at Shrovetide, a practice that could be interpreted as a token of serfdom. As Andreas Alois Wiest wrote in 1835, 'the natural history of juristic hens is still to be written.'

19 Klotten 1511 (Krämer and Spiess 1986:265, no. 61). This is an extraordinary *Weisung* recorded in writing. It is not clear whether the jurors' statement in a usual *Weisung* was also modified to suit the lord's version; it was enough for the jurors to use the shorter formula 'St Peter' instead of the fuller one – 'St Peter of Cologne' – in order to give room for diverging interpretations.

20 Klotten 1652 (Krämer and Spiess 1986:no. 67).

21 'und daz wisetum gedan ee myns herrn wisetum, und enhan ich noch myns herrn vaged noch nymans sie nach dem wisetum zu male nit gefraget und meynen, daz sie daz unmoglich gedan haben, diewile sie myns herrn scheffen sint und zu den heyligen gesworen hant, daz sie kein urteyl wisen sollen me dan sie mit irem eyde ermanet und gefraget werden. Item darnach hant sie zum rechten gewist und hant gesprochen als es won iren aldern off sie komen sy' (Fankel 20 January 1422: Krämer and Spiess 1986:198, no. 46).

22 Krämer in Krämer and Spiess 1986:96; Goerz [1861] 1969:170.

23 For this dimension, see Grimm 1840–78:II,132.

24 The Count of Sponheim was trying to assert his rights against the archbishop of Trier. In an earlier session that year, Trier officials were present, and Sponheim's agent had to put up with the jurors' reply that they were unaware of Sponheim's rights in the village, whereas in the succeeding session discussed above, no Trier agents were mentioned.

25 For a subtle analysis of the issues involved, see Goffman 1981.

26 Ensheim 1465 (Weizsäcker 1957–73:397); Blieskastel 1570 (ibid.:144); Bruttig 1469 (Krämer and Spiess 1986:68, no. 17).

27 See Ensheim 1435 (Weizsäcker 1957–73:388–9). The case is analysed in detail in Algazi 1996:chap. 1.

28 An example is Schweppenhausen 1407 (Grimm 1840–78:11,84–5).

29 Encrevé and Formel 1983:3–30.

30 'Am ersten ist der scheffen beladenn worden zu recht, ob ys zyt sye von stun[del] vnd dage, daß man dem hern jargedinge besitzen sulde'; the jurors' answer: 'want es mynen herrn von Wad[egassen] dhunckt zytt sin vonn dage stunde, so sie es is zyt.' Ensheim, 8 October 1511, 1 October 1520 (Weizsäcker 1957–73:399, 405).

31 'Darvff Henrich der scheffen von syner mitgesellen vnd syn antwort bracht alβo: Der scheffen thut eyn frage vnd begert zu wissen, ob myn herr apt von Wadagassen den scheffen vnd das gericht by irem alten herkumen vnd gebruch laβen wolle; darvff hat der probst inen also antwort geben: Myne herr apt zu Wadagassen ist nyt des willens oder vornemens, vch einichen alten rechten, gebruych oder herkommens zu smaelen oder zu nemmen, dan synβ

vermoegens darby wie recht zu handtfesten vnd behalten.' Ensheim, 30 September 1538 (Weizsäcker 1957–73:411–12). The evidence of the 1537 *Weisung*, apparently with few witnesses present and reported by the Wadgassen scribe, seems doubtful; see especially questions 10 and 25–28 (Weizsäcker 1957–73:408–10). In some communities, similar counter-questions by jurors were part of the routinized sequence of the *Weisung*; such does not seem to have been the case in Ensheim, though it cannot be excluded that a Wadgassen promise to respect peasants' customary rights had been omitted from earlier records.

32 Helmut and Alexander Wilhelm, *Ortschronik Ensheim* (Ensheim, Saarbrücken, n.d. [1977]), 41. The situation of the Wadgassen lordship in the years following the revolt can be gauged from the fact that it had to rely on peasant cooperation in order to reconstruct records listing its claims in the villages, which had been destroyed during the revolt.

33 'Daroff hant sie eynen berait geheischen, sich zu bedenken, und hant geantwert' (Krämer and Spiess 1986:198, no 46). See Bruttig, 1469 (ibid.:no. 17).

34 Bruttig 1468 (Krämer and Spiess 1986:no. 13). Lords also occasionally asked 'the community' to confirm jurors' consequential answer. See Briedel, 1468 (Grimm 1840–78:II,414–15); Freiensteinau, 1452 (Grimm 1840–78:III,884–6).

35 Jurors could also ask for time in order to go to another rural court (*Oberhof*) and get an authorized answer from the local jurors there, which they were later to pronounce as their own statement in a subsequent session. The practice (*Rechtszug*) should not be confused with an appeal; it did not take place on the initiative of some party questioning a verdict, and the law 'fetched' was strictly local, not implying some formal hierarchy of courts and legal knowledge (Weitzel 1981).

36 Bruttig 1461–4 (Krämer and Spiess 1986:40, no. 11).

37 'Item wann der scheffenn ein gemude nemmet ein zeit vnn kemme nit vsser dem gemude inn der zeit, als das vffgenommen wer, gieng cost vnnd schadenn darvff, wer das geltenn solde, des hat der scheffenn auch ein gemude genommen ein monat Ianngk.' Gersheim 1533 (Weizsäcker 1957–73:631–3); Eder 1978:55, note 171, suggests that the text should be dated to 1453. For the jurors' answers on the same questions concerning serfdom, see the *Weisung* of 1508 (Weizsäcker 1957–73:628); it may be an allusion to the behaviour of the jurors of Breitfurt, who reacted similarly (Weizsäcker 1957–73:194).

38 An exceptional *Weisung* containing a relatively detailed list of peasant claims only underlines the rule: it is a case of three lords who came to divide the lordship over the community of Bliesmengen (1580). In this case, questions did not serve to remind peasants of their obligations but actually to elicit authoritative information on local procedure and usage. Accordingly, instead of a series of detailed questions by lords, we find them asking, 'Which question should the lords now pose?' a query that actually cedes conversational control over the definition of topic to the jurors. To one such question the jurors replied by demanding that the lords be asked whether they were willing to respect the old usage of the community; to which the local officials of the lords answered in the affirmative. Near the end of the long *Weisung*, the jurors were asked again what should happen next. They took the opportunity to declare mainly their own rights in the woods, though they also mentioned the lords' right in it (Weizsäcker 1957–73:150–1; see also Eder 1978:65).

39 On assemblies held during rebellion, see, for example, Franz 1963:165, 138; Liliencorn 1865–6:III, no. 285, lines 78–82, 88–9.

40 Such as service to some lord, illness, or departure for pilgrimage.

41 Many village courts used a simple system of fines, distinguishing the 'small fine' (often ten pfennig or a quarter or *sester* of wine) and the 'high fine' (often five or ten marks in the fifteenth century), though such practice does not imply that these were the sums actually paid.

42 Bruttig, no date (Krämer and Spiess 1986:82–4, no. 21; compare no. 28).

43 See Buschoven 1547 (Grimm 1840–78:II,664). A late document from Fankel (1666–73) can be adduced here for the rare explicit statement that it contains about the dangers for lordship which the practice of *Weisung* was to encounter: the monastery of Engelport asked for permission to establish in Fankel an assembly with a regular *Weisung* following the tumults of the Thirty Years' War, during which 'peasants did as they pleased without fear' ('ohne forcht gehaußet undt gethan, waß sie gewölt'). The Fankel peasants tried to resist the attempt (Krämer and Spiess 1986:no. 53).

44 Grinberg (1988) makes a similar point concerning French seigniories of a later period.

45 On the crucial role of 'conditionally feasible social alternatives' in forming judgment concerning existing social relations, see Roemer 1986:102–5. The accessibility of imagined social alternatives and its implications for the late-medieval German peasants is dealt with in Algazi 1966:chap. 5.

46 See, for example, Rastatt 1370 (Grimm 1840–78:I,441); Gillenbeuren 1555 (Krämer and Spiess 1986:21–5, no. 8); Gillenfeld 1561 (Grimm 1840–78:II,412–14).

47 See the case of Hägbach 1487 (Grimm 1840–78:I,397–403).

48 Buschoven 1547 (Grimm 1840–78:II,662–4); see also Muggenheim 1555 (ibid.:IV,767).

49 See, for instance, Schifferstadt (Grimm 1840–78:V,589).

50 Klotten 1571 (Krämer and Spiess 1986:277, no. 65).

51 Rights of the Abbey of Saint-Vincent de Metz in Norroy-le-Veneur; fourteenth-century manuscript cited in Perrin 1946:33.

52 Klotten has some of the most detailed descriptions (Krämer and Spiess 1986:nos. 57–71).

53 See Gersheim 1508 (Weizsäcker 1957–73:627). For a more complex case, see Ensheim 1435, discussed in my *Herrengewalt und Gewalt der Herren*, chap. 1. The jurors of Bacharach did answer in 1407 a question about the due punishment for their own infringements, but asked the lord's agent not to pose this question in the future, that is, not to make it part of the customary repertoire of questions in the *Weisung* (Grimm 1840–78:II,218).

54 Alflen 1507 (Grimm 1840–78:II,407–9); Bruttig 1609 (Krämer and Spiess 1986: no. 21).

55 See, for instance, the recent German agrarian history by Edith Ennen and Walter Janssen, *Deutsche Agrargeschichte: Vom Neolithikum bis zur Schwelle des Industriezeitalters* (Wiesbaden: Franz Steiner, 1979), 208–9.

56 For the argument, see Algazi 1996:chap. 2, 6.

57 'Item praescriptio praescribenti tantummodo prodest, sed consuetudo populo etiam aliquando nocet: quia potest contra populum, per ipsum populum consuetudo induci' (Zasius 1550:I, cols. 396–409, here col. 399).

58 Marx [1872] 1987:523–34, esp. 524–5, 533–4; 1964:798–801; Bois 1976:352–6; Kuchenbuch and Michael 1977:694–761, esp. 710, 732; Kriedte 1980:1–10.

59 The structural role of the lords' violence and its ideological effects are more fully discussed in Algazi 1996.

60 See, for example, Unrest 1957:93, 99, 85.

61 For different modes of 'self-forgetting,' the models of 'self' embedded in them, and the contradictory consequences of attempts to reject ascribed 'selves,' see Algazi 1995:387–400.

62 Fankel 1554 (Krämer and Spiess 1986:219, no. 52).

63 For Brauweiler's attempts to obtain information, see Klotten 1511 (Krämer and Spiess 1986:267–8, no. 61); see no. 69 and the differences with Brauweiler's note (no. 57). The assembly on St Valerius' Day served as the occasion for organized action against lords

226   Gadi Algazi

(Eckertz 1868:244–6). A parallel in Elsace for the role of the community assembling as *Waldgenossenschaft* in organizing resistance is discussed in Saarbrücker Arbeitsgruppe 1980:138, 148.

64 Franz 1977:206, no. 73. For an English parallel, see Faith 1981.
65 Waas 1938–9. This assertion cannot be sustained and relies on a misleading use of the term *Weistum*.
66 For an example of peasants contrasting 'former times' (*vor zeiten*) with the near past extending into the present (*zu zeiten, jetzt*), see the grievances of the community of Lauenheim (1525) in Merx 1923:I/1,282–3, no. 366.
67 Jacob Grimm, Wilhelm Grimm, et al., *Deutsches Wörterbuch* (Leipzig, 1854–1948), vol. 16, by Rudolf Meiszner, cols. 1994–9.

REFERENCES

Algazi, Gadi
1993 The Social Use of Private War: Some Late Medieval Views Reviewed. *In* Tel Aviver Jahrbuch für deutsche Geschichte, pp. 253–73.
1995 'Sich selbst vergessen' im späten Mittelalter: Denkfigur und soziale Figurationen. *In* Memoria als Kultur, Otto Gerhard Oexle, ed. pp. 387–427. Göttingen: Vandehoeck & Ruprecht.
1996 Herrengewalt and Gewalt der Herren im späten Mittelalter. Frankfurt am Main, New York: Campus.
Bastide, Roger
1970 Mémoire collective et sociologie de bricolage. L'Annee sociologique, 3rd ser., 21:65–108.
1978 The African Religions of Brazil: Toward a Sociology of the Interpenetration of Civilizations. Helen Sebba, trans. Baltimore: Johns Hopkins University Press.
Beyerle, Franz
1934 Weinkauf und Gottespfennig. *In* Festschrift Alfred Schultze zum 70. Geburtstag, Walther Merk, ed. pp. 251–82. Weimar: Hermann Böhlaus Nachfolger.
Blickle, Peter, ed.
1978 Deutsche ländliche Rechtsquellen: Probleme und Wege der Weistumsforschung. Stuttgart: Klett-Cotta.
Bois, Guy
1976 Crise du féodalisme: économie rurale et démographie en Normandie orientale du début du 14e siècle au milieu du 16e siècle. Paris: Presses de la fondation nationale des sciences politiques/Éditions de l'EHESS.
Bourdieu, Pierre
1980 Le sens pratique. Paris: Minuit.
Burchard, Kurt
1893 Die Hegung deutscher Gerichte im Mittelalter. Leipzig.
Douglas, Mary
1986 Institutionalized Public Memory. *In* the Social Fabric: Dimensions and Issues, James F. Short Jr, ed. pp. 63–76. Beverly Hills: Sage.
Eckertz, Godefridus, ed.
1868 Chronicon Brunwylrense. Annalen des Historischen Vereins für den Niederrhein 19:220–61.

Eder, Irmtraut
    1978 Die saärlandischen Weistümer – Dokumente der Territorialpolitik. Saarbrücken:
        Minerva-Verlag Thinnes & Nolte.
Encrevé, Pierre, and Michel de Formel
    1983 Le sens en pratique: construction des la référence et structure sociale de l'interaction
        dans le couple question/réponse. Actes de la recherche en sciences sociales 46:3–30
Erler, Adalbert
    1971 Botenwein. *In* Handwörterbuch der deutschen Rechtsgeschichte, Adalbert Erler and
        Ekkehard Kauffmann, ed. vol. I, pp. 492–3. Berlin: Erich Schmidt.
Faith, Rosamond
    1981 Class Struggle in Fourteenth-Century England. *In* People's History and Socialist
        Theory, Raphael Samuel, ed. pp. 50–9. London: Routledge and Kegan Paul.
Feigl, Helmut
    1974 Rechtsentwicklung und Gerichtswesen Oberösterreichs im Spiegel der Weistümer.
        Archiv für österreichische Geschichte, 130. Vienna.
Franz, Günther, ed.
    1963 Quellen zur Geschichte des Bauernkrieges. Darmstadt: Wissenschaftliche
        Buchgesellschaft.
    1977 Der deutsche Bauernkrieg: Ein Aktenband. 4th ed. Darmstadt: Wissenschaftliche
        Buchgesellschaft.
Friedensburg, Walter
    1887 Der Reichstag von Speier 1526 im Zusammenhang der politischen und kirchlichen
        Entwicklung Deutschlands im Reformationszeitalter. Berlin: Gaertners
        Verlagsbuchandlung.
Goerz, Adam
    [1861] 1969 Regesten der Erzbischöfe von Trier. Trier; reprint, Aalen: Scientia.
Goffman, Erving
    1981 Replies and Responses. *In* Forms of Talk, pp. 5–77. Oxford: Oxford University Press.
Goody, Esther N.
    1978a Introduction. *In* Questions and Politeness: Strategies in Social Interaction, Esther N.
        Goody, ed. Cambridge: Cambridge University Press.
    1978b Towards a Theory of Questions. Ibid. pp. 17–43.
Grimm, Jacob
    1840–78. Weisthümer. Reprint, Darmstadt: Wissenschaftliche Buchgesellschaft.
Grinberg, Martine
    1988 Dons, prélévements, échanges: à propos de quelques redevances seigneuriales. Annales
        ESC 43:1413–32.
Hinsberger, Rudolf
    1989 Die Weistümer des Klosters St. Matthias in Trier: Studien zur Entwicklung des
        ländlichen Rechts im frühmodernen Territorialstaat. Stuttgart: Gustav Fisher.
Koch, Ernst August, ed.
    1745 Neue und vollständige Sammlung der Reichs-Abschiede. Frankfurt am Main.
Krämer, Christel, and Karl-Heinz Spiess, eds.
    1986 Ländliche Rechtsquellen aus dem kurtrierischen Amt Cochem. Wiesbaden: Franz Steiner.
Krebs, Richard
    1903 Die Weistümer des Gotteshauses und der Gotteshausleute von Amorbach. Alemania
        31:193–242.

Kriedte, Peter
   1980 Peasants, Landlords and Merchant Capitalists. Leamington Spa: Berg.
Kuchenbuch, Ludolf, and Bernd Michael
   1977 Zur Struktur und Dynamik der 'feudalen' Produktionsweise im vorindustriellen Europa.
       In Feudalismus – Materialien zur Theorie und Geschichtee, Ludolf Kuchenbuch and
       Bernd Michael, eds. pp. 694–761. Frankfurt am Main: Ullstein.
Laufner, Richard
   1957 Das ehemalige St. Pauliner Hofgut in Kesten. Jahrbuch des Vereins für Rheinische
       Denkmalpflege und Landschaftsschutz, 39–52.
Liliencorn, Rochus von, ed.
   [1865–6] 1966 Die historischen Volkslieder der deutschen vom 13. bis 16. Jahrhundert.
       Leipzig; reprint, Hildesheim.
Marx, Karl
   1964 Das Kapital. Vol. 3. Marx Engels Werke, vol. 25. Berlin/DDR: Dietz.
   [1872] 1987 Das Kapital: Kritik der politischen Ökonomie. Vol. 1. Marx Engels
       Gesamtausgabe, vol. 2, part 6. Berlin/DDR: Dietz.
Merx, Otto, ed.
   [1923] 1964 Akten zur Geschichte des Bauernkriegs in Mitteldeutschland. Leipzig. Reprint,
       Aalen: Scientia.
Patzelt, Erna
   1924 Entstehung und Charakter der Weistümer in Österreich. Budapest.
Perrin, Charles-Edmond
   1946 Chartes de franchise et rapports de droits en Lorraine. Le Moyen Age 4th ser., 52:
       11–42.
Razi, Zvi
   1987 Family, Land and the Village Community in Later Medieval England. *In* Landlords,
       Peasants and Politics in Medieval England, T.H. Aston, ed. pp. 360–93. Cambridge:
       Cambridge University Press.
Ringholz, Odilo
   1904 Geschichte des Fürstlichen Benediktinerstiftes U.L.F. v. Einsiedeln. Einsiedeln:
       Waldshut
Roemer, John
   1986 New Directions in the Marxian Theory of Exploitation and Class. *In* Analytical
       Marxism, John Roemer, ed. pp. 81–113. Cambridge: Cambridge University Press.
Saarbrücker Arbeitsgruppe
   1980 Huldigung und Herrschaftsstruktur im Hattgau (Elsaß). Jahrbuch für westdeutsche
       Landesgeschichte 6:117–55.
Sabean, David
   1972 Landbesitz und Gesellschaft am Vorabend des Bauernkriegs: Eine Studie der sozialen
       Verhältnisse im südlichen Oberschwaben in den Jahren vor 1525. Stuttgart: Gustav
       Fischer.
Stockmann, Doris
   1975 Der Kampf um die Glocken im deutschen Bauernkrieg. *In* Der arm man 1525:
       Volkskundliche Studien, Hermann Strobach, ed. pp. 309–41. Berlin: Akademie Verlag.
Toch, Michael
   1986 Asking the Way and Telling the Law: Speech in Medieval Germany. Journal of
       Interdisciplinary History 16:667–82.

Unrest, Jakob
1957 Österreichische Chronik. Karl Grossmann, ed. Weimar: Hermann Böhlaus Nachfolger.
Vanja, Christina
1986 'Verkehrte Welt': Das Weibergericht zu Breitenbach, einem hessische Dorf des 17.
       Jahrhunderts. Journal für Geschichte 5:22–9.
Waas, Adolf
1938–9 Die große Wendung im deutschen Bauernkrieg. Historische Zeitschrift 158:457–91;
       159:22–53.
Weber, Max
1972 Wirtschaft und Gesellschaft. 5th ed. Johannes Winkelmann, ed. Tübingen: Mohr.
Weitzel, Jürgen
1981 Über Oberhöfe, Recht und Rechtszug: Eine Skizze. Göttingen: Muster-Schmidt.
1985 Dinggenossenschaft und Recht: Untersuchungen zu Rechtsverständnis im
       fränkische-deutschen Mittelalter. Cologne: Böhlau.
Weizsäcker, Wilhelm, ed.
1957–73 Pfälzische Weistümer. Speyer: Veröffentlichungen der Pfälzischen Gesellschaft zur
       Förderüng der Wissenschaften.
Werkmüller, Dieter
1972 Über Aufkommen und Verbreitung der Weistümer. Berlin: Erich Schmidt.
Wunder, Heide
1985 Die bäuerliche Gemeinde in Deutschland. Göttingen: Vandenhoeck & Ruprecht.
Zasius, Ulrich
[1550] 1964–5 Opera omnia. Lyon; reprint, Aalen: Scientia.

From Peasant Wars to Urban 'Wars': The Anti-Mafia Movement in Palermo

JANE SCHNEIDER AND PETER SCHNEIDER

In Palermo, we are living a kind of civil war ... There are two social blocs against one another. On the one hand, there are efficient magistrates; on the other there are inefficient magistrates in collusion with the Mafia. You have people who want a civil society and who want to rebel against the Mafia, and then there's a polluted civil society that works with the Mafia. It's the same for the police and the politicians. This is the fight.

Costantino Garaffa, quoted in the *New York Times*, 26 October 1992

Costantino Garaffa is an official in Palermo's association of merchants and shopkeepers whose mission has been to break the system of the *pizzo*, or tribute, that mafiosi extort from merchants and industries as a price for doing business in their respective territories. His statement to a reporter for the *New York Times* captures the frustration of many anti-mafia activists, who see themselves confronting a social world with no clean institutions, trade unions, or political parties – no obvious points of reference to anchor their struggle and deepen its social base. Rather, within each institution, union, and party they must discover those persons whose behaviour appears uncorrupted by entanglements with the mafia, its protectors and friends, and the political regime that has supported it.

In this sense, the anti-mafia movement of today has departed radically from its precursor of the post-war years, when landless peasants were considered the foremost victims of mafia violence. Anti-mafia leaders of those days singled out the Italian Communist Party, the prime advocate of land reform on behalf of these poorest peasants, as a clean political organization. In contrast, they defined the governing Christian Democratic Party as the fount of corruption. Today the tables are ever so slightly turned. The Christian Democratic Party (now the Partito Popolare) bears the taint of pervasive corruption, but is recognized to have an emergent, reformist wing. Conversely, the Communist Party, its main branch renamed the Democratic Party of the Left (PDS), is accused of incidents of collusion, even though it is still held up as the 'least compromised.' In any case, the days are gone when intellectuals could locate mafia in the class structure of agrarian Sicily and imagine its demise as the vindication of landless against propertied classes in the countryside. A comparable 'class analysis' does not exist among anti-mafia activists today.

This paper shows how, historically, the sharp, clear language of class relations and class struggle has been lost to anti-mafia activism in Sicily. We do so first by sketching the class-formation processes of the last twenty years, which, as in so much of the developed world, have yielded social groups not easily categorized on the basis of their relations to the means of production. But the dissolution of an old social structure and its replacement by another that seems unfamiliar is only one aspect of the disappearance of the class concept from the thinking and planning of anti-mafia activists in recent years. These activists more or less share a class position, but they are deeply divided with regard to cultural formation, some having come from Communist, others from anti-Communist, family and intellectual backgrounds. Overcoming this divide has necessitated suppressing the very words that in the past evoked it, among them 'social class.' That in recent years some members of the Sicilian Communist Party colluded with mafia interests has eased the transition for other members, many of whom have disaffiliated not only from the party, but also from its class-oriented vision of the world as a source of personal identity and belonging. For them, as for activists of Catholic background, anti-mafia is increasingly about moral concerns – the 'clean' versus the 'corrupt' - so much so that issues of social and economic, or distributive, justice seem relegated to the dust heap of history, for retrieval, perhaps, at some future time.

Finally, our paper asks about the implications of this singular abandonment. Issues of social and economic justice fester today as in the past, although in a different guise. We suggest that they have constituted a rich terrain for the formation of an anti-anti-mafia backlash whose intellectuals and leaders cleverly label movement activists as ambitious careerists, disloyal to their Sicilian roots. In addition, we propose that these issues underlie an otherwise perplexing factionalism within the movement itself – a factionalism derived not only from the divergent cultural formations of the activists, but also from their present relationships to Palermo's work-deprived poor. In conclusion, we argue that, awkward as they may seem, the concepts of class, class relations, and class struggle remain crucial to understanding mafia, its present weakness, and what might happen should those who would defeat it achieve their goal.

This conclusion, as will be noted, contradicts the trend in recent social theory to analyse social movements that are not overtly about class as 'new' and substantially different from the labour movements of an earlier epoch. In attending to issues of social and economic justice, we enter a terrain that new-movement theorists would attribute to 'old' labour conflicts and relegate to the past. We shall argue, by contrast, that although anti-mafia activists self-consciously distance themselves from the language of class struggle and class relations, their central target for reform – the clientelistic structure of the Italian state – is deeply implicated in resource distribution. Clientelism, in their view, aids and abets mafia power in ways that are morally disgusting. It is also, objectively speaking, the source of employment and income for thousands upon thousands of Sicilians, including many of genuine anti-mafia persuasion.

Notwithstanding our difference from 'new movement' theorists, we have borrowed their research strategy of looking closely at the sociocultural dimension of social-movement formation. This means paying attention to 'the micro-mobilization context,' an intermediate space between latent reservoirs of potential protest created by structural change and the manifest decisions of social actors to become involved (e.g., McAdam 1988). Whereas in the past, analysts were prepared to move directly from preconditions to action, there is now an ever-better understanding of various mediating processes. One is framing: the diagnosis of problems and the posing of solutions in ways that build (or fail to build) consensus (Snow and Benford 1988). Another is motivating individual behaviour by tapping the social energy of pre-existing, community-level groups (Klandermans 1988; McAdam 1988).

Based on an ethnographic study of 'new movements' in Milan, Alberto Melucci (1989) shows how collective identities are the tenuous and fragile outcome of ongoing social construction. Through consciousness-raising argument and negotiation, small groups and networks, 'submerged,' as he puts it, 'in everyday life,' build up the kind of solidarity that earlier scholars of 'old' movements, above all the labour movement, once attributed to structural preconditions and more or less took for granted. Our fieldwork has taken a similar track. During a series of summer stays in Palermo beginning in 1987, we have followed a wide range of anti-mafia groups, ad hoc coalitions, and social networks. Research methods have included repeat interviews with movement participants and other knowledgeable persons, observing many hours of meetings, and attending public events, as well as keeping up with an exploding literature in newspapers, magazines, and books. Our sojourn in Palermo during the summer of 1992 was bracketed by the tragic assassinations of two anti-mafia magistrates, Giovanni Falcone and Paolo Borsellino. Although our research has continued since then, we use this moment of intense mobilization as the culmination of the events herein described.

Late Capitalism: Its Dangerous Traffics and Social Dislocations

Since the early 1970s, global capitalism has vastly increased the volume and velocity of resource transfers: capital flight, labour migration, and industrial relocation and restructuring. Emerging in tandem with this 'speed-up' is a set of unprecedented traffics generating global markets in armaments, drugs, and speculative capital. Clearly there is a relationship between these invasive markets and the accelerated pace of destabilizing resource transfers, although little systematic attention has been paid to their interaction.

There are, as well, other processes at work in the evolution of these dangerous traffics. One is the political economy of the Cold War era, which nurtured proxy insurgencies and counter-insurgencies, the parties to which were armed and encouraged not only by the foreign-policy establishments of the two super powers, but by a clandestine network of secret-service operatives and transnational weapons dealers, some of whose goals were purely commercial (Peleg 1990). Coincidentally, the oil crisis and global recession of 1973–4 led to a vast expansion of capital that, discouraged from productive investment, sought returns through speculation – on interest-rate spreads, currency-exchange fluctuations, inflationary trends in real estate, stocks, and bonds, and a giddy lending boom (from 1973 to 1981) to Third World countries (see Moffitt 1983; Spero 1980). Together with income of all kinds in search of short-term liquid assets and tax havens, this 'hot' or 'stateless' money has circulated ever more energetically thanks to the electronics revolution in information technology, which permits round-the-clock banking on a global scale, and thanks also to bank secrecy laws (Naylor 1989).

Throughout the 1970s Switzerland-like enclaves proliferated 'off shore' on Caribbean and Pacific islands, each competing for the branches and subsidiaries, as well as the blessing, of respectable commercial houses (Blum 1984; Naylor 1989; Permanent Subcommittee 1983). The decade as a whole saw international banking expand by 'more than 25 percent per year, much faster than world production and world trade' (Moffitt 1983:217). Opportunities to launder dirty money expanded in tandem. As Canadian economist Thomas Naylor has argued, because the new fiscal paradises are integrated with, and have the support of, legitimate international financial institutions, they work well to hide narco-dollars. Criminal money, to borrow his words, 'joins with and submerges itself into an enormous mass of speculative capital that races around the world ... at the touch of a computer key' (1989:62, 69).

There is, then, a connection between traffic in speculative investments, in hot money, and in drugs. A reciprocal traffic of drugs for arms is also well documented (see Arlacchi 1983; Arlacchi and dalla Chiesa 1987; Naylor 1989; Pierre 1982; Sampson 1977), as is the utility to arms merchants and secret-service operatives of off shore banks – the CIA-asset Nugent Hand Bank of Australia and the Bank of Credit and Commerce International are familiar examples (Kwitny 1987; McCoy 1991). Such institutions obscure activities (insurgency and counter-insurgency, arms and drug dealing) that secret-service operatives want to hide, whether from legislative bodies that are legally obliged to oversee foreign policy or from the official makers of foreign policy themselves. The consequence is a triangulation of global markets for hot money, arms, and narcotics whose powerful interactions and potential for accumulation have reoriented governments and disrupted societies around the globe.

Sicily is a case in point. Its geography and prior history of organized crime favoured it to become the capital of heroin distribution after the break-up of the French Connection in the early 1970s. How this affected mafia is outlined below; here we consider more general distortions. Last among Italian cities in per capita income, Palermo climbed to fifth place in consumer spending during the early 1980s, in part through the circulation of narco-profits (Mercadante 1986:89–90). Those years also saw increased mafia involvement in public works and construction. Alongside of banks, which multiplied locally in the same period, narco-dollars helped to capitalize several construction firms (Centorrino 1986:89–90). Although employment increased in this sector, it was at the price of an increasingly tangled web of connections between local politicians and contractors: the one extending political protection, illegal variances, and rigged auctions, the other promising the votes of their mafia-allied and mafia-influenced dependents (see Crisantino 1990:181, 221–39; Chubb 1982; Santino and La Fiura 1990:366–91, 455–63).

Problems in other areas became more intense. Palermo's manufacturing base, historically artisanal and weak (see Guarrasi 1978), had declined in the 1960s when dockyards for shipbuilding yielded to Japanese competition. A subsidiary industry, railroad-car manufacture, simultaneously lost ground to the automobile (Barbadoro 1966:83–4). City and regional governments, compromised by mafia ties, allowed speculation on real estate to fill the void of viable economic activity, with mounting un- and underemployment except in the construction trades (Chubb 1982). In some Palermo neighbourhoods, extensive kinship ties continue to provide security to working-class residents who are quick to demonstrate against neglect by the municipal government. But in much of the inner city and the marginal slums of the periphery, children grow up shunning school to hone skills at purse snatching and dope peddling, for now the most accessible ways to earn income for their families and prestige for themselves. Housing is degraded, social services unevenly distributed through clientelistic mechanisms, and the rates of drug and alcohol addiction, teenage pregnancy, and the brutalization of women alarmingly high (see Crisantino 1989:105–39).

Palermo's working classes and marginal poor have not been alone in floundering, however. Sicily represents an instance of post-peasant transformation in which many end up, or aspire to end up, in the salaried middle classes. A land reform of the late 1950s and early 1960s led to extensive agricultural mechanization and some abandonment of arable land, with diminishing opportunities for the formerly land-poor rural population. Industrial development, although widely touted as the best solution for rural unemployment, took the form of capital-intensive petrochemicals and automobile assembly, on the one hand, and of numerous failed projects, often for reasons of corruption, on the other – a pattern replicated by tourism a decade later. Confronted with these limitations, thousands of Sicilians emigrated, most of them to northern Italy and other parts of Europe. For those who stayed, there were schools to attend and rapidly expanding regional, provincial, and local governments promising employment. In the 1950s and 1960s migrants to Palermo were overwhelmingly displaced peasants who entered the construction trades and petty commerce. Since then the city's tertiary sector, attractive to people with schooling, has grown into an 'excessive, pathological weight' (Chinnici 1989:44; Crisantino 1989:181–2).

Palermo's middle classes lost the moorings of a predictable future during the 1980s. For Italy as a whole, the two previous decades had been marked by worker-student movements, a steady expansion of left voting, and a policy climate favourable to the protection of both salaries and wages (see Ginsborg 1990; Tarrow 1989). Labour contract negotiations for tertiary-sector workers responded to demands for anti-inflation clauses and generous benefits, while a stepped-up level of public spending on health, education, and welfare gave government employees and members of the helping professions continually expanding resources for performing their jobs. The 1980s, however, brought a more centrist government to power whose representatives began grumbling about redistributive policy as Italy's budget deficit climbed to the highest in Europe (see Clark 1984; Ginsborg 1990; Lumley 1990). Never able to absorb more than a small portion of the high school, technical school, and college graduates of Sicily and southern Italy, the public sector – national, regional, local – ceased to expand: indeed, came to seem hollowed out. In Palermo, public-sector workers express anxiety about 'living on borrowed time' – and not only because the jobless urban poor seem ever more predatory and violent.

Other harbingers of a downturn include the further integration of the European market, which is forcing the Italian government to legislate wage and benefits austerity, and the emergence in northern Italy of regionalist movements that blame the nation's fiscal woes on 'welfaristic' southerners.

But economic insecurity is hardly the only issue; middle-class families also face a crisis of social reproduction. Whereas peasants, unless they were paupers, aimed to set up their offspring with a 'resource bundle' of movable and immovable property, for 'post-peasants' education is the most desired resource that parents can bestow. A form of cultural capital, it is, like land, pivotal in the structuring of marriage choices, even if old forms of match making, with their strong role for parental supervision, have disappeared. Yet reproduction through education is now problematic, raising the possibility that sons and daughters will become downwardly mobile in wealth and status. The reasons parallel those familiar elsewhere: the escalating cost of schools, their lack of adequate funding, and conflicts over curriculum. As Bourdieu has observed (1984), once education becomes a mass phenomenon, it ceases to count in the making of elites, except in an ever more refined and expensive form. In Sicily, as more generally, mothers now seek employment as a way to confront rising costs, only to find their children distracted by new entertainment and communications options and new consumer temptations – narcotics included. It is fair to say that moral outrage over the new traffics, their agents, and the escalation of violence and crime that accompany them is a crucial element in the formation of the contemporary anti-mafia movement. So were changes in mafia and in the mafia-state relation, to which we now turn.

Mafia and State, 1970–90

It is no easy task to define 'mafia.' The shift away from a class-related interpretation, documented in this paper, is only the latest in a series of transformations. We could also have focused on how class analysis supplanted a folkloric understanding. To members of the contemporary anti-mafia movement, the definition found in nineteenth-century police reports comes close, except that they would insist on a role for regional and national, as well as local, politics. These reports represented mafia as 'a network of politically protected extortion rings ... as groups of criminals who terrorized a local community, living off extortion and other illegal gains, and controlling access to jobs and local markets. These groups, however, were always connected to local political parties and factions, whom they supported, and from whom they drew protection' (quoted in Fentress and Wickham 1922:189). Called *cosche* (singular, *cosca*) in Italian, the groups in question are often referred to a 'families' in English. Though each might have included one or more nuclei of closely related male kin, they are not, on the whole, based on kinship and often contradict real family loyalties.

However we define it, mafia, like the larger society in which it is embedded, has evolved in tandem with the processes of late capitalism, displaying, in fact, some of the same stresses and strains. In 1963 a conflict between rival *cosche* led to the explosion of a car bomb in the Palermo suburb of Ciaculli, in which several officers of the police and *carabinieri* were killed. This event provoked mass arrests, a major trial, and the activism of a parliamentary 'anti-mafia commission.' The trial, though, did not result in convictions, and the new commission disappointed its advocates by investigating only small fish (see Chubb 1982). Meanwhile, as Antonino Calderone, brother of an important boss of Catania, has now told the world in a startling 'confession', the mafia was 'saved by drugs.' According to him, the arrests of 1962–3 and the subsequent cost of lawyers undercut mafiosi to the point that many were 'starving.' One, the infamous Totò Riina, 'cried when he told me that his mother couldn't come visit him in prison in 1966 or 1967 because she couldn't pay for the train ticket' (quoted in Arlacchi 1993:75). 'Then we all became millionaires. Suddenly, within a couple of years. Thanks to drugs' (ibid.:76).

The shift, though, was neither inclusive nor smooth. Early to enter the traffic in drugs was a coalition of Palermo bosses led by Gaetano Badalamenti, whose properties near the city's airport and deep involvement in that facility's construction and operations added up to a logistic advantage. Even before the displacement of heroin-refining operations from Marseilles to Palermo and environs, Badalamenti and a few of his close associates had begun accumulating profits from drug shipments to the United States. Among those whose ire and envy were thereby provoked was a large and growing contingent of somewhat younger bosses from the provinces. Unable to participate in the narcotics market without first raising money on their own, they staged a series of kidnappings for ransom. But the targets of this activity were not simply rich men. The provincial upstarts sought to kidnap well-heeled construction impresarios who were closely allied to the Badalamenti group – who, in fact, depended upon members of this group for protection. To kidnap them was to throw down the gauntlet to what was increasingly being defined as an internal enemy.

Although control over the narcotics traffic was not the only issue, it was an important element in the second 'mafia war,' which exploded between 1979 and 1983. At that time, a group of mafiosi originally identified with the interior rural town of Corleone, but for some years resident in Palermo and its suburbs, organized a takeover of the city's principal mafia families by assassinating their leaders and those leaders' closest associates. During these 'hot years' the aggressors also assassinated some fifteen police officers, magistrates, and government officials whose involvement in criminal justice or political reform could otherwise have blocked the takeover (see Chinnici and Santino 1986, 1989; Falcone 1986:181–209).

The coincidence of the 'war' with continued assaults on representatives of the state provoked a second, and this time more decisive, crackdown: in particular, the appointment of the veteran of the 1970s police suppression of terrorism in northern Italy, General Carlo Alberto dalla Chiesa, to prefect of Palermo province and high commissioner against mafia. When dalla Chiesa and his wife were gunned down in September 1982, state action intensified. Between 1982 and 1986 nearly 15,000 men were denounced throughout Italy for 'association of a mafia type,' with some 707 being investigated by the instructional magistrates and 460 brought to a trial in Palermo that lasted from February 1986 to December 1987. The dramatic trial, known as the *maxiprocesso*, took place in a specially constructed high-security bunker courthouse built inside the walls of the nineteenth-century Ucciardone Prison, to which over 3,000 police, military, and judicial personnel were assigned. In all, the state's hand was strengthened by evidence from mafiosi who had turned 'state's witness' – an unprecedented new development for which the Sicilian magistrate Falcone has received much credit – and by the La Torre law, named for the Sicilian Communist leader Pio La Torre, who had been slain by the mafia in April 1982. Among other provisions, this legislation empowered the police and magistrates to trace bank records for evidence of criminal activity and to confiscate illegally gained assets.

Although the energy and resources for the crackdown on mafia were provided by elements of the Italian state, it is crucial that we not imagine this institution as univocal and ideologically or structurally homogeneous. For more than a century, it had been governed by regimes enjoying one or another form of mafia support. The Fascists, it is true, challenged this relation, but at the end of the Second World War it was vigorously reinstated, some argue with the help of American and British officials involved in the Allied landing in Sicily and the subsequent reconstruction of post-Fascist institutions. Because of the pattern, many local and state officials are conditioned by connections with mafia *cosche*; others are tarnished simply for never having questioned the role of mafia votes in stabilizing the Christian Democratic and other governing parties. Because of the importance of this relationship between mafia and politics, high-ranking police officers engaged in critical investigations some-times found themselves transferred to a distant place or charged with 'serious procedural errors' – charges that took weeks and months to resolve. There were, as well, administrative obstacles to effective judicial action. In the late 1980s, for example, organizational decisions were made that had the effect of dismantling and demoralizing the anti-mafia 'pool' that a group of investigating magistrates had established in Palermo at the time of the 'maxi-trial.' In the aftermath of this debacle, Judge Falcone, Sicily's most prominent anti-mafia prosecutor and the pool's informal leader, requested that he be transferred to an administrative post in the Ministry of Justice in Rome.

Nor was 'outside' political interference with the anti-mafia investigations of the police and the judiciary the only problem. Within these institutions one also found career functionaries who were conditioned by a relationship to mafia and political corruption. Furthermore, among magistrates and police investigators whose attitudes were not so conditioned, there could be genuine disagreements about judicial and investigative procedures, especially with regard to civil liberties and due process, not to mention how aggressive a magistrate should be when pursuing linkages between mafia and politics. These are among the reasons why, in spite of the extraordinary response of the state to the events of the early 1980s, the men, called *mandanti*, who ordered the most important political murders are only now being arrested and tried. Uncertainty and distrust are widespread among police officers and judges prosecuting organized crime. Indeed, a Pirandellian atmosphere pervades Palermo, in which people and the press talk constantly about the city's 'mysteries,' about 'poisonous rumours' that circulate in the Palace of Justice, and about 'dust clouds' of unconfirmed or false accusations that add to the confusion and are never completely dissipated.

The Contemporary Anti-Mafia Movement

The police and judicial effort does not exist in a societal vacuum, however; on the contrary, citizen action, above all in Palermo, has pressured the state to remove ever more of the personnel and structures that have heretofore constituted obstacles to effective prosecution. The assassination of General dalla Chiesa marked the onset of this pressure, provoking an outpouring of public sentiment against organized crime. Shocked by the murder of this distinguished outsider and by the killing of his young wife, Palermitani engaged in unprecedented demonstrations, including a spontaneous candlelight procession in honour of his memory. In January 1984 representatives of the city's political party sections and trade unions, responding to still other assassinations, formed themselves into a Coordinamento Antimafia. Virtually paralysed by ideological disputes related to party background, however, this body was replaced in 1986 by a new *coordinamento* that invited people to participate as individuals rather than as representatives of previously existing groups.

By the late 1980s the second *coordinamento* had over three hundred co-signers and several thousand followers. Led by Carmine Mancuso, a police officer whose father, also a police officer, had been killed by the mafia in 1979, it set about organizing conferences, book presentations, and demonstrations, especially on behalf of mafia victims. In 1986 the *coordinamento* took over the planning of what was by then an annual event, the candlelight procession for General dalla Chiesa on 3 September. *Coordinamento* members and others like them also raised funds to change Palermo's symbolic landscape, which since 1982 has come to include plaques at several assassination sites and a twenty-foot-tall modernist steel 'monument to the victims of mafia' in a piazza near the port.

The *coordinamento* by no means represents the anti-mafia movement as a whole. Protean and multifaceted, it is best described as a growing organism, widening and branching out in response to events, above all assassinations of anti-mafia heroes and authorities, then contracting under the returned weight of 'normalcy.' Overall, from the early 1980s to the present, it has filled an ever wider swath of social and political space. In addition to the *coordinamento*, whose influence has waned in recent years, the following have been, in our estimation, the most significant elements of the movement to date.

Closely allied with Mancuso and his associates in the early days of the movement was Leoluca Orlando, mayor of Palermo from 1985 until 1990 and for a while its most visible and charismatic figure. Initially a member of the moderate left, reformist current of the Christian Democratic Party, Orlando developed his anti-mafia stance in 1979 after his close friend, the Christian Democratic president of the region of Sicily, Piersanti Mattarella, was killed. Under Orlando, city hall became a focal point of anti-mafia activity. Not only did he, as mayor, personally support *coordinamento*-sponsored events; some of the administrative departments of his regime also allocated funds and personnel for related initiatives. An unusually energetic environmentalist and feminist headed the Department of Parks and Sanitation, which staged a blitz of tree planting, city park clean-ups, and dedicated garbage collection that began to cancel signs of past neglect. Other departments responded to national and regional calls for an anti-mafia curriculum in the schools and to a European Community promise of investment capital for the restoration of Palermo's historic centre. So dynamic were the beginnings of the new, *coordinamento-*

supported administration that the years 1985 and 1986 have been dubbed 'the Palermo springtime' (la primavera di Palermo).

A third branch is manifested in grass-roots activities in the city's popular quarters and working-class suburbs, especially the San Saverio parish of the Albergheria quarter. Here in the mid-1980s an activist priest, Catholic lay volunteers, members of the helping professions, and former neighbourhood organizers founded a centro sociale. Aimed at removing children from lives of drugs and crime on the streets, the centre also provides services for their families. Among its most significant initiatives are after-school programs, apprenticeships to teach artisanal skills, a health clinic, summer camps, and each July, several days of youth 'Olympic Games.'

Important to the mission of the Albergheria social centre is cultural re-education, with an emphasis on two themes. One is the cluster of attitudes around 'taking offence,' harbouring grudges, and vindicating wrongs on one's own. Aspects of a long tradition of self-help justice in Sicily, these orientations are held by social centre workers to foster the mafia-linked code of omertà: silence before the law. Social workers of Catholic background further define them as 'un-Christian.' Proselytizing for an alternative stance toward local-level conflict, centre leaders interject both the gospel of Christian love and the international ethics of sportsmanship and team play into projects involving the young. The second theme to engage their energy is the patriarchal gender system that pervades the popular quarter. Evidence for this concern resides in the studied gender integration of the neighbourhood teams that compete in the mock Olympic Games and in the centre's sponsorship of a textile-dyeing course mainly for the purpose of giving neighbourhood wives and mothers extended social time away from home.

Overlapping with the social centre of San Saverio is a small coalition of intellectuals, anchored by a research centre on mafia named for a martyred journalist and activist, Giuseppe Impastato. The coalition's self-appointed mission is to monitor closely the reform politicians as they attempt to displace the old and corrupt regimes that have governed not only Palermo but the region of Sicily and the nation of Italy since the war. Shortly after Orlando was elected mayor of Palermo in 1985, participants in this coalition formed themselves into a watchdog group whose acronym, COCIPA, roughly stands for 'Committee on Transparency in Government.' At first welcomed by the new administration, COCIPA eventually became a thorn in its side, the more so as it pressed for specific budget information from city agencies. In 1990 Orlando was re-elected mayor in a landslide victory, but he was prevented from reconstituting his municipal administration by local opponents and their allies in the national Christian Democratic Party. Soon after, he left this party to found another one

– a cross between a party and a movement called La Rete (The Network). It was under this banner that he recaptured the mayoralty, again with a large majority, in 1993.

Yet another group is the 'Committee of the Sheets' (Comitato dei Lenzuoli), traceable to a kinship network of three sisters and their daughters who hung slogan-painted sheets from the balconies of their neighbouring apartments on the night that Falcone was killed. This spontaneous expression of grief and rage resonated with two rather contradictory dimensions of Sicilian culture: the traditional role of embroidered bedlinens in every respectable bride's trousseau, symbolizing not only her family's status but her sexual purity, and the emergence in Palermo of feminist groups with the courage to make public statements. Either way, the idea of sheets as a medium of communication was compelling. Capturing the immediate attention of others, it led to the formation of a cohesive group of about twenty women and six men – numbers that could have grown considerably had the original core wanted to expand. Meeting as a whole and in sub-groups, the committee became responsible for series of media-savvy events from slogan T-shirts to subsequent displays of sheets to television spots and speech making. Garnering national and even international coverage, members of the group have had as their goals to pressure the state on behalf of its own anti-mafia elements and to raise the consciousness of ordinary citizens regarding the adoption of anti-mafia patterns of behaviour.

If the anti-mafia struggle is a multifaceted, branching phenomenon, its various constituencies consist of people with shared social experience. Most are in their forties or younger. A number of key figures either are students or were politicized by the trajectory of protests that followed the peasants' quest for land in the 1950s and 1960s. Campus unrest, widespread in northern Italy in 1968, invaded the University of Palermo a year later. The formation of activist clergy often included exposure to the socially aware curricular reforms that were inspired by Vatican II in the 1960s and participation in protests of the 1970s against the church's close alliance with Christian Democracy (see Stabile 1989). Still other movement figures participated in the alliance of the 1970s between students and Palermo shipyard workers. Subsequently, urban Sicily has harboured a growing number of feminist, environmentalist, and peace organizations. Anti-mafia activism is especially continuous with the peace and feminist groups. Not only was the Committee of the Sheets founded by women; key inner-circle participants of other branches of the movement are women as well. Moreover, women often outnumber men at demonstrations and other events. Significantly, women who were affiliated with Palermo's feminist press brought organizing skills and the social energy of their friendships to the movement (Cascio 1989).

Regarding class, some activists are from comfortable and long-established professional families: the kind of family which, in Palermo, is likely to own or dominate an apartment building over two or three generations, its various nuclei occupying three or four large and comfortable apartments, repositories of heirlooms and antiques. Others are of lower status, their peasant or labouring parents not having gone beyond elementary school. Notwithstanding this split, however, we find a preponderance of university-educated intelligentsia – people with careers or aspirations for careers in social work, teaching, law, government, journalism, health care, and the clergy. Dense networks cut across these categories. It is our impression, in fact, that old high school ties are salient 'building blocks' (McAdam 1988:136) of anti-mafia organization.

From Peasant Wars to Urban Wars

Class-formation processes of the last twenty years have blurred the contours of social structure in Palermo as they have nearly everywhere else, seeming to render the old categories of propertied and unpropertied social groups obsolete. Of all the constituents of the anti-mafia movement, the group of intellectuals seeking transparency in government is perhaps the best equipped to address this change and articulate its meaning. Most of them are schooled in Marxist theory, whether through the lay or Catholic left. But, as we will see below, much of the work of building a movement has involved the suppression of words and concepts that could evoke Cold War divisions, silencing the contributions that such intellectuals might make.

This emphasis contrasts with the form that opposition to mafia took in Sicily in the 1950s and 1960s. In those years the island was still a predominantly rural society, and the vast cereal and pastoral latifundia of the western interior were targets of a peasant mobilization for land. Although mafia *cosche* parasitically extorted tribute from a wide swath of the regional economy, anti-mafia discourse focused on the land question. With a few exceptions, to be 'anti-mafia' in the 1960s meant to follow one of the left political parties – usually the Communist Party – that were promoting peasant claims. It was also to risk intimidation or violence from the backbone of the rural mafia, a coterie of stewards and estate guards in the employ of the landed class. The late Leonardo Sciascia, internationally acclaimed Sicilian novelist, set the agenda when in 1961 he defined mafia as an 'association for crime with the aim of enriching its members and posing itself as an element of (parasitic) mediation between property and labour.' We know this, he added, because we know 'against whom it shoots' – martyred peasant leaders and left intellectuals (1961:165).

Today's roster of martyrs is different; it includes reform Christian Demo-
crats, magistrates, policemen, and businessmen – figures whose positions of
power or privilege have prompted their designation as 'elite cadavers' (*cadaveri
eccellenti*) in the press. By the same token, contemporary anti-mafia activists
argue for transcending party affiliations, above all those of Communism and
Christian Democracy, so divisive in the Cold War years. Those of Communist
background insist on their identity as 'free citizens,' while Catholics joke about
having been told as children that Communists might 'eat them.' At the San
Saverio social centre, activists display their 'non-confessional' stance by inviting a secular definition of the church, whose pews face the altar for Sunday
services but are turned towards the right for public meetings and to the left for
dramas and concerts. According to a church-affiliated leader, when someone is
sick, 'we listen to anyone with a prescription' (even if the doctor is an atheist).
In another participant's words, it is an 'eloquent sign of the times to find
Catholic and Marxists side by side, both repenting the dogmatic ideological
choices that kept them apart ten or twenty years ago' (Cavadi 1989:156).

The reconstituted Coordinamento Antimafia of 1986 similarly claimed a
non-ideological pedigree, its nine founding members having abandoned a par-
liament-like, representative structure in favour of chartering themselves as 'independent citizens.' Appropriately, they decided to meet in a sports club rather
than in quarters offered by the Communist Party, even though, at the time, a
majority were of Communist background. Then came their rapprochement with
the Christian Democrat mayor, Orlando. Mancuso, leader of the *coordinamento*,
was once a militant Communist: his father was named Lenin, as is his son.
Orlando, by contrast, is the son of a wealthy landowner, attended a Jesuit high
school, and has been influenced by the Jesuit political theorists Ennio Pintacuda
(1988) and Bartolomeo Sorge (1989). On assuming the office of mayor, however, he publicly joined the *coordinamento* and made the city council chambers available for various anti-mafia functions – gestures that dissolved the
diffidence of many former Communists toward him and opened an alliance
with Mancuso.

In speeches and interviews (see Perriera 1988), Orlando has described the
left-right spectrum of party affiliations (*appartenenze*) as a residue of past
conflicts which must now yield to the non-collectivist values of individual
merit and commitment. It is the person and not the label that counts. Ideological badges remind him of 'tribalism' – the debilitating claims of lineages on
the body politic as if it were a 'camp of tents' with nothing going on between
them. In another of his favourite metaphors, the *appartenenze* of the political
parties and their respective factions are like stacking Russian dolls or Chinese
boxes, in which the surface quality of the individual is removed, only to reveal

another surface that can be removed, down to the core, which is equally super-ficial. With mock pride, Orlando related in an interview with us how his teenage daughter refused to answer questions about the family names of her friends, responding, 'I'm going out with "Maria Maria" and "Giovanni Giovanni," that's who.'

During his first tenure as mayor, the press parodied Orlando's sixteen-member cabinet as 'anomalous' (*la giunta anomala*) or the 'Sicilian fruitcake' (*cassata Siciliana*) because its key members did not represent any of the five political parties that had formed Italian governments, local as well as national, since the Second World War: Christian Democrats, Socialists, Social Demo-crats, Republicans, and Liberals. One was a Green; a second gained election through a Jesuit-sponsored 'City for Humanity' (*Città per Uomo*) ticket, which stands for 'apolitical' civic reform with a Catholic left orientation (and was the source of another nickname, 'the Jesuit pastiche'). A third, the vice-mayor, was a former magistrate elected as an independent on the Communist Party list. In 1989 two Communists were added.

In emphasizing their independence from the 'system of *appartenenze*,' anti-mafia activists are explicit that the struggle against mafia no longer expresses the secular, anticlerical politics of class antagonism as during the time of the land reform. Rather than appeal to class solidarity, leaders claim to represent communities. According to Nando dalla Chiesa, sociologist son of the martyred general and prefect, the movement is enhanced by an opening up of the left to 'profound cultural issues.' A former Communist and a resident of Milan, he recalled in one interview being moved by the condolences he had received from Catholics and feeling impatient with Communist scepticism about Orlando's Christian Democratic and landed-gentry heritage. In an essay with Pino Arlacchi, he describes anti-mafia initiatives as 'considerably more ethical and civil than political' – an expression of aspirations for liberty against the vestiges of an arbitrary feudalism (1987:129–31).

Anti-Mafia Frame (as of Summer 1992)

Needing to suppress the ideological chasm between Communism and Christian Democracy inherited from the Cold War era, and reflecting their broad com-monalities of middle-class social experience, most of today's participants in the struggle against mafia diagnose the 'emergency of Palermo' in moral-political, rather than political-economic, terms. Like the progressives of the early 1900s in the United States, activists seek not only the elimination of organized crime, but also the reform of a corrupt political regime believed to be the lifeline of the criminals. In speeches, manifestos, and publications, as well as in interviews, they deride the politics expressed in a Sicilian proverb: 'Better to have a friend than a right.' The most fundamental problem, they believe, is the clientelist structure of Italian political parties and the Italian state. To the extent that *clientelismo* lies at the centre of the diagnosis, the treatment must emphasize, or at least include, severing clientelist ties (see Snow and Benford 1988).

Anti-mafia discourse warns against the return of a past condition when respectable citizens had no compunctions about including mafiosi in their social networks. In the past, for example, it was 'normal' for owners of rural holdings to engage mafiosi as security guards and to maintain multi-stranded relationships with their families. Attending a mafioso's wedding or standing as a godparent at the baptism of his child was not at all uncommon. The movement has stigmatized and where possible criminalized such behaviour. Additionally, fearing a return to the normal, its most vocal participants seek to raise citizens' consciousness about complicity in a wider sense. Using words such as 'break' and 'split' (*rottura* and *spaccatura*), they advocate dissociation in the present from all those whose networks include mafiosi, their friends, or their protectors, or who, for whatever reason, seem disinclined to abandon compromising social or political connections.

That such a strategy came to fill much of the movement agenda is illustrated by events following the killing on 23 May 1992 of the leading anti-mafia magistrate, Giovanni Falcone. As we noted earlier, he had recently become a functionary in the Italian Ministry of Justice, his work in Palermo being frustrated by national as well as local political manoeuvring. Falcone's assassins placed a great quantity of dynamite in a culvert under the expressway that connects Palermo with its airport, and on one of his return trips from Rome, they detonated the explosives by radio command, slaughtering not only the judge but his wife (also a judge) and their three police bodyguards.

The event re-energized the anti-mafia movement. Old groups reconvened and new ones formed, their immediate aim being to pressure the state into an escalation of the crackdown. On 23 June, the one-month anniversary of the killing, some 10,000 Palermo citizens formed a human chain that connected Falcone's apartment building (its entrance had already become a shrine to which people brought fresh flowers and testimonial letters almost daily) with the Hall of Justice, and four days later Palermitani turned out en masse for a demonstration organized by the national trade-union confederations. On this occasion some 50,000 to 70,000 people from all over Italy flooded Palermo in a giant show of solidarity with the city.

Neither the killers of Falcone nor their *mandanti*, had yet been apprehended. Rather, by early July the usual clouds of dust, rumours, and poisons were thickening, fed by the circulation of a remarkable anonymous letter theorizing a conspiracy between a faction of mafia and certain leaders of the Christian Democratic Party. According to this letter, which was mailed to a seemingly arbitrary selection of thirty-nine politicians, magistrates, and journalists, the conspirators had masterminded several assassinations, that of the judge being only one piece of a larger puzzle. Then, stunning the world, on 19 July Falcone's successor in Palermo, Judge Paolo Borsellino, together with his police body-guards, was killed in another explosion in front of his mother's apartment house. This tragedy greatly deepened the anguish and confusion, while amplifying the anger and resolve, of those who would fight back.

In Palermo during the weeks that separated these two clamorous killings, we were witness to endless hours of meetings, small group discussions, demonstrations, and assemblies, as well as the beneficiaries of a general eagerness on the part of movement participants and supporters to discuss their ideas at length. Of particular interest were meetings of a 'cartel,' formed to bring the Orlando group into a cooperative alignment with the intellectuals who had monitored his mayorship, insisting on 'transparency'; meetings at which the followers of Orlando, who had by then formed La Rete, voted on a constitution for their party/movement; and meetings of the Committee of the Sheets. In every case, participants addressed the problem of 'drawing the line between good and evil,' this issue continuing to consume much intellectual and emotional energy.

The problem is first of all manifest in an ongoing and inexorable process of classification. Where does being mafioso leave off and being 'clean' or 'honest' begin? What about the grey areas between these moral poles? What about, as well, those who claim to be honest and clean but lack the commitment or courage to translate this claim into action? The questions seem to require an ever richer vocabulary for ranking the category of people who, although not 'made members' of mafia, are suspected of collusion with it. Expressions that occur frequently in conversation include 'smelling of mafia' (*in odore di mafia*) and 'a subject of mafia gossip' (*chiacchiarata* or *in chiacchiara di mafia*). Whether such labels should apply to all Socialist Party politicos – argued to have increased their use of mafiosi as vote getters during several recent elections – was among the questions debated at length in many different contexts. Oralando, the consummate politician of rupture, at one point characterized the former Socialist minister of justice, Claudio Martelli, as 'philo-mafioso.' Yet it was precisely Martelli who had invited Falcone to join his staff in Rome. Many activists, for whom Falcone was the consummate anti-mafia hero, interpreted this as evidence, if not of Martelli's prior innocence, then of a recent conversion, and they were critical of Orlando for his polemic.

More upsetting was Orlando's direct criticism of the judge himself, in the months before the assassination, for not going far enough to expose the 'third level' of complicity between mafia and politics. According to Orlando, Falcone had kept evidence of political involvement 'locked up tightly in his desk drawer,' reluctant, if not afraid, to use it. That he, Orlando, would make public speeches about Falcone's martyrdom after the massacre rubbed numerous activists the wrong way. 'Those are crocodile tears," they argued. The expression 'crocodile tears' was also applied to other politicians who had once sharply criticized Falcone for being 'too ambitious.' Commemorative ceremonies in which space was given to such former critics of the man being eulogized, above all to Orlando, were instantly controversial; indeed, many activists debated with themselves and each other whether they could, in good conscience, attend the ceremonies.

As one might imagine, the complex process of classification extends to the dead as well as the living, for the victims of mafia violence range all the way from such martyrs of struggle as Falcone and Borsellino to mafiosi themselves. Indeed, until the late 1970s, the great majority of mafia killings developed out of intra- and inter-*cosca* competition. In the days following Falcone's murder, the Committee of the Sheets raised money to place several spots on television, but an argument over the list of mafia victims in one of the spots nearly cost the group its otherwise remarkable solidarity. The list, prepared by a subgroup, included the name of a Christian Democratic politician, Salvo Lima, who had been a foremost protector of mafia before he was killed (most certainly by mafiosi) a month before Falcone. That these two names were, for reasons of chronology, placed in juxtaposition greatly angered other committee members not involved in setting up the spot.

If the process of classification breeds tension, so too do discussions of what is to be done. We heard several interesting arguments over proposals to organize boycotts of particular merchants and to initiate a letter-writing campaign against a media figure whose name had come up in the recently published confession of mafioso Antonio Calderone. The question of where to draw the line in these cases provoked some participants to warn against the danger of witch-hunting. How could one really know whether a merchant was clean or dirty? If he or she were forced to pay protection money, could this be called collusion? And what would it mean if the executives of the national television network fired a comedian 'smelling of mafia,' given that they themselves could have figured in a vast scheme of pay-offs between politicians and industry concurrently being exposed in northern Italy?

Also complicated is what activists should reasonably expect from other elements of the intelligentsia. Do mafiosi not have a right to a lawyer? Are their attorneys 'dirty' by definition? Those who share pizzas with their clients in prison, and who receive and transmit phone messages for them, are perhaps clear cases, but should their 'bad example' be taken as characteristic of moral degradation among mafia defence lawyers generally? And what about their physicians? Most interesting were the discussions that we heard regarding priests. Movement activists celebrate priests who refuse to give last rites to mafiosi, but sometimes hesitate as the circle expands – for example, to the case of a priest refusing to preside over the first communion of a mafioso's daughter. The church does not condone these acts of conscience on the part of its clergy, and their incidence is unusual although increasing. A recent circular from the bishop of the province of Agrigento asks parish priests to scrutinize the names that parishioners propose as godparents for their children. Persons 'smelling of mafia' should be excluded from this role. (The Agrigento bishop, by the way, was prompted to act after the murder of a young magistrate in his province, and he has also talked of proposing the magistrate for Vatican beatification.)

We come, finally, to the debates surrounding personal comportment: what activism should entail in terms of individual behavioural change. Should 'dirty behaviours' be identified and listed? If so, what would be included and what not? Is it compromising to succumb to demands for protection money, for bribes, for recommendations, or for an extra-legal fee just to park your car? Should an activist give in to the 'micro-mafioso' prepotent bullying that characterizes a few of their colleagues at work? Indeed, should workplaces such as government offices and the university set up commissions to hear complaints? And how should a clean and honest citizen relate to others classified as smelling of mafia so as to make them feel socially unacceptable? Should they refuse to greet, as well as to conduct business with, them? Could a single guideline on this question serve two people who live in such dramatically different neighbourhoods as the gentrified streets of the new Palermo and the mafia suburb of Ciaculli? Both might have neighbours who are 'collusive' with mafia, but the decision not to greet them might take more courage in Ciaculli than in a bourgeois apartment house.

Eventually, the Committee of the Sheets did publish a handout entitled 'Nine uncomfortable pieces of advice for the citizen who would combat the mafia.' According to these *consigli*, citizens should learn to claim their rights vis-à-vis the state, not beg for them as favours. They should educate their children in democracy and respect for the law. Workplace suspicions of bribery, corruption, extortion, favouritism, and the waste of public money should be reported to legally constituted authorities. So should irregularities in the delivery and billing of medical, legal, and other services, as well as other illegal acts. Before, after, and during elections, citizens should refuse any exchange of favours for votes. 'Nothing will change if we continue to vote for parties that have governed us for many decades, allowing the mafia to poison public life, consigning pieces of the state to the mafia's hand' (Comitato 1992).

A fascinating debate preceded the committee's arrival at this set of guidelines, in which several members fell back on the most mundane and immediate of behaviours that might be expected to change: how they themselves disregard both the law and all informal codes of politeness and civility when driving their car. This observation in turn led to the following reflection: 'What if I criminalize a whole range of behaviours and yet continue to double park?' And then, quoting Falcone, 'but if everything is mafia, then nothing is mafia,' and the movement cannot go on.

Observations about driving etiquette crop up among anti-mafia activists more often than one might imagine, for, as we have seen, 'drawing the line' concerns not only politics but everyday life. Meanwhile, class analysis, once at the centre of anti-mafia discourse, has virtually disappeared. And yet the problem of class inequality – of social and economic justice – lurks in the background, affecting the movement from both within and without. This is because outside the corral of reformed consciousness and behaviour are thousands of well-meaning people who owe their very employment to a patron's favour or who seek such a favour on behalf of someone else, perhaps a daughter or son.

In other words, although innocent and morally compelling on the surface, the anti-mafia attribution of blame to *clientelismo* and the promotion of *spaccatura* is double-edged. Not many people in Palermo's schools, professions, public-sector jobs, and construction trades can rearrange their sociopolitical relationships, severing all compromised social ties, without destroying all that they have by way of position and connections for themselves and their children. More than inconvenient, the requirement threatens to destabilize the 'resource bundles' of the city's unpropertied middle and working classes, to some extent robbing the movement of potential constituents. In the pages to follow, we explore how anxiety over employment opportunities has interacted with moral outrage to intensify both an anti-anti-mafia backlash and the emergence of two broad factions within the movement.

Backlash

The ideological rigidity of a clean break with anyone 'tainted by mafia' invites the counter-accusation that the activists themselves are self-interested careerists, overeager to remove those who do not agree with them from the magistracy, the schools, the priesthood, and the various departments of city government, with the goal of taking their place. That activists are younger, and more of them are women, than those with 'normal' clientelistic relations only reinforces the perception that they are personally ambitious.

Among the first to articulate this perception was the late Leonardo Sciascia. Responding to a *coordinamento*-sponsored congress honouring three murdered police officers in 1986, he spoke out against imputing 'third level' – that is, political – guilt by association. Rather than blame Italian *clientelismo*, Sciascia interpreted the narco-trafficking mafia as Sicily's version of a crime and violence epidemic, on the loose in modern cities throughout the world. A follow-up article in the *Corriere della Sera*, Milan's main daily, accused anti-mafia leaders of careerism, as if they were philo-mafiosi themselves. The novelist also claimed in the press (but then retracted the accusation) that Magistrate Borsellino was promoted out of the line of seniority as a reward for his unrelenting effort to expose 'third level' corruption. In 1961 Sciascia had denounced mafia as an enemy of social justice, countering the then-prevalent folklorist definitions that viewed it as simply a part of the Sicilian atmosphere. Although he had also at the time criticized attempts to name political collaborators on the grounds that collusion was an old and hard-to-prove story (1961:178–9), his 1986 'mafia of the anti-mafia' accusation was unanticipated and provoked an abiding bitterness among movement activists.

Other sources of anti-anti-mafia sentiment were, or could have been, anticipated: the older generation of power-holders in such institutions as the University of Palermo, the Sicilian Council of Bishops, the main currents of the national and regional Christian Democratic Party, the clientelistic regional Socialist Party, and the *Giornale di Sicilia*, Palermo's only surviving daily, whose anti-mafia reporters, a small team, had already been laid off or marginalized by 1987. Coinciding with reports of Sciascia's first missive, this paper listed the names and addresses of the founding members of the *coordinamento*, a move interpreted by many as intended to intimidate activists and expose them to the risk of mafia reprisal.

One way that the backlash discourse attributes ulterior motive to anti-mafia activists is through use of the verb *strumentalizzare*, 'to instrument.' Penitents who turn state's witness are said to *strumentalizzare* the judicial process. Not only are they not contrite; they must surely be manipulating the prosecutors who take their confessions. The families of victims do the same to public opinion, their grief and outrage drawing attention to what should be a private affair: the loss of a loved one. Particularly mean-spirited is the innuendo that certain widows have publicly joined the movement in order to cover their present or prior indiscretions. Another critique proposes that a rump Communist Party has 'instrumented' the movement's attack on local contractors. From an anti-mafia perspective, owners of construction firms have a strong 'organic permeability' to mafia corruption (see Santino 1989:36). Voices of the anti-anti-mafia warn, rather, that this hard-nosed view will lead to capital flight and loss of jobs.

In attacking careerism, the labelling process of the anti-anti-mafia backlash creates a climate of demoralization in which the goals of cultural, let alone political, reform seem unachievable. An example is Giuseppe Cipolla's account of reform in the schools. A regional education law of 1980 sought the formation of a 'civil and democratic consciousness' in children by setting aside funds for the development of bibliographic and didactic materials with anti-mafia content, for hiring consultants, and for mounting relevant projects and exhibitions. A few teachers wrote grant proposals to receive these funds, for the most part younger teachers of left persuasion who were employed in the 10 per cent of affluent schools. But the number of proposals, which increased from 182 in 1980–1 to 331 in 1986–7, fell off thereafter, for reasons that Cipolla attributes to the backlash (1989:132). In such a context, teachers who questioned why the subject of mafia should enter the curriculum, and who resented having their reservations construed as 'philo-mafioso,' were able to put the committed (and shrinking) minority on the defensive. A similar isolation befell activist clergy in the Sicilian church (Stabile 1989).

In addition to asserting an ulterior motive of personal ambition for career or power, anti-anti-mafia discourse often sounds a Sicilianist chord, reminiscent of the declaration of the former archbishop of Palermo, Cardinal Ruffini, that 'the mafia exists only in the minds of those who wish Sicily ill.'[1] The appeal to ethnicity gains impetus from egregious slurs by outsiders, which the *Giornale di Sicilia* diligently reports: for example, the remark of an Emilian minister who, upon seeing two Sicilian politicians in Rome greet each other with the customary kiss rather than a handshake, was heard to remark, 'Look at the Sicilian mafiosi!'[2] Such comments remind Sicilians of the many humiliations that they have experienced while travelling or working and living in northern Italy, or at the hands of north Italians in the south.

In many respects, however, the anti-mafia movement is Italian or European as well as Sicilian. Among its most vocal leaders are young professionals with colleagues in Italy and elsewhere on the continent who also express affinity with the civil-society values of 'individualism' and the 'rule of law.' Symbolic of their cosmopolitanism is the new monument to the victims of mafia in Palermo. Starkly abstract, it is also surrounded by a lawn that remains green through Sicily's arid summers only by dint of constant watering. Significantly, national peace and environmental activists have contributed resources to initiatives in Palermo, much as northern United States civil-rights advocates did in the American south. All of which leaves unmentioned the ethnic interactions that occurred in the context of the maxi-trial when the national government 'sent down' enough *carabinieri* and military equipment to give Palermo the appearance of an armed camp, an appearance that it acquired again after the Borsellino killing. While Sicilian judges and lay jurists courageously heard the evidence that Sicilian prosecuting magistrates presented against men who had been arrested by (for the most part) Sicilian police officers, they did so in the national language, often joining in northerners' bemusement with the dialect and manners of the men on trial.

Disdain for the regional culture and language can be troubling even to committed opponents of mafia, especially if they harbour nostalgia for a rural childhood or love for less-educated kin whose Italian is awkward or absent. A high school teacher in the forefront of reform activities lamented to us about how saddened he is by his students' derision of the dialect phrases he draws to their attention in class. But the anti-anti-mafia backlash is not just about nostalgia. Its 'cultural defence of Sicily against negative influences coming down from the north' is also self-consciously presented as a defence of employment opportunities (Priulla 1989:75). Central to this message is a not-so-subtle appeal to working- and middle-class Sicilians who rightly or wrongly fear exclusion if clientelistic criteria for hiring and advancement are to be overthrown in favour of a faceless – that is, Italianized, Europeanized – meritocracy.[3]

Internal Conflicts

In addition to feeding anti-anti-mafia accusations of careerism and disloyalty, the movement strategy of breaking with mafia and all those 'tainted by mafia' is a pervasive source of conflict among activists themselves. Here too, underlying issues of employment and justice are at stake. During our first summer of fieldwork in 1987, the movement displayed little internal tension; on the contrary, much was made of the mutually supportive roles of the various anti-mafia constituencies, especially the *coordinamento*, Orlando, and the neighbourhood social centres. Debate was already surfacing, however, around the call for *rottura* or *spaccatura*. To some, only the pursuit of a clean break could demonstrate a person's commitment; others, rather than face the social and practical dangers of rupturing normal relations, began to drift away. Indicative of the malaise, the candlelight ceremony on 3 September, once a galvanizing occasion, became an object of controversy, as groups and individuals with questionable credentials joined in. In 1988 Orlando and Mancuso boycotted it to organize an alternative, purified manifestation, while many others stayed home.

After 1987 the leaders of the *coordinamento* and the social centres became alienated from each other in ways that reflect the different class constituencies with which each is most involved. Volunteers and professionals attached to the centres are in touch with, and often live in, Palermo's popular quarters, where the Sicilian dialect has more currency than Italian and people's family traumas are an everyday reality. With some exceptions, members of the *coordinamento* and, more broadly, the new political party of Orlando earn their livings in offices where mainly Italian is spoken. Although Orlando himself speaks with notable charismatic appeal to 'all of Palermo,' office workers are generally at some distance from the poor, whom they perceive as both parasitic and threatening. One *coordinamento* ideologist told us that he attributed the city's high unemployment to the fact that 'no one wants to work any more, save the new immigrants from Africa,' an interpretation that is anathema to grass-roots volunteers.

Whereas during the period under study, the social-centre advocates saw themselves engaged in a compassionate effort to rebuild Palermo from the bottom up, for *coordinamento* and Rete members, the prior task was top-down political reform. As one might expect, based on the discussion of *spaccatura* presented above, the reform that they envisioned placed those who were considered to be compromised outside the bounds of 'civil society.' Restructuring is not a 'question of ideology,' one *coordinamento* member told us, adopting the polarizing vocabulary of inclusion and exclusion: it is a question of 'acceptable and unacceptable people.' On the surface innocent, top-down reform implies a profound, if unacknowledged, shift in the distribution of economic resources. Advocating the dismissal from local government of all who dispense public-works contracts, construction variances, and favours in exchange for votes, Orlando and his close associates imagine a redeemed Palermo that will attract European Community investments and be a 'Palermitizing' model for the rest of Italy. Were their program to be accomplished, it could, however, pave the way for still-wider disemployment. Indeed, it could contribute to the generalized instability of even white-collar positions that seems desired by cutting-edge employers for the twenty-first century – investors who intend to remain competitive by dint of technologies and labour practices that are 'lean and mean.'

Clearly, the policy of *spaccatura* pursued to this extent has different consequences for the divergent audiences of the anti-mafia movement. To those surrounding Orlando, it has meant the inconvenience and social risk of alienating friends and kin through whistle-blowing in office, refusing gifts and favours, rejecting recommendations, and even sacrificing one's sense of humour about the clever 'wheeling and dealing' strategies of politicos and entrepreneurs. In general, vast numbers of the publicly employed who won their jobs through patronage must be held in contempt, even though, at an earlier time, gaining employment by this route was both necessary and 'normal.' To those around the social centres, this version of *spaccatura* is wrong-headed because of the humiliation that it causes ordinary citizens, alas dependent on the mediation of party functionaries and union officials to obtain such benefits as health insurance, housing, diplomas, licences, and jobs. If such people 'prostitute themselves through the subtle channels of clientelism,' necessity continues to be a reason (Vitale 1989:94).

During the 1970s construction companies reputed to have mafia connections and access to narco-dollars ingratiated themselves with Palermo's trade unions – Communist and Socialist, as well as Christian Democrat – and with the regional Communist and other parties. The pursuit of a 'historic compromise' with Christian Democracy on the part of the national Communist Party provided a context in which such corruption came easier. Together the changes confused the once-powerful image of the left as a vanguard against mafia and was later a source of bad feelings between the *coordinamento* and the unions. The grass-roots community organizers, by contrast, have on occasion seemed reluctant to sacrifice good relations with union leaders who control the kinds of positions that their people need, forcefully arguing that segments of the unions are or could be clean.

Under Orlando the municipal government in 1987 embarked on a split with local contractors, quite pointedly at a time when German and northern Italian companies were poised to take their place. *Coordinamento* members then accused leaders of the San Saverio centre of extreme political naivety for their reluctance publicly to denounce union demonstrations that were called in response, even after the demonstrators trumpeted the slogan 'Viva la mafia!' and displayed such intimidating symbols as two empty coffins labelled 'mayor' and 'vice-mayor.' Grass-roots organizers point out that they did, however, break with the unions after the demonstrations. At the time, they also accused the *coordinamento* and Orlando of purposely withholding municipal contributions for neighbourhood centres, having become too 'intellectual' – more interested in words than acts. According to them, the reformer-mayor had merely installed a new structure of clientelism, from which the social centres and other local initiatives were excluded.

A Tentative Conclusion

Theorists of new social movements point to certain features of late capitalism as an underlying structural condition: the end of the 'Keynesian settlement' that produced the welfare state; the transformation of Fordist mass production into decentralized, computer-driven, flexible and mobile worksites; and the swelling of an information-oriented, knowledge-based service class. New forms of protest, disconnected from national political parties and the national political process, are held to characterize, in particular, the members of this service class, who feel both oppressed by the expanded capacity of modern mass society to impinge on everyday life and disillusioned by the failure of workers' organizations – considered paradigmatic of 'old' social movements – to realize their goals in the political arena (see Aronowitz 1988; Habermas 1986; Klandermans et al. 1988; Melucci 1981, 1982, 1988, 1989; Touraine 1988).

Tarrow criticizes this approach for being ahistorical (1991:57–69). A look back in time would show that movement characteristics touted as 'new' – for example, the emphasis on cultural, as distinct from political, action – in fact shaped the labour struggle at an early stage of its development. Nor are the new movements, in Tarrow's analysis, as removed from the upheavals of the past, or from party politics, as they seem. The latter point is well taken with regard to the movement against the mafia in Palermo. Many participants, probably the majority, are veterans of past political protest on the left; the labour and student movements of the late 1960s and 1970s were an integral part of these activists' political formation.

But this history is not fully shared. Other anti-mafia activists derive from a Catholic experience which, however populist in orientation, usually implied antagonism toward the secular traditions of socialism and communism in Italy. Because the contemporary anti-mafia movement depends for its strength on coalition building, its constituents must invest considerable energy in establishing their respective distances from all political parties, movements, and ideologies of the past. To claim their mantle or heritage would render impossible the project of creating a common front against mafia. This is part of the context for suppressing, and forgetting, the struggles around inequality that so marked Sicilian history not only in the decades after the Second World War, but in 1848 and during the Fasci uprising of the 1890s.

It is an interesting question, now, how much of this history can in fact be ignored. The preceding analysis has focused on events in Palermo between the 'spring' of 1986 and the assassinations of Falcone and Borsellino in the summer of 1992. In subsequent years Italy has seen its remnant fascist party, the Movimento Sociale Italiano, suddenly grow in size, acquire a new name (the Alleanza Nazionale), and begin a national political campaign for respectability and position. In the Sicilian context, this development has meant appropriating an anti-mafia stance, indeed, reminding voters of Mussolini's harsh repression of the mafia during the 1930s, and the more recent presence among courageous magistrates of a small number of MSI adherents (no less than Magistrate Paolo Borsellino belonged to the MSI). As of this writing (from Palermo in February 1996), an intense debate is unfolding with regard to the wisdom, or folly, of a recently declared alliance of university students from the PDS (the former Communist Party) and the AN (former Fascists) 'against the mafia.'

Over and above the problems of alliance building is the question of how to define the enemy so as to oppose it effectively. The concept of a social bloc articulated by Constantino Garaffa in the quotation that introduces this paper is widely adopted by activists as a convenient shorthand. By it is meant not only the mafia, but all those who have in one degree or another facilitated its operations or sustained its system of power. This 'mafia bloc' cuts, by definition, across classes. Not only do mafiosi themselves occupy different social locations – expressions of a highly conflictual internal process of differentiation – but their supporters extend from the artisans and labourers in the building trades of a city whose major industry, construction, was colonized by the mafia to the elite politicians and magistrates who 'condition' mafia trials. In between is the entire 'polluted civil society' referred to by Garaffa, from lowly clerks and storekeepers to physicians and financiers.

No doubt because Palermo's 'mafia bloc' cuts across so many strata and institutions, defining its boundaries is nothing less than a nightmare of contradictions. We have seen how activists must struggle with an ongoing moral dilemma: that their desire to cleanse could misfire, unjustly incriminating what were once 'normal' behaviours. Can they zealously seek to uncover complicitous arrangements without endangering civil liberties? Have they incapacitated people of goodwill who would raise questions about strategy or tactics except for fear of being labelled 'philo-mafioso?' Considerable energy within the movement is expended here too, in an endless, yet necessary, analysis and argument over where to draw the line.

To the degree that the 'mafia bloc' is transverse, cutting across all social classes, so too should be the anti-mafia bloc. But in fact it is not. Regardless of their political formation (Communist, Catholic-populist, even Fascist), activists tend to be middle or upper middle class, the beneficiaries of at least a high school and most often a university education, and employed or seeking employment in public-sector jobs or the free professions. Their various overlapping coalitions include labour leaders as well, but these leaders are simultaneously pulled in another direction. To comprehend that other direction, it is necessary to appreciate that since the Second World War Palermo's working classes have been substantially shaped, not by industrial development, but by a construction boom controlled by mafia entrepreneurs and their political friends. These people are now under judicial investigation or in jail. The rivers of cement that once poured from the mixers have subsided to a trickle, lifting cranes no longer puncture the horizon, and the official rate of unemployment is over 25 per cent.

There are important cultural reasons why working-class Palermitani might feel alienated from the anti-mafia movement. With time, they will be increasingly marked by what used to be considered common: Sicilian ways of being and talking, a Sicilian set of cultural practices, and a Sicilian dialect. To the extent that they become, or become viewed as, exclusive or remnant practitioners, this once-shared culture and language will seem to them debased – less rich than it was in the past. For sure, they will suspect, even know, that in anti-mafia circles their ways of being and talking have become objects of criticism and ridicule. The hurt may be the worse for the failure to acknowledge, in these same circles, that working-class Sicilians also have a tradition of opposition to the mafia.

But the differentiation and alienation of class cultures in Sicily is only one part of our story. From a working-class perspective in the Palermo of today, *la mafia dava lavoro* (the mafia gave work), and the anti-mafia has taken work away. In other words, although the language of class – class relations and class struggle – has been, with great effort, put under wraps or shelved, the most serious problem confronting today's anti-mafia movement is how to seek the moral reform of an entire society and its institutions, given that Palermo's underemployed, marginalized working classes remain vulnerable to inclusion in, and victimization by, mafia networks. The problem, as argued above, is another source of intra-movement dissension.

To these observations we would add one more. A feature of late capitalism that has received little attention in the literature on new social movements is the development, since the mid-1970s, of what we might call an 'underworld system' – a global arena in which arms, drugs, and stateless money circulate with impunity, hardly obstructed or controlled by the 'world system' of national states. If 'new' participants in collective action seem little interested in, or are disgusted by, national political parties, their attitude in part reflects a high point in the subversion of national political institutions by these global trends. Unfortunately, the trends have become implicated in the way of life of thousands, indeed, millions of people around the globe – a route, and in many instances the only route, to one or another form of local viability and prestige. To define such people as collusive with an evil system, even if not evil themselves, is perhaps too easy, for it does not answer the question of what will become of them if the (historically very recent) system of 'dangerous traffics' were, indeed, to be interfered with or displaced by something else. Here, we suggest, there remains an especially compelling role for class analysis.

NOTES

The research project on which this paper is based has received support from the H.F. Guggenheim Foundation and the National Science Foundation. In conducting fieldwork with anti-mafia activists, we have taken much care to consider the risks that they face. The men and women identified in this paper are public figures who want their story to be told, have published books and articles, and regularly speak to the press about these issues. Several of them, representing different perspectives, have kindly read and commented on an earlier draft. We are grateful for their criticisms, which we have taken into account in making revisions. We also wish to thank the editors, Gerald Sider and Gavin Smith, for their critical insights.

1 In the 1950s Silvio Milazzo, the regional president, declared that the very creation of a parliamentary anti-mafia commission would cast a shadow on the Sicilian people.
2 Also highlighted was a story about Danish and French entrepreneurs making a parody of Sicilian tourism, the former by publishing a map depicting the Mount Etna volcano erupting, the earthquake in the Belice valley, navigation accidents in the straits of Messina, and the locations of several homicides; the latter by advertising a 'heart in your throat *lupara* tour' with scheduled views of magistrates under armed escort, the bunker courthouse of the maxi-trial, and famous sites of violence. According to the advertisement, the lucky tourist might even witness a murder. Press attention to such items reinforces Graziella Priulla's conclusion, based on content analyses, that what others say about Sicily's problems often figures more prominently than the problems themselves (1989:77).
3 Given their defence of Sicilian culture against universalist values, it is ironic that ideological opponents of the anti-mafia movement have also spoken out in favour of civil liberties. From the first days of the maxi-trial, the *Giornale di Sicilia*, for example, portrayed mafiosi as casualties of Italy's slow pace of legal and prison reform, emphasizing the uncomfortable facts of their being held in jail until prosecuted, tried en masse in lengthy proceedings, and convicted under conspiracy laws of 'guilt by association.' That their arrests were, in many cases, prompted by evidence from confessed mafiosi fuelled the effort to construct them as victims, as did their families' letters to the newspaper and petitions to the prisons lamenting the conditions of incarceration. Promoting a sympathy vote for these families, the newspaper wrote of 'judicial error,' decried proposals to reward 'penitence' with reduced sentences, and predicted a degeneration of round-ups into witch-hunts. It also supported a national referendum to reform the judiciary, which, when passed in 1988, left the magistracy weakened vis-à-vis 'organized' crime (see Di Federico 1989; Santino 1989).

REFERENCES

Arlacchi, Pino
    1983 La mafia imprenditrice: l'etica mafiosa e lo spirito del capitalismo. Bologna: Il Mulino.
    1993 Men of Dishonor: The First Inside Account of the Sicilian Mafia. New York: William Morrow and Company.
Arlacchi, Pino, and Nando dalla Chiesa
    1987 La palude e la città: si può sconfiggere la mafia. Milano: Arnaldo Mondadori.
Aronowitz, Stanley
    1988 Foreword to Alain Touraine, Return of the Actor, pp. vii–xxi. Minneapolis: University of Minnesota Press.

Barbadoro, Idomeneo
  1966 Le industrie di Palermo. Palermo: Libri Siciliani.
Blum, Richard H.
  1984 Offshore Haven Banks, Trusts, and Companies: The Business of Crime in the
    Euromarket. New York: Praeger.
Bourdieu, Pierre
  1984 Distinction: A Social Critique of the Judgement of Taste. Cambridge: Harvard
    University Press.
Cascio, Antonia
  1989 Donne e mafia. *In* Santino 1989: 99–102.
Cavadi, Augusto
  1989 L'esperienze del Centro sociale S. Saverio. *In* Santino 1989:155–8.
Centorrino, Mario
  1986 L'economia mafiosa. Catanzaro: Rubbetino Editore, Saverio Mannelli.
Chinnici, Giorgio
  1989 Omicidio e guerra di mafia. *In* Santino 1989:41–8.
Chinnici, Giorgio, and Umberto Santino
  1986 L'omicidio a Palermo e provincia negli anni 1960–1966 e 1978–1984. Collano di studi
    statistico-sociali e demografici, 1. Palermo: Istituto di Statistica Sociale e Scienze
    Demografiche e Biometriche, Università di Palermo.
  1989 La violenza programmata: omicidi e guerra di mafia a Palermo dagli anni '60 ad oggi.
    Milano: Franco Angeli.
Chubb, Judith
  1982 Patronage, Power, and Poverty in Southern Italy: A Tale of Two Cities. Cambridge:
    M.I.T. Press.
Cipolla, Giuseppe
  1989 Tradizione e innovazione nell'esperienza educative antimafia. *In* Santino 1989:128–39.
Clark, Martin
  1984 Modern Italy, 1871–1982. London and New York: Longman.
Comitato dei Lenzuoli
  1992 Nove consigli scomodi al cittadino che vuole combattere la mafia. Palermo.
Crisantino, Amelia
  1989 Un progetto di ricerca su Palermo. *In* Santino 1989:80–7.
  1990 La città spugna: Palermo nella ricerca sociologica. CSD quaderni, 2. Palermo: Centro
    Siciliano di Documentazione Giuseppe Impastato.
Di Federico, Giuseppe
  1989 The Crisis of the Justice System and the Referendum on the Judiciary. *In* Italian
    Politics: A Review, Robert Leonardi and Piergiorgio Corbetta, eds. pp.25–49. New
    York and London: Pinter Publishers.
Falcone, Giovanni
  1986 Rapporto sulla Mafia degli Anni '80. Intervista-racconto a cura di Lucio Galluzzo,
    Francesco La Licata, and Saverio Lodato. Palermo: S.F. Flaccovio.
Fentress, James, and Chris Wickham
  1992 Social Memory. Oxford: Blackwell.
Ginsborg, Paul
  1990 A History of Contemporary Italy: Society and Politics 1943–1988. London: Penguin
    Books.

Guarrasi, Vincenzo
   1978 La condizione marginale. Palermo: Sellerio.
Habermas, Jurgen
   1986 The New Obscurity: The Crisis of the Welfare State and the Exhaustion of Utopian
       Energies. Philosophy and Social Criticism 2:1–18.
Klandermans, Bert
   1988 The Formation and Mobilization of Consensus. In Klandermans et al. 1988:173–97.
Klandermans, Bert, Hanspeter Kriesi, and Sidney Tarrow, eds.
   1988 From Structure to Action: Comparing Social Movement Research Across Cultures.
       Greenwich, Conn.: JAI Press.
Kwitny, Johnathan
   1987 The Crimes of Patriots: A True Tale of Dope, Dirty Money, and the CIA. New York:
       W.W. Norton.
Lumley, Robert
   1990 States of Emergency: Cultures of Revolt in Italy from 1968 to 1978. London: Verso.
McAdam, Doug
   1988 Micromobilization Contexts and Recruitment to Activism. In Klandermans et al.
       1988:125–55.
McCoy, Alfred
   1991 The Politics of Heroin. New York: Lawrence Hill.
Melucci, Alberto
   1981 New Social Movements, Terrorism and the Political System. Socialist Review 56.
   1982 L'invenzione del presente. Bologna: Il Mulino.
   1988 Getting Involved: Identity and Mobilization in Social Movements. In Klandermans et al.
       1988:329–49.
   1989 Nomads of the Present. Philadelphia: Temple University Press.
Mercadante, Vito
   1986 La nuova mafia da Lucky Luciano a Michele Greco. Caltanisetta: Vaccaro Editore.
Moffitt, Michael
   1983 The World's Money: International Banking from Bretton Woods to the Brink of
       Insolvency. Touchstone Book, New York: Simon and Schuster.
Naylor, R. Thomas
   1986 The Problem of Illegal Capital Movements in the International Financial System.
       Unpublished paper prepared for the seminario di studio, Tendenze della Criminalità
       Organizzata e dei Mercati Illegali Internazionali, Instituto Italiano per gli Studi
       Filosofici, Naples, 10 November 1986.
   1989 Drug Money, Hot Money, and Debt. European Journal of International Affairs
       2:55–70.
Peleg, Ilan
   1990 Models of Arms Transfer in American Foreign Policy: Carter's Restraint and Reagan's
       Promotion, 1977–1987. In Arms, Politics, and the Economy, Rogert Higgs, ed. 132–54.
       New York: Holmes and Meier.
Permanent Subcommittee
   1983 Crime and Secrecy: The Use of Offshore Banks and Companies. Staff study made by
       the Permanent Subcommittee on Investigations of the Committee on Governmental
       Affairs, U.S. Senate. 98th Congress, First Session. Washington: U.S. Government
       Printing Office.

Perriera, Michele
    1988 Orlando: intervista al Sindaco di Palermo. Palermo: La Luna.
Pierre, Andrew J.
    1982 The Global Politics of Arms Sales. Princeton: Princeton University Press.
Pintacuda, Ennio
    1988 Breve corso di politica. Milano: Rizzoli.
Priulla, Graziella
    1989 Informazione e mafia: dal silenzio al rumore. In Santino 1989:69–79.
Sampson, Anthony
    1977 The Arms Bazaar: From Lebanon to Lockheed. New York: Viking Press.
Santino, Umberto, ed.
    1989 L'antimafia difficile. Palermo: Centro Siciliano di Documentazione Giuseppe Impastato.
Santino, Umberto, and Giovanni La Fiura
    1990 L'impresa mafiosa: dall'Italia agli Stati Uniti. Milan: Franco Angeli.
Sciascia, Leonardo
    1961 Pirandello e la Sicilia. Caltanissetta: Salvatore Sciascia.
Snow, David A., and Robert D. Benford
    1988 Ideology, Frame Resonance, and Participant Mobilization. In Klandermans et al.
        1988:197–219.
Sorge, Bartolomeo
    1989 Uscire dal tempio: intervista autobiografica. Ed. Paolo Giuntella. Genova: Casa Editrice
        Marietti.
Spero, Joan Edelman
    1980 The Failure of the Franklin National Bank: Challenge to the International Banking
        System. New York: Columbia University Press.
Stabile, Francesco M.
    1989 Chiesa e mafia. In Santino 1989:103–27.
Tarrow, Sidney
    1989 Democracy and Disorder: Protest and Politics in Italy, 1965–1975. Oxford: Clarendon
        Press.
    1991 Struggle, Politics and Reform: Collective Action, Social Movements, and Cycles of
        Protest. Western Societies Program, Occasional Paper, no. 21. 2nd ed. Ithaca: Center for
        International Studies, Cornell University.
Touraine, Alain
    1988 Return of the Actor: Social Theory in Postindustrial Society. Trans. Myrna Godzich.
        Minneapolis: University of Minnesota Press.
Vitale, Salvo
    1989 Dopo la morte di Peppino: resistere a mafiopoli. In Santino 1989: 91–8.

Work and the Production of Silence

LOUISE LAMPHERE

I'll tell you this, If I ever work anywhere else, I'll never get involved with a union. I have learned that a union is good. But let somebody else do the dirty work. ... I've learned companies are very oriented against unions and to them, once you get involved in that or whatever, you're like their worst enemy and they have a fear of you.

Maria, female worker fired during union drive at HealthTech

The isolation was the worst part. I didn't have a disease. They [other women workers] wanted to talk to me, but they were afraid. They said, 'But we don't want to get involved.' But I said, 'You're not getting involved in anything by talking to me.'

Lorraine, female union activist at HealthTech

Lorraine and Maria, Hispana women workers employed at the newly built HealthTech plant in Albuquerque, echoed each other's disillusion and sense of defeat in 1983, several months after they had participated in a union drive that resulted in a vote of 141 against the union and only 71 for it. The history of the union campaign, which we glimpsed at several different points, illustrates the process that encapsulates the exercise of power, the creation of resistance, and the production of silence in the workplace. The interviews conducted by Guillermo Grenier, a sociologist pursuing research for his dissertation in sociology during the union campaign, and those conducted by myself, Patricia Zavella, and Jennifer Martinez as part of a National Science Foundation project studying working mothers in the sunbelt give us a sense of the relationship between the exercise of power, the making of histories, and the creation of silences, gaps, and forgettings.

What I will emphasize in telling the story of the HealthTech union drive is the creation of gaps and fissures that constitute silences – portions of histories that get suppressed in the later reconstruction of History. At one level this is a series of local recountings or histories of one union drive in a southwestern American city. But I will present a more unified story which itself is a construction: a piecing together of partial recountings and observations, not by workers or management, but by myself using interviews and field notes produced by my co-researchers and Guillermo Grenier.[1]

In constructing this history, I have taken the view that there are two competing histories: one put forward by management and the other by workers who favoured the union. This not simply a matter of two dichotomous groups and stories that did not mesh, but of a dialectical process where some workers come to share the management's story and others sharpen a counter-history in an attempt to draw additional workers to their side. The voices of unionists such as Bonnie, Annette, Andres, Lorraine, and Maria tell an activists' history, while that of Lucille articulates a history sympathetic to the management vision. Still others felt that they could not actively embrace either version, but preferred to assent to the side that was least likely to jeopardize their jobs.

The outcome in this struggle was that one of these histories was effectively silenced, partly through the removal of union activists from the labour force in the months that followed the union defeat. But the defeat also left no institutional basis for a continued reiteration of the activists' side of the story (i.e., an active union organization legitimately inside the plant). This silencing did not just 'happen'; rather, the exercise of power in the workplace forcefully drove the activists' histories underground or out of the plant. Ultimately, we can see the suppression of these counter-histories in the way in which struggles against participant-management schemes have been silenced and a paradigm for 'flexible, non-hierarchical' management-worker relations has become nearly hegemonic and enshrined in Labor Secretary Robert Reich's policies within the Clinton administration during the 1990s.[2]

The Ambiguous Relationship between Consent and Resistance

To understand the dynamic interplay between these two histories, we need to interrogate the dynamics of resistance and consent on the shop floor. This focus on the labour process is crucial, I would argue, because it is through the experience of the day-to-day tasks of work which are structured by management that workers come either to agree with management's history or to forge a counter-history or histories.

The capitalist industrial workplace, where corporations own the means of production and where workers sell their labour for a wage, is a site where power is exercised in the everyday operation of the labour process. Power and control are diffused through the organization of production (for example, in the use of assembly lines or batch processing), the placement of workers in relation to machines, the use of a particular kind of wage system (piece rates, quota-bonus systems, learning curves), the implementation of work discipline, and the hiring and firing of workers. A worker's active engagement with this system is always inherently ambiguous, containing elements of both consent and resistance (Kondo 1990:218–25). Management control systems (whether they are based on simple, technological, and/or bureaucratic control; see Edwards 1979) push towards individualizing the worker, isolating her from co-workers, and driving her towards higher and higher levels of productivity (engendering coping and consent with the system).

Yet such an exercise of power also creates resistance. (Foucault 1980:142; Dreyfus and Rabinow 1983:147). Workers attempt to exercise autonomy and control over their work, undercutting the rules, cutting corners, and coping with the system of control. Some of this opposition can be manifest in a highly individualized way, as described by James Scott in *Weapons of the Weak* (1985). In other cases, resistance becomes collective. Workers develop a shared set of tactics, a vision of the management that sets them in opposition to the firm, or a set of work rules that cuts through management's ability to extract higher levels of production. The creation of a counter-history that summarizes this opposition often revolves around those recountings of moments when resistance becomes collective rather than individual. It also involves the cultural reinterpretation of management ideology – the appropriation of key terms and their redefinition.

When resistance becomes full-blown and collective, management then takes steps to break that resistance, reasserting its history and at the same time attempting to persuade other workers of its vision of the labour process. Yet this is not simply a matter of two competing stories or histories, since relations among workers change as some become aligned with management, others join the activists, and still others sit on the sidelines.

A union drive results in either success or failure; while a successful drive may keep alive the two counterpoised stories, a defeat usually means the submersion of the counter-vision. It remains, I will argue in the conclusions of this paper, in the possibility of everyday acts of resistance (tied to a concrete labour process, system of pay, and set of management policies) that a collective counter-history can emerge. Women workers' accounts of their everyday coping and resistance, as well as their comments on management's exercise of power, their own experience of that power, and their participation in counter-tactics, give us a sense of how the exercise of power can create silences or fragmented stories of resistance and also a sense of defeat. In the conservative climate of the 1980s, when few union struggles were successful and when corporate hegemony was supported by the state, it is important to examine the forces that disperse histories, as well as those that help to resurrect memories and break silences.[3]

The Construction of Two Histories

The union drive at HealthTech took place in 1982 and 1983 in a new branch plant located in Albuquerque. Within the last twenty years the city has begun to attract branch plants of large corporations, primarily in apparel manufacture and electronics. A number of these plants have introduced aspects of participative management, making Albuquerque somewhat of a 'laboratory' for the management of the future. Thus when HealthTech opened its doors in 1981, it was one of the most innovative plants in the city, operating on what management termed a 'high-involvement' philosophy and also hiring a workforce that was 90 per cent female and 65 per cent Hispanic.

The 'high-involvement' philosophy at HealthTech, which became the dominant theme of management's recounting of the plant's unique history, had several ingredients. We learned from interviews with the plant manager and plant psychologist that benefits for production and clerical employees were equal, there were no time clocks, and workers could be late and make up time at the end of the day.

The plant manager and plant psychologist emphasized the innovative structure of the plant, including its open-door policy and team organization. Each department was divided into 'production teams' of twelve to fourteen workers. The plant operated on two shifts, and each team decided on a rotation schedule, which normally meant that individuals worked two weeks on days and two weeks on nights. Team-mates often took breaks or lunch together. The 'team concept' also meant a massive restructuring of the cultural categories through which management-worker relations were interpreted. Each team had a 'facilitator,' not a supervisor. The facilitator was thus not a 'boss' but someone who helped improve the interpersonal relationships on the team and aided individuals with their productivity. The team itself was supposed to have an important role in decision making. Two team members interviewed prospective employees (after they had been interviewed by management), and if the team members brought back a negative evaluation, the person was not hired. These ideal-typical accounts emphasized the positive aspects of this new organization, and it was only after the union campaign and after we had access to Grenier's data that we came to the view that management, through the team structure, had co-opted the 'informal work group' long ago discovered by the human-relations school of management psychology (Mayo 1933; Roethlisberger and Dickson 1939).

Workers' recountings of their relationship to management and the union drive emerged slowly. Jennifer Martinez and I began interviewing in October 1982, and by mid-January 1983 (when I returned to Rhode Island) we had completed eight interviews. At the time of some of our first interviews in October, the union drive had begun to 'heat up,' and Jenny, a shy and very quiet nineteen-year-old mother whose husband was chronically unemployed, dropped the comment that 'the union's trying to get in too ... and it's terrible.' I did not pursue her remark, remembering my promise to the plant psychologist (who was providing me with the names of working mothers) that I would not ask questions or mention the union drive to any of the interviewees.

During my next interview on 26 October, Annette, a young single parent, told me of her role as a member of the organizing committee. I turned the tape recorded off for most of this conversation, not wanting to jeopardize my interviewee, should the tapes ever become part of a legal proceeding. We discussed the leaflet that the organizing committee had distributed that week, as well as the fact that her facilitator had stopped having team meetings because of the pro-union sentiment among team members. A week later I was also visited by the union organizers, who had heard that I was conducting research and who wanted my help in obtaining names and addresses of women workers. I learned that the firm had attempted to remove one of the pro-union workers from the compensation committee. In November Dolores discussed the way in which union sentiments were being expressed in team meetings. After the interview she told Jennifer that she was 'not keen on union activity in general.' However, she was inclined to vote for the union, if it could do away with the rotating shift schedule, which, as a mother, she found particularly difficult. In January 1983 Jennifer also interviewed Lorraine, and she told Jennifer of her role in a committee to fight against the union.

During the spring, while I was in Rhode Island, I received a newspaper clipping concerning a community meeting at which a sociologist read a statement claiming that the firm had deliberately fired members of the organizing team and engaged in additional union-busting tactics. Then I leaned that the union had lost the vote in May. When I returned to Albuquerque the following month, I met the sociologist, Guillermo Grenier, who after his statement had been barred from the plant, but had continued work on his dissertation, concentrating on the union drive.

During the last two months of the campaign and into the summer months of 1983, Guillermo Grenier interviewed a number of the union activists. His taped discussions were wide-ranging (in contrast to our use of specific questions about the labour process asked of each interviewee). He was interested in discovering how activists were drawn to the union and what the current management tactics (particularly after the union loss) were. In contrast, our interviews provided a window on each woman's successes and struggles with the labour process and tapped a wider range of female employees (including four who had not voted for the union and a very active anti-union organizer). In sum, we knew more about women's work and family relationships, while Guillermo's interviews gave us much more insight into the exercise of power by the management and its impact on pro-union women.

Over the next few months, I worked with Guillermo to put together an article on the union drive. It soon became apparent that union support was concentrated in two of the channel-swaging and several of the drill-swaging teams, while teams that had been formed by newly recruited workers during the winter and spring of 1983 had remained solidly anti-union. The role of the channel and drill workers in starting the union drive led us to examine the labour process in these departments and the ways in which everyday work experiences are intimately connected with the evolution of individual tactics of resistance, the emergence of a group consciousness, and the development of a counter-history.

Shop-Floor Resistance and the Emergence of a Counter-History

Workers at HealthTech made surgical sutures. Trainees attached surgical thread on curved steel needles (a process called 'swaging') through the use of 'learning curves.' Each week the trainee was given a production goal of completing so many dozen swaged needles each day; the number increased until the employee reached '100 per cent efficiency.' Employees were not paid by the piece (as is often the case when learning curves are used) but by the hour. Nevertheless, workers were 'pushing against a clock' and trying to 'make their numbers,' increasing their production on a daily basis, since their six-month evaluation and subsequent raises depended on maintaining productivity.

Drill and channel swaging were two different methods of attaching a surgical needle to a gut or silk cord. Since the channel technique involved a step in which the needle was curved (drill needles had been curved in a previous process), it took eighteen months to master, while the drill technique took twelve. Learning curves were used to train women in both swaging and 'winding,' that is, the winding of the surgical thread in a figure-eight pattern preparatory to its being placed in a foil envelope. Both drill and channel workers had to 'demonstrate' or maintain the 100 per cent efficiency level for a period of thirteen weeks at the end of their training period before they received a bonus raise. Then workers were supposed to enter a year's 'payback period' during which they worked at 100 per cent efficiency at either drill or channel swaging before they were allowed to learn another job. In practice, only a few workers in the drill department had completed their demonstration period when Jennifer and I were conducting interviews, and virtually no workers had attempted demonstration in the channel department.

Those in the other two departments (foil and overwrap, where needles were wrapped in foil, and devices, where 'staples' to be used in surgery were packaged) found their jobs much easier. Since most of the jobs entailed loading machines or watching the progress of the foil wrapping, the quotas did not seem difficult to achieve. Workers also rotated jobs, breaking the monotony of working on an assembly line. Clearly, the women in channel and drill swaging faced a different kind of work process and much more pressure to achieve 100 per cent efficiency, a difficult goal, especially for those working with the trickier technique of channel swaging.

These differences in the labour process led us back to our interviews with Annette and Bonnie. In them we could see the ambiguous nature of the work itself, the way that it engendered both coping and resistance. Workers attempted to forge tactics to produce more ('make the numbers'), both exerting some control over the labour process and also drawing themselves more tightly into it as they raised their productivity. They also developed a sense of the unfairness of management's attempt to extract greater levels of productivity. Resistance may have started at the point of production, but it was honed and became both collective and public in the context of team meetings, where individual facilitators often created an atmosphere that was far from being 'participative' and 'democratic.'

Bonnie has been among the first workers hired when HealthTech moved to Albuquerque in 1981. She was chosen from more than nine hundred initial applicants and was on one of the first teams formed. She told Guillermo in March 1983 that at first she was quite nervous about doing well in her job. 'I was really scared at first. Because it's very tedious, you know. Right down into the machine ... It really took me a month or so to get into it. You only had so

many days to produce that much. And if you don't make it ... well, "goodbye."
So I was really kind of panicked, but I picked up on it ... There was so much to
learn that it was quite scary.' However, Bonnie did well enough to become a
trainer of new employees. She was one of only two of the original twelve team
members who were still employed by the spring of 1983.

My interview with her revealed her everyday tactics on the job, her efforts
to pace her work, and the difficulties she had with her machine. She explained
that 'every half hour; I'd try to do 25 dozen every half hour ... The needles,
they weren't perfect. So you had to hold your needles differently sometimes.
And you had to be real careful not to get fins on them ... when it flares out at
the sides ... And if the needle wasn't cut right, then you have to try and work
with those needles and that sometimes slows you down a bit.'

Bonnie also explained the difficulties that she had with her machine and
how she would cope with them. 'A lot of times it would jam up on you. Or
they'd get out of alignment real easy. If you tried to tighten them up, they'd
come down real hard and before you knew it, your machine was out of alignment. And then you'd have to clock out again on machine breakdown or
whatever and sit there and put in new dies.' Since she had to make the same
quota each day, excessive repairs and machine difficulties often kept her numbers down.

Annette, the young widow and single parent whom I interviewed on 26
October, had been hired in September 1981 and became a member of channel
team B. In my interview with her, she described a number of difficulties.
'Because I was taught with the smallest needle there is in channel. And I had
problems with keeping my hands steady, because you just like ... shake trying
to aim for those little grooves.' Annette struggled on her own and was able to
'pick up' the technique by herself.

She had slightly different problems with her machine. As she explained,
'Well, in channel swaging, you get a stubborn product and the dies and the
needles don't want to go together and you get defects until you get one that
will run with your needle ... The facilitator had me trying different dies to find
out which dies the needles worked best with and stuff like that. So my numbers
dropped then too.'

Annette explained that she had recently been put on probation. If her numbers did not improve within two weeks, she would face a three-day suspension.
She felt this was really punishment for her pro-union activities. 'Because they
are getting kind of nervous because the union wants to get in. So they are
doing anything to get rid of people that are like for [the union]. Like I'm on the
union committee.'

Bonnie's and Annette's accounts of the labour process and their individual tactics for coping with it illustrate the ambiguous nature of women's strategies. They emerged from struggles with the machine, the needles, the dies, and the silk or gut thread. As such, these were attempts to take control of the labour process, but since they also brought measure of success, they pulled the worker more clearly along the road to higher and higher production. In some workplaces, such as the apparel plant that I studied in Rhode Island, women devised a set of work rules that limited management's attempts to increase productivity. They also developed a well-honed critique of management, who lowered the piece rates so that workers had to complete more garments in order to make the same wages (see Lamphere 1987).

At HealthTech individual tactics developed into a collective critique in a different context, that of the team meeting. Facilitators used the meetings to create and communicate management's history of the firm, stressing the uniqueness of its participative structure. At the same time, they used peer pressure to get workers to perform. The contradictions between the ideology of participation and the management's tactics to control helped workers develop a collective critique. Not only did they hear one another relate their tactics, struggles, and difficulties, but they experienced the way that these recountings were used against each of them. Bonnie's interview with Guillermo and my discussions with Annette revealed these dynamics clearly.

Bonnie told Guillermo that she had initially responded favourably to the team philosophy. As Bonnie said, 'I thought it was kind of nice. It might be kind of fun. It was all new to me: to have somebody ... if you had a problem in your team you could have somebody to help you out.' However, Bonnie became disillusioned with the team process. Jim, one of the early facilitators for the channel department teams A and B, often tried to provoke conflict among workers. 'It got really hairy in there. We just dreaded to go into those meetings. And they'd last two or three hours. I'd get home at six ... He just really got a kick out of tearing people over. Oh, people would just sit there and cry. He'd get them into tears. It was a mess ... a total mess.' Under these circumstances, Bonnie felt that it was embarrassing for workers to have to justify their low production numbers or explain their troubles with the machines during a public meeting.

Participating in a firing was also a difficult process for Bonnie, as was clear when she told Guillermo about the decision to fire one male team member. 'Well, it's terrible. That person is sitting right there ... It was for his numbers. He really was a good worker and a good person ... But his numbers weren't there. He'd had some trouble with his machine, and I guess it had just gotten down to the wire and they had to fire him. I guess we all agreed that if this was what we are supposed to do, we've got to do it. If you don't make your numbers, you've got to go ... It was awful.' Annette, on team B, said the following about Jim's meetings: 'It would be just like one big "tattle-tale session." That's the way our other facilitator ... the one before José. He had the meetings being conducted like that. It got to where everybody was fighting with each other and everything.'

When José was assigned to be the facilitator of teams A and B (and Jim was fired), members of team B acted to put the brakes on José's use of peer pressure and more openly confront him. 'He's ask us our opinion in the team meeting and when we gave it to him, we'd be considered bitchy ... So he got really mad one week and he said "no more team meetings." Because we just weren't getting anything out of them any more ... But what he wanted was for everyone to rat on each other ... we're not [willing to do that].' By October Annette's team had developed its own support system. 'We have team support as far as helping each other goes and everything ... we kind of back each other up ... We back each other up, not only in the production area, but I guess in other problems too – personal problems.'

The high-involvement philosophy and the team structure at first enlisted cooperation from Bonnie and Annette, but as they confronted the underlying sources of control (the demand to produce more under difficult conditions), they began, not just to use individual tactics to deal with the labour process, but also to participate in collective resistance. The stories that they recounted to Guillermo and me told of two competing histories in the making, one of management's vision of the firm and the other of the increasingly militant team members whose experience both on the shop floor and in the team meetings produced a counter-history.

The Successful Exercise of Power

Management's history became much clearer from conversations that Guillermo had with the plant psychologist and various facilitators. They revealed an over-all management strategy that was being orchestrated by the plant psychologist, which in turn allowed many facilitators to be much more successful than Jim and José in controlling their teams. In talking with Guillermo, the psychologist mentioned the company's 'proactive approach,' in which each facilitator orchestrated and initiated the discussion of the union at team meetings and communicated anti-union ideas to the employees. In addition, the psychologist and facilitators used what was called the 'individual conflict approach': attempting to isolate individuals already known to be pro-union. Both these approaches demonstrate management's ability to exercise power through subtle, cohesive forms. They often had the impact of silencing workers in team meetings, turning potential resistance into agreement with the company perspective.

Dennis, who was the facilitator for drill teams A, B, and C, was particularly successful in using these tactics. Where channel teams A and B had been able to silence their supervisor, the reverse was true in Dennis's drill teams. The histories that we collected from members of his teams showed the role of management in developing splits within the workforce, drawing some members to their side and effectively silencing others. In drill team A, Lucille was active in forming the pro-company organization, as she told Jennifer when she was interviewed in January 1983.

Well, there was quite a bit of conflict, because there was a couple on our team that wanted the union. And the rest didn't want the union, and there was some that didn't care one way or the other or didn't know enough about it to care ... We changed the minds of the ones that wanted the union ... about six or seven weeks ago. The union stopped being pushy ... What we did was, several of us from different departments got together and started an anti-union committee. And we had our own meetings and passed out our own flyers.

Andres, another team member, described to Guillermo how Dennis had utilized Lucille's anti-union stance as early as September 1982 to silence others. At that meeting, Lucille had asked, 'How far would the union go to get into the plant?' In response, Dennis pulled out a piece of paper and said something like 'Oh, by the way, I've got something to read you about the union.' He read out an account that a union in New York had gotten its members a twenty-five-cent raise. 'Is this the kind of union you want representing you?' he asked. Andres retorted, 'Why don't you stick to the facts of what the union had done at other HealthTech plants and what it can do here, and not some other union at another place?'

Elena, another anti-unionist, responded, 'If you're not happy with the company, why don't you resign?' She continued her attack, almost yelling at Andres. Dennis did not speak up. 'He allowed the wolf pack to attack me,' Andres commented. Such acrimonious conflict meant that workers became reluctant to speak out, afraid of being ridiculed or even fired.

In drill team B, pro-union support seemed stronger and was quietly developing among the group who consistently worked on the day shift (all women, including Dolores and Valerie, two Hispana mothers whom Jennifer and I interviewed). Guillermo was present at a team meeting on 17 September 1982 when Dennis, the facilitator, took action to bring out any anti-union views that might be expressed publicly by team members. He mentioned a television show of the previous evening: 'Speaking of TV, did anyone see the piece on Coors on "60 Minutes" last night?' A couple of workers responded that they had, as did a female personnel administrator whom Dennis had invited to come to the meeting. He encouraged her to give her views.

It showed how the union keeps trying to get in at the Coors plant in Colorado, even when the workers don't want anything to do with it. It was real funny because they showed how they got all the employees in a great big room asking them what they thought of the company, and every single one of them said how much they liked working for the company, how much the company was trying to help them and all that stuff ... They showed all the stuff the company was doing for the workers – the gym they had set up, the benefits and all that ... And it was a really good show.

The administrator's speech was sufficient to bring out anti-union sentiments from three other workers.

In team C, Dennis managed the resignation of a union supporter from a plant committee through public intimidation. His target was Rosa, the pro-union employee on the compensation committee, whom I had heard about from the union organizers in October 1982. Guillermo interviewed Rosa with her mother, Margarita, who also worked at HealthTech, in June 1983 after the union's loss. Rosa recounted the history of her painful experience, telling Guillermo that during a team meeting the previous October Dennis had discussed the leaflet that the union had just distributed. He 'tore the leaflet apart' and then asked for comments. As Rosa reported,

Tracy spoke up. She said, 'I don't feel Rosa should be on the compensation committee because I don't feel she is trustworthy enough not to express what we feel or want.' She said my name had been on the union leaflet with other people she thought were not trustworthy enough because we were not for the HealthTech philosophy ... When she got through I said that I'd voluntarily step down from the committee. I didn't want to be on it if people felt that way about it. Plus, I suspected that I was being set up. Tracy had always been my friend. People said we were like sisters, that we even looked like sisters.

Dennis refused to let Rosa step down and said that the other teams should have a chance to decide this issue. The next day at a meeting of about seventy-five members of the whole drill department, he raised the issue of Rosa's resignation and asked for comments. Tracy again stood up and accused Rosa, 'almost yelling.' Finally, Anne, a team-mate, defended Rosa's performance on the committee. Rosa finally retorted, 'I feel I'm being harassed for my political opinion and that is discrimination.' Anne later reported to Guillermo, 'They totally humiliated her in this mass meeting. They called her a hypocrite ... She was very upset afterwards. She couldn't do anything that night. She was in tears and to me that was humiliating.'

Dennis's tactic of setting up the public intimidation of a pro-union worker in front of seventy-five employees was clearly designed to break the growing solidarity of the organizing committee and show more neutral workers the severe penalties that union activism would bring. It was an orchestrated exercise of power and a successful effort to push an activist off the compensation committee and demonstrate to other workers the risks of resistance.

Beginning in December 1982, the management turned to illegal tactics such as firing union supporters and carefully screening out potential employees for pro-union views. The firings were the ultimate exercise of power, the termination of a worker's connection with the company and hence an end to her or his resistance. Management also used the tactics of a tough legal campaign, showing anti-union movies, putting anti-union material in pay envelopes, and isolating union supporters by employing the motto 'Be a winner! Vote No.' The climate of fear created by the firings made it difficult to recruit new union supporters, especially among those recently hired, who were not inclined to join a union anyway. In addition, many women workers felt that this was the best job they had ever had; most were supporting children (either as part of a couple or as a single parent) and could not risk their jobs. The initial collective resistance never spread to a number of the newer teams. The company spent $1 million on the campaign and was rewarded with a vote against the union by a two-to-one margin. (See Lamphere and Grenier 1988, as well as Grenier 1988, for a full account of the drive.)

The election was not the end of the company's attempt to silence pro-union workers, however. After the drive was defeated, some facilitators had private interviews with each team member, often intimidating the pro-union workers. As Anne, who had supported Rosa, told Guillermo in June 1983, 'Dennis has been going through all his team members ... each individual. And I had my meeting. And I was there three and a half hours.' Later in the interview she said, 'I think the company is going to weed out as many as they can without getting into further charges [with the National Labor Relations Board]. They are being careful.'

In addition, some of the quality-control workers who were anti-union continued to harass union activists by giving them rejections. Lucille, for example, moved to quality control and was still carrying out the anti-union campaign a month after the election was over, according to Anne. 'I don't know why she

[Lucille] has it out for her. But Margarita [Rosa's mother] is really feeling the pressure. More pressure is put on the person who is disliked and they were still mentally harassed. Lucille has not given up the union campaign ... She's still using those tactics ... And she's a QC and she can do it ... She's giving daggers at everybody.'

The isolation and harassment was difficult for some activists to deal with. Lorraine, who had been close to a number of facilitators, felt that she had been particularly ostracized. After she became pro-union, 'They ignored me. Before the campaign started, they were always inviting me to go here and there. Then afterwards ... not even a "hi." They made dirty faces at me. Like when I would approach them ... I kept on ... I tried not to care, but I did care ... And that would bother me, because they had never done it before.' She was also isolated from her co-workers in her department, where many were anti-union. The quotation that begins this paper recounts the success of management in getting workers to refrain from talking to Lorraine and other union activists.

After the union lost, Lorraine suffered increased harassment, eventually leading her to quit. She told Patricia Zavella in August 1983, 'And like at the end, they wouldn't even let me go to work ... Like clock in, when I used to go in, they wouldn't let me clock in, make you go in through a back room and start harassing me, telling me that I was not worth a shit.'

Lorraine was, in fact, quite relieved when she decided to quit her job and found another one. When Patricia asked her how she felt about leaving HealthTech, she replied, 'I felt good ... I mean, I knew, it was like something was coming out of me and I was free again, I didn't have to worry about it. Before I'd come home and I'd cry and I'd cry and I'd cry. And I'd hate what it did for my condition. My body just couldn't take it. I was sick a long time the last months there. Headaches, all different types of things.'

Not all activists reacted as Lorraine did. Bonnie took the union drive in stride, quit her job in the summer of 1983, and seemed to leave the HealthTech experience behind her. Anne, who had sympathized with Rosa, felt that she was tougher than many of her co-workers. She told Guillermo: 'Some people react different to scare tactics. Me – I stand up and fight. That's the way I am. If someone threatens me, I ... especially if I am boxed in a corner, I come out fighting. Some people don't. They give into the threat. And I think that's what a majority of people do. They were afraid. Afraid of losing their jobs. Afraid of the humiliation you were put through ... and you were humiliated.' Maria, who was quoted at the beginning of this article, said that she would still vote for a union but would not be on an organizing committee. She told Guillermo, 'Never again will I ever get involved like that. I know.'

The union filed over fifty grievances with the National Labor Relations Board, especially in an effort to reinstate the four workers who had been fired.

However, the hearings were delayed four times. Finally, in February 1984, almost a year after the election, the NLRB ordered the company to pay $50,000 to the four fired employees and to four others who were refused jobs because of union sympathies (Grenier 1988:157). By this time, many of the union activists had left the firm, often worn down by the interpersonal struggle waged by the management.

The wearing down of union activists is also vividly reported in Rick Fantasia's description of a union drive at a hospital in New Hampshire (1988:121–79). The use of anti-union consultants and attempts to isolate and intimidate union activists were reminiscent of the HealthTech case. Despite the fact that the Licensed Practical Nurses and Technicians won an election in 1982, the hospital was successful in delaying the negotiation of a contract. The organizing committee met for three years, but with normal job attrition and continued delays, the local rank and file had essentially given up by 1987.

Intimidation, harassment, and the exercise of myriad forms of everyday control often push activists out of workplaces after a union drive or strike. Those who manage to stay are frequently the ones who had less of a stake in the transformation of the workplace or who sided with the firm during the conflict. I have drawn upon contemporary ethnographic material to illustrate the production of silence in contemporary times, when companies have hired a battery of psychologists, lawyers, and consulting firms and relied on a sympathetic NLRB to delay elections, negotiations for a contract, or hearings on grievances. Although these ethnographic examples illustrate the power and tactics of firms in a modern, capitalist setting, they do, I think, give us some insight into the dynamics of worker-management relations and the production of silence in the past.

The Excavation of Resistance

The same power relations that create resistance on the shop floor are also those that produce consent and silence. If the labour process, the extraction of surplus labour, and management control of work relationships create resistance, the exercise of power within this same context often produces silence. On the other hand, if resistance in one period is thwarted, the conditions that produced it often remain, since they are embedded in the way that work is organized and managed. It is this everyday set of resistance strategies that is likely to reoccur or even be remembered by those who are relatively unsympathetic to larger forms of collective resistance. Where the exercise of power has silenced whole stories of resistance (erasing them from History), fragments of histories are sometimes evidenced in the recountings of everyday acts on the shop floor.

We can see how this might be the case by examining a historical example based on the research conducted by myself and Ewa Hauser in Central Falls, Rhode Island (Lamphere 1987; Hauser 1981). Hauser initially worked on my research project on working mothers and then returned to conduct oral history research about the Central Falls Polish community for her dissertation. She found it extremely difficult to get her consultants to discuss the strikes of the 1920s and 1930s in Central Falls. In addition to the 1934 work stoppage, there was an important strike of silk workers at the Royal Weaving and General Fabrics mills in July 1931. Unlike the 1934 event, in which few women were to be seen in the crowds confronting the National Guards, the 1931 strike was organized by Ann Burlak, 'the Red Flame,' a Ukrainian woman who was a member of the National Textile Workers Union (a union affiliated with the Communist Party). Women were active on the picket lines and were arrested during the mass picketing. Burlak was arrested and sent to Boston for deportation, despite the fact that she was an American citizen. Hauser repeatedly tried to contact the sister of one of her Polish informants about the strike, but the woman (who had apparently led workers from the mill at the beginning of the strike and had been Burlak's personal secretary) refused to be interviewed (Hauser 1981:320). Burlak herself, in returning to Central Falls to talk with community members in the process of writing her memoirs, found that those who had worked with her during the strike refused to speak with her.[4]

Hauser contrasts her informants' memory of class difference in Poland with the deletion of strikes from their histories of Central Falls. The narratives of life before immigration are filled with evidence of class consciousness and a sense of the different interests between peasants, on the one hand, and landlords and clergy, on the other. In comparison, interviewees on the 1920s and 1930s, when members of the Polish community were actively engaged in protests and strikes, were conspicuously silent on these matters. 'Their memories of the moment of class struggle are either effaced or concealed. In my analysis of the oral histories and direct communication with members of the group about their past, the traces of the pattern of concealment emerge, sometimes in the content, sometimes in the distortion, and sometimes in the anxious laughter or rapid speech of the informant.' Hauser goes on to attribute this concealment to several factors, particularly the 'crushing defeat that the labor movement suffered in America' (Hauser 1981:342). Her position here is that the exercise of power not just on the shop floor but at a later period and throughout the whole society had silenced these histories.

On the other hand, some of our difficulties in excavating and recovering these silences may have been related to our initial lack of knowledge. In 1977 we knew little about the 1931 and 1934 strikes and even less about those at individual mills in the 1920s. Thus Hauser's questions were vague and on the order of 'Did you ever participate in any of the strikes?' Without a better sense of the location and chronology of these events in connection with the work history of any particular interviewee, it was difficult to probe further if he or she gave a negative or evasive answer.

We were more successful in getting descriptions of everyday resistance, but even here I had not yet put together a good account of the labour process in textile mills or a good history of the firms in Central Falls and their decline in the 1920s and 1930s. Thus Hauser's questions about previous work histories often did not reveal a clear picture of the shop floor or everyday resistance since she did not know what each job entailed, how they were interrelated, what the history of the mill had been, and how foreman and agents controlled the work itself. Only during the early 1980s, while collecting the material for chapters 2, 3, and 4 of my book on the rise and decline of the textile industry in Central Falls, did I begin to know enough about the local industry to ask the appropriate questions of oral history interviews collected by Hauser and others. A much more concrete grasp of the labour process, the history of particular firms, and the structure of power might have helped us excavate some of the fragmented histories long silenced.

Conclusions

The ethnographic material that I have used from interviews and observations on the shop floor in Rhode Island and New Mexico gives us a sense of the forces at work in the creation of gaps and silences in labour history. In constructing two contesting histories (one articulated by management and the other by workers), I have begun with the labour process, because it is both the place where power is always exercised at work and the site of resistance and consent. I have examined a union drive in detail to show how these contesting histories emerge and how, when resistance becomes collective, the exercise of power and the struggle over contending stories move into other arenas (in this case, at team meetings, but also at breaks, during lunch periods, and in larger meetings). I have emphasized that these histories are dynamic and changing and that workers are often drawn to management's vision of the firm or conversely to the activists' version which opposes it. Other workers may avoid commitment to either history, keeping to the sidelines or disengaging as soon as possible. Still others are forcefully silenced for their articulation of support for the activists' histories. The passages quoted at the beginning of this article blame neither the union nor the workers for the defeat; rather, they articulate a sense of being silenced, of dealing with loss and isolation, of becoming an object of power, of telling a story, but one whose coherence and unity might well be dispersed, fragmented, and rarely told again.

Further removed from such silenced histories, the investigator is often faced with excavating fragments and reassembling pieces from archival materials, newspaper clippings, or oral histories. Here an investigation of the labour process itself, the organization of management control, and the stories of everyday work life can breathe spirit into these fragments. Ordinary workers can be quite articulate concerning every day acts of resistance, even if they have never participated in more-collective forms of organization. Such recountings are a way of breaking through the silences that the exercise of power within the workplace both in the past and in the present has created. We perhaps can never recover these silenced histories, but we can glimpse the forces that both foster acquiesence and unleash resistance, and we can better understand the complexities of power relations at work.

NOTES

1 This essay focuses on a union drive in the United States under historical circumstances when union organizing was particularly different. Resistance and organizing take on very distinct characteristics in various national contexts, for example, in England and Canada, which have a much more militant trade union past; see, for example, Wenona Giles's study of Portuguese hotel workers in London (1992) or collections edited by Jackie West (1982) and Audrey Kobayashi (1994). A great deal of attention has been given to women's resistance and accommodation in new Third World industrial zones on the U.S.–Mexican border, Malaya, Indonesia, and other parts of southeast and east Asia. See Kopinak 1996 and Pena 1996 for two recent studies of women in Mexican Maquiladoras, and Wolf 1992 and Turner 1995 for recent research in Indonesia and Japan on women and industrial work. Ong 1991 provides an excellent review of the material on Third World women and industrialization with special attention to women's resistance in southeast Asia, Mexico, and Korea.
2 With the election of John J. Sweeney, former head of the Service Employees International Union, to the head of the AFL-CIO, the labour movement is shifting attention to increasing its membership and organizing the unorganized. The SEIU itself is beginning a campaign to stress organizing using member-organizers, encourage more active involvement by the membership, and increase political education. Since there has also been a change in the responsiveness of the National Labor Relations Board (partly because of President Clinton's appointments), organizing drives over the next few years may meet with more success, a change from the 1980s and the period discussed in this essay.
3 There is a vast literature on shop-floor resistance and on women and unions in the United States, much of which points to the active presence of immigrant women and women of colour in union struggles and strike activity. Two collections that deal with some of this research are Sacks and Remy 1984 and Bookman and Morgen 1988. Some of the best research on Chicana/ Hispana working women includes monographs by Zavella (1987), Romero (1992), and Ruiz (1987) and the recent collection edited by De la Torre and Pesquera (1993). The history of

male-dominated unions and their ambivalence towards women has also been well documented; see, for example, Milkman 1987, Kessler-Harris 1982, and Milkman 1985.

4 Polish immigrants to Rhode Island did not bring with them a tradition of labour radicalism, since most were from small peasant villages in Galicia. Other groups, for example, the Jewish, Italian, and English immigrant populations, contained those who carried with them European radical traditions as a basis for continuing to resist and protest in the United States. Paul Buhle, Scott Molloy, Gary Gerstle, Judith Smith, and other members of the Rhode Island Labor History Forum during the 1970s did a great deal to uncover and publicize the history of labour protest, the role of Italian-American radicals, the importance of French-Canadian unionists, and the connections between work, family, and gender among Rhode Island immigrant communities (*Radical History Review* 17 [spring 1978]). Even though the French Canadians, Poles, and Portuguese – to use three prominent examples – were often thought of as quiescent conservative peasants, members of these groups, including many women, became mobilized in labour protests throughout the early decades of the twentieth century, particularly during the 1922 and 1934 textile strikes (Lamphere 1987). I would argue that the Cold War and the conservatism of the labour movement in the post-war period did much to silence memories of this activism.

REFERENCES

Bookman, Ann, and Sandra Morgen, eds.
   1988 Women and the Politics of Empowerment. Philadelphia: Temple University Press.
De la Torre, Adela, and Beatriz M. Pesquera
   1993 Building with Our Hands: New Directions in Chicana Studies. Berkeley: University of
         California Press.
Dreyfus, Hubert L., and Paul Rabinow
   1983 Beyond Structuralism and Hermeneutics. 2d ed. Chicago: University of Chicago Press.
Edwards, Richard
   1979 Contested Terrain: The Transformation on the Workplace in the Twentieth Century.
         New York: Basic Books.
Fantasia, Rick
   1988 Cultures of Solidarity. Berkeley: University of California Press.
Foucault, Michel
   1980 Power/Knowledge: Selected Interviews and Other Writings, 1972–77. Ed. Colin
         Gordon. New York: Pantheon Books.
Giles, Winona
   1992 Gender Inequality and Resistance: The Case of Portuguese Women in London.
         Anthropological Quarterly 65: 67–128.
Grenier, Guillermo
   1988 Inhuman Relations: Quality Circles and Anti-Unionism in American Industry.
         Philadelphia: Temple University Press.
Hauser, Ewa Krystyna
   1981 Ethnicity and Class Consciousness in a Polish American Community. PhD dissertation,
         Johns Hopkins University.
Kessler-Harris, Alice
   1982 Out to Work: A History of Wage-Earning Women in the United States. Oxford: Oxford
         University Press.

282 Louise Lamphere

Kobayashi, Audrey, ed.
1994 Women, Work and Place. Montreal and Kingston: McGill-Queen's University Press.
Kondo, Dorrine
1990 Crafting Selves. Chicago: University of Chicago Press.
Kopinak, Kathryn
1996 Desert Capitalism: Maquiladoras in North America's Western Industrial Corridor. Tucson: University of Arizona Press.
Lamphere, Louise
1987 From Working Daughters to Working Mothers: Immigrant Women in a New England Industrial Community. Ithaca: Cornell University Press.
Lamphere, Louise, and Guillermo Grenier
1988 Women, Unions and 'Participative Management': Organizing in the Sunbelt. In Women and the Politics of Empowerment, Ann Bookman and Sandra Morgen, eds. Philadelphia: Temple University Press.
Mayo, Elton
1933 The Human Problems of an Industrial Civilization. New York: Macmillan.
Milkman, Ruth
1985 Women, Work, and Protest: A Century of US Women's Labor History. Boston: Routledge & Kegan Paul.
1987 Gender at Work: The Dynamics of Job Segregation by Sex during World War II. Urbana: University of Illinois Press.
Ong, Aihwa
1991 The Gender and Labor Politics of Postmodernity. Annual Review of Anthropology 20:279–309.
Pena, Devon
1996 The Terror of the Machine. Austin: CMAS Books/University of Texas Press.
Radical History Review
1978 Labor and Community Militance in Rhode Island. No. 7 (spring).
Roethlishberger, F.J., and W. Dickson
1939 Management and the Worker. Cambridge: Harvard University Press.
Romero, Mary
1992 Maid in the U.S.A. New York: Routledge.
Ruiz, Vicki
1987 Cannery Women, Cannery Lives. Albuquerque: University of New Mexico Press.
Sacks, Karen Brodkin, and Dorothy Remy, eds.
1984 My Troubles Are Going to Have Trouble with Me. New Brunswick: Rutgers University Press.
Scott, James
1985 Weapons of the Weak: Everyday Forms of Peasant Resistance. New Haven: Yale University Press.
Turner, Christena L.
1995 Japanese Workers in Protest: An Ethnography of Consciousness and Experience. Berkeley: University of California Press.
West, Jackie, ed.
1982 Work, Women and the Labour Market. London: Routledge and Kegan Paul.
Wolf, Diane L.
1982 Factory Daughters: Gender, Household Dynamics, and Rural Industrialization in Java. Berkeley: University of California Press.

Zavella, Patricia
    1987 Women's Work and Chicano Families: Cannery Workers of the Santa Clara Valley.
          Ithaca: Cornell University Press.

The So-Called Laichingen Hunger Chronicle

An Example of the Fiction of the Factual, the Traps of Evidence, and the Possibilities of Proof in the Writing of History

HANS MEDICK

The document discussed in the following pages was published for the first time in the *Württembergische Jahrbücher für Statistik und Landeskunde* in 1917. The editor was a teacher, Christian August Schnerring, who was born the son of a hand weaver in the Swabian Alps in 1870 and died in Stuttgart in 1951. Schnerring published the document as an appendix to a longer scholarly treatise on 'scarcity and famine in Württemberg in 1816–17' (Schnerring 1917).[1] He had discovered the 'handwritten record of an Alps dweller concerning years of expensiveness and starvation in 1816–17,' as he described it,[2] during his folklore researches on the Alps. He introduced the publication of the document with these words: 'The man who left the following description lived and wrote in Laichingen in the Swabian Alps. On more than forty now very yellowed pages, he wrote down what that hard period of need had brought him each day. The directness of his exact description exercises a certain fascination; historical investigation supports each of his statements. Unfortunately, the first page, or perhaps the first several pages, of the manuscript has been torn away' (Schnerring 1917:72).

The complete publication of the 'record' was preceded in the years of 1913 and 1916 by extracts presented partly in paraphrase (Schnerring 1913, 1916–17). But it was only Schnerring's publication of the whole document with footnotes and explanations in the respected *Jahrbücher*, issued by the Central Statistical Office of Württemberg, that made it known and to a certain degree 'respectable' to historically interested laymen and scholars. Above all, the 'Hunger Chronicle,' as it was and still is called, became a pillar of local historical consciousness in Schnerring's birthplace. Its effect was supplemented and reinforced by a historical novel that the teacher published a year after the appearance of the document under the title *Du suchest das Land heim: Geschichtlicher Dorfroman aus einer Teuerungs- und Hungerzeit* (You punish the land: a historical village novel from a period of scarcity and famine; Schnerring 1918). The centre of action in the novel is the village of Webringen, that is, Laichingen, the Württemberg linen-weaving village par excellence. The novel is set in the years 1816 to 1817. In it the author also frequently supports his description by the use of references to the 'record of an Alps dweller,' which he himself had published, as the authentic source of information for the event that he now related in fictional form.

The reception of both texts in the village itself took place in a similar way. However highly the novel was regarded, the deeply religious Protestant people of Laichingen wanted to distinguish clearly between fiction and fact. The chronicle, known to every reader of the novel, was considered the more authoritative text. Public evening readings of the 'Hunger Chronicle' can be documented in the 1950s.[3] They show how a printed text can become an important part of the orally transmitted collective memory of the locality. Thirty years later, the text was placed on a more permanent, 'material' foundation in the local tradition. In the weaving museum of the village, a room dedicated to the story of the famine years at the beginning of the nineteenth century was set up in 1984. In this room the visitor cannot escape being reminded of the 'Hunger Chronicle' and the continuing belief in its relevance until the year 1997. He or she will discover a frieze with an inscription: 'Starvation year 1816 at Laichingen, as experienced by a citizen and written down in 1817.' It is a place of commemoration, a *lieu de mémoire*, where the recollection of the afflictions and misery of all the crises of the nineteenth century are brought together in the representation of the famine years of 1816–17.

The influence of the 'Laichingen Hunger Chronicle' was not at all limited to local historical consciousness. Especially after the Second World War, it was cited in numerous scholarly publications, among which were two that I myself wrote on the history of hunger and nutrition (Medick 1985a:101; 1985b:43). Personal searches around the area for the location of the original manuscript had long been unsuccessful. They led only to the information that Schnerring had published the document after he had left Laichingen, several years before 1914, in order to take up a position as a teacher, first in Crailsheim and later in Kirchheim unter Teck. Still, considering the well-regarded place of publication and the form of publication itself, which came close to an edition, there was little to contradict consideration of the document as authentic. Another interest of mine was also involved: the chronicle referred to the locality in which my work on the history of rural, proto-industrialized cottage weaving was based.[4]

Günter Moltmann, late emeritus professor of early-modern and modern history in Hamburg, certainly did the most before 1987 to promulgate the chronicle as an apparently authentic contemporary source. He published the complete text anew in 1979 in the context of an extensive work on Friedrich List and emigration to America from Baden and Württemberg in 1816–17 (Moltmann 1979).[5] In 1985 another complete re-edition followed (Köpf 1985). Finally, the 'Laichingen Hunger Chronicle' was made known to a wider audience when central passages of the text were displayed at the top of a reconstructed hunger pyramid in an exhibition entitled 'Baden and Württemberg in the Napoleonic period,' organized by the state of Baden-Württemberg in 1987 at a cost of millions of marks.[6]

The broad dissemination of the chronicle and the continuing interest in the text did not come from out of the blue. For one thing, its authenticity and coherence appeared to be beyond doubt. 'Every datum of the chronicle' was supported, as the editor stressed in 1917, 'by historical research' (Schnerring 1917:72). In the article concerning the years of famine and scarcity that preceded the printed version of the chronicle, he attempted to demonstrate this by comparing its contents with other sources. The credibility of the editor appeared to be even less in doubt, since, in the introduction of the documentation and in the article itself, he pleaded for a critical and careful handling of manuscript records. As he stressed, such records could be used only when they 'withstand scientific-statistical criticism' (Schnerring 1917:45).

The extraordinarily detailed depiction of local events during one of the last great crises of scarcity and famine in central Europe lent credence to the narrative. The reports of the chronicle extend from March 1816 until the end of 1820, with numerous exactly dated, continuous, chronological statements. The 'record of an Alps dweller' offers an impressive picture of the events and course of the crisis, from weather observations to the description of the scarcity or lack of food, the depiction of governmental and political measures to mitigate hunger and need, and their effectiveness or lack thereof in the locality.

A closer reading shows that the document's structure, arrangement, and form of narration put it somewhere between a chronicle and a narrative historical description. The text is formally constructed in the form of a diary, in which facts are lined up in a temporally ordered sequence. But behind the linear chronological course of events, hidden in the chronicle, is a dramatic historical narrative in which events are described in a way that creates suspense. At the beginning stands an extensive description of unusual weather signs in the spring and early summer of 1816, together with their interpretation by the chronicler and other village inhabitants as harbingers of a coming disaster. The climatic catastrophes of the summer and fall of 1816 and the resulting harvest failures, together with the activities of usurious traders and grain speculators, are described as the causes of the scarcity, resulting in a famine and starvation that affected rich and poor alike. Only the intervention of the state in the winter and spring of 1816–17 in the form of deliveries of grain and foodstuffs and price and market controls rescued the locality from a catastrophe. 'One can breathe easier again,' the chronicler already reported by the end of February 1817, 'The king and queen have comforted us. They have punished the corn Jews and thereby done so much good for the people, who can never thank them enough' (Schnerring 1917:75). The conclusion of the narrative history – but not of the chronicle, which continued summarily and with gaps until the year 1820 – was marked by a report on the Thanksgiving service held on 18 August 1817, when the whole population of the village united in thanks to God and the government for their survival of scarcity.

A certain quite legitimate 'fiction of the factual' appears to operate here. At any rate, the chronicler built a fictional narrative structure under the chronological report. This narrative structure gave an additional coherence and urgency to the chronicle's description, a quality that certainly enhanced its reception without putting its authenticity and authority into question from the beginning. The language of the early nineteenth century in which the document appeared to be composed and also the numerous phrases from the dialect of the Swabian Alps appeared as additional authentication. Above all, the document's experiential, 'personal' manner of description, the chronicler's report on the suffering of his own children, as well as on the effects of starvation on the population of the village, his urgent and contemporary-sounding description of hunger, not only as a scarcity of foodstuffs but also as a loss of the possibility of acquiring and preparing traditional bread and grain dishes – all these appeared to make the document an especially valuable witness. It is thus not surprising that, for example, the Swiss scholar Markus Mattmüller, at a meeting in preparing for a section of the German Historical Association conference in Berlin in 1984, expressed the opinion that the chronicle was a 'unique source' for the history of hunger. In Switzerland at any rate, he claimed, there was nothing like it.

Another aspect may have promoted the increasing interest in the 'Laichingen Hunger Chronicle' in recent years, as interpretation of the hunger crisis of 1816–17 given in the report of the chronicler corresponded to new trends in research. For the crisis, in the description of the chronicler, first appears to have been set off and driven forward by natural factors, such as catastrophic weather conditions and the resulting harvest failures. But the deeper causes were traced to human actions and to the influence of the most inclusive, translocal, social, economic, and political conditions. 'Hunger is man-made': this programmatic statement of Josué de Castro, a political economist and researcher into the causes of contemporary mass starvation in the Third World, could also stand as a motto for the 'Hunger Chronicle.' Above all, the chronicler's specific description of the causes for the rise in grain prices supports an interpretation of the famine as 'man-made.' He described the scarcity and worsening of the famine situation as caused by usury and speculation. And he labelled clearly a group of the 'guilty': outsiders, Jewish traders, and grain hoarders from the two villages of Buttenhausen and Jebenhausen near Laichingen, small territories at one time independent within the Holy Roman Empire, but since 1805 part of Württemberg.

From this role ascribed to the Jews arose crucial objections that led to the discovery that the chronicle is, in fact, a forgery. It was not a professional historian but a layman interested in history, the economist Günter Randecker, who first unmasked the chronicle as a forgery and initiated the ensuing discussion.[7] In the context of a public-works project in the city of Münsingen, he researched the history of the Jewish community of Buttenhausen up to its expulsion and destruction after 1933. His knowledge of the economic conditions of the Buttenhausen Jews at the beginning of the nineteenth century as mostly small traders and pedlars led him to the opinion that the role assigned to the Jews of Buttenhausen and Jebenhausen in the chronicle not only did not correspond to the facts, but also could only be understood as a projection of a twentieth-century anti-Semitic perspective onto a completely different historical context.

The possibility of proving this suspicion improved when the 'impassioned' detective succeeded in discovering a handwritten version of the chronicle in the possession of Schnerring's son-in-law. In the teacher's testamentary writing to his heirs that accompanied the manuscript, it was identified clearly as the original record of a Laichingen master craftsman with the supposed name of Peter Bürkle the Elder. The handwriting and paper quality of the manuscript dit not at first appear to contradict this assertion, which had the authority of a dying bequest. But there were terminological and textual discrepancies between the printed version of the chronicle and the manuscript. For example, the term 'profit Jew' (*Profitjude*), which only became current in the twentieth century, is found in the manuscript, but the printed version of 1917 exhibits the older term 'corn Jew' (*Kornjude*), by no means limited to Jews. In both versions of the text, descriptions of the weather and the dates of events do not tally with the data available in other primary sources. These mistakes and anomalies, as well as the anti-Semitic tendency – to which Randecker, as a historian of the town of Buttenhausen (Randecker 1987), was more finely attuned than others – led him to regard the chronicle as a forgery and to publicize this claim in the summer of 1987. He not only criticized the credulity of professional historians, but also advanced a broader, problematic thesis, which he later maintained in the face of opposition, saying that the manuscript was, in essential parts, created about 1933 as a 'post-construction' of the printed version and that the latter was also a forgery. This precise dating of the manuscript unmasked, as he drastically put it, the author of the 'Hunger Chronicle' as a Nazi 'armchair perpetrator' and composer of crude 'inflammatory anti-Semitic pamphlet.'[8]

This vehemently accusatory thesis had an immediate consequence. Schnerring's heirs removed the manuscript of the chronicle from inspection by interested researchers. It was sent to the Central State Archives in Stuttgart and kept there under lock and key. My own task after the 1987 appearance of the forgery thesis, which I first and unexpectedly confronted during the discussion after a lecture in Laichingen, was not simple. It consisted first in having to take a position as an 'expert,' relatively conversant with sources for the history of the village, on the charges of forgery, without, however, being able to look at the manuscript, which was locked up. I was directed to questions of internal criticism and at the same time limited to them. Testing the factual claims from the printed version of the text against local sources was initially my only possible approach. (Only later have I been able to draw on a copy of the manuscript.)

As far as the important question of the activity of Jewish traders in the village during the famine years is concerned, I could only confirm Randecker's thesis. From the 1770s, numerous cases of Jewish traders in the locality are to be found in the sources. They paid passage and protection money for the privilege of trading in haberdashery, textiles, and leather, and came almost exclusively from the Jewish villages of Buttenhausen and Jebenhausen mentioned in the chronicle. Although they could show official licences, these Jewish traders frequently ran into opposition from local artisans and merchants, who sought to defend themselves against the penetration of foreign competitors. Conflict with Jewish traders was carried on very much more roughly than with non-Jewish pedlars and traders. Jewish grain merchants, hoarders, and creditors, however, do not appear in the sources. If the activities maintained in the chronicle actually had taken place, they would almost certainly have appeared in the sources, especially since after the autumn of 1816 an ordinance was promulgated and enforced against grain trading in rural areas outside city grain barns.

Regarding numerous other factual claims, the chronicle again demonstrates itself to be a fiction that cannot have been based on observations and reports of a contemporary from the village. For example, the data on mortality and its causes during the crisis can be examined. Here we can compare the chronicle with accurate information in the parish records and the details about age that can be reconstructed from them. The chronicle speaks frequently of an increased infant, child, and old-age mortality as particular signs of the exacerbation of the crisis, for example, in June 1816, January 1817, and February and March 1817. This mortality model corresponds to a widespread popular idea about age-specific mortality in hunger crises, but it is not corroborated by the data from the parish registers for the crisis months in question or the crisis in general. Mortality for infants and children up to six years old was, on the contrary, noticeably reduced in the famine year 1816–17 when compared to the previous normal year of 1815–16, while the mortality of the aged rose only insignificantly.

Typical for the mortality of the hunger crisis of 1816–17 in Laichingen (and a significant indication of insufficient nutrition and extreme hunger as a cause of death) are the increased mortality of adults at the ages capable of marriage and reproduction and the greatly increased mortality of children and youth between six and twenty-five, in comparison with the previous and following years. The scarcity and famine crisis of 1816–17 especially affected the reproductive core of the Laichingen population. The causes of this greatly increased mortality were the typhus produced by hunger – what contemporaries called 'hot fever' (*hitziges Fieber*) – and hunger oedema, the so-called stomach dropsy (*Wassersucht*). The high point of mortality, not mentioned at all in the chronicle, was in the months of March, April, and May 1817, in the period of the most strained food situation. A list of the poor from May 1817, which denoted 86 per cent of the listed inhabitants of the village as completely without bread and foodstuffs, makes this fact clear. Also, with respect to the incidence of child dysentery and mortality, which the chronicler mentioned as typical famine disease and causes of death for January 1817, there is no substantiation at all in the exact date from the Laichingen parish registers, especially since infectious dysentery normally appeared and appears in the summer months anyway.

These and numerous other kinds of independent evidence from local sources make it clear that the 'record of an Alps dweller' cannot be a document originating in Laichingen contemporaneously with the events of 1816–20, although the author suggests such an appearance. Already the printed version of the text thus appears as an illegitimate fiction of the factual historical evidence. On the basis of its narrative structure and mode of description, the chronicle may appear as an example of legitimate fiction of the factual. But such fictions of the factual find their limit where they consciously suggest the false appearance of historical evidence, realities, or possibilities, and this is the case with the document discussed here.

The distinction made here between legitimate and illegitimate 'fictions of the factual' is inspired by theoretical suggestions about narrative historical description developed by the American philosopher of history Hayden White

(White 1985). White, however, deals only with *legitimate* fictions of the factual, that is, those fictions 'in play' in every description of history as poetic-fictional interpretative constitution of the factual only applied to representations of history as *text* but not to *what is represented*. He does not raise the problem of *illegitimate* fictions of the factual, whether on the level of falsification or of methods – methods understood here in the sense of research methods one-sidedly prejudicing the things under consideration. Carlo Ginzburg has critically remarked on this issue: 'Testing the claim to truth, which is inherent in historical narrative as such, should have entailed discussing questions tied to sources and the techniques of research, which individual historians ask during their work. If one neglects these elements, as Hayden White does, then historical writing becomes pure ideological discourse' (Ginzburg 1984:204).

Let us return to the more mundane level of our own testing and continue to follow the 'fiction of the factual' in the case of the chronicle. The internal criticism of this text is to be drawn from a very large number of local sources and cannot content itself with merely testing particular factual claims. It must also turn to the interpretations connected to these factual claims. A few indications will have to suffice here.

In the chronicle, a commonality of experience of both rich and poor in the crisis is repeatedly claimed. It is supposed to have arisen from the equalizing (*durchschlagende*) effect of harvest failure, usury, scarcity, and hunger. But investigating the living conditions and behaviour of the inhabitants of the village leads to a contradictory picture: lists of the poor, tax lists, and marriage and estate inventories show that the crisis led to a polarization of rich and poor. Since January 1817, 61 per cent of the 1,637 inhabitants no longer had the cash to purchase bread or grain, meeting the very strict criteria for poor relief; by May the figure had risen to 86 per cent. By contrast, a small group of the local elite – bakers, innkeepers, butchers, merchants, substantial agricultural producers, and even the pastor, Carl Wilhelm Blech – understood how to make a profit from this situation of distress. That they did so is shown by the numerous cash loans which this group offered the needy at interest, while offerings to the poor-relief association ceased. An investigation of the tax lists clearly reveals that members of this group were the only ones to acquire significant amounts of additional real estate during and immediately after the crisis.

The Laichingen cottage industrial weavers, never mentioned at all in the chronicle, were intensely affected by the distress. For them, a marketing crisis for their products (as a consequence of the loss of the traditional markets for Württemberg linen in France and southern Europe) coincided with the effects of the harvest failure and scarcity. The extent of unemployment and the loss of property and wealth, although only temporary, show that the Laichingen linen weavers reached a low point of impoverishment and misery in the years 1816–17 and immediately after, one that would never again be matched in the nineteenth century.

The gap that developed during the crisis between those who continually had control over resources in foodstuffs, money, and land, and who understood how to increase them, and those who completely lost the possibility of feeding themselves through their own work was mirrored in the area of everyday behaviour. Several conflicts over the division of foodstuffs show a temporary suspension of moral standards and solidarities that had seemed self-evident before the crisis. If one was poor and hungry, one did not hesitate even to steal from neighbours and relatives. If one belonged to the socially and economically powerful, at the distribution one might appropriate church and communal emergency grain stores to one's own possession.

The excessively positive role depicted for the state's emergency assistance in the crisis also appears in an ambivalent light in the sources. Grain distribution from the state storehouses at the high point of the crisis in May 1817 followed only after the *Schultheiss* of the village – with the lovely name of Johann Christian Kraft (*Kraft* being a term for power or force) – threatened a violent hunger march of all Laichingen inhabitants.

With these clarifications, we have come far from the picture that the 'Hunger Chronicle' offers. At the same time, however, another aspect of reality has become clearer, one screened out in the fiction of the chronicle. The state does not appear as an uninterested and sovereign helper in need in the crisis, nor can the causes of scarcity and hunger be derived primarily from the activities of 'foreign' usurers. Rather, members and groups of the local elite leap into view. Still, the general description of these conditions interests us in the context less than the questions of causes, motives, and intents of a fictive historical representation such as that given in the chronicle, which diverges so much from ours.

Who was the author, when was the manuscript original of the printed version composed, and what – if ascertainable – were the motives that the author associated with his fiction? These are the questions to be pursued. Scrutiny of the manuscript has demonstrated Schnerring himself to be the 'original' author of the chronicle. This examination was carried out by Hans Martin Maurer and Wolfgang Schmierer from the Württemberg Central State Archives in Stuttgart, which kept the manuscript locked up. The results were first made public at a conference in Münsingen at the end of March 1988,[9] where the varying interpretations and opinions about the chronicle confronted each other. The examination of the manuscript by the archivists was crucial to the extent that it now is certain that it is a forgery and that the author was not a Laichingen master craftsman but Schnerring himself.

The investigation of the writing characteristics and form of the chronicle was crucial. It showed that although Schnerring had cleverly attempted to imitate a handwriting from the early nineteenth century on the basis of contemporary examples, he was not completely successful. With the more obvious capital letters he succeeded in adopting the old handwriting and disguising his own; with the less-suspicious lower-case letters, however, his personal writing characteristics came through. Also, the regular and swift writing strokes points to the authorship of the teacher – at least it does not correspond to that of an artisan.

After the identification of the chronicle as a forgery, there still remained many open and contested questions at the Münsingen conference, above all that of the exact dating of the manuscript and of its relation to the printed version, and – certainly more important – that of the motives of the author. Was the manuscript a 'later composition' created after 1933 primarily from anti-Semitic motives, as the discoverer of the forgery maintained, or was the forgery from 1916–17, as the archivists believed? This question, unresolved in the discussion up to this point, is – so I found – answered by the author of the forgery himself. I discovered the answer in the only one of his writings that he composed as fiction and acknowledged publicly as such, which until now, given the dominant focus on the chronicle text, found no consideration.

I refer to Schnerring's historical novel about the famine period from 1816–17 in Webringen, or Laichingen, and Württemberg, *Du suchest das Land heim* (Schnerring 1918). Unlike the chronicle, but also unlike his scholarly treatise, the novel represents the crisis of these years in a personalizing form as a political-moral conflict. Against the representatives of moral solidarity and mutual assistance in the community stand corrupt patricians. The latter, in league with an outside trader, clearly depicted as a Jew, rob the community of its last emergency stores. This conflict is seen against the background of a more inclusive political-social conflict inside Württemberg. There are found the corrupt representatives of a despotic state apparatus, which characterized Württemberg under the so-called Swabian Tsar, King Friedrich I, who ruled by the grace of Napoleon. This regime is contrasted with the reform-oriented forces that actually came to power with the accession of King William I in October 1817. Of interest here is the fact that Schnerring depicts himself in a twofold manner: once in the form of a positive ideal figure as the weaver Christian Ring (alias Schnerring). He is one of the chief defenders of the values of the village 'moral community' against those who spread corruption in the crisis. At the end of the novel, Ring begins composing a chronicle in November 1816 (Schnerring 1918:371).

At the same time, Schnerring also appears to have established himself as a negative figure, represented by the person of the county under-clerk (*Amtsschreiber und Substitut*) Hufnagel. This individual is presented not only as a politically negative symbolic figure, but also as the local administrator of the despotic regime of King Friedrich I. As clerk, he also carries on wholesale document forgeries, which he uses for political denunciations and to rob almost completely the moral heroes of the novel, including Christian Ring himself, of their political-moral existence. In the course of the novel it becomes clear that the person who, as clerk, is responsible for the correct administration of the archives (of Webringen-Laichingen) and for the verified and trustworthy use of documents – such were the legal tasks and duties of the clerks in contemporary Württemberg – is the one who completely falsified and corrupts this record.

The novel is therefore to be read as a *roman-à-clef*. Together with the personalized description of a famine crisis, the discovery of an enormous forgery is one of its chief subjects. It contains, at least indirectly, an admission by the author Schnerring that he was completely conscious of the moral problem of the hunger document as a forgery. He described his personality as split into good and bad halves in the face of this encumbered experience. If one takes this 'admission' into account, then the certain publication date of the novel in 1918 makes it possible also to draw secure conclusions about the period of composition of the chronicle and, beyond that, about the motives behind Schnerring's historical representation (to which the Stuttgart archivists first pointed). The forgery, in any event, cannot have originated *after* 1918, especially not during the Nazi period as a 'later composition' from the printed document. The chronicle is, rather, a literal 'forgery of the century' *Jahrhundertfälschung*) in a restricted sense, since it originated exactly one hundred years after the crisis of 1816–17 and directly before and after the 'turnip winter' of 1916–17, when the potato harvest failure led to a dramatic worsening of the food situation already strained by the war in the German empire. The government sought to manage scarcity and mass hunger through the control of production and distribution of food by price setting and rationing.

Schnerring's motive, to which he alluded in the introduction to his article on the hunger years of 1816–17, seems to have been to offer 'many points of comparison,' as he wrote (Schnerring 1917:45), for the experiences of the present through a model historical example described as perfectly as possible. With this example, he apparently wanted to encourage the readiness of his readers for the imperial government's coercive economic measures in the food sector. It was only in this modern connection, in which black-marketing and usury blossomed, that he brought anti-Semitic expressions into his forged chronicle (and not, by contrast, into his scientific article). In the first publication of a paraphrased version of the 'Hunger Chronicle' in the year 1913, anti-Semitic expressions are lacking, with the exception of a reference to Jewish usurers, for which the explanation ran: 'the Christian Jews are said to be the worst' (Schnerring 1913:27).

This exact contextualization of Schnerring's forgery and its anti-Semitic passages in no way relativizes its anti-Semitism, nor does it render them more harmless. But in a way it allows us to localize the appearance of anti-Semitism on the surface of the text in a specific situation. Further, it shows that Schnerring's forged and reality-effacing use of the stereotype of the Jewish usurer cannot be ascribed to him alone, but rather that it was part of the everyday anti-Semitism of his time. Not only did he share this anti-Semitism, but he actively resorted to its clichés to lend his 'historical' description more authority and public effect.

As the publication of the first chronicle text in 1913 shows, Schnerring's interest in the history of the famine years cannot be reduced either to his anti-Semitic expressions or to his topical political-pedagogical interest in the depiction of a model historical case in the context of the turnip winter of 1816–17. A supposition still to be verified would be that, stimulated by the folklore studies of his time, he wanted to establish in a written text the oral memory of the famine years of 1816–17 still current in Laichingen and the Swabian Alps in the years before the war. The oral tradition was losing its vividness during this period of rapid economic, social, and cultural change and transportation, so that its contours, becoming ever more scanty, had to be filled out. Written testimony of local folk traditions, which Schnerring used, was not sufficient for him. Reading through the volumes of the government information sheets and the parliamentary reports in the Stuttgart State Library, which still contain his marginalia today, probably did not satisfy his historical fantasy either. Still, why he used a forgery as a tool for achieving a 'thick description' remains difficult to explain, especially if one considers the considerable research effort he invested in his forgery.

Perhaps the ban on research and writing of social and cultural history in imperial Germany, which resulted from the bitter '*Historikerstreit*' (historians' dispute)[10] between Karl Lamprecht and Georg von Below and their respective followers around the turn of the century, could provide an explanation. Representations of subjects in social and cultural history came under attack from political historians and were marginalized or even tabooed as a result. It became increasingly easier to publish them in the form of historical fiction or documentary evidence than in the essay or monograph forms that were current and 'normal' in periodicals and other media controlled by the guild of German historians. These guild historians increasingly considered a straightforward history of power in the tradition of Ranke as the only legitimate form of historical representation. Under the conditions of historical study prevailing in Germany at the time, the 'fiction of the factual' in the form of an invented source could represent a marginal, but at least incontrovertible, means of finding some credibility and attention.

For us there remains the text to deal with. The case of the so-called Laichingen Hunger Chronicle stimulates us to ask, self-critically and ever more precisely, about the constitutive conditions for the authority, efficacy, and evidence of historical representations and texts, to demonstrate possibilities for their verification, and to call into question falsified claims for their validity.

I learned a great deal from my experience with the 'Hunger Chronicle' – not least when a supra-regional daily newspaper appropriated the unpublished first manuscript of my study of this text without my permission (Seibt 1988; Medick 1988). This unauthorized, distorted use of my text and the characterization of my experience as that of 'duped rigour' was especially painful: on the one hand, because I had indeed been deceived by a forged text and, on the other hand, because the article ignored my attempt to work through and describe something that is a critical experience for historians, and not just myself.

With his insight that 'Surtout un mensonge en tant que tel, est à sa façon un témoignage,'[11] Marc Bloch puts his finger on only part of the problem that confronted me in grappling with the 'Hunger Chronicle.' Bloch could still point first of all to the fallibility of primary sources, from which, as a critical historian, he hoped to draw useful conclusions; but today, after the linguistic-rhetorical turn in historical discourse, the issue is also the fallibility of historians' judgment and elucidations, including the use of these elucidations in a public arena moulded by the media. At any rate, a historian can no longer maintain the belief that 'method' alone can shield him from 'error.' Here too, Bloch thought ahead on the basis of his own experiences: 'Among all the kinds of lie, self-deception is not the rarest, and the word "uprightness" is so many-sided that it allows many uses' (Bloch 1993:132f). Nonetheless, he championed an 'apology for history' as a communicative 'craft' whose motto is 'Veritas est vinum vitae.'[12]

At the end of this case and in all my work, I too am left with little more than the insight that the 'constitutive relation to experience for historiography' (Jörn Rüsen) is not to be sought only in the method of presentation or in text analysis, however subtle, but rather, most of all, in critical research that also questions itself. This is a kind of historical research that goes beyond the source-credulous positivism of the nineteenth century, but also beyond the new historicism's exclusive fixation on cultural texts and their circulation in the sphere of self-presentation. This kind of historical research takes the sources seriously as the historian's final court of appeal, but enters into dialogue with them in two ways: with questions posed to the source, but also with an avid search for multiple legacies on the same issue and the release of the critical interpretive energy arising from the process's own interactive commentary and questioning. In this way, historical research arrives at an intensified reconstruction and depiction of its findings. It opens itself to the view of a broad, complex historiographical landscape populated by historical people with their stances, ideas, artefacts, and other legacies, but also by the historians themselves, who devote their attention, work, and grappling to these historical people across tremendous discontinuities and stretches of time.

NOTES

I wish to express my warmest thanks to Mitch Cohen and David Sabean for their help with the translation. This is a developed and expanded version of a text that first appeared in *History Workshop Journal* 40 (1995).

1 The Chronicle is reprinted in Schnerring 1917 72–7.
2 'Handschriftliche Aufzeichnungen eines Älblers über die Teuerung und Hungersnot 1816/17' (Schnerring 1917:72).
3 See the notice in *Schwäbische Albzeitung* (Laichingen), 7 February 1950.
4 A monograph has meanwhile been published: Medick 1996.
5 The chronicle is reprinted on 48–64; a new edition of this collection, published at Stuttgart in 1989 under the title *Aufbruch nach Amerika: Die Auswanderungswelle 1816/17*, no longer contains the chronicle.
6 A copious quotation from the chronicle can be found in Baden and Württemberg 1987: I, 477.
7 See his version of the discovery of the forgery and his interpretation of its aims: Randecker 1990.
8 Stated during a conference at Münsingen on 25 March 1988 and in Randecker 1990:33.
9 Held in the town hall of Münsingen on 25 March 1988; see the report in *Schwäbische Zeitung* (Laichingen ed.), 26 March 1988.
10 On this controversy among German historians and a corresponding debate in France at the same time (which there, however, produced a very different result: the birth of the '*Annales*' school of historians), see the insightful essay by L. Raphael (1990).
11 Bloch 1993:128; in English, 'But above all, a lie, as such, is also testimony in its own way.' I thank Peter Schöttler for drawing my attention to this observation.
12 Compare Raulff 1995:371 ff: 'Arbeiter im Weinberg' (workers in the vineyard).

298 Hans Medick

REFERENCES

Baden und Württemberg
 1987 Baden und Württemberg im Zeitalter Napoleons: Ausstellung des Landes Baden-
   Württemberg unter der Schirmherrschaft des Ministerpräsidenten Dr. h.c. Lothar Späth,
   3 vols. Stuttgart.
Bloch, Marc
 [1944] 1993 Apologie pour l'histoire ou métier d'historien. Édition critique preparée par
   Etienne Bloch. Paris.
Ginzburg, Carlo
 1984 Postscriptum. In Die Wahrhaftige Geschichte von der Wiederkehr des Martin Guerre,
   by N.Z. Davis, pp.185–213. Munich.
Köpf, Ulrich
 1985 Hungerchronik und Bild aus Laichingen. In Die Hungerjahre 1816/17 auf der Alb und
   an der Donau, Ulrich Köpf, ed. pp. 36–44. Ulm.
Medick, Hans
 1985a 'Hungerkrisen' in der historischen Forschung, Beispiele aus Mitteleuropa vom 17.–19.
   Jahrhundert. Sozialwissenschaftliche Informationen für Unterricht und Studium 14:95–
   103.
 1985b Teuerung, Hunger und 'moralische Ökonomie von oben': Die Hungerkrise der Jahre
   1816–17 in Württemberg. Beiträge zur historischen Sozialkunde (Vienna) 2:39–44.
 1988 Ein fahrlässiger Umgang [A negligent treatment]. Letter to the editor, Frankfurter
   Allgemeine Zeitung 173 (28 July 1988).
 1996 Weben und Überleben in Laichingen 1650–1900: Lokalgeschichte als Allgemeine
   Geschichte. Göttingen. 2d ed., 1997.
Moltmann, Günter
 1979 Aufbruch nach Amerika, Friedrich List und die Auswanderung aus Baden und
   Württemberg 1816/17: Dokumentation einer sozialen Bewegung. Günter Moltmann, ed.,
   in cooperation with Ingrid Schöberl. Tübingen.
 1989 Aufbruch nach Amerika: Die Asuwanderungswelle von 1816/17. Günter Moltmann, ed.
   Stuttgart 1989 (2d ed. of Moltmann 1979).
Randecker, Günter
 1987 Die Juden und ihre Heimat Buttenhausen. Günter Randecker, ed. Münsingen.
 1990 Die 'Laichinger Hungerchronik' – Ein Lügengewebe. In Gefälscht! Betrug in Politik,
   Literatur, Wissenschaft, Kunst und Musik, Karl Corino, ed. pp. 74–90. Frankfurt am
   Main: Eichborn Verlag.
Raphael, Lutz
 1990 Historikerkontroversen im Spannungsfeld zwischen Berufshabitus, Fächerkonkurrenz
   und sozialen Deutungsmustern: Lamprecht-Streit und französischer Methodenstreit der
   Jahrhundertwende in vergleichender Perspektive. Historische Zeitschrift 251:325–63.
Raulff, Ulrich
 1995 Ein Historiker im 20. Jahrhundert. Marc Bloch. Frankfurt/Main.
Schnerring, Christian August
 1913 Hungersnot und teure Zeit. C. Schn. [i.e., Christian August Schnerring].
   Württembergische Volksbücher 9:23–33.

1916–17 Handschriftliche Aufzeichnungen eines Älblers über die Teuerungs- und Hungerjahre 1816/17 mitgeteilt von C.A. Schnerring. Blätter des Schwäbischen Albvereins 28:210–20, and 29:50–2.

1917 Die Teuerungs- und Hungerjahre 1816 and 1817 in Württemberg. Württembergische Jahrbücher für Statistik und Landeskunde 1916:45–78.

1918 Du suchest das Land heim: Geschichtlicher Dorfroman aus einer Teuerungs- und Hungerzeit. Stuttgart.

Seibt, Gustav

1988 Düpierte Strenge: Eine Fälschung wird entlarvt. Frankfurter Allgemeine Zeitung 131 (8 June 1988).

White, Hayden

1985 The Tropics of Discourse: Essays in Cultural Criticism. Baltimore.

Further Thoughts on the Production of History

DAVID WILLIAM COHEN

Historians, together with anthropologists concerned with the past and with history, will in future years have to confront more directly the ways in which popular and official constructions of the past, as well as political suppressions of historical knowledge, shape and deform the processes of knowledge production – and also the general knowledge of the past – in the world. Historians have become aware that they must give attention not only to their traditional object – the reconstruction of the past – but also to the nature and work of their audiences. In looking at ways in which language and social practice give form to the relationships between scholar and audience, scholars are opening a vital path in the reconstitution of history as a field and as a discipline, recognizing an area of practice that we may term 'the production of history.'[1]

The production of history, a frame of reference that augments the conventional senses of meaning of history and historiography, refers to the processing of the past in societies and historical settings all over the world and in struggles for control of voices and texts in innumerable settings which animate this processing of knowledge of the past. This field of practice – the production of history – encompasses conventions and paradigms in the formation of historical knowledge and historical texts: the organizing sociologies of historicizing projects and events, including commemorations and exhibitions; the structuring of frames of record-keeping; the culturally specific glossing of texts; the deployment of powerfully nuanced vocabularies; the confronting of patterns and forces underlying interpretation; the workings of audience in managing and responding to presentations of historical knowledge; and the contentions and struggles which evoke and produce texts and which also produce historical literatures. As a concept, 'the production of history' evades, yet at the same time serves to bring under closer observation, the narrow frames of reference constituted within the practice of 'historiography' and the culturally and historically anchored lines of historiographical criticism and debate.

This conceptualization of a field termed 'the production of history,' as it is used here, developed in 1985 and 1986 during the planning for the Fifth International Roundtable in Anthropology and History, and was articulated in the round-table position paper (David William Cohen, 'The Production of History'), completed 31 March 1986 and circulated to round-table participants and others involved in a broader discussion concerning the values and opportunities of a refreshed discussion of the workings of history as practice and as representation of the past. Although 'The Production of History' paper was distributed to all the participants in the fifth and sixth round tables, and xeroxed copies of the 'final' text have circulated more widely, it has never been published intact. However, it forms the framing structure of a book-length treatment, *The Combing of History*, published by the University of Chicago Press in mid-1994.

When we look back to 1985, there was, in the particular conceptualization of this notion of 'the production of history,' an analogy being drawn to processes of labour, work, and production that had been the central concerns of the earlier round tables in anthropology and history. The challenge that the organizers of the fifth and sixth round tables set for themselves and other participants was how as 'producers' they could stand both within and outside the production process, drawing attention to both the inner dimensions of production – relating, for example, to the definition of topic, the conceptualization of audience, research methods, archival practices, writing, and publication – and the outer dimensions of production, relating to guild routines and constrictions, official regulation, capitalization of research, the workings of audience, debate and contest, the dissemination of knowledge, and so forth. Here was an opportunity for the coupling of a reflexive concern for the ways in which academic practice disguises its very own organization of production and a similarly sensitive and critical attention to the ways in which histories of various kinds are produced outside the academy. At the same time, there was an interest in the walls and passageways that have closed and opened chambers of guild and non-guild history production to one another.

Now, some ten or more years hence, it is possible to look, or look back, critically across some of the ideas, issues, and approaches entangled within 'the production of history' discussions organized in and around the fifth and sixth round tables, at a moment when some of the work developing from, or animated by, the round tables is coming into published form under the joint editorship of Gerald Sider and Gavin Smith. From 1985 to 1989, several obser-

vations emerged, through the development of the 1986 position paper, the Fifth
Roundtable meeting in Paris, and subsequent planning for a follow-up meeting
at Bellagio in September 1989. Several of these points were developed within
the call for papers for the Sixth Roundtable at Bellagio:

1 Silences, particularly within families, villages, and whole societies, may
   make the open expression of certain historical knowledge appear to be, or
   actually be, dangerous.
2 There is power in silences. There may be critical distinctions between 'not
   speaking of' and 'not remembering' the past.
3 History production masks the legitimation practices that give authority to
   histories. But, in the *evaluation* of productions of history both outside and
   inside the guild, claims to authority and priority may be challenged and
   debated through such questions as 'whose history?' or 'who has a right to
   speak?'
4 While some historians or philosophers of history may argue the importance
   of distinguishing between *past* and *history*, they are often, and also
   powerfully, conflated in practice both within and outside the guild.
5 There are responsibilities and risks in the production of history, across a
   broad range of issues from the building of a Holocaust memorial in a south
   German village to the poignant absence of one colleague from Kenya who
   was not able to attend the Fifth Roundtable as a result of restrictions placed
   on travel and his professional activities.
6 Languages of gender and property invade historical discourse at many
   levels, both within and outside guild practice.
7 There are, within the production of history, complexities of time and
   temporalities, in which the very harmonic of historical practice – a common sense of time – may cover or efface powerful and competing senses of
   time, temporality, and temporicity, between and within cultures, among
   social groupings, classes, and households, and within the experience of the
   individual.

As a position paper to suggest lines of inquiry to prospective round-table
participants, 'The Production of History' drew attention to a collection of
debates and struggles over the authority of knowledge of the past that had
crossed this author's desk between the end of September 1985 and early March
1986. Although the paper was 'commissioned' by several of the scholars responsible for the organization of previous round tables, the present writer only
began to find a clear path towards a position paper through the opportunity to
read, as a daily subscriber to the *Baltimore Sun*, news reports of a contest that

had broken out in the United States over the historicity and authenticity of a Budweiser beer commercial.[2] It may have been the very 'ludic' aspect of the debate – with what at the time I thought were unimaginably minimal stakes – that made it possible to recognize some of the dilemmas involved in communicating knowledge of the past, and representations claiming authenticity, to audiences who themselves command knowledge and alternative notions of the authentic and true. Although the participants vested themselves in the critique of the Budweiser advertisement as if it were a debate with two sides, on reflection the positions were structured in something other than a bipolar fashion. And the contest over the question of the 'true account' was seen to require a host of agreements, or silences, relating to contextualization within the advertisement and to the purpose of the 'text' that was, or was within, the advertisement.

In the weeks and months following, the author's attention was brought to other contests, each one at least partly outside the academy, over the representation of the past, including discussions about the possibility of producing replications of slaves and slave experience within the living exhibits of Colonial Williamsburg, debates over the representation of African and African-American culture in the film *The Color Purple*, an emergent moment in the struggle between Native American groups and the Smithsonian over the museum's holdings of skeletal remains, and reports of debates among historians and others as to whether Mau Mau in Kenya was best thought of as an embarrassment. It could hardly be said that research effort needed to be deployed to uncover these contests; they were rendered overt and public through reports in the everyday press, on radio, and on television. Further inquiry, in the nature of research, revealed greater complexity and subtlety, but no less demanding terms of settlement for claims to historical truth or to authority over the relics and interpretations of the past. In the author's 1994 volume *The Combing of History*, some of these earlier encounters were further elaborated, but many of these contests observed briefly in 1985 and 1986 had their own continuing development into the 1990s and were revisited and brought somewhat up to date in the 1994 volume.

The position paper was a repository of many suggestive pieces of contest and ambiguity over the representation of the past. A core piece was the treatment of 'a story of a story of a story.' This work began when, in February 1985, a group of anthropologists and historians, including several active in the round tables in anthropology and history from their inception in the late 1970s, met in Baltimore. Over a luncheon at a Chinese restaurant, they drew out some ideas for a fifth round table on 'histories and historiographies' and asked Gerald Sider and the present writer to take responsibility for planning and convening the meeting. At that lunch Hans Medick referred to a contribution that Professor Herbert Gutman made at the Second Roundtable in Anthropology and History about a woman who had in her youth experienced a dreadful and deforming injury in the workplace but had not, over her lifetime, said a word to her own daughter about her experience – even as the daughter had for years combed her mother's hair every day to cover the scar from the injury. The question posed by Gutman, and suggested by Medick as a possible centre-piece for the Fifth Roundtable, was 'How does class consciousness evolve if the traumatic experiences of class are suppressed even within the households of those who directly experience them?'[3] Over the following months, colleagues associated with the round tables, among others, provided more insight into Gutman's telling of the story, which not only betrayed his enchantment with it but demonstrated the ways in which Gutman, a historian's historian, could, through such stories, enchant and challenge others. Attention was focused on the role of Paul Cowan, a reporter for the *Village Voice*, who visited Lawrence, Massachusetts, where the woman had been injured. Cowan found the daughter and interviewed her; over several years he wrote articles for the *Voice* about Lawrence, about the mother and daughter, about the mother's role in the great mill strike of 1912, about memory and silence, and about the breaking of silence and 'the reawakening of the past in Lawrence in 1979 and 1980.'

The treatment of Herb Gutman's retelling of Paul Cowan's stories in the original position paper and in the discussions that surrounded it[4] had heuristic and analytical values. The presence of Gutman's story among a group of round-table colleagues provided a bridge between earlier round tables and the one then, in 1985–6, being planned. His story was also, in a sense, a legacy of challenge to the group, since Herb Gutman died in the summer of 1985. Beneath the surface of his more overt question concerning class consciousness, there stood, as the story of the story of the story came to be elaborated, significant questions concerning the boundaries of action and history (Paul Cowan both observed and intervened in the 'silences' of Lawrence) and the boundaries of academy and publics that both were disclosed and breached in the respective work of Gutman and Cowan (and still further complicated in the discussion by the present author within the original 1986 position paper).

Although the treatment of the story of the story of the story in the original position paper drew attention to the complexities of the ways in which Cowan 'read' Lawrence, Gutman read Cowan, and Gutman's colleagues 'read' his treatment of the story, it left unattended (though hardly unremarked) the events in Lawrence itself. This was, after all, not a treatment of the 1912 strike, and its approach to the constitution of silences in Lawrence hinged on the 'readings' of Cowan, Gutman, and the present writer. Recently, Gerald Sider has gone to

Lawrence, looked more closely at the processes of memory and silence there, and revised Cowan substantially,[5] while taking off explicitly from the treatments of Cowan, Gutman, and the present writer as developed in the original 1986 position paper and in *The Combing of History*.[6] His 'anthropology' looks within Lawrence at the 'complex web both of continuities and memory breaks' from the time of the strike in 1912 and 1976 when Paul Cowan first visited the town. Sider's is a persuasive treatment that corrects the stories which Cowan and Gutman told. What his treatment evades is the *work*, the *production*, of these stories as they crossed many boundaries of discourse from Cowan's first reporting – and Herb Gutman's reading of it – to the animation of the work of the Fifth Roundtable. In a profound way, Sider's intervention – or, better, this reading of Sider – restages the simplistic and ludic encounter over the beer commercial: mistakes are exposed in the search for the authentic, yet the power and purpose of the extant historical treatments – and by analogy, the power of representations of the past – are left unproblematic. This is the essential tension of history, or historical research, writing, and representation: between the telling of stories – the representation of the past – and their retelling (whether by critique, revision, scientific method, or art). Although Sider's treatment unearths the sociology of knowledge in Lawrence, it leaves unattended the sociologies of knowledge stretching from within Lawrence across the round tables and beyond.

Looking back to the time of the Sixth Roundtable in September 1989 and the months immediately following, I recall several rather poorly formed observations which seemed to be present and influential to 'the production of history,' but which did not seem easily susceptible to definition and to which I have returned without satisfaction over the seven ensuing years:[7]

1 Where I had originally seen the Budweiser beer contest as a salutary, if insignificant, opening to get at the complexities of history production between 'author' and 'audience,' I was, just four years later, feeling that the 'public sphere' had become saturated by such contests and struggles. The rubric 'Silences of the living, orations of the dead,' suggested to me by the medieval historian Gabrielle Spiegel (herself a participant in the Fifth Roundtable), emerged as a mode of encapsulation of what appeared to be some of the most prevalent programmatic turns: the sustenance of critical silences and the 'making of the dead' to speak with unique authority. I wondered about the 'economy' of production of these contests across the globe, the forces and programs feeding energy into these struggles over secrets and bodies. Yet it was only a simplistic hypothesis that the order

and rate of such struggles had changed; certainly, my readiness to be
subjected to such experience had grown to nearly a pathologically acute
stage. But had the world changed – or perhaps only the propensity of media
to report such contests and my own propensity to breathe this stuff like
oxygen?

2   Where I had, with the contest over historical truth in the beer commercial,
been intrigued by the programs of historical documentation and historical
representation evinced in the workings of various parties to the contest –
there are, after all, rules and programs relating to the constitution of truth
outside the academy – I was intrigued by the ways that debates over the
past seemed to work as surrogates for other struggles over interest, value,
and meaning (and also property) that somehow were not equally susceptible to elaboration, appropriation, or defence in that their articulation could
find no workable contest. (An example would be the legal contest that
worked its way up through the Busoga and Uganda courts nearly five
decades ago and was always about much more than the courts intended to
hear.)[8] I was further intrigued by the enormous power potential in silences
and the extraordinary vacancies that seemed to inhabit the commemorations and celebrations of the past, from museum exhibits to replications, to
documentary films and photographs, to national monuments and anniversa-
ries, to commissions of inquiry and truth commissions. The stronger and
more successful the claims for the official authorization, sanction, and
instantiation of claims to historical truth and historical meaning, the
seemingly more commensurate the loss of force of those truths and those
meanings.

3   Nine weeks after the Sixth Roundtable, the Berlin Wall began to come
down and so much with it. I could only intuit, but not credibly argue, that
our collective papers from two round tables were seriously at risk as a
consequence of this change in the world. The point was not that the papers
presented to the 1986 and 1989 round tables were suddenly out of date or
naive – far from it – but that the realm of debate and conflict over the
representation of the past captured in the papers had expanded exponen-
tially almost overnight. I may have been wrong, or right, but in the seven
years since then, the academic world has been visited by an extraordinary
volume of revisionist contests across the globe. To what extent have these
changes forced a very different address to the phenomena under discussion
at the Paris and Bellagio conferences?

4 There is an uncertain sense that the challenges of reconstructing and representing the African past give a particularly salient quality to the questions and approaches underlying the concept of 'the production of history.' For the present writer, this sense, this hypothesis, has of course very weak legs, since it was he, a historian of Africa, who was, with Gerald Sider, invited to develop the position paper on 'the production of history' and help to organize the fifth and sixth round tables on 'the production of history.' Also, it was he whose research and writing on Africa – for example, the several projects done in tandem with E.S. Atieno Odhiambo – was both informing of and being informed by wider discussions under the umbrella of 'the production of history.' Apart from the great shifts in India and China in the 1940s and the serial effects of the fall of the Wall in central Europe in November 1989, no region of the world has been more affected since the Second World War by the transformations in authority and power than Africa. Such transformations were inscribed, perhaps over-inscribed, not only in the dramatic changes in the writing of history and the revaluation of the past, but also in the displacement, by historians and historical scholarship, of the primary position occupied by anthropologists as interlocutors between the lived experience of Africans and many and different audiences. The imaginations of coherent and unified histories to be written for and about Africans and African nations came apart as history and the representational programs of history themselves became a central competitive arena for the elaboration of interest, right, property, status, and power.

The questions and approaches drawn into the notion of 'the production of history' have additional salience for Africanists as one considers the enlarged attention given to oral and other non-documentary sources within the practices of historians working on the African past. When a formal field of African history emerged in research universities outside Africa in the late 1950s and early 1960s (and as it relieved itself of some of the burdens of anthropology and imperial history, as it would later on in South African universities), the issue of the authority of African historical traditions – constructed, debated, and revised within specific political, cultural, and social settings in Africa – entered the academy directly, coming to the fore in the elaborations of methodologies for handling oral materials and oral traditions, in the training of students in these methodologies, and in the development of research and the writing of dissertations. In the first programmatic writings within the academy on methodology of oral tradition, and in the first generation of dissertations based on these materials, the overwhelming metaphor was freeing a continent from the silences of immovable and inflexible Western historiography, unable to see beyond the written document. The project of writing Africa's history from oral accounts would parallel the political emancipation of the continent occurring in other spheres, and like it, reveal a number of significant contradictions.

5   I was, and continue to be, intrigued by the resistances of individual scholars and cohorts of scholars to the problematization of the historian's craft through discussion and research on 'the production of history.' Some professional historians have expressed alarm or consternation that one would propose to read 'historians' such as themselves with the same critical tools that most would bring to reading a diary or a text from an archive. Some were alarmed at the interposition of the methods and epistemes of historical scholarship in the academy with those approaches that one might take to examining or representing historical inquiry and historical representation outside it. Professionally, some have sought to police any reflexive or self-reflexive writing from the historical academy. And some have reckoned the questions and approaches suggested within the framework of 'the production of history' as fundamental attacks on broadly held ideas concerning science, truth, objectivity, and reason. The threat seems to lie in the fact that the focus is directed toward academic historians and other interested producers of history and their audiences. Yet these questions and approaches are hardly novel, for they are located within the familiar practices of intellectual historians, social historians, and others well established in the guild. Some of the questions and approaches have been commonplace within the practice of historical anthropology for three decades.[9] Or is there more at stake in this 'debate': perhaps the unlocking of other narratives and other forms of narrative?

6   It is also curious how such questions and approaches as those that underlie the concept of the production of history are taken to exemplify postmodernism, for some meaning the abject negation of the possibility of truth and for others unveiling the internalities by which an externality, such as a text, an exhibit, a film, or a building, come to be constituted; for the former nothing but a babel of histories or claims to history with no concept of objectivity, and for the latter an opening to 'reading' authorial practice. I have not found comfort in either inclination, because of the accessibility of so much good work that brings enduring and respected tools of evidence to the programs and procedures of representing the past

both within and outside academic practice, without losing sight of the importance of the historical matter that is at the centre of the historian's attention. Laments by senior historians for the loss of the narrative aside, it seems possible for scholars with interests in the reconstruction and representation of the past to find layers and fragments of historical representation that not only attend to the reconstruction but also unveil the sociologies and economies of doing so; to restore the elements to their (our) monographs and dissertations that were removed to produce 'a clean text' or one 'observing the conventions' of professional history; and to reveal the 'back stages' of collective inquiry, debate, consensus. To work an analogy noted in the 1986 position paper from the photographer Richard Avedon, talking about his own practice as a portraitist, 'These disciplines, these strategies, this silent theater, attempt to achieve an illusion: That everything embodied in the photograph simply happened, that the person in the portrait was always there, was never told to stand there, was never encouraged to hide his hands, and in the end was not even in the presence of a photographer.'[10]

NOTES

1   This discussion draws on the author's *The Combing of History* (1994), 243–6, which in turns draws upon an unpublished position paper, 'The Production of History,' prepared for the Fifth Roundtable in Anthropology and History, Paris, July 1986, and the call for papers for the Sixth Roundtable, Bellagio, Italy, September 1989 (see discussion below).

2   Over several days, the *Baltimore Sun* followed the story. A Budweiser beer commercial shown during the 1985 World Series represented Americans huddled around radios listening to the seventh game of the 1960 World Series. The radio caught the announcer's call of the last play, Pittsburgh Pirate Bill Mazeroski's sensational final-inning home run, which stole the series from the New York Yankees. The announcer, Chuck Thompson, was heard to say that Art Ditmar pitched that ball to Mazeroski. In 1985, in the hours and days following the airing of the Budweiser commercial, sports fans and writers drew attention to this 'mistake' in the advertisement and suggested that it be corrected (Ralph Terry actually pitched the ball that Mazeroski hit out of the park). But the 'mistake' was in the original recording – Thompson had called it that way – and after much discussion among the beer company, ABC Television, and the advertising agency, the decision was made to leave the soundtrack of the commercial largely intact, to maintain the authenticity of the moment when the decisive home run was hit. Of course, it was the 'authenticity' of the radio broadcast, not of the event at Forbes Field in Pittsburgh.

3   This narrative draws on the present writer's discussion in the 1986 'production of history' position paper and on Cohen 1994: xvii, 1–23.

4   As well as in Cohen 1994.

5   Sider 1996; and see adjoining and surrounding pieces in the special number of *Radical History Review*.

310   David William Cohen

6 Though Sider has chosen not to mention the 1986 paper or the discussion in New York on 14 March 1986 of a draft of the position paper, at which both he and Paul Cowan were present.
7 And some of these 'further thoughts' were drawn onto paper for a presentation to a conference in July 1996 at the University of the Western Cape on 'The Future of the Past: The Production of History in a Changing South Africa.'
8 Cohen 1991.
9 See Kalb, Marks, and Tak 1985.
10 Avedon 1985.

REFERENCES

Avedon, Richard
    1985 Foreword. *In* In the American West. New York: Abrams.
Cohen, David William
    1991 A Case for the Basoga: Lloyd Fallers and the Construction of an African Legal System. *In* Law in Colonial Africa, Kristin Mann and Richard Roberts, eds. pp. 238–54. Portsmouth, NH: Heinemann.
    1994 The Combing of History. Chicago: University of Chicago Press.
Kalb, Don, Hans Marks, and Herman Tak
    1996 Historical Anthropology: The Unwaged Debate. Focaal: Tijdschrift voor antropologie, special number, 26/27.
Sider, Gerald M.
    1996 Cleansing History: Lawrence, Massachusetts, the Strike for Four Loaves of Bread and No Roses and the Anthropology of Working-Class Consciousness. Radical History Review 65:48–83.

Contributors

Gadi Algazi, Senior Lecturer in Medieval History, Department of History, Tel Aviv University. Recent publications include *Herrengewalt und Gewalt der Herren im späten Mittelalter: Herrschaft, Gegenseitigkeit und Sprachgebrauch* (Frankfurt am Main/New York: Campus, 1996); 'Violence, mémoire et pouvoir seigneurial au moyen âge tardif,' *Acts de la recherche en sciences sociales* 105 (1994); and '"Sich selbst vergessen" im späten Mittelalter: Denkfigur und soziale Figurationen,' in *Memoria als Kultur*, ed. Otto Gerhard Oexle (Göttingen: Vandehoeck & Ruprecht, 1995). His current research interests are the social and cultural history of the late-medieval and early-modern peasantries, historical semantics and discourse analysis, and oral traditions and scribal practice.

David William Cohen, Professor of History and Anthropology and Director of the International Institute, University of Michigan. Among his recent publications are *The Combing of History* (Chicago: University of Chicago Press, 1994); 'Historical Anthropology: Discerning the Rules of the Game,' *Focaal* (Netherlands) 26/27 (1996); and two books co-authored with E.S. Atieno Odhiambo: *Burying SM: The Politics of Knowledge and the Sociology of Power in Africa* (Portsmouth, NH: Heinemann, 1992) and *Siaya: The Historical Anthropology of an African Landscape* (London: James Currey, 1989). He is currently studying the multiple investigations into the disappearance and murder of Robert Ouko, the Kenyan minister of foreign affairs and international cooperation, and is continuing work on the constitution and fate of international expertise.

Karin Hausen, Professor of History at the Technische Universität Berlin and Director of the Center for Interdisciplinary Studies on Women and Gender. Her recent publications include 'Arbeiterinnenschutz, Mutterschutz und gesetzliche Krankenversicherung im Deutschen Kaiserreich und in der Weimarer Republik,' in *Geschichte der Frauen im Recht*, ed. Ute Gerhard (Munich, 1997); 'Frauenerwerbstätigkeit und erwerbsfähige Frauen seit 1945 in Deutschland,' in *Frauen arbeiten*, ed. Gurilla Budde (Göttingen, 1997); and 'Geschlecht und Ökonomie,' in *Moderne Wirtschaftsgeschichte: Eine Einführung für Historiker und Ökonomen*, ed. G. Ambrosius et al. (Munich, 1996). Her research interests centre on gender and the changing rituals and ceremonies of daily life in twentieth-century Germany.

Louise Lamphere, Professor of Anthropology at the University of New Mexico. Among her publications are *Structuring Diversity: Ethnographic Perspectives on the New Economy* (Chicago: University of Chicago Press, 1992) and two recent co-edited volumes: *Situated Lives: Gender and Culture in Everyday Life* (forthcoming, 1997) and *Sunbelt Working Mothers: Reconciling Family and Work* (Ithica: Cornell University Press, 1993). Her research interests include women's work, ethnicity and immigration, and Native North America.

Alf Lüdtke, Max-Planck-Institut für Geschichte, Göttingen. His recent publications include his edited volume, *The History of Everyday Life* (Princeton: Princeton University Press, 1995); *Eigen-Sinn: Fabrikalltag, Arbeitererfahrungen und Politik vom Kaiserreich in den Faschismus* (Hamburg: Ergebnisse, 1993); 'The Appeal of Exterminating "Others": German Workers and the Limits of Resistance,' *Journal of Modern History*, special issue, 1992; and 'Coming to Terms with the Past: Illusions of Remembering – Ways of Forgetting Nazism in West Germany,' *Journal of Modern History*, 1993. His current research interests concern the inner fabric of dictatorship, especially in Nazi Germany and East Germany, and issues of theory in anthropology and history, history and memory, and the history of everyday life.

Hans Medick, Max-Planck-Institut für Geschichte, Göttingen. He has recently published *Weben und Überleben in Laichingen 1650–1900: Lokalgeschichte als Allgemeine Geschichte* (Göttingen: Vandenhoeck & Ruprecht, 1996; 2d ed., 1997) and *Interest and Emotion: Essays on the Study of Family and Kinship*, co-edited with David Sabean (New York: Cambridge University Press, 1984). His current research interests are the history of mentalities and the everyday in the Thirty Years' War, 1618–46, and various kinds of autobiographical materials.

E.S. Atieno Odhiambo, Professor of History, Rice University. Among his publications are *Iaramogi: The Political Biography of Oginga Odinga, 1911–1994* (Nairobi: East African Educational Publishers, forthcoming) and two books co-authored with David W. Cohen, *Burying SM: The Politics of Knowledge and the Sociology of Power in Africa* (Portsmouth, NH: Heinemann, 1992) and *Siaya: The Historical Anthropology of an African Landscape* (London: James Currey, 1989). His current research interests are African perspectives on development and the Luo in anthropology and history.

Sumit Sarkar, Professor of History, Delhi University. Recent publications include *Writing Social History* (Delhi: Oxford University Press, 1997); 'Orientalism Revisited: Saidian Frameworks in the Writing of Modern Indian History,' *Oxford Literary Review* 16 (1994); 'A Marxian Social History beyond the Foucauldian Turn? – Peter Linebaugh's "The London Hanged,"' *Economic and Political Weekly*, 29 July 1995; and *Khaki Shorts, Saffron Flags: A Critique of the Hindu Right* (Delhi: Orient Longman, 1993). His current research interests include the social history of late-colonial Bengal, particularly the rise and decline of languages and the formation of caste, and contemporary right-wing Hindu communalism.

Jane Schneider, Professor of Anthropology, the Graduate School and University Center, City University of New York. Her publications include *Festival of the Poor: Fertility Decline and the Ideology of Class in Sicily, 1860–1980*, written jointly with Peter Schneider (Tucson: University of Arizona Press, 1996); *Articulating Hidden Histories: Exploring the Influence of Eric R. Wolf*, co-edited with Rayna Rapp (Berkeley: University of California Press, 1995); and *Cloth and the Human Experience*, co-edited with Annette Weiner (Washington, DC: Smithsonian Press, 1989). Her current research interests focus on cultural transformations in Sicily.

Peter Schneider, Professor of Anthropology, Fordham University. With Jane Schneider, he has recently published *Festival of the Poor: Fertility Decline and the Ideology of Class in Sicily, 1860–1980* (Tucson: University of Arizona Press, 1996), and he is completing a long-term research project on the changing relationships between the Sicilian mafia and the Italian state, and between the mafia and the anti-mafia movements.

Gerald Sider, Professor of Anthropology, College of Staten Island and the Graduate School and University Center, City University of New York. Recent publications include 'The Making of Peculiar Local Cultures: Producing and Surviving History in Peasant and Tribal Society,' in *Was Bleibt von Marxistischen Perspectiven in der Geschichtsforschung?* ed. Alf Lüdtke (Göttingen: Vandehoeck & Ruprecht, 1997), 'Anthropology and History: Opening Points

314 David William Cohen

for a New Synthesis,' *Focaal* (Netherlands) 26/27 (1996); 'Cleansing History: Lawrence, Massachusetts, the Strike for Four Loaves of Bread and No Roses, and the Anthropology of Working Class Consciousness,' *Radical History Review* 65 (1996); and *Lumbee Indian Histories: Race, Ethnicity and Indian Identity in the Southern United States* (New York: Cambridge University Press, 1993). His current research focuses on the history of inequality in the Sahel and on differential mortality in famines.

Gavin Smith, Professor of Anthropology, University of Toronto. Among his recent publications are 'Las contornos de la actividad colectiva: el rol de la organización y de la interpretación,' *Proceedings of the XVI Colloquio de Antropologia e Historia Regionales: Las disputas por el Mexico rural*, ed. Pieter de Vries and Sergio Zendejas (Zamora, Mexico: El Colegio de Michuacan, 1997); 'Western European Informal Economies in Historical Perspective,' in *Artful Practices: The Political Economy of Everyday Life*, ed. Henri Lustiger-Thaler and Daniel Salée (Montreal: Black Rose, 1994); 'Towards an Ethnography of Idiosyncratic Forms of Livelihood,' *International Journal of Urban and Regional Research* 18 (1994); and *Livelihood and Resistance: Peasants and the Politics of Land in Peru* (Berkeley: University of California Press, 1989).

Michel-Rolph Trouillot, Distinguished Professor of Anthropology and Director, Institute for Global Studies in Culture, Power and History, Johns Hopkins University. Recent publications include *Open the Social Sciences*, jointly with Immanuel Wallerstein et al. (Stanford: Stanford University Press, 1996); *Silencing the Past: Power and the Production of History* (Boston: Beacon Press, 1995); and *Haiti: State against Nation: The Origins and Legacy of Duvalierism* (New York and London: Monthly Review Press, 1989). His current research interests are the paradox of race and colour in Haiti, and orality and the production of history.